Corporate Social Responsibility and Opportunities for Sustainable Financial Success

Julia Margarete Puaschunder
Columbia University, USA & The New School, USA

A volume in the Advances in Human Resources Management and Organizational Development (AHRMOD) Book Series

IGI Global
DISSEMINATOR OF KNOWLEDGE

Published in the United States of America by
IGI Global
Business Science Reference (an imprint of IGI Global)
701 E. Chocolate Avenue
Hershey PA, USA 17033
Tel: 717-533-8845
Fax: 717-533-8661
E-mail: cust@igi-global.com
Web site: http://www.igi-global.com

Library of Congress Cataloging-in-Publication Data

Names: Puaschunder, Julia Margarete, 1979- author.
Title: Corporate social responsibility and opportunities for sustainable financial success / by Julia Margarete Puaschunder.
Description: Hershey : Business Science Reference, [2019] | Includes bibliographical references.
Identifiers: LCCN 2018031997| ISBN 9781522576198 (hardcover) | ISBN 9781522576204 (ebook)
Subjects: LCSH: Social responsibility of business. | Business ethics.
Classification: LCC HD60 .P813 2019 | DDC 658.4/08--dc23 LC record available at https://lccn.loc.gov/2018031997

This book is published in the IGI Global book series Advances in Human Resources Management and Organizational Development (AHRMOD) (ISSN: 2327-3372; eISSN: 2327-3380)

British Cataloguing in Publication Data
A Cataloguing in Publication record for this book is available from the British Library.

Advances in Human Resources Management and Organizational Development (AHRMOD) Book Series

ISSN:2327-3372
EISSN:2327-3380

MISSION

A solid foundation is essential to the development and success of any organization and can be accomplished through the effective and careful management of an organization's human capital. Research in human resources management and organizational development is necessary in providing business leaders with the tools and methodologies which will assist in the development and maintenance of their organizational structure.

The **Advances in Human Resources Management and Organizational Development (AHRMOD) Book Series** aims to publish the latest research on all aspects of human resources as well as the latest methodologies, tools, and theories regarding organizational development and sustainability. The **AHRMOD Book Series** intends to provide business professionals, managers, researchers, and students with the necessary resources to effectively develop and implement organizational strategies.

COVERAGE

- Human Relations Movement
- Personnel Retention
- Workplacc Culture
- Performance Improvement
- Workplace Discrimination
- Compliance
- Entrepreneurialism
- Employee Benefits
- Recruitment Process
- Employee Relations

The Advances in Human Resources Management and Organizational Development (AHRMOD) Book Series (ISSN 2327-3372) is published by IGI Global, 701 E. Chocolate Avenue, Hershey, PA 17033-1240, USA, www.igi-global.com. This series is composed of titles available for purchase individually; each title is edited to be contextually exclusive from any other title within the series. For pricing and ordering information please visit http://www.igi-global.com/book-series/advances-human-resources-management-organizational/73670. Postmaster: Send all address changes to above address.

Titles in this Series

For a list of additional titles in this series, please visit:
https://www.igi-global.com/book-series/advances-human-resources-management-organizational/73670

Managerial Competencies for Multinational Businesses
Macarena López-Fernández (University of Cádiz, Spain) and Pedro M. Romero-Fernández (University of Cádiz, Spain)
Business Science Reference • ©2019 • 364pp • H/C (ISBN: 9781522557814) • US $215.00

Organizational Culture and Behavioral Shifts in the Green Economy
Violeta Sima (Petroleum-Gas University of Ploiesti, Romania)
Business Science Reference • ©2018 • 334pp • H/C (ISBN: 9781522529651) • US $205.00

Disruptive Technologies for Business Development and Strategic Advantage
Anatoly V. Zhuplev (Loyola Marymount University, USA)
Business Science Reference • ©2018 • 364pp • H/C (ISBN: 9781522541486) • US $195.00

Attracting and Retaining Millennial Workers in the Modern Business Era
Meng-Shan Tsai (Clouder Technology Inc., Taiwan)
Business Science Reference • ©2018 • 249pp • H/C (ISBN: 9781522562641) • US $185.00

Handbook of Research on Knowledge Management for Contemporary Business Environments
Armando Malheiro (University of Porto, Portugal) Fernanda Ribeiro (University of Porto, Portugal) George Leal Jamil (Fumec University, Brazil) Jose Pocas Rascao (Polytechnic of Setubal, Portugal) and Oscar Mealha (University of Aveiro, Portugal)
Business Science Reference • ©2018 • 438pp • H/C (ISBN: 9781522537250) • US $295.00

Advances in Data Communications and Networking for Digital Business Transformation
Debashis Saha (Indian Institute of Management Calcutta, India)
Business Science Reference • ©2018 • 358pp • H/C (ISBN: 9781522553236) • US $225.00

Online Collaboration and Communication in Contemporary Organizations
Ditte Kolbaek (Aalborg University, Denmark)
Business Science Reference • ©2018 • 348pp • H/C (ISBN: 9781522540946) • US $225.00

For an entire list of titles in this series, please visit:
https://www.igi-global.com/book-series/advances-human-resources-management-organizational/73670

IGI Global
DISSEMINATOR OF KNOWLEDGE

701 East Chocolate Avenue, Hershey, PA 17033, USA
Tel: 717-533-8845 x100 • Fax: 717-533-8661
E-Mail: cust@igi-global.com • www.igi-global.com

Table of Contents

Section 3
Discussion

Preface

The 2008/09 World Financial Recession heralded the "Age of Responsibility" as the societal call for responsible market behavior reached unprecedented momentum. Responsibility is part of the human nature and complements corporate activities and financial considerations. The economic, legal, social and philanthropic responsibilities within the corporate sector are attributed in Corporate Social Responsibility (CSR). Sustainable Financial Social Responsibility is foremost addressed by Socially Responsible Investment (SRI). Globalization, political changes and societal trends, but also the current state of the world economy, have leveraged a societal demand for ingraining responsibility into market systems.

Corporate Social Responsibility and Opportunities for Sustainable Financial Success explores corporate and financial social responsibility by the cases of Corporate Social Responsibility (CSR) and Socially Responsible Investment (SRI) in order to draw attention to contemporary and prospected future opportunities for sustainable financial success. Theoretical descriptions discuss the human constituents of responsibility and the international emergence of CSR with special attention to multi-stakeholder partnerships. The rise of SRI in the international arena in the wake of stakeholder activism and intrinsic socio-psychological motives is outlined. Empirically expert interviews with public servants about CSR reveal opportunities of flexible corporate social service provision but also shed light on deficiencies of corporate social conduct. The potentials and downfalls of international public private partnerships are analyzed by the case of a currently launched UN multi-stakeholder network fostering international development. A meta-analysis of the impact of political divestiture from South Africa studies attributes methodological deficiencies of event study designs. Expert interviews about SRI feature the innovative potential but also disclose a lack of information and doubts about the efficiency and fiduciary predicaments. Recommendations target at ingraining social responsibility in economic systems by global governance, multi-stakeholder management and governmental assistance of the implementation and administration of corporate and financial social responsibility. Transparency and accountability are key for monitoring corporate and financial social responsibility. As for the ongoing adaptation and adoption of CSR and SRI in the wake of the 2008 financial crisis, future research must attribute the newly defined role of social responsibility in the interplay of public and private actors given concurrent anti-globalization trends.

The aftermath of the 2008/09 World Financial Recession has been referred to as the "Age of Responsibility" in back-then US president Barack Obama's inauguration speech on January 21, 2009 (Washington Post, 2009). In the wake of the 2008 financial crisis, Obama called for a new spirit of responsibility that serves the greater goals of society. According to former World Bank President Robert Zoellick the "new era of responsibility" features "changed attitudes and co-operative policies" steering responsible corporate conduct and socially responsible investment as means of societal progress (Financial Times, 2009).

In July 2010 the US Congress approved a sweeping expansion of federal financial regulation in response to the 2008 "the financial excesses" causing the "worst recession since the Great Depression." The 2,300-page legislative catalog of repairs and additions to the financial regulatory system reflects the current mistrust in deregulated markets (Appelbaum, 2010). The US government sets to ensure responsibility in financial markets and protect from human ethical decision-making failures in this "most important Wall Street reform legislation in 75 years" in the words of the National Economic Council Director Lawrence Summers (2010). It is on us to not interpret this as an end to the idea of liberal market economies; but rather appreciate the crisis' potential to create a future built upon a renewed attention to social responsibility.

Only by understanding the past, we can excel in the future. Studying the emergence of social responsibility will allow us perfecting future economies of free and responsible humankind. In such an attempt, let us examine the emergence of human social responsibility in modern economies. Thereby we may not rest at the accomplishments, but must also address the downfalls of human bounded ethicality in a search for future advancements.

Throughout recent decades, Corporate and Financial Social Responsibility have steadily leveraged into concepts of worldwide recognition in the wake of globalization, political and societal trends. During the last century, markets have been proven as the most prominent form to distribute scarce resources. Within global markets, international corporations have continuously increased in scale, scope, output and economic influence into the most powerful resource allocation form to spread innovation and prosperity around the world (Chua, 2003; Fitzgerald & Cormack, 2007; Micklethwait & Wooldridge, 2003; Rothkopf, 2008). The ascent of multinationals strengthened the corporate role in society and placed a greater share of social responsibility onto the corporate sector.

In recent decades, globalization featuring the progressive deterritorialization of social, political, economic interaction concurrently raised societal concerns raised beyond the power, control and influence of national governments. In a globally interlinked world, governmental agencies' ability to protect citizenship rights, fulfil social obligations and avert global crises gradually declined and imposed new levels of social responsibility onto corporate actors.

Governmental liberalization trends also geared social responsibility. Since the 1970s liberal markets were praised as optimum frameworks for exchange and drivers of innovation, in which the mere pursuit of self-interest of responsible market actors was believed to bring along societal progress and social welfare (Jones & Pollitt, 1998; Smith, 1776/1976). To let market forces float freely, a libertarian deregulation course was pursued featuring lowered regulatory control of trust-based market systems, which fostered the influence of corporate social service provision.

In addition, a societal call for responsible corporate conduct developed in advanced societies, in which the expectations of corporate conduct and market obligations sophisticated. With the IT revolution providing heightened degrees of easily-accessible information, corporate societal impacts became subject to scrutiny to an affluent, internationally-focused "Weltgesellschaft" who demanded to consumer with respect for business ethics around the globe (Nelson, 2004; Sichler, 2006, p. 8; Werther & Chandler, 2006). The emergence of NGOs further contributed to corporate conduct disclosure and the integration of social responsibility into corporate practices.

As for all these trends, multinational corporate conduct started exhibiting higher levels of responsibility vis-à-vis society. Having gained in economic weight and political power, the majority of corporations tapped into improving the societal conditions by contributing to a wide range of social needs beyond the mere fulfillment of shareholder obligations and customer demands (De Silva & Amerasinghe, 2004; Kettl, 2006). Global players stepped in where traditional governments refrained from social service provision – foremost through privatization or welfare reforms. International corporations also filled opening governance gaps when governments could not administer or enforce citizenship rights, new regulations were politically not desirable, feasible or even when governments had failed to provide social services (Steurer, 2010). By striving to meet citizenship goals, corporate executives integrated responsibility into ethical leadership that served multiple stakeholders by balancing economic goals with societal demands (DeThomasis & St. Anthony, 2006).

Today Corporate Social Responsibility (CSR) has leveraged into a pivotal factor to align profit maximization with concern for societal well-being and environmental sustainability. Corporations contribute to social causes beyond mere economic and legal obligations (Elkington, 1998; Lea, 2002; Livesey, 2002; Matten & Crane, 2005; Wolff, 2002). By ingraining economic, legal, ethical, and societal aspects into corporate conduct, CSR attributes the greater goal of enhancing the overall quality of life for this generation and the following (Carroll, 1979).

Nowadays almost all corporations have embedded social responsibility in their codes of conduct, introduced CSR in their stakeholder relations and incorporated social conscientious practices in their management (Crane, Matten & Moon, 2004; Werther & Chandler, 2006). The emergence of CSR as a corporate mainstream is accompanied by CSR oversight by stakeholders advocating for corporate social conduct. In line with these trends, CSR has become an *en vogue* topic in academia. Academics challenge Milton Friedman's proclamation of profit maximization as the primary intention for business activities and investigate innovative public private partnerships (PPPs) to contribute to social welfare (Moon, Crane & Matten, 2003; Nelson, 2004; Prahalad & Hammond, 2003). Under the guidance of international organizations, CSR has developed into a means of global governance social service provision in innovative PPPs that tackle social deficiencies. International organizations thereby bridge the gap between ethical standards and institutionalized ethical corporate conduct.

Concurrent with corporations having started to pay attention to social responsibility, ethical considerations have become part of the finance world. Developing an interest in corporate social conduct, conscientious investors nowadays fund socially responsible corporations (Ahmad, 2008; Sparkes, 2002). In Socially Responsible Investing (SRI) securities are not only selected for their expected yield and volatility, but also for social, environmental and institutional aspects. In the special SRI case of political divestiture, socially responsible investors refrained from contributing to politically incorrect market regimes.

With trends predicting continuing globalization, corporate conduct disclosure and societal crises beyond the control of single nation states, the demand for corporate and financial social responsibilities is believed to continuously rise (Beck, 1998; Bekefi, 2006; Fitzgerald & Cormack, 2007; Livesey, 2002; Scholte, 2000).

In the wake of the 2008 World Financial Recession, the call for responsibility within corporate and financial markets has reached unprecedented momentum. Since August 2008 financial markets have been engulfed in an extraordinary sequence of events. The neglect of corporate and financial responsibility in a liberal market climate featuring an absence of regulatory and accountability control have weakened the world economy. Media coverage of corporate scandals, fiduciary breaches, astronomic CEO remunerations and financial managers' exuberance perpetuated stakeholders' skepticism in the performance of unregulated, trust-based market systems. The announcement of the recapitalization of the banking system in October 2008 halted world-wide liberalization trends and created a demand for ingraining social responsibility in the corporate and finance world that is regulated by a watchful eye over the market place. Governmental bail-outs in the wake of corporate bankruptcy have contributed to stakeholder pressure and hold the potential to re-establish governmental oversight in the corporate and financial worlds (Greenspan, 2007). In the current shift of public and private sector forces in addressing social responsibility, the optimum balance of public and private social contributions as well as the degree of trust in disciplined market actors and regulatory oversight of economic transactions are yet to be determined. With US President Barack Obama dedicating his inauguration speech to responsibility as a means to re-establishing trust in market systems in the aftermath of the 2008 financial downturns, but also in the light of the following recapitalization of the banking system; the roles of governmental, financial and corporate actors in addressing social responsibility has been redefined (Duchac, 2008).

What can we do to prevent similar events in the future? To avoid a recurrent scenario in the future, sustainable financial success appears to be key. In order to generate more sustainable financial leadership, transparency of private sector activities, accountability of financial market operations and responsibility of market actors are demanded by political and financial leaders. Mainstream economic theories have been preoccupied with demonstrating how markets are largely efficient, unregulated market forces working towards the best interest of the single market participant and the collective of societal constituents.

Financial crises theories have largely ignored socio-psychological notions of economic systems, emotional facets of market participants and their emotional decision making fallibility imposing risk onto economic systems. As for gaining an accurate understanding of economic markets, future research must widen the interdisciplinary lens and consider socio-psychological motives in corporate, economic and financial theories and models.

Depicting the socio-psychological causes, historic roots and political frameworks of responsibility within corporate and financial markets provides an opportunity to understand the interplay of trust in responsible market actors and governmental oversight control as vital ingredients for functioning market economies and democratic societies. Reflecting on responsibility within market systems may serve to better understand real-market responsibility phenomena in order to find a well-tempered balance of public and private social contributions within modern market economies. In the interplay of public and private responsibility, legislation can only create favorable structures for social responsibility, but within complex, trust-based market systems; social conscientiousness must be nurtured to grow in socially conscientious leaders who will attract others to follow their paths.

As a first step in this direction, this book is dedicated to explore the concept of responsibility within modern market economies. Overall the monograph is targeted at describing historical, socio-psychological, cognitive, political and economic processes that impact on social responsibility within corporate and financial markets in order to draw inferences how to sustainable economies.

The theoretical part sheds light on the foundations of human responsibility and ethicality. Social responsibility within market systems is foremost addressed by CSR which is of value to multiple constituents. CSR is introduced as a culture-dependent phenomenon, which emerged in the US and Western Europe. As a means of global governance provision, CSR contributes to social services in public private partnerships (PPPs) and serves multi-stakeholder management and conflict resolution purposes. The United Nations Global Compact (UNGC) offers CSR best practices principles and fosters corporate social conduct as a feature of global governance provision in multi-stakeholder partnerships. The Global Alliance for Information and Communication Technologies and Development (GAID) is a recent example of an innovative PPP that implements social responsibility under the auspice of the UN.

Sustainable Financial Social Responsibility attributes the consideration of CSR in investment decisions, which is the basis for Socially Responsible Investment (SRI). The most common forms to align financial investments with ethical, moral and social causes are socially responsible screenings, shareholder advocacy, community investing and social venture capital funding. SRI is a multi-stakeholder phenomenon that comprises economic, organizational and societal actors. The emergence of SRI in the Western World within recent decades can be traced back to a combination of historical incidents, legislative compulsion and stakeholder pressure. As a culture-dependent phenomenon, financial social responsibility features international differences in SRI conduct. The UN plays a pivotal role in promoting SRI in initiatives and actions. Financial investment strategies are coupled with political activism in the case of political divestiture, which refers to the removal of investment from socially irresponsible markets with the greater goal of accomplishing socio-political changes. Financial social responsibility is proposed to be based on socio-psychological SRI motives that supplement rational profit maximization endeavors. The theoretical part then discusses the role of leadership between trust and CSR the leadership person behind intergenerational corporate social conscientiousness. The role of CSR and SRI for financial reporting and fraud prevention as well as CSR as global risk management tool are outlined.

Empirically the presents the reflections of public and private actors on CSR and SRI in the aftermath of the 2008/09 World Financial Recession. Gaining insight on the common body of knowledge but also critically evaluating the implementation and efficiency of corporate and financial social responsibility in this unique time is targeted at outlining strengths and weaknesses of the public and private sectors' attribution of social responsibility. Depicting current trends in CSR and SRI conduct delineates circumstances under which social responsibility is likely to occur, yet also shed light on risks imbued in private sector social welfare contributions. Describing UN multi-stakeholder partnerships with a special attention to the start-up phase concludes on the efficiency and downfalls of public and private global governance provision. The body of knowledge on political divestiture is meta-analyzed to draw predictions about the impact of political activism on corporate value. Qualitative expert interviews with financial leaders that were conducted during the outbreak of the 2008/09 World Financial Recession outline socio-economic losses imbued in market agents' hesitance to consider social responsibility in financial investments.

Overall the book explores innovative ways in which corporations and financial markets can create sustainable value for society. The research is targeted at outlining potentials and resolving deficiencies in the implementation of Corporate and Sustainable Financial Social Responsibility. The empirical results derive conclusions for the ongoing adaptation and adoption of CSR and SRI with a special attention to the interplay of public and private contributions. In sum the book may help guide-lining the administration of CSR and SRI to foster the overarching goal of improving the living conditions for this generation and the following.

REFERENCES

Ahmad, M. (2008, January 24). Global CEOs at World Economic Forum cite sovereign wealth funds as the new power broker. *BI-ME.*

Appelbaum, B. D. (2010, July 15). *Financial Overhaul Signals Shift on Deregulation*. Retrieved from https://www.nytimes.com/2010/07/16/business/16regulate.html

Beck, U. (1998). Wie wird Demokratie im Zeitalter der Globalisierung möglich? In U. Beck (Ed.), *Politik der Globalisierung* (pp. 7–67). Frankfurt am Main: Suhrkamp.

Bekefi, T. (2006). *Business as a partner in tackling micronutrient deficiency: Lessons in multisector partnership. Report of the Corporate Responsibility Initiative*. Cambridge, MA: Harvard University Press.

Carroll, A. B. (1979). A three-dimensional model of corporate social performance. *Academy of Management Review*, *4*, 497–505. doi:10.5465/amr.1979.4498296

Chua, A. (2003). *World on fire: How exporting free market democracy breeds ethnic hatred and global instability*. New York: Anchor.

Crane, A., Matten, D., & Moon, D. (2004). Stakeholder as citizens? Rethinking rights, participation and democracy. *Journal of Business Ethics*, *53*(1/2), 107–122. doi:10.1023/B:BUSI.0000039403.96150.b6

De Silva, S., & Amerasinghe, F. (2004). *Corporate social responsibility: Issues, problems and challenges*. Colombo: Lake House.

DeThomasis, L., & St. Anthony, N. (2006). *Doing right in a shrinking world: How corporate America can balance ethics and profit in a changing economy*. Austin, TX: Greenleaf.

Duchac, J. (2008, December 5). The perfect storm: A look inside the 2008 financial crisis. WU talks special notes, Vienna, Austria.

Elkington, J. (1998). *Cannibals with forks: The triple bottom line of 21st century business. Gabriola Island*. New Society.

Financial Times. (2009, January 25). *Time to herald the Age of Responsibility*. Retrieved from https://www.ft.com/content/1348d34e-eb0d-11dd-bb6e-0000779fd2ac

Fitzgerald, N., & Cormack, M. (2007). *The role of business in society: An agenda for action*. Retrieved from the internet at http://www.hks.harvard.edu/mrcbg/CSRI/publications/report_12

Greenspan, A. (2007). *The age of turbulence: Adventures in a new world*. New York: Penguin.

Jones, I., & Pollitt, M. (1998). *The role of business ethics in economic performance*. London: Macmillan. doi:10.1057/9780230379794

Kettl, D. F. (2006). *The global public management revolution*. Washington, DC: The Brookings Institution.

Lea, R. (2002). Corporate social responsibility: Institute of Directors (IoD) member opinion survey. IoD.

Livesey, S. (2002). The discourse of the middle ground: Citizen Shell commits to sustainable development. *Management Communication Quarterly*, *15*(3), 313–349. doi:10.1177/0893318902153001

Matten, D., & Crane, A. (2005). Corporate citizenship: Toward an extended theoretical conceptualization. *Academy of Management Review*, *30*(1), 166–179. doi:10.5465/amr.2005.15281448

Micklethwait, J., & Wooldridge, A. (2003). *A future perfect: The challenge and promise of globalization*. New York: Crown Business Press.

Nelson, J. (2004). *Leadership, accountability and partnership: Critical trends and issues in corporate social responsibility. Report of the Corporate Responsibility Initiative*. Cambridge, MA: Harvard University.

Prahalad, C. K., & Hammond, A. (2003). *Serving the world's poor profitably. Harvard Business Review on Corporate Responsibility*. Cambridge, MA: Harvard Business School.

Rothkopf, D. (2008). *Superclass: The global power elite and the world they are making*. New York: Farrar, Straus & Giroux.

Scholte, J. A. (2000). *Globalization: A critical introduction*. Basingstoke: Palgrave.

Sichler, R. (2006). *Autonomie in der Arbeitswelt: Psychologie und Beruf*. Göttingen: Vandenhoeck & Ruprecht.

Smith, A. (1976). *The theory of moral sentiments*. Oxford: Clarendon. (Original work published 1759)

Sparkes, R. (2002). *Socially responsible investment: A global revolution*. Wiley.

Steurer, R. (2010). The role of governments in corporate social responsibility: Characterising public policies on CSR in Europe. *Policy Sciences*, *43*(1), 49–72. doi:10.100711077-009-9084-4

Summers, L. (2010, July 21). *CNBC News Closing Bell*. Speech presented at CNBC's Closing Bell in the New York Stock Exchange, New York, NY.

Trevino, L. K., & Nelson, K. A. (2004). *Managing business ethics: Straight talk about how to do right*. Hoboken: Wiley.

Washington Post. (2009, January 21). *In Obama's Moment, Many in Crowd Feel Echoes of Their Own Stories*. Retrieved from http://www.washingtonpost.com/wp-dyn/content/article/2009/01/20/AR2009012004466.html

Werther, W. B., & Chandler, D. (2006). *Strategic corporate social responsibility: Stakeholders in a global environment*. Thousand Oaks, CA: Sage.

Wolff, M. (2002). Response to "Confronting the critics." *New Academy Review*, *1*, 230–237.

Acknowledgment

After theoretical research on corporate and financial social responsibility at the University of Vienna in 2006; I was a Fulbright scholar at the Maxwell School of Citizenship and Public Affairs in 2007 and 2008 with placements in Washington D.C. and New York City. While interviewing New York financial experts in the late summer of 2008, I learned about financial global governance at the Open Society Institute and Soros Foundation.

Louisa van Baalen and Judy Kugel enabled me to conduct research at Harvard University from 2008 on. A Max Kade Foundation scholarship granted by the Austrian Academy of Sciences supported research as faculty associate at the Harvard University Center for the Environment as well as Harvard University Faculty of Arts and Sciences and Harvard Business School and Harvard Kennedy School. The Harvard Law School Law and Mind Sciences Initiative provided invaluable insights from 2012. In 2013 responsible leadership aspects got refined at the Vienna University of Economics and Business. From 2014 a Prize Fellowship in the Inter-University Consortium of New York allowed generous research and studies at The New School New York, Columbia University and Princeton University. During the summer of 2016, global governance aspects of the presented topic were fortified at the International Institute for Applied Systems Analysis and as an invited Alpbach-Laxenburg Group member. During the summer of 2018, the George Washington University Center for International Business Education and Research became my intellectual home for finishing the book.

The author remains most grateful for colleagues' noble gifts of time and kind share of expertise as well as the generous aid of the mentioned institutions and foundations in granting access to august communities and freedom of thought, thanks to which the following idea of Corporate Social Responsibility and Sustainable Financial Success exists.

Section 1
Theoretical Background

Chapter 1
Social Responsibility

ABSTRACT

Responsibility refers to the human care about others' wellbeing. Motives for responsible behavior are connected to altruism—as a search for meaning beyond the self—and positive reinforcement of sympathy within society. Responsibility is part of human nature and learned within the societal context. Leaders are role models who face an extraordinary obligation to responsibility in balancing multiple stakeholder needs. Responsibility considerations underlie human decision-making fallibility. This chapter explores social responsibility.

INTRODUCTION

Dating back to antique and religious roots, responsibility has been addressed in philosophical, legal and libertarian writings. Ancient Greek philosophers outline responsibility as an essential feature of human commitment and care for others (Reese-Schäfer, 1995 in Sichler, 2006). Immanuel Kant defined responsibility as an internal moral mainspring for ethicality and duty as a universal privilege of society (Gunkel, 1989 in Sichler, 2006; Kant, 1787/1974, 1788/1974). According to Kant (1787/1974) free, self-determined individuals become responsible when reflecting about others' free will (Berlin, 1969 in Sichler, 2006; Hayek, 1944/2007). Grounding responsibility on self-reflection and social perspective taking, Kant's categorical imperative therefore advises to solely act in ways one wants to be treated by others. Free-willed responsible individuals exhibit pro-social behavior. In the social compound, collective

DOI: 10.4018/978-1-5225-7619-8.ch001

responsibility therefore fosters an overall trust-based social climate (Luf, 2009; Sichler, 2006). Collective responsible caring breeds the so-called 'social glue' – an implicit form of societal order beyond regulations and legal enforcement. The related 'Gesellschaftsvertrag' or social contract of socially responsible actors steers social progress and economic stability (Sichler, 2006). Underlying this implicit social compound, responsibility thus coordinates and structures our living.

Legal writings outline responsibility as a feature of ethicality and an expression of natural law (Sichler, 2006). Responsibility is believed to have emerged from the obedience to externally imposed norms into an intrinsic endeavor of a disciplined, modern humankind (Luf, 2009). Post-conventional forms of morality and ethicality attribute individuals to be responsible when they base their individual decision making with respect for others' free will (Auhagen & Bierhoff, 2001; Sichler, 2006).

Based on the ethics of morality, responsibility depicts an internal care for others that stems from altruism – the ianternal need to benefit others whilst lowering the level of personal fitness (Trivers, 1971). Underlying motives for altruism are self-fulfilment by contributing to matters beyond the self and the so-called 'warm glow' – a positive emotion attributed to caring for and giving to others (Andreoni, 1989; Jenkins, 2007). In an unconscious search for reflective meaning in life and seeking warm glow-reinforcement, humans exhibit responsible behavior and ethical decision making (Sennett, 1998). Deciding in line with personal ethics notions is experienced positively as for determining our character to ourselves and others, which grants positive self-worth (Sennett, 1998).

Karl Marx was the first to depict responsibility as a central motivating factor in working tasks (Sichler in Weber, Pasqualoni & Burtscher, 2004). Responsibility leads to the perception of an internal locus of control and helps identifying with working tasks (DeCharms, 1992 in Sichler, 2006). When responsibility is connected to profound reasons that are central to a persons' identity, individuals identify themselves with these purposes and feel obliged to act in sync with their values. Social responsibility is a motivating factor in group work tasks (Weber, 1997). Self-imposed responsibility goals become compelling drivers for actions and can leverage into professional endeavors (Damon, Menon & Bronk, 2003; Gardner, 2007; Sichler, 2003). By stringency of values and actions, responsible working tasks bestow individuals with identity and grant working relations symbolic meaning (Müller, 1990 in Sichler, 2006). Modern working situations are depicted as for requiring a high degree of responsibility from individuals and responsibility being a determinant of success and self worth (Sichler, 2006). This is especially the case with social entrepreneurs and propreneurs, who apply economic acumen to societal causes about which they personally care. Propreneurs are individuals who strive for aligning working situations with personal values, lifestyles and ethical goals (Fischer, 1995 in Sichler, 2006).

In the corporate domain, social responsibility is a feature of business ethics. Business ethics foster the responsibility of corporate actors by setting moral anchors in corporate codes of conduct. Corporate codes of ethics constitute norms of what is right, just and fair that reflect the law and moral convictions of society (Hennigfeld, Pohl & Tolhurst, 2006). When business ethics match personal responsibility endeavors with the corporate culture, work becomes a self-actualizing motivation factor that fosters productivity (Colby & Damon, 1992; Gerson, 2002; Sichler in Weber et al., 2004). Exhibiting commonly shared social responsibility in line with business ethics strengthens group cohesion and the ability to work harmoniously (Fukuyama, 1995).

In corporate settings, responsible leadership has gained unprecedented importance in the light of the heightened self-regulation of groups featuring an autonomous planning of working times, work relations and high degrees of individual group coordination, decision making and goal accomplishment strategies (Sichler, 2006). An extraordinary obligation to responsibility is attributed to leaders as for serving as role models and incorporating the aspirations of multiple constituents, whose wants and needs leaders balance (Lenk & Maring, 1992; Nelson, 2004). Corporate, financial and political leadership disproportionately impacts on the lives of present and future generations (Lennick & Kiel, 2007). In many cases leadership thus requires a disciplined focus on long-term goals to ensure sustainability (Sichler, 2006). More than others are leaders change agents who can foresee and respond efficiently to future anticipations. In addition, leaders' hierarchical positioning and established power bases grant the opportunity to institutionalize responsibility and bestow subordinates with transformational aspiration of responsibility (Aronson, 2001; Biermann & Siebenhüner, 2009; de Woot, 2005; Lennick & Kiel, 2007). Within society, political leaders and institutional role models hold the potential to ignite and strengthen social responsibility. As such, in his historic inauguration speech, the former US president Barack Obama openly called for responsibility (Gebert & von Rosenstiel, 1996; Porter & Kramer, 2003). Concurrently former World Bank president Robert Zoellick addressed the "new era of responsibility" featuring sustainable globalization in line with the United Nations Millennium Development Goals (UNMDGs) (Financial Times, January 25, 2009). In the light of the 2008

World Financial Recession, both these role models call for responsibility in their public addresses as an underpinning of a vital and modern market economy. In addition to political leaders, academics and intellectual leaders attributed the role of disciplined responsibility in the age of global capitalism (Centeno & Cohen, 2010; Roberts, 2010).

Paying attention to responsible leadership is beneficial for leaders and society. When leadership decisions are subject to public scrutiny, responsibility enhances the constituents' acceptance of their outcomes, which fosters their implementation and in reverse contributes to the success of leaders. For corporate leaders, responsibility is a crucial component of business performance as for strengthening employee motivation and ensuring long-term positive stakeholder relations (Gross, 2018; Lennick & Kiel, 2007). Financial ethical leadership is an implicit means of reducing the likelihood of fiduciary breaches in principal-agent-relations and in the following a prerequisite of economic stability.

As a part of the human nature, responsibility underlies fallibility. Responsibility deficiencies arise when moral individuals are not aware that their decision making implies ethical considerations or negative societal externalities. If individuals make moral judgments quickly and intuitively – solely based on their gut feelings of right and wrong – they are prone to believe that their behavior is ethical, yet at the same time fall prey to unconscious biases and accidental unethicality (Banaji, Bazerman & Chugh, 2003; Bazerman & Banaji, 2004; Haidt, 2001). Based on Simon's concept of bounded rationality – comprising a model in which human rationality is very much bounded by the situation and mental capacity limitations – bounded ethicality attributes human fallibility in ethical decisions (March & Simon, 1958; Murnighan, Cantelon & Elyashiv, 2001; Simon, 1957). Bounded ethicality describes unintentional deviations from morality and ethical behavior, by which systemic and predictable psychological processes lead people to engage in ethically questionable behavior inconsistent with their conscious ethical notion (Banaji et al., 2003; Bazerman, & Banaji, 2004). Recently bounded ethicality has become subject to descriptive and experimental scrutiny. An exploratory examination of bounded ethicality phenomena is provided by Table 1.

Exploratory evidence describes bounded ethicality to stem from uncertainty and **information deficiencies** in the way we collect, process and use information in our decision making. Decisions are made behind a "veil of ignorance" of perceivable information (*bounded awareness*) due to mental capacity limitations and biased cognitions (*ethical fading*) (Rawls, 1971 in Luf, 2009, p. 91; Tversky & Kahneman, 1974).

Table 1. Overview of bounded ethicality phenomena

	Bounded Ethicality
	Information deficiencies
Bounded Awareness refers to systematic information deficiencies that prevent individuals from noticing or focusing on relevant data.	***Bounded Awareness***: As a misalignment between the information needed for a rational decision and the information included in the standard decision processes, bounded awareness refers to systematic information deficiencies that prevent people from noticing or focusing on useful, observable and relevant data (Bazerman & Chugh, 2005). Bounded awareness is most likely to occur when the unethical behavior is unclear, distant and erodes over time (Gino, Moore & Bazerman, 2008). The incremental manner, in which the information is neglected, increases the likelihood to fall prey to predictable surprises (Bazerman & Watkins, 2004). Boundedness even holds for beholders who have the tendency to overlook unethicality in others (Gino et al., 2008).
Ethical Fading is a process by which a person does not realize that decisions have ethical implications.	***Ethical Fading***: The extent to which decision makers perceive the ethical aspects of decisions affect their behavior. In the case of ethical fading, individuals do not realize that decisions have an ethical impact as moral implications and negative externalities are not activated at the time of the decision making (Tenbrunsel & Messick, 2004). Framing and sanctions imposed on unethical behavior moderate the degree to which ethicality is cognitively available or fades.
	Ignorance of one's own unethicality
Ethical Detachment occurs when self-interested individuals have difficulty approaching ethical dilemmas without self-serving bias.	***Ethical Detachment***: Individuals who hold vested self-interests are prone to approach situations self-biased and tend to ignore their self-centeredness (Ross & Sicoly, 1979). In conflicts between acting in one's self-interest and being socially responsible, self-serving options appear more natural than ethical considerations, which may include complex meta-cognitions about others and uncertain future perspectives (Moore, Loewenstein, Tanlu & Bazerman, 2004).
Memory Revisionism attributes that individuals selectively and egocentrically revise their memory as for threats of perceiving themselves as being nethical.	***Memory Revisionism***: A process by which people selectively revise their memory as for threats to a positive self-image (Epstein, 1973; Markus & Wurf, 1987). When values are challenged by actual behavior, individuals' perception gets biases in order to refrain from unethical notions of the self (Chaiken, Giner-Sorolla & Chen, 1996). Through a selective memory filter, individuals search for biased self-supporting evidence (Baron, 1995; Nisbett & Ross, 1980; Pyszczynski & Greenberg, 1987; Snyder & Swann, 1978). Whilst the selective memory sustains positive self perceptions, it impedes the ability to strive for higher levels of ethicality (O'Banion & Arkowitz, 1977; Zuroff, Colussy & Wielgus, 1983).
Moral Disengagement implies motivated forgetting of moral rules and unethical information cues of the self.	***Moral Disengagement***: Motivated forgetting of moral standards avoids distress of immorality, yet at the same time allows guiltless unethicality to remain uncensored (Bandura, 1999; Baumeister & Heatherton, 1996; Shu, Gino & Bazerman, 2009). Moral salience and the need for justification reduce moral disengagement (Mazar, Amir & Ariely, 2008).
Slippery Slope refers to a potential decline in ethicality as for a chain of unnoticed deviations from regular moral standards.	***Slippery Slope***: Individuals compare their actions to their past behavior. If their unethicality represents a small deviation from the standard, the change remains unnoticed and a potentially slightly more unethical behavior becomes the new reference point (Tenbrunsel & Messick, 2004). The potential gradual decline of ethicality follows a slippery slope featuring incremental change. In sync, beholders are more likely to accept others' immorality if their unethical behavior erodes slowly and develops gradually over time rather than occurs in an abrupt shift (Gino & Bazerman, 2005).

continued on following page

Table 1. Continued

	Bounded Ethicality
Focus on the present whilst being blinded by future uncertainty	
The ***Availability Heuristic*** lets decision makers overweight current, vivid happenings.	***Availability Heuristic***: Temporal perspectives impact on decision making. The distant future is viewed as abstract and subordinate, while the present appears more detailed and concrete (Rogers & Bazerman, 2007). Close events that affect us immediately are more easily recalled and seem more available (Tversky & Kahneman, 1974). The availability heuristic lets decision makers overweight vivid instances and neglect future considerations. Outcomes that demand the anticipation of the future are less vivid, harder to process and require more involvement. When outcomes are not vivid, humans tend to avoid action (Bazerman & Watkins, 2004). The lack of vividness of environmental decay and climate change lets decision makers refrain from noticing future resource constraints and intergenerational fairness predicaments. Falling prey to the availability heuristic is especially crucial for corporate and political leaders, whose decision making extraordinarily impacts on future societal conditions.
Intergenerational Anonymity holds that individuals have difficulty envisioning future generations as potential victims of today's consumption.	***Intergenerational anonymity*** holds that individuals have difficulty envisioning anonymous future generations as potential victims of today's consumption (Bazerman, Messick, Tenbrunsel & Wade-Benzoni, 1997). Future generations are a vague group of people living in a distant time (Bazerman, 2008). The more distant and uncertain future negative impacts are, the less likely individuals consider them. In the environmental domain, the lack of future anticipation causes neglect of environmental resources preservation.
The ***Status Quo Bias*** addresses that individuals strive to maintain their current position which results in an overall ignorance of the necessity to change.	***Status Quo Bias***: Individuals have an aversion to deviations from their status quo (Samuelson & Zeckhauser, 1988; Thaler, 1980). The status quo bias addresses that individuals strive to maintain their current position as for information awareness deficiencies and ignorance of the necessity to change. The status quo bias becomes stronger when multiple parties place different weights onto various concerns. In the environmental context, the status quo bias is an irrational barrier to preventing predictable surprises. Governmental officials refraining from improving obsolete policies imply long-term societal constraints (Bazerman, Baron & Shonk, 2001).
Temporal Trade-Off Predicaments arise when short-term self-interests stand at odds with long-term societal concerns.	***Temporal Trade-Off Predicaments***: Dilemmas arise when self-interests stand at odds with societal responsibility (Tenbrunsel, Wade-Benzoni, Messick & Bazerman, 1997). In temporal trade-off predicaments, individuals tend to overweight present consumption at the expense of future generations (Wade-Benzoni, 1996). When immediate losses loom larger than prospective future gains, we tend to fail to act in time and miss opportunities for creating long-term value. As sustainability policies have immediate costs, their current implementation may be refrained from although it would result in net societal savings.
Discounting the Future implies that people tend to overweight short-term considerations rather than evaluating options with a long-term perspective.	***Discounting the Future***: In daily decisions, humans have a general tendency to discount future problems. The discount function resembles the shape of a hyperbola, which implies that people overweight short-term considerations rather than evaluating options from a long-term perspective (Frederick, Loewenstein & O'Donoghue, 2002; Laibson, 1994). Future discounting gets more skewed, the more uncertain and distant future perspectives are (Wade-Benzoni, 1999). Future discounting results in overweighting the immediate costs of environmental conscientiousness and people refraining from necessary action (Ackerman & Heinzerling, 2004; Wade-Benzoni, 1996). As for policy implementations, citizens were found to support environmental policies with initial costs and long-term benefits when the policies were to be implemented in the future rather than immediately (Rogers & Bazerman, 2007).

continued on following page

Table 1. Continued

	Bounded Ethicality
Want / Should Conflicts comprise intrapersonal dilemmas between immediate gratification and future benefits.	***Want / Should Conflicts***: While game theory sheds light on economic facets of common goods dilemmas, scarce is the knowledge on concomitant emotional facets of social dilemmas. The *want / should* distinction depicts emotional facets of human decision making predicaments between egoistic and socially responsibility (Bazerman, Tenbrunsel & Wade-Benzoni, 1998). Hot headed *want* choices are emotional, affective and impulsive; whilst emotionally cooler *should* decisions are characterized as rational, cognitive and thoughtful. The *want* self is related to self-interests and a disregard of ethical considerations, whilst the *should* self encompasses ethical intentions and moral principles (Bazerman et al., 1998). *Want* needs feature immediate gratification, while *shoulds* address future benefits (Ainslie, 1975; 1992; Shefrin & Thaler, 1988; Winston, 1980). Prior to ethical decision making, individuals believe to act in line with the *should*; in the aftermath of an unethical decision, they distort the perception of our *want* behavior to hold themselves ethical in sync with the *should*. Exploratory evidence indicates that people learn about their *want / should* biases with experience and gain the capacity to curb its influence (Milkman, Rogers & Bazerman, 2009). As for policy implications, individuals have an increased willingness to support *should* policies when they are to be implemented in the distant rather than in the near future (Rogers & Bazerman, 2007).
Tuning refers to an adaptation of preferences based on availability and circumstances.	***Tuning***: The human tendency to mentally mold preferences, tastes and habits in accordance to available resources and circumstances (Bazerman et al., 1997). As for reducing the likelihood of necessary changes, tuning implies vulnerability to predictable surprises of future resource constraints.
Behavioral Forecasting Errors occur when individuals are overly confident in their future performance.	***Behavioral Forecasting Errors***: Human forecasts of behavioral consequences are often inaccurate (Osberg & Shrauger, 1986; Sherman, 1980). In general, individuals are overly confident in their predicted future performance – especially when socially desirable and moral choices are involved (Diekmann, Tenbrunsel & Galinsky, 2003; Epley & Dunning, 2000; Sherman, 1980; Vallone, Griffin, Lin & Ross, 1990).
	Positive illusions about the future
Positive Illusions imply unrealistic optimism based on the belief that the future will be better and brighter than possible.	***Positive Illusions***: describe unrealistic optimism based on the belief that the future will be better and brighter than realistically possible (Bazerman et al., 2001; Taylor, 1989). Positive illusions about the self protect the self-esteem, enhance commitment and allow people to persist difficult tasks. At the same time, positive illusions reduce rationality (Taylor, 1989). In the false believe of control of uncontrollable events, positive illusions foster ignorance for the urgency of change, which counterweights environmental protection (Crocker, 1982).
Future Uncertainty exacerbates biases as for difficulty in imagining future options.	***Future Uncertainty***: crucially impacts on decision making as for exacerbating ethical ignorance and biases (Wade-Benzoni, Tenbrunsel & Bazerman, 1996). Lacking imagination of future perspectives forces people to mentally separate decision choices – that is to process them one by one – which fortifies human fallibility (Bazerman, White & Loewenstein, 1995). Future uncertainty causes unethicality to remain unnoticed during the decision making and lets individuals favor irrational *want* choices (Gino et al., 2008; Milkman et al., 2009).

continued on following page

Table 1. Continued

	Bounded Ethicality
The ***Fairness Bias*** attributes that we think that we are fairer than others and more critical of others' ethicality.	***Fairness Bias***: The human view of fairness is biased by self-interest. The fairness bias attributes that we think that we are more honest, trustworthy and fair than others and we are more critical and suspicious of others' ethicality (Alicke, 1985; Baumhart, 1968; Epley & Caruso, 2004; Epley & Dunning, 2000; Messick & Bazerman, 1996; Messick, Bloom, Boldizar & Samuelson, 1985). Humans preferably notice and attend information that supports their self-interests, recall self-supportive evidence more easily and overweight self-serving views in personal judgments (Babcock, Loewenstein, Issacharoff & Camerer, 1995; Lord, Ross & Lepper, 1979; Messick & Sentis, 1979, 1985; Thompson & Loewenstein, 1992).
Misperception of others' ethicality and related negotiation biases	
Reactive Egoism occurs when group members, who are made aware of their unfair claim of collective goods, become more egoistic.	***Reactive Egoism***: Groups members often claim a selfishly-biased unfair share of collective resources and believe that they deserve an unfair credit for collaborative efforts (Babcock & Loewenstein, 1997; Leary & Forsyth, 1987; Ross & Sicoly, 1979). This cognitive bias can be overcome if individuals are made to consider others' perspectives. However, this perspective taking invokes cynicism and egoistic behavior – a phenomenon called reactive egoism (Babcock & Loewenstein, 1997; Caruso, Epley & Bazerman, 2005a; Paese & Yonker, 2001). Perspective taking also reduces the interest in future collaborations among those who belief that they contributed more than others (Caruso, Epley & Bazerman, 2005b). Reactive egoism gets more accentuated in competitive contexts. Competing parties hold the honest believe that it is fair for them to bear less responsibility and act accordingly.
Mythical Fixed Pie of Negotiation depicts negotiators' failure to look for solutions that heighten the pool of resources and/or degrees of freedom.	***Mythical Fixed Pie of Negotiation***: In negotiations individuals tend to think that they debate over finite resources. Negotiators thereby fail to look for alternatives that enlarge the pool of resources and degrees of freedom. As for sustainability, the search for environmental protection innovations holds long-term advantages and positive externalities that can easily be overshadowed by narrow-minded, short-term foci (Porter & van der Linde, 1995).
Bounded Responsibility addresses the fact that responsibility gets diffused the more constituents are involved.	***Bounded Responsibility***: Responsibility is most blatant in one-on-one relationships and gets diffused the more constituents are involved (Bandura, 1999). Responsibility gets blurred the more distant victims and outcomes appear and the less identifiable negative externalities are. The different scales of responsibility and the remedies to counterweight the consequences of biases become apparent when studying the nature and enforcement of responsibility. Whilst in nuclear families' responsibility is based on mutual trust; within society social responsibility is foremost regulated by contracts and governmental control.
	Blurred collective responsibility
Collective Responsibility implies collectively shared problems featuring a lowered degree of individuals' attention for individual solution finding.	***Collective Responsibility***: Collectively shared problems feature a lowered degree of individuals' attention to finding solutions on an individual basis. If collectively shared problems are 'psychologically outsourced,' individuals think that others will take care of their solution. The illusion of others addressing challenges crowds out the individual motivation to tackle problems and respectively change behavioral patterns.
Mispricing of Natural Resources refers to underestimating the price of environmental preservation.	***Mispricing of Natural Resources***: People view the preservation of environmental assets as voluntary contribution rather than strategic advantages. Future intangible preferences and predicted expected utility are hard to imagine, which reduces the willingness-to-pay for the preservation of environmental goods and leads to long-term societal losses and intergenerational equity constraints (Bazerman et al., 1997).

continued on following page

Table 1. Continued

	Bounded Ethicality
Public Goods Detachment addresses a hunch that collectively shared common goods go hand in hand with lowered degrees of loss aversion.	***Public Goods Detachment***: Individuals have an aversion to losses from their endowments (Samuelson & Zeckhauser, 1988; Thaler, 1980). This loss aversion may be higher for individual property of tangible goods than for intangible common goods. Psychological detachment of ownership of goods is yet to be tested for natural resources.
Negative Goal Attainment outlines that extrinsically imposed goals may crowd out intrinsic motivation and efficient, flexible solution finding.	***Negative Goal Attainment***: Externally imposed standards influence people's decision making (Tenbrunsel, Wade-Benzoni, Messick & Bazerman, 2000). An over-reliance on regulatory goals creates a dominant wish to meet given standard (Hoffman & Bazerman, 2007). However, if these standards are obsolete or inefficient, they can crowd out intrinsic motivation for change and hinder flexible solution finding. Extrinsically motivating goal attainment can thus lower the motivation to preserve natural resources and overshadow efficient environmental protection (Schweitzer, Ordónez & Douma, 2004).
In ***Principal-Agent Predicaments*** leaders direct subordinates to contribute and/or bear responsibility for their unethicality.	***Principal-Agent Predicaments***: Collectively shared responsibilities can blur the focus on ethicality. Diffusion of responsibility becomes most crucial when leaders direct subordinates to contribute to and/or bear responsibility for their unethicality (Darley & Latane, 1968).
Indirect Agency attributes that agents may indirectly be forced to unethicality by the organizational structure.	***Indirect Agency***: Attributes agents' failure to consider potential unethicality of commands (Paharia, Kassam, Greene & Bazerman, 2009). Agents may indirectly be forced to unethicality by external settings whilst being blindfold to the ethical consequences of their actions (Cushman, 2008; Young, Cushman, Hauser & Saxe, 2007). If agents face ethical infringements, they have the choice of command obedience, resistance or whistle blowing.

We tend to **ignore unethicality cues regarding ourselves** (*ethical detachment*, *moral disengagement*). As we are prone to adjusting our self-perception to meet our conscious ethical standards (*memory revisionism*), unethicality can unnoticingly slip into our behavior (*slippery slope*).

With a **focus on the present** (*availability heuristic*), we ignore future generations as potential victims of today's consumption (*discounting the future*, *intergenerational anonymity*, *temporal trade-off predicaments*). Our tendency to reside in the status quo (*status quo bias*) and adapt our perception and needs to slightly changing conditions (*tuning*) makes us vulnerable to lurking crises. This is especially crucial in sustainability considerations, in which we tend to underestimate the exponential cost increase of environmental protection and climate change. When refraining from discipline today, we miss opportunities for improving our future conditions (*want / should conflicts*) (Puaschunder, 2017a).

Discounting future events includes perspectives about the future into our everyday economic decision making as a prerequisite for sustainable development. However, if we anticipate the **future in discounting, we hold positive illusions** (*behavioral forecasting errors, positive illusions*) and *future uncertainty* exacerbates this view.

We have **misperceptions and a biased judgment of others' ethicality**. When it comes to others, we unreasonably raise the standards of responsibility (*fairness bias*) and selfishly claim disproportionate shares of common goods (*reactive egoism*). In negotiations we fail to see alternative solutions to ethical predicaments (*mythical fixed pie of negotiation*).

Collectively shared responsibility gets blurred among constituents (*bounded* and *collective responsibility*). Diffusion of responsibility leaves the individual with inefficient rigor to fulfilling externally imposed, standardized goals (*negative goal attainment*). Citizens' *public goods detachment* and *mispriced values of natural resources* hinder environmental protection. Organizational command structures and information deficiencies impact on subordinates' social responsibility (*indirect agency, principal-agent predicaments*).

Unnoticed human decision making fallibility implies responsibility deficiencies for society. As an avenue for change, 'libertarian paternalism' currently promises efficient public polistrategies to surmounting bounded ethicality (Thaler & Sunstein, 2008). Libertarian paternalism features policies that account for how people make decisions and invisibly steer decision making in a more socially responsible direction. 'Paternalism' thereby stands for manipulating people to act according to the preferences of the policy makers; 'libertarian' attributes that changes do not limit the individual freedom. By offering 'behavioral nudges,' policies influence behaviors within the given institutional framework whilst upholding personal freedom. Examples for nudges are opt-in and opt-out solutions, in which citizens face either actively or passively framed choices that implicitly influence decision outcomes (Bazerman & Moore, 2009; Thaler & Sunstein, 2008). This implicit guidance has proved as a successful means to trigger organ donations and financial social responsibility (Bazerman & Moore, 2009; Thaler & Sunstein, 2008). Bounded ethicality is most crucial when social responsibility deficiencies have economic impacts within market systems.

SOCIAL RESPONSIBILITY IN MARKETS

Adam Smith proposed unregulated market forces as the optimum means to propel economies and advance society. Following this notion, libertarianism holds open markets as the most efficient societal system to allocate scarce resources and progress society by the collective striving of self-interested market agents. Libertarians depict market mechanisms as the optimum means to distribute scarce resources. In the libertarian view, governmental market interference and control of corporate conduct are unnecessary hindrances of free market forces (Friedman, 2002). The individual pursuit of self-interest in combination with unbound market mechanisms are believed to lead to a spontaneous order fostering the overall economic development and societal advancement.

The scenario of self-interested market agents pursuing profit maximization, however, does not address social responsibility (Bekefi, 2006; Soros, 2000; Simon, 2004). As societies cannot exist without a social compound, governmental social welfare and evolutionary-grown social responsibility notions are essential for human well-being (Rodrik, 2007; Soros, 2000).

As a prerequisite for societal stability, social welfare is guidelined by democratically-enacted governmental control and regulation (De Soto, 2000). Democratic market economies feature a mix of governmental intervention and laissez-faire market forces that complement another in the provision of social services. Governmental regulations implement CSR in legal frameworks that ensure social responsibility throughout the entire value chain – e.g., in the International Organization for Standardization (ISO)'s and Eco Management and Audit Scheme (EMAS) certifications. Public officials also regulate CSR interactions by multi-stakeholder management means. However, the free choice to engage in social responsibility raises ethical predicaments for decision makers (Taylor, 1988).

In addition to legislative oversight, many market transactions are primarily based on trust (Zak, 2008). Responsible market participants ensure correct business performance and natural rule obedience which breeds trust in the well-functioning of markets. The collective trust in the responsibility of market actors eases business transactions by replacing the constant need for law enforcement and minimizing contracting, performance and monitoring costs (Andreoni & Miller, 2002; Batson, 1991; Yamagishi & Yamagishi, 1994). As a means to the end of market efficiency, trust in the responsibility of market actors is a pivotal ingredient of market economies (Newton & Ford, 2008).

Trust in the responsibility of market participants is associated with market cooperation (Kramer & Tyler, 1996; Ostrom & Walker, 2003), social capital (Putnam, 2000; Putnam, Leonardi & Nanetti, 1993), governmental stability (Inglehart, 1999; LaPorta, Lopez-de-Silanes, Shleifer & Vishny, 1997) and economic growth (Knack & Keefer, 1997; Zak & Knack, 2001). Without trust in market actors' responsible performance, the psychological hesitancy and institutional costs of market transactions would limit economic activities.

Trust, at the same time, implies vulnerability as for the exposure to risks of default in ethical dilemma decisions and bounded responsibility constraints (Kramer, 1999; Mansbridge, 1999). Ethical dilemmas arise as responsible markets participants are naturally inclined to self-interest. Personal ethical dilemmas of market decision making can be overcome by concurrently pursuing market profit maximization and altruistic philanthropy. Combining rational market performance with a civilian role is a feature of corporate philanthropists such as, for example, George Soros, who maximizes profits in asset allocations, yet at the same time fosters social welfare in non-profit activities – among others by the Open Society Institute and Soros Foundation.

When individuals who face ethical dilemmas are not aware of decision making fallibility, their responsibility is bounded. In the corporate setting, ethical predicaments may not become apparent if executives are not trained in responsible decision making. Bounded responsibility also stems from dysfunctional incentives. Corporate goal settings can implicitly shield individuals from perceiving business ethics as a corporate advantage. Organizational command-and-control structures and competitive remuneration systems can accentuate individual profit maximization that counterweights societal concerns. Short-sighted evaluation periods draw attention from long-term perspectives and let managers over-discount the future in environmental sustainability considerations. Information deficiencies lower the degree of social responsibility as for decreasing the possibility to consider the potential future implications of decisions.

As for turning to higher levels of responsibility, ingrained organizational cultural norms, status quo biases and economic sunk costs prevent corporate executives from addressing change. Established power bases, habitual work practices and taken-for-granted managerial command-control hierarchies may cause resistance to reforms, particularly when the outcomes are uncertain.

Collectively shared corporate social responsibilities can blur the focus on ethicality, which emphasizes the importance of ethical leadership. Responsible leadership decisions demand taking multiple perspectives, constituents' needs, social externalities and future anticipations into consideration. Within the organizational context, ethical leadership can be bounded, when leaders face multiple obligations on ethical predicaments that impact on their decision making quality.

Leaders' bounded responsibility bears extraordinary levels of risks as value-based leadership triggers the trust of self-actualized subordinates. Trusting leaders implies exposure to the risk of neglecting useful information, refraining from critical assessments and alternative solution seeking. In group think phenomena, trust in irresponsible leaders lets followers fall prey to leaders' accidental fallibility, which galvanizes the outcomes of decision making errors (Janis & Mann, 1977; Kramer, 1999; Mansbridge, 1999).

Current knowledge-based market structures and fast-paced market systems increase the risk of leaders' bounded ethicality. The negative impacts of bounded rationality, speedy information and capital transfer are outlined in Paul Krugman's estimations of Austria's bankruptcy likelihood being publicly announced in April 2009. Later found to have been based on erroneous data, the quick information dissemination of his predictions led to a costly foreign investment drain for the Austrian Republic. Finding the optimal balance between value-laden leadership and rational decision making, but also informing leaders and subordinates about decision making fallibility appear to be essential strategies to minimize negative outcomes of leaders' bounded ethicality in causing societal crises.

Diffusion of responsibility becomes most crucial when corporate executives direct their subordinates to contribute to irresponsible corporate conduct (Darley & Latane, 1968). In this indirect agency, the agents may implicitly be steered towards immoral behavior whilst being blindfold to the ethical consequences of their action (Cushman, 2008; Young et al., 2007). Agents who recognize moral infringements face trade-offs between command obedience, resistance or whistle blowing.

Today's complex global governance systems shift attention away from individual responsibility (Milkman, Chugh & Bazerman, 2008). In a currently globalizing world featuring international corporations and a ceasing role of governmental global crises prevention, responsibility can get diffused among anonymous market participants. The tightening of the political, economic and cultural web increases the cognitive load of more and more time-pressured key decision makers who determine the fate of present and future constituents. This tendency may be enhanced as responsibility is a feeling towards a group and less an obligation towards society.

The crucial role of bounded responsibility in triggering societal crises is addressed by the metaphor of predictable surprises (Bazerman, in speech, April 2009). Predictable surprises imply that individuals collectively face obstacles to respond efficiently to avert crises as for neglecting information and anticipating future negative events. Leaders who do not consider the evolving consequences of unreflected unethicality and/or whose preventive actions are hindered by external constraints can accidently fall prey to predictable surprises (Bazerman & Watkins, 2004; Winship & Rein, 1999). As such the 2008 World Financial Recession was partially triggered by executives who did not foresee the cumulative effects of their singular irresponsible decisions on the overall economic stability and societal condition. Although representatives of financial institutions – such as the International Monetary Fund and the European Central Bank – had warned of systemic undervaluation of risks in the years prior to the crisis, no counterweighing actions were taken (Tumpel-Gugerell, 2009). Future risk evaluations and coordinated foresight are meant to prevent future predictable surprises.

Anonymous responsibility diffusion is crucial in principal-agent relations, in which an agent is engaged to responsibly act on behalf of and in line with the best interest of the principal. Agents feature specialized knowledge and skills or overcome physical and temporal constraints within market systems. Information asymmetries between principals and agents in the form the principal's limited ability to observe the agent's action can result in principal-agent responsibility predicaments.

On an aggregate level, corporate executives face quasi-principal-agent dilemmas in responsibility towards share- or stakeholders. CEO duties typically refer to the best interest of the corporation, but whether this attributes solely to corporate shareholders or a wider range of stakeholders – potentially even future constituents – is not well defined (Cox & Haven, 2003). In 1970 the US economist Milton Friedman held shareholder primacy as the sole responsibility of corporations. As employees to owners, corporate executives were meant to entirely focus on maximizing shareholder equity. This premise was backed up by classic finance theory (Ehrlich, 2005; Fisch, 2006; Friedman, 1970; Renneboog, Horst & Zhang, 2007; Springer 1999). However, the legal basis for shareholder primacy varies throughout national legislations. Whilst the overall judicial records are most often supportive of a duty to maximize shareholders profits, it leaves room for the possibility that corporations sacrifice in the public interest. Some corporate laws – such as the French – give managers discretion to comply with social norms even if this lowers shareholder profits (Elhauge, 2005). Growing legislations backed up by codes of loyalty and corporate ethics principles promote CEOs responsibility to a variety of stakeholders and corporate obligations to the larger society (Gabaldon, 2006; Sheehy, 2005, 2015). In an attempt to capture the concurrent unstandardized legal foundations within the international arena, in December 2001 the OECD held a round table discussion on stakeholder influences on corporations as well as trade-off predicaments between share- and stakeholder responsibilities (Clark, 1986; Nourick, 2001; Simons, Powers & Gunnemann, 1972).

In the finance sector, fiduciary duties imply principal-agent dilemmas. Originated from a person entrusted to another one's property, fiduciaries advise clients on investments or keep custody of client funds. Fiduciaries are individuals who have a fiduciary responsibility that entrusts them to act in the interest of the client without gaining any personal benefit except with the knowledge and consent of the client. Fiduciaries face moral and ethical dilemmas if self interests conflict with social responsibility for the client and the wider stakeholder community.

Fiduciary responsibility to a variety of stakeholders is attributed by the US Statement of Investment Principles (Goodpaster & Matthews, 2003). Since the 2000, trustees have been required to disclose – as a part of their Statement of Investment Principles – the extent to which social, environmental or ethical considerations are taken into account in the selection, retention and realization of investments. This measure was introduced to encourage socially responsible investments in pension funds (Hennigfeld et al., 2006).

Fiduciaries serving anonymous market participants can create a situation of psychological detachment from blurred responsibility. As outlined by the 2008 World Financial Recession, corporate irresponsible conduct and fiduciary responsibility failures in combination with heightened degrees of societal trust without regulatory and accountability controls triggered a worldwide financial turmoil. In the aftermath of the crisis outbreak, corporate executives' and fiduciary duties to share- or stakeholders have become subject to scrutiny (Deegan & Blomquist, 2006; Kotler & Lee, 2005; Lee & Kotler, 2013). Obligations to multiple stakeholders are currently foremost ensured by soft-law voluntary corporate and financial social responsibility models that promote to consider the overall stakeholder community in corporate conduct and investment decision making (Rodrik, 2007; Steurer, 2010).

CORPORATE SOCIAL RESPONSIBILITY (CSR)

Today economist Milton Friedman's proclamation of corporations' primary goal being shareholder equity maximization is challenged. Nowadays corporate conduct increasingly address societal and philanthropic responsibilities. As an *en vogue* concept, Corporate Social Responsibility (CSR) has gained unprecedented momentum (Livesey, 2002; Matten & Crane, 2005).

Originally drawing upon governmental and political theories that focus on the relationship of the individual to the state, CSR depicts the relation of individuals and corporations. Based upon business ethics, CSR overlaps corporate philanthropy, corporate citizenship and sustainability. As a "concept whereby companies integrate social and environmental concerns in their business operations and interaction with the stakeholders," CSR comprises the voluntary and pro-active corporate commitment to operate in an economically, socially and environmentally responsible and sustainable manner whilst balancing the interests of diverse stakeholders (Commission of the European Communities Report 2001, p. 6; De Silva & Amerasinghe, 2004). CSR comprises the *economic responsibility* for the corporation in terms of return on the investment; the *legal responsibility* to abide by the laws of society as the codification of societal moral commitments; the *ethical responsibility* to do what is right, just, and fair beyond economic and legal obligations; and the *philanthropic responsibility* to contribute to various kinds of social, educational, recreational and cultural purposes to improve the overall societal quality of life (Carroll 1979, 1991, 1999).

In the wider sense, CSR can be seen as a quasi-democratic principle to attribute stakeholder demands within the corporate world. CSR is shaped by progressive corporations, societal pressure and partnership favoring public policies (Steurer, 2010). As a voluntary engagement, CSR activities complement hard-law social regulations. As a form of "mandated self-regulation," CSR rather stems from social pressure than regulatory state power (Bartle & Vass, 2007 in Steurer, 2010).

CSR policies pronounce ethical values and moral goals in the domains of environmental protection, health and safety standards, diversity management and human rights. CSR policy instruments comprise *legal* (e.g., legal and constitutional acts, regulations on reporting and information disclosure, prohibitions and sanctions for investments), *economic* (e.g., subsidies, grants, export credits, incentives), *informal* (e.g., research and educational activities, information resources such as websites, brochures and reports, guidelines and codes of conduct, campaign material), *partnering* (e.g., networks, partnerships, agreements, multistakeholder forums, contact points) and *hybrid* means (e.g., centers, platforms, programs, labels, action plans, multi-stakeholder initiatives, awards and blacklists, certifications, policy coordination, sustainable and socially responsible procurement) (Steurer, 2010).

CSR is implemented by the compliance with discretionary regulations, integration of voluntary norms and ethical principles in leadership models, but also the attention to risks imbued in economic, social and environmental externalities of corporate conduct (Steurer, 2010). CSR social programs and instruments achieve social responsibility goals and weight social impacts of responsible working practices. In particular, CSR themes feature *raising awareness and building capacities* for social and environmental causes; *improving disclosure and transparency* on reliable information on the economic, social and environmental performance of corporations to stakeholders; *fostering socially responsible investment* by considering CSR, social and environmental externalities and ethical criteria in capital allocations; and *leading by example* regarding socially responsible corporate practices (Steurer, 2010).

In the international arena, CSR pro-actively sets the standards to continuously enhance corporate contributions to economic, social and environmental development (Sachs, 2007; World Development Report, 2005). In this light, CSR is an important forerunner for innovative and future-oriented legislations that help averting future prisoners' dilemmas in the light of scarce environmental resources.

Within the last decades, CSR has continuously leveraged into a mainstream corporate phenomenon (Wolff, 2002). Today almost all major corporations have embedded CSR in their codes of conduct, incorporated CSR practices in human resources management and embraced CSR in their stakeholder relation. Especially corporations that feature transparent outputs and end-customer contact have integrated CSR in their customer relation. Professional CSR reporting on social, ethical, and environmental performance (e.g., standardized ISO or EMOS norms) serves as a best practice guideline that is accompanied by an emerging stream of academic literature and professional auditing on CSR (Livesey 2002, Matten & Crane 2005). Steurer (2010) categorizes the CSR literature to foremost comprise case studies that focus on single CSR initiatives (e.g., Barkemeyer, 2007; Holgaard & Jørgensen, 2005; Konrad, Martinuzzi & Steurer, 2008); conceptual analyses that capture business-government relations and political aspects of CSR (e.g., Moon, 2002, 2007; Midttun, 2005) as well as exploratory comparative CSR policy analyses (e.g., de la Cuesta & Martinez, 2004; Moon & Vogel, 2007). The disparate ways to address CSR are bundled by respective policy frameworks and initiatives – such as the OECD Guidelines for Multinational Enterprises, the United Nations Global Compact (UNGC), the Global Reporting Initiative, AA1000 reports of corporate social impacts, the ISO quality standards and the SA 8000 (Steurer, 2010; Waddock & Graves, 1997). Corporate global governance policies are foremost pioneered at international conventions and conferences – e.g., at the World Summit on Sustainable Development, the World Summit on the Information Society and the World Economic Forum.

In recent decades, CSR has risen to prominence in the course of globalization, political and societal trends as well as economic and demographic changes.

In the wake of **globalization**, the progressive deterritorialization of social, political, economic interaction has leveraged many aspects of societal welfare beyond the power, control and influence of nation states. Global economic interdependence has undermined the capacity of governments to control economies and led to global societal deficiencies out of reach for nation states that demand for multi-stakeholder solutions (Sichler, 2006).

Globalization has heightened the outreach of international corporations and triggered the transnational diffusion of market interactions (Sichler, 2006). Open society trends have *expanded markets worldwide*. In the wake of outsourcing trends, global players have spread production chains around the world that require for social quality control on an international basis (Prahalad & Hammond, 2003; Sichler, 2006). Corporate conduct in politically fragile and ideologically differing territories is challenged by unstandardized regulatory frameworks and culture-dependent business practices. Arising social deficiencies increase the demand for standardized, internationally-applicable social norms of corporate conduct which ensure that social best practices are addressed in headquarters and subsidiaries alike. As for facing these challenges, international corporations have grown into social enterprises and global governance entities. Beyond the voluntary fulfillment of corporate social standards, multinational corporations have become "governmental stand-ins" in the provision of social services in underdeveloped markets (Livesey, 2002, p. 314; Stiglitz, 2003).

Globalization intensified worldwide communication and interaction (Sichler, 2006). Access to information on corporate standards around the globe was fostered by technological revolutions featuring extended *media coverage of corporate conduct* and peculiarities of production sights (Bonß, 2000 in Sichler, 2006; Waddock & Graves, 1997). The transparency of corporate activities in combination with heightened degrees of autonomous decision making of corporate executives has perpetuated stakeholder activism (Sichler, 2006). Especially corporations operating in competitive international markets with transparent products and/or services are pressured to pay attention to social responsibility (Bagnoli & Watts, 2003).

In the wake of disclosure of corporate failures, *non-governmental organizations* (NGOs) have evolved. Benefiting from new levels of transparency of corporate activities and access to high-tech media, these voluntary civil society organizations of activist groups monitor corporate operations and disseminate information about CSR. NGOs call for accountability of CSR conduct by taking advantage of facebook, twitter and blogs for information dissemination, networking and coordinating activities among stakeholders.

The world-wide corporate expansion has opened *governance gaps* – implying imbalances between corporations and nation state policies. Global governance gaps are blatant in the human rights domain and applicable in environmental constraints when. Gaps open when subsidiary governments refrain from implementing social or environmental protection standards as for the fear of foreign capital flight and losing attraction as low-cost production sites. This has been particularly the case in developing countries in which governments lack the institutional capacity to enforce national laws and regulations against powerful global players doing unethical business within their territory. The negative impact of multinational corporations on subsidiary host countries also becomes apparent in agreements between host governments and corporations to freeze social protection as well as foreign investors claiming competitive loss compensations for worker welfare expenditures (Ruggie, 2008). As a remedy, stakeholder-demanded CSR ensures human rights and labor standards as well as sustainability attention in every part of the international supply chain. Problematic oversight deficiencies imply the fact that if infringement cases go to international arbitration, they are generally treated as commercial disputes and thus conducted under closure for the sake of commercial confidentiality (Ruggie, 2008).

Apart from the inability of nation states to manage global governance issues without the help of corporations, CSR emerged in situations when governments retreated from social service provision (Matten & Moon, 2004). **Political trends** of governmental *privatization* and *market liberalization* have steadily lowered the degree of public social welfare. Starting as a policy trend in the 1970s, privatization transferred public services onto the corporate sector (Brown, Potoski & Van Slyke, 2006; Farrington, Curran, Gori, O'Gorman & Queenan, 2017; Van Slyke, 2003). In combination with the stringent deregulation of markets throughout the 1980s and the 1990s –

exemplified by Thatcherism and Reaganomics – private actors' social welfare contributions rose continuously.

During the 1990s *New Public Management* (NPM) introduced private sector market dynamics in public service provision (e.g., by voucher programs) and outsourced state obligations to private contractors (Kettl, 2006). Privatization, welfare reform and outsourcing triggered social responsibility in economic markets. In recent years, CSR – that started out as a neo-liberal concept in the wake of downscaled government regulations – matured into a more progressive approach of societal co-regulation (Steurer, 2010).

Societal trends attributed to CSR feature changed *consumption behavior*. Post-materialistic consumers who are concerned about human rights and environmental protection want corporate conduct to be in line with legislative frameworks and personal standards of ethics (Sparkes, 2002). Post-materialistic consumers consider CSR in their purchase decision and influence corporate conduct by consumer activism and boycotts (Jones & Pollitt, 1998). *Humanization trends* – featuring an increasing autonomy and self-regulation of employees who demand self-determination – fostered responsibility in working situations (Paulus, 1994 in Sichler, 2006). As the core of autonomy, self-determination describes the opportunity to choose processes, control and time frames in fulfilling working tasks (Sichler, 2006). Self-determination is a means to enhance the self-image by fulfilling working tasks responsibly within the social compound (Sichler, 2006). In addition, the rising trend of individualization and participation of an educated workforce and the harmonization of work with lifestyle attitudes have led to the steady growth of CSR (Kettner, 1998 in Sichler, 2006).

CSR-contributing **economic trends** comprise heightened competition due to a shift from producer- to consumer-dominated markets (Giesler & Veresiu, 2014). The focus on *consumer demands* has perpetuated social responsibility as a branding feature that fosters corporate competitiveness (Sichler, 2006).

Additionally *technical revolutions* have shifted technical work towards high-end cognitive production. In modern work situations, manual demands have become replaced by social responsibility obligations. Coordination, management and planning of future-oriented decision making are nowadays the core of leadership demands (Weber et al., 2004). In combination with heightened levels of autonomy, which leveraged the degrees of freedom of corporate conduct, social responsibility has become a central part of everyday's decision making of corporate executives who are responsible to multiple stakeholders (Weber et al., 2004).

Demographic trends of heightened market segmentation raising niche products and services, but also population trends in the Western World are drivers of CSR. Endowed with high levels of purchasing power, the aging baby boomers have leveraged into a high-end, postmaterialistic consumption group that pays attention to intangible product features and CSR branding such as eco-labelling. The management revolution in combination with a consumer needs-led production, have assigned CSR a pivotal feature in today's workforce and production chain.

Today CSR has become an up-to-date issue on the agenda of multinational corporations operating in the Western World, but also of societies that undergo economic transitions and development. In the light of global problems out of reach for nation states, but also as for the ongoing rise of international joint ventures and strategic alliances; the worldwide importance of CSR is predicted to grow in the following years to come. With a continuously rising role of international corporations in global governance, CSR has become an issue of relevance for a wide range of constituents to whom social responsibility is of value.

THE VALUE OF CSR

Primarily corporations are profitability-dependent entities that increase shareholder return by efficient product and/or service provision (Fullerton & Henderson, 1989). In 1970 the US economist Milton Friedman claimed the sole responsibility of corporations being the shareholder value maximization and managers focusing on any other purpose than profits to neglect shareholder obligations. In Friedman's argumentation social services are solely governmental responsibilities that corporate executives should refrain from as they are neither trained to set and achieve social goals, nor democratically elected to doing so (Hennigfeld et al., 2006).

Contrary to Friedman's notion, business ethics feature social and environmental considerations of corporate conduct. The so-called 'triple bottom line' advocates for the concurrent corporate pursuit of economic goals, social responsibility and sustainability endeavors (Elkington, 1998). For the last decade, academics and practitioners have investigated the interrelation of corporate profit maximization with social and environmental responsibility, yet no generalizable pattern has been identified yet (Griffin & Mahon, 1997; Waddock & Graves, 1997).

Some empirical evidence finds a positive relation between CSR and corporate financial performance (CFP) (Kotler & Lee, 2005). Orlitzky, Schmidt and Rynes (2003) meta-analyzed 52 studies on CSR and CFP featuring a sample of over 33,800 observations and report a positive relation of CSR and CFP across various industries for the past 30 years (McWilliams & Siegel, 2001). Some studies show a positive correlation of environmental conscientiousness and economic performance – especially for innovative industries – which is explained by the innovative character and the reduction of litigation risks (Bragdon & Marlin, 1972; Gore, 1992; Holman, New & Singer, 1985; Porter, 1991; Russo & Fouts, 1997; Spicer, 1978). However, unsolved remains whether corporations with better CSR financially outperform because of their social responsibility or whether already extraordinarily profitable corporations are in the position to contribute more to society – thus responsible corporations may be those that can afford CSR based on their overall profitability and market leadership position (Barnett, 2005; Brammer, Brooks & Pavelin, 2006; Hennigfeld et al., 2006; Margolis, Elfenbein & Walsh, 2007).

Other research outlines no clear connection between CSR and corporate profitability (e.g., Bauer, Koedijk & Otten, 2005; Cummings, 2000; Fogler & Nutt, 1975; Hamilton, Hoje & Statman, 1993; Rockness, Schlachter & Rockness, 1986; Stone, Guerard, Gületkin & Adams, 2001; Tippet, 2001). In 167 meta-analyzed studies on the relationship between CSR and CFP, Margolis et al. (2007) count in 27 percent a positive, in 58 percent a non-significant and in 2 percent a negative relationship of CSR and CFP.

Overall the current body of knowledge on the relationship between CSP and CFP does not offer a generalizable pattern (Jones & Wicks, 1999 in Orlitzky et al., 2003). The inconsistent relationship between CSR and profitability can be explained by intertemporal costs and benefits of CSR that may cancel out over time and across investigations (Margolis et al., 2007; Reinhardt, 2000). The unsolved relationship of CSR and profitability may also stem from CSR offering multiple tangible and intangible values to various constituents (Clarkson, 1995; Cornell & Shapiro, 1987; Donaldson & Preston, 1995; Freeman, 1984; Mitchell, Agle & Wood, 1997).

Within corporations CSR fosters conscientious use of resources, which reduces operating expenses. CSR builds social capital by attracting loyal workers whose social competencies are enhanced (Barney, 1991; Greening & Turban, 2000; Russo & Fouts, 1997). Aligning corporate standards with employees' goodwill motivates employees, in whom CSR builds pride and nurtures self-fulfilment (Moskowitz, 1972; Sichler, 2006; Thomson & Wheeler, 2004). Attention to human rights and safety standards improves the working conditions, which raises human productivity (Hennigfeld et al., 2006; Weinreb, 2004).

Throughout the value chain, attention is paid to CSR. For producers of intermediary goods, meeting CSR and ISO 14000 standards is necessary to attract customers. For end-consumers symbolic CSR brand equity differentiates existing products and services (Kotler & Lee, 2005; Margolis et al., 2007; Puaschunder, 2006). By transporting social values that are in sync with the consumer's worldview, CSR brands trigger consumer-corporation identification processes (Aaker, 1996; Keller, 2003; Matten & Moon, 2004). Beyond the mere act of consumption, purchase decisions allow customers to engage in something that is crucial to their personal lives (Puaschunder, 2006). With goods not only being purchased for primary product features, but also for their emotion-laden symbolic meanings; the strategic alignment of brand images in accordance to individuals' worldviews stimulates corporate sales (Bhattacharya & Sen, 2003).

Access to information about corporate activities helps consumers integrate CSR in their purchase decisions (Mohr & Webb, 2005). Evaluating CSR as an influencing factor in decision making, Puaschunder (2006) surveyed the brand representations of 370 European and North American consumers revealing the influence of CSR on brand preferences. Especially nineteen to twenty-seven-years old and internally attributing, self-determined respondents paid attention to CSR.

From a grass-roots perspective, consumers are a driving force for corporate social conduct in their brand preferences. Brand choices can be seen as an additional conduit through which post-materialistic consumers express their worldviews in society (Aaker & Joachimsthaler, 2000). Thereby consumption leverages into a personal statement and means of exercising quasi-democratic rights to reward socially responsible corporate conduct (Werther & Chandler, 2006).

In terms of stakeholder relations, CSR determines the relationship between corporations and society. Fostering a socially accepted corporate identity, CSR nurtures a positive reputation of the corporation, improves public relations and decreases the likelihood of stakeholder sanctions (Aaker, 1996; Fombrun, 1996; Keller, 2003). CSR attentive corporations benefit from strategic partnerships with competitors, suppliers, public entities, nonprofit organizations, foundations, NGOs and interest groups that offer support in form of endorsements, expertise, networks, shared distribution channels and human capital. CSR is directly related to pro-social lobbies that advance legislature and policy making regarding social issues of concern and can therefore become a means of political influence. As for positively contributing to society, CSR can be regarded as an indirect long-term investment in a safer and more stable community that serves as a fruitful breeding ground for profitable corporate conduct (Hennigfeld et al., 2006; Windsor, 2001). Today a growing body of shareholders factor ethics into investment decisions. Attention to CSR whole-roundedly enhances shareholder satisfaction. Not operating in sync with corporate social standards decreases the possibility to attract investment capital and divestiture (Davis, 1973; Greening & Turban, 2000; Rivoli, 2003; Spicer, 1978).

CSR implies leadership and long-term strategic advantages when triggering corporate innovation and accounting for future risks. As a pro-active stance, CSR can foster early adoptions of future policies and thereby grant first-mover advantages (Kotler & Lee, 2005). Participating in policy dialogues with governmental officials provides opportunities to shape future legislations and adapt to policy regulations early-on. Apart from tax exemptions for socially responsible corporate conduct, CSR decreases the likelihood of regulatory supervision, legislative infringements, litigations and governmental fines. While neglecting CSR raises insurance expenditures, corporate conduct in sync with societal expectations counterweights stakeholder confrontations and sanctions such as purchase boycotts.

From a macroeconomic viewpoint, social responsibility trends hold the potential to lift entire market industries onto a more socially conscientious level. Leaders in the field that set corporate social standards enjoy first-mover advantages, customer support and stakeholder relation benefits. Other corporations following CSR patterns may shift entire markets onto a more socially responsible level. In this feature, CSR could offer a "third way" between socialism and capitalism by providing social protection whilst strengthening a nation's economic competitiveness at the same time (Haufler, 2001 in Steurer, 2010).

As for downsides of CSR, the implementation of social responsibility implies immediate expenses. In addition, positive changes towards social responsibility are long-term processes that must be guidelined, administered and reviewed (Kotler & Lee, 2005). Partnerships with constituents can bring along time-consuming coordination obstacles. Stakeholder management and multiple goal settings may draw corporate executives' attention away from core corporate obligations (Kotler & Lee, 2005). Serving unfitting causes off track the regular corporate portfolio may raise consumers' scepticism about altruistic corporate activities and harm the overall corporate reputation. When attributing social causes, CSR may at the same time crowd out direct help for social deficiency alleviation – such as charity (Graff-Zivin & Small, 2005). This instance is crucial as CSR remains a second-class corporate obligation with the heightened default risks of corporate bankruptcy. CSR also features accountability limitations. Contrary to governments that are directly enacted by their citizens and governmental responsibility being approved by democratic elections, CSR is subject to lower scrutiny and corporations are only indirectly evaluated for their socially responsible performance by consumers' purchase behavior. Until today one of the major deficiencies of corporate social conduct remains the lack of standardized CSR conduct, which becomes apparent in international comparisons.

INTERNATIONAL DIFFERENCES

In today's globalized market economies, corporations expand operations worldwide and feature international production and supply chains. International corporate conduct builds globally comprehensive corporate structures that account for stakeholder demands around the globe (de Sam, Dougan, Gordon, Puaschunder, St.Clair, 2008). Corporate conduct is inseparably linked to cultural settings (Meyer & Höllerer, 2005; Van Maanen & Laurent, 1993). Cultural frameworks feature specific governmental regulations, legal obligations, managerial practices and societal norms that constitute corporate conduct (Porter & Kramer, 2003; Whitley, 1997). CSR is contextualized by a nation state's legal and regulations, governmental entities, political landscape, industrial relations, labor conditions, economic circumstances and societal values. Describing intercultural differences in corporate social conduct based on historical, legislative and regulatory differences allows to shed light on CSR triggers as well as predictions about current and future trends of corporate social conduct (Kotler & Lee, 2005).

Historically CSR developed in the Western World hosting the world's largest stock of capital and the most vital economies that feature business ethics and philanthropy (Powell, 2008; Rodrik, 2007). Continental Europe and North America are the main incubators of implicit and explicit CSR notions (Powell, 2008; Rodrik, 2007; Williams & Aguilera, 2006).

European CSR models emerged out of guilds, royal codes of conduct and post war settlements. First European corporate social conduct is traces back to the German guild tradition that required corporations to educate not only for profit maximization, but also for attention to societal well-being. The Hapsburg monarchy stressed consensus among market actors. In 1612 British jurists firstly addressed business ethics in the light of social infringements of the East Indian Company (Porter & Kramer, 2003). In the 1790s, first consumer boycotts of slave-harvested sugar were staged in Great Britain. Benevolent capitalism started in the United Kingdom (UK) around the 1850s and first publications on the fundamentals of corporate citizenship appeared at the turn of the 19th century. At the same time, Sweden's constitutional monarchy advocated for stakeholder conflict resolution. Legal writings on sacrificing corporate profits for the sake of public endeavors began in the 1930s (Berle, 1932 in Reinhardt, Stavins & Vietor, 2008; Dodd, 1932). In the wake of industrialization, the British government developed a regulatory framework and inspectorates to disclose anti-social corporate conduct. During the 1970s and 1980s, philanthropy became popular. In the UK, the impact of the Thatcher era on the British welfare state and the revival of entrepreneurial spirits in the 1980s spearheaded the European CSR movement (Handy, 2006; Moon, 2004). Environmental concerns grew in the wake of the 1989 Exxon Valdez oil spill and steadily rose in the wake of attention to climate change. In 1987, the Brundtland Commission channelled the common endeavor to provide an at least as favorable standard of living as enjoyed today in a Sustainable Development Summit. Sustainability became a demand expressed in taxation models, natural resources consumption plans, renewable energy supply but also financial market options. During the 1990s, the first mainstream CSR models emerged as corporate practices complementing philanthropy (Smith, 2003). The increased importance of business ethics was underlined by investors' raising demand for socially screened funds. Consumer boycotts as an expression of stakeholder activism peaked in the wake of the Shell Corporation considering sinking oceanic oil rigs. Continental European legal frameworks started attributing social responsibility to the wider constituency group of corporations. Employment empowerment fostered these endeavors.

In terms of regulatory frameworks, European CSR was originally based on mandatory requirements, which are assigned by the entirety of a country's formal and informal public entities (Matten & Moon, 2004). Corporate boards featuring employee representatives considered corporate impacts on multiple stakeholders (Corfield, 1998; Marinov & Heiman, 1998; Reinhardt et al., 2008). Foremost the German legislation does not even explicitly obligate to maximize shareholder value, but stresses the role of corporations within society. German *Mitbestimmung* laws entitled union representatives access to corporate supervisory boards and the Austrian voluntary *Sozialpartnerschaft* emphasized the role of stakeholders in determining corporate conduct

(Puaschunder, 2017b). French loyalty codes of conduct obliged corporate executives to care for their employees and include the interest of multiple constituents into corporate decision making (Fanto, 1998).

In contrast to North America, Europe features an elaborate welfare infrastructure that enforces social service provision by taxation. Explicit market controls are accompanied by implicit oversight control of trade unions and industry associations. The European legislation and regulation systems require corporations to take over a significant amount of social responsibility (Strebel, 1980). As a matter of fact, many European corporate activities that account for CSR in North America are not labelled as CSR in Western Europe, as they are mandatory. The resulting implicit CSR understanding features a relative low salience and absence of outspoken CSR.

During the last decades, however, CSR has become a viable alternative to governmental social welfare provision in Europe. The ongoing Americanization of management concepts in Western Europe created a European explicit CSR notion, foremost visible in the media attention, rise of vanguard organizations, CSR reporting and publicly promoted socially responsible investment indices (Crane et al., 2004). On the interrelationship between public and private sector social welfare provision, Puaschunder (2015) found corporate social activities being negatively associated with governmental social service provision.

The European Union plays a pivotal role in building trans-national CSR capacities in networking and partnering approaches as well as economic incentives (de la Cuesta & Martinez, 2004). For the European Union, CSR remains a voluntary corporate endeavor. Clear regulations and blacklisting of CSR bad practice, which was discussed at the EU in the early 2000s, never came into effect (European Commission, 2002, 2006 in Steurer, 2010).

European CSR features national implementation nuances. Western European CSR regulations and public policy frameworks are spearheaded in the UK, Denmark and France. In the UK CSR was already discussed as early as in the 1970s (Steurer, 2010). The Thatcher government downsizing the role of the state and cutting regulatory social service provision flourished CSR during the 1980s period of high employment, urban decay and social unrest. The UK regulatory framework was the first to mandatorily require corporate social and environmental conduct disclosure for pension fund trustees (Nelson, 2004). The UK Minister for Competitiveness at the Department for Business, Enterprise & Regulatory Reform launched the European Alliance for CSR as an umbrella network to bring together key CSR constituents to discuss advancements (Moon, 2004).

Since the turn of the millennium, the spread of CSR across Europe was fostered by the Lisbon European Council and the European Commission promoting transparency and convergence of CSR across Europe (Steurer, 2010). The transition of the Commission in 2004, however, halted the pro-active EU CSR policy and re-emphasized business selfregulation on social responsibility (Steurer, 2010). At the EU local level, Western European countries' CSR efforts thus remain national approaches rather than systematically planned and enforced EU matters.

The Nordic region features partnership models in Sweden comprising several national ministries to advocate for human rights, decent labor conditions, environmental protection and anti-corruption in corporate endeavors. Denmark and the Netherlands have established national CSR Centers that coordinate social responsibility activities by promoting dialogues and information exchange in partnerships.

Access to CSR information is ensured by national disclosure and transparency laws. For example, the 2001 French 'New Economic Regulations' policy and similar laws in Denmark, the Netherlands, Sweden and Spain require corporations offering publicly-traded shares to include information on social and environmental performance in annual reports (Holgaard & Jørgensen, 2005; Steurer, 2010). However, the accuracy of the information provided remains unchecked. In sync, positive examples of CSR disclosure are more often awarded than negative examples are blacklisted (Steurer, 2010). Certified labels (e.g., Blue Angel, EU Eco-label) are a pivotal instrument to foster corporate transparency as for combining access to information with economic incentives for corporations (Steurer, 2010).

Within Eastern Europe CSR is growing and has foremost been implemented by expanding international corporations. For Eastern European transforming economies, CSR grants foreign investment prospective, international partnerships and corruption prevention. Eastern European governments regulate CSR policies, endorse privately-led social initiatives and monitor fairly regulated corporate compliance. Awareness for CSR and transparency is fostered by awards and information campaigns (Steurer, 2010). Challenges in Eastern Europe comprise information deficiencies and misperceptions – for example, a survey of 475 Bulgarian, Croatian and Romanian corporate managers revealed that CSR is understood as a means to solely abide by governmental control and CSR is still undermined by corruption (World Development Report, 2005).

In the **United States** (US), the Quakers addressed social responsibility and value-based corporate conduct since the 17th century. Already Tocqueville (1835/1959) described corporate social conduct. In the 1950s the Supreme Court removed legal restrictions that limited corporate social involvements and legislators intentionally incentivized policy gaps to be filled by non-governmental social service provision (Carroll, 1999; Moon, 2005; Steurer, 2010). In the 1960s stakeholder activism increased US corporations to exhibit social responsibility, which led to the widespread establishment of corporate in-house foundations and charity programs. Academics paid attention to CSR when the United Student Against Sweatshops (USAS) movement demanded manufactured goods to publicly disclose the names and addresses of production sites (Roddick, 2001). Within the US, CSR is more popular in Democratic than Republican-led states, which is explained by CSR-compliance in order to please pro-social-stakeholders and conservative US administrators ignoring CSR (Aaronson, 2002; Liston-Heyes & Ceton, 2007 in Steurer, 2010; Mathis, 2008).

Since the breakdown of communism, predominately Anglo-American management models have been adopted throughout the world (Hennigfeld et al., 2006). Under the guidance of international organizations – such as the United Nations (UN), World Bank, International Monetary Fund and the World Trade Organization – democratic, open market society values exported corporate social standards on an international basis (Chua, 2003; Friedman, 2002). Featured by the largest and most powerful nation-state economy for centuries, today the US has established itself as an innovative forerunner in CSR management practices as a means of global governance. Concurrently a trend towards financial social responsibility featuring socially attentive securities has emerged.

The US legal framework is based on the Anglo-Saxon ***Common Law*** that emphasizes shareholder demands. The Canadian Common Law legislature requires corporate executives to act in the corporate interest with respect for shareholders (Reinhardt et al., 2008). The Australian Corporate Law holds CEOs to make decisions in the best interest of the corporation, yet a statutory business judgment rule grants considerable discretion to serve the greater good (Corfield, 1998). As a European Common Law country, the UK's legislation permits corporate managers to engage in philanthropy as long as acting in the interest of shareholders (Lynch-Fannon, 2007).

North America ***regulatory frameworks*** are significant for a tradition of low governmental oversight and social welfare. In combination with hosting the most powerful corporate sector that accounts for a relatively large percentage of the nation's economic productivity, North American corporations feature sophisticated CSR conduct (Palazzo, 2002; Smith, 2003). In North America CSR is much more a discretionary issue with the government mainly offering incentives through negative tax exemptions. As for a tradition of participation and self-help, in North America high levels of civic participation have led to CSR being directly enacted by mostly voluntary corporate policies which are openly promoted as CSR. The respective explicit CSR features self-interest driven corporate strategies to address societal deficiencies. As for low levels of oversight and unstandardized quality control, corporations have flexibility in fulfilling self-imposed social responsibilities.

In the **Developing World**, CSR conduct is still bound by emerging, weak or absent legal frameworks, unenforceable legislations, democracy infringements and corruption. Governance gaps and CSR failures are likely to occur in overseas subsidiaries of multinational corporations that feature a lack of compliance with local laws and regulatory as well as oversight challenges (Reinhardt et al., 2008).

While CSR emerged out of neo-liberal concepts that facilitate the downscaling of governmental regulations, in recent years, CSR has matured from a philanthropic idea to a more comprehensive concept of a pro-active strategic management move that engages in global governance around the world (Steurer, 2010). As of today, CSR initiatives around the globe already tackle a wide range of global problems out of reach for single nation states. With more and more transnational corporate conduct and an ongoing rise of international joint ventures and strategic alliances, this trend is believed to continue.

Overall, CSR remains a politically-dependent concept that varies from culture and time (Steurer, 2010). As for the future, the optimum balance of social responsibility provision in between the public and private sectors given respective national and international frameworks is yet to be determined. While liberalization trends have led to a rising importance of corporate social contributions, governmental bail-outs and recapitalizations of the corporate sector in the wake of the 2008/09 World Financial Recession have re-established governmental control over corporate social conduct. Investigating public and private roles in social service provision will help well-balancing social welfare contributions in global governance. Most recent extensions are in the domains of global intergenerational leadership of contemporary CSR models (Puaschunder, 2017a, 2018).

REFERENCES

Aaker, D. J. (1996). *Building strong brands*. New York: Free Press.

Aaker, D. J., & Joachimsthaler, E. (2000). The brand relationship spectrum: The key to the brand architecture challenge. *California Management Review*, *42*, 8–23.

Aaronson, S. A. (2002). How the Europeans got a head start on policies to promote global corporate responsibility. *Corporate Environmental Strategy*, *9*(4), 356–367. doi:10.1016/S1066-7938(02)00107-0

Andreoni, J. (1989). Giving with impure altruism: Applications to charity and Ricaridan equivalence. *Journal of Political Economy*, *97*(6), 1447–1458. doi:10.1086/261662

Andreoni, J., & Miller, J. (2002). Giving according to GARP: An experimental test of the consistency of preferences for altruism. *Econometrica*, *70*(2), 737–753. doi:10.1111/1468-0262.00302

Aronson, E. (2001). Integrating leadership styles and ethical perspectives. *Canadian Journal of Administrative Sciences*, *18*(4), 244–256. doi:10.1111/j.1936-4490.2001.tb00260.x

Auhagen, A. E., & Bierhoff, H. W. (2001). *Responsibility: The many faces of a social phenomenon*. London: Routledge. doi:10.4324/9780203468739

Bagnoli, M., & Watts, S. (2003). Selling to socially responsible consumers: Competition and the private provision of public goods. *Journal of Economics & Management Strategy*, *12*(3), 419–445. doi:10.1162/105864003322309536

Banaji, M. R., Bazerman, M. H., & Chugh, D. (2003). How (un)ethical are you? *Harvard Business Review*, *81*(12), 56–64. PMID:14712544

Barkemeyer, R. (2007, July). Beyond compliance – below expectations? Cross-border CSR, development and the UN Global Compact. In *Corporate Responsibility Research Conference*. University of Leeds.

Barnett, M. L. (2005). Stakeholder influence capacity and the variability of financial returns to corporate social responsibility. *Academy of Management Review*, *32*(3), 794–816. doi:10.5465/amr.2007.25275520

Barney, J. (1991). Firm resources and sustained competitive advantage. *Journal of Management*, *17*(1), 771–792. doi:10.1177/014920639101700108

Bartle, I., & Vass, P. (2007). Self-regulation within the regulatory state: Towards a new regulatory paradigm? *Public Administration, 85*(4), 885–905. doi:10.1111/j.1467-9299.2007.00684.x

Batson, C. D. (1991). *The altruism question: Toward a social psychological answer*. Hillsdale, NJ: Erlbaum.

Bauer, R., Koedijk, K., & Otten, R. (2005). International evidence on ethical mutual fund performance and investment style. *Journal of Banking & Finance, 29*(7), 1751–1767. doi:10.1016/j.jbankfin.2004.06.035

Bazerman, M. H. (2008). *Barriers to acting in time on energy and strategies for overcoming them.* Working paper 09-063. Cambridge, MA: Harvard Business School.

Bazerman, M. H., & Banaji, M. R. (2004). The social psychology of ordinary ethical failures. *Social Justice Research, 17*(2), 111–115. doi:10.1023/B:SORE.0000027544.56030.04

Bazerman, M. H., & Moore, D. (2009). *Judgment in managerial decision making*. Hoboken, NJ: Wiley.

Bekefi, T. (2006). *Business as a partner in tackling micronutrient deficiency: Lessons in multisector partnership. Report of the Corporate Responsibility Initiative*. Cambridge, MA: Harvard University Press.

Berle, A. A. (1932). From whom corporate managers are trustees: A note. *Harvard Law Review, 45*(8), 1365–1372. doi:10.2307/1331920

Berman, S. L., Wicks, A. C., Kotha, S., & Jones, T. M. (1999). Does stakeholder orientation matter? The relationship between stakeholder management models and firm financial performance. *Academy of Management Journal, 42*(5), 488–506.

Bhattacharya, C. B., & Sen, S. (2003). Consumer-company identification: A framework for understanding consumers' relationships with companies. *Journal of Marketing, 67*(2), 7688. doi:10.1509/jmkg.67.2.76.18609

Biermann, F., & Siebenhüner, B. (2009). *Managers of global change: The influence of international environmental bureaucracies.* Cambridge, MA: MIT Press. doi:10.7551/mitpress/9780262012744.001.0001

Bragdon, J. H. & Marlin, J. A. T. (1972). Is pollution profitable? *Risk Management, 19*(4), 918.

Brammer, S., Brooks, C., & Pavelin, S. (2006). Good reputations can be bad investments: Corporate reputation and stock returns: Are good firms good for investors? *Professional Investor*, *10*, 21–25.

Brown, T. L., Potoski, M., & Van Slyke, D. M. (2006). Managing public service contracts: Aligning values, institutions, and markets. *Public Administration Review*, *66*(3), 323–331. doi:10.1111/j.1540-6210.2006.00590.x

Carroll, A. B. (1979). A three-dimensional model of corporate social performance. *Academy of Management Review*, *4*, 497–505. doi:10.5465/amr.1979.4498296

Carroll, A. B. (1991). The pyramid of corporate social responsibility: Toward the moral management of organizational stakeholders. *Business Horizons*, *34*(4), 39–48. doi:10.1016/0007-6813(91)90005-G

Carroll, A. B. (1999). Corporate social responsibility: Evolution of a definitional construct. *Business & Society*, *38*(3), 268–295. doi:10.1177/000765039903800303

Centeno, M. A., & Cohen, J. N. (2010). *Global capitalism*. Hoboken, NJ: Wiley.

Chua, A. (2003). *World on fire: How exporting free market democracy breeds ethnic hatred and global instability*. New York: Anchor.

Clark, R. (1986). *Corporate law*. Boston: Little, Brown & Company.

Clarkson, M. B. E. (1995). A stakeholder framework for analyzing and evaluating corporate social performance. *Academy of Management Review*, *20*(1), 92–117. doi:10.5465/amr.1995.9503271994

Colby, A., & Damon, W. (1992). *Some do care: Contemporary lives of moral commitment*. New York: Free Press.

Commission of the European Communities Report. (2001). *Green paper: Promoting a European framework for corporate social responsibility*. Brussels: European Union Commission.

Corfield, A. (1998). The stakeholder theory and its future in Australian corporate governance: A preliminary analysis. *Bond Law Review*, *10*(2), 213–232.

Cornell, B., & Shapiro, A. (1987). Corporate stakeholders and corporate finance. *Financial Management*, *16*(1), 5–14. doi:10.2307/3665543

Cox, J., & Haven, T. (2003). *Corporations*. New York: Aspen.

Crane, A., & Livesey, S. (2002). Are you talking to me? Stakeholder communication and the risks and rewards of dialogue. In J. Andriof, S. Waddock, S. Rahman, & B. Husted (Eds.), *Unfolding Stakeholder Thinking* (pp. 39–52). Sheffield: Greenleaf.

Crane, A., Matten, D., & Moon, D. (2004). Stakeholder as citizens? Rethinking rights, participation and democracy. *Journal of Business Ethics*, *53*(1/2), 107–122. doi:10.1023/B:BUSI.0000039403.96150.b6

Cuesta de la, G. M., & Martinez, V. C. (2004). Fostering corporate social responsibility through public initiative: From the EU to the Spanish case. *Journal of Business Ethics*, *55*, 275–293. doi:10.100710551-004-0994-y

Cummings, L. A. (2000). The financial performance of ethical investment trusts: An Australian perspective. *Journal of Business Ethics*, *25*(3), 167–177.

Cushman, F. (2008). Crime and punishment: Distinguishing the roles of causal and intentional analyses in moral judgment. *Cognition*, *108*(2), 353–380. doi:10.1016/j.cognition.2008.03.006 PMID:18439575

Darley, J. M., & Latane, B. (1968). Bystander intervention in emergencies: Diffusion of responsibility. *Journal of Personality and Social Psychology*, *8*(4), 377–383. doi:10.1037/h0025589 PMID:5645600

Davis, K. (1973). The case for and against business assumptions of social responsibilities. *Academy of Management Journal*, *16*, 312–317.

de Sam, M., Dougan, B., Gordon, J., Puaschunder, J., & St. Clair, C. (2008). *Building a globally competent citizenry in the United States*. Washington, DC: United States Department of Education.

De Silva, S., & Amerasinghe, F. (2004). *Corporate social responsibility: Issues, problems and challenges*. Colombo: Lake House.

De Soto, H. (2000). *The mystery of capital: Why capitalism triumphs in the west and fails everywhere else*. New York: Perseus Books.

De Woot, A. (2005). *Should Prometheus be bound? Corporate Social Responsibility*. London: Palgrave Macmillan. doi:10.1057/9780230502062

Deegan, C., & Blomquist, C. (2006). Stakeholder influence on corporate reporting: An exploration of the interaction between WWF-Australia and the Australian minerals industry. *Accounting, Organizations and Society*, *31*(4-5), 343–372. doi:10.1016/j.aos.2005.04.001

Dodd, E. M. (1932). From whom are corporate managers trustees? *Harvard Law Review*, *45*(7), 1145–1163. doi:10.2307/1331697

Donaldson, T., & Preston, L. E. (1995). The stakeholder theory of the corporation: Concepts, evidence and implications. *Academy of Management Review*, *20*(1), 65–91. doi:10.5465/amr.1995.9503271992

Ehrlich, C. (2005). Is business ethics necessary? *DePaul Business & Commercial Law Journal*, *4*(3), 55–67.

Elhauge, E. (2005). Corporate managers' operational discretion to sacrifice corporate profits in the public interest: Environmental protection and the social responsibility of firms. In B. Hay, R. Stavins & R. Vietor (Eds.), Environmental Protection and the Social Responsibility of Firms. Washington, DC: Resources of the Future.

Elkington, J. (1998). *Cannibals with forks: The triple bottom line of 21st century business.* New Society.

European Commission. (2002). *Communication from the commission concerning corporate social responsibility: A business contribution to sustainable development*. COM.

European Commission. (2006). *Implementing the partnership for growth and jobs: Making Europe a pole of excellence on corporate social responsibility: Communication from the Commission*. COM.

Fanto, J. A. (1998). The role of corporate law in French corporate governance. *Cornell International Law Journal*, *31*, 31–45.

Farrington, T., Curran, R., Gori, K., O'Gorman, K., & Queenan, C. J. (2017). Corporate Social Responsibility: Reviewed, rated, revised. *International Journal of Contemporary Hospitality Management*, *29*(1), 30–47. doi:10.1108/IJCHM-05-2015-0236

Fisch, J. E. (2006). Robert Clark's corporate law: Twenty years of change: Measuring efficiency in corporate law: The role of shareholder primacy. *The Iowa Journal of Corporation Law, 31*(3), 637.

Fogler, H. R., & Nutt, F. (1975). A note on social responsibility and stock evaluation. *Academy of Management Journal, 18*, 155–160.

Fombrun, C. (1996). *Reputation: Realizing value from the corporate image*. Cambridge, MA: Harvard Business School.

Freeman, R. E. (1984). *Strategic management: A stakeholder approach*. Mashfield, MA: Pitman.

Friedman, M. (1970). The social responsibility of business is to increase its profits. *New York Times Magazine, 13*, 33-38.

Fukuyama, F. (1995). *Trust: The social virtues and the creation of prosperity*. New York: Free Press.

Fullerton, D., & Henderson, Y. K. (1989). The marginal excess burden of different capital tax instruments. *The Review of Economics and Statistics, 71*(3), 435–442. doi:10.2307/1926900

Gabaldon, T. A. (2006). Like a fish needs a bicycle: Public corporations and their shareholders. *Maryland Law Review (Baltimore, Md.), 65*, 538–578.

Gardner, H. (2007). *Responsibility at work: How leading professionals act (or don't act) responsibility*. San Francisco, CA: Jossey-Bass.

Gebert, D., & Rosenstiel, L. v. (1996). *Organisationspsychologie: Personen und Organisationen*. Stuttgart: Kohlhammer.

Gerson, K. (2002). Moral dilemmas, moral strategies and the transformation of gender: Lessons from two generations of work and family change. *Gender & Society, 16*(1), 1, 8–28. doi:10.1177/0891243202016001002

Giesler, M., & Veresiu, E. (2014). Creating the responsible consumer: Moralistic governance regimes and consumer subjectivity. *The Journal of Consumer Research, 41*(10), 849–867.

Goodpaster, K. E., & Matthews, J. B. (2003). *Can a corporation have a conscience? Harvard Business Review on Corporate Responsibility*. Cambridge, MA: Harvard Business School.

Gore, A. (1992). *Earth in the balance*. Boston: Houghton-Mifflin.

Graff-Zivin, J., & Small, A. (2005). A Modigliani-Miller theory of altruistic corporate social responsibility. *Journal in Economic Analysis and Policy, 5*(1), 1–19.

Greening, D. W., & Turban, D. B. (2000). Corporate social performance as a competitive advantage in attracting a quality workforce. *Business & Society*, *39*(3), 254–280. doi:10.1177/000765030003900302

Griffin, J. J., & Mahon, J. F. (1997). The corporate social performance and corporate financial performance debate: Twenty-five years of economic and organizational factors. *Strategic Management Journal*, *10*, 399–411.

Gross, R. (2018). *Corporate Social Responsibility and employee engagement: Making the connection*. Retrieved from http://www.mandrake.ca/bill/images/corporate_responsibility_white_paper.pdf

Gunkel, A. (1989). *Spontaneität und moralische Autonomie. Kants Philosophie der Freiheit*. Bern: Haupt.

Haidt, J. (2001). The emotional dog and its rational tail: A social intuitionist approach to moral judgment. *Psychological Review*, *1089*(4), 814–834. doi:10.1037/0033-295X.108.4.814 PMID:11699120

Hamilton, S., Hoje, J., & Statman, M. (1993). Doing well while doing good? The investment performance of socially responsible mutual funds. *Financial Analysts Journal*, *49*(6), 62–66. doi:10.2469/faj.v49.n6.62

Handy, Ch. (2006). *What's a business for? Harvard Business Review on Corporate Responsibility*. Cambridge, MA: Harvard Business School.

Haufler, V. (2001). *A public role for the private sector: Industry self-regulation in a global economy*. Washington, DC: Brookings Institution.

Hayek, F. A. (2007). *The road to serfdom*. London: The University of Chicago Press. (Original work published 1944) doi:10.7208/chicago/9780226320533.001.0001

Hennigfeld, J., Pohl, M., & Tolhurst, N. (2006). *The ICCA handbook on corporate social responsibility*. West Sussex: Wiley.

Holgaard, J. E., & Jørgensen, T. H. (2005). A decade of mandatory environmental reporting in Denmark. *European Environment*, *15*(6), 362–373. doi:10.1002/eet.397

Holman, W. R., New, J. R., & Singer, D. (1985). The impact of corporate social responsiveness on shareholder wealth. In L. Preston (Ed.), *Research in Corporate Social Performance and Policy* (pp. 137–152). Greenwich, CT: JAI.

Inglehart, R. (1999). *Trust, well-being and democracy: Democracy and trust*. Cambridge, MA: Cambridge University Press. doi:10.1017/CBO9780511659959.004

Janis, I. L., & Mann, L. (1977). *Decision making: A psychological analysis of conflict, choice, and commitment*. New York: Free Press.

Jenkins, B. (2007). *Expanding economic opportunity: The role of large firms. Economic opportunity series*. Cambridge, MA: Harvard Kennedy School.

Jones, I., & Pollitt, M. (1998). *The role of business ethics in economic performance*. London: Macmillan. doi:10.1057/9780230379794

Keller, K. L. (2003). Brand synthesis: The multidimensionality of brand knowledge. *The Journal of Consumer Research*, *29*(4), 595–600. doi:10.1086/346254

Kettl, D. F. (2006). *The global public management revolution*. Washington, DC: The Brookings Institution.

Knack, S., & Keefer, Ph. (1997). Does social capital have an economic payoff? A crosscountry investigation. *The Quarterly Journal of Economics*, *112*(4), 1251–1288. doi:10.1162/003355300555475

Kotler, P., & Lee, N. (2005). *Corporate social responsibility: Doing the most good for your company and your cause*. Wiley.

Kramer, R. (1999). Trust and distrust in organizations: Emerging perspectives, enduring questions. *Annual Review of Psychology*, *50*(1), 569–598. doi:10.1146/annurev.psych.50.1.569 PMID:15012464

Kramer, R., & Tyler, T. (1996). *Trust in organizations*. Thousand Oaks, CA: Sage.

LaPorta, R., Lopez-de-Silanes, F., Shleifer, A., & Vishny, R. W. (1997). Trust in large organizations. *The American Economic Review*, *87*, 333–338.

Lee, N., & Kotler, Ph. (2013). *Corporate social responsibility doing the most good for your company and your cause*. Hoboken, NJ: Wiley.

Lenk, H., & Maring, M. (1992). *Wirtschaft und Ethik*. Stuttgart: Reclam.

Lennick, D., & Kiel, F. (2007). *Moral intelligence: Enhancing business performance and leadership success*. Upper Saddle River, NJ: Wharton School Publishing.

Liston-Heyes, C., & Ceton, G. C. (2007). Corporate social performance and politics. *Journal of Corporate Citizenship*, *25*(25), 95–108. doi:10.9774/GLEAF.4700.2007.sp.00010

Luf, G. (2009). *Grundfragen der Rechtsphilosophie und Rechtsethik. Einführung in die Rechtswissenschaften und ihre Methoden*. Wien: Manz.

Lynch-Fannon, I. (2007). The corporate social responsibility movement and law's empire: Is there a conflict? *The Northern Ireland Legal Quarterly*, *58*(1), 1–22.

Mansbridge, J. (1999). Altruistic trust. In M. E. Warren (Ed.), *Trust and democracy* (pp. 290–309). Cambridge, MA: Cambridge University Press. doi:10.1017/CBO9780511659959.010

March, J., & Simon, H. (1958). *Organizations*. New York: Wiley.

Margolis, J., Elfenbein, H., & Walsh, J. (2007). *Does it pay to be good? A meta-analysis and redirection for research on the relationship between corporate social and financial performance*. Working paper, Harvard Business School.

Marinov, B., & Heiman, B. (1998). Company law and corporate governance renewal in transition economics: The Bulgarian dilemma. *European Journal of Law and Economics*, *6*(3), 231–262. doi:10.1023/A:1008606211793

Mathis, A. (2008). *Corporate social responsibility and public policy-making: Perspectives, instruments and consequences*. Twente: University of Twente.

Matten, D., & Moon, J. (2004, July). *"Implicit" and "Explicit" CSR: A conceptual framework for understanding CSR in Europe*. 20th EGOS Colloquium, Ljubljana, Slovenia.

McWilliams, A., & Siegel, D. (2001). Corporate social responsibility: A theory of the firm perspective. *Academy of Management Review*, *26*(1), 117–127. doi:10.5465/amr.2001.4011987

Meyer, R. E., & Höllerer, M. A. (2005, August). *From value management to values management: Contrasting views or just two sides of the same coin: Shareholder value and corporate social responsibility in Austrian publicly listed corporations. 18th NFF Meeting*, Aarhus School of Business, Aarhus, Denmark.

Midttun, A. (2005). Policy making and the role of government: Realigning business, government and civil society. *Corporate Governance*, *5*(3), 159–174. doi:10.1108/14720700510604797

Mitchell, R. K., Agle, B. R., & Wood, D. J. (1997). Toward a theory of stakeholder identification and salience: Defining the principle of who and what really counts. *Academy of Management Review*, *22*(4), 853–888. doi:10.5465/amr.1997.9711022105

Mohr, L. A., & Webb, D. J. (2005). The effects of corporate social responsibility and price on consumer responses. *The Journal of Consumer Affairs*, *39*(1), 121–147. doi:10.1111/j.1745-6606.2005.00006.x

Moon, J. (2002). The social responsibility of business and new governance. *Government and Opposition*, *37*(3), 385–408. doi:10.1111/1477-7053.00106

Moon, J. (2004). *Government as a driver of corporate social responsibility: The UK in comparative perspective*. Nottingham: Research paper series of the International Centre for Corporate Social Responsibility.

Moon, J. (2007). The contribution of corporate social responsibility to sustainable development. *Sustainable Development*, *15*(5), 296–306. doi:10.1002d.346

Moon, J., & Vogel, D. (2007). Corporate social responsibility, government and civil society. In A. Crane, A. McWilliams, D. Matten, J. Moon, & D. S. Siegel (Eds.), *The Oxford Handbook of Corporate Social Responsibility* (pp. 1–19). Oxford: Oxford University Press.

Moskowitz, M. (1972). Choosing socially responsible stocks. *Business & Society*, *1*, 71–75.

Murnighan, J. K., Cantelon, D. A., & Elyashiv, T. (2001). Bounded personal ethics and the tap dance of real estate agency. *Advances in Qualitative Organization Research*, *3*, 1–40.

Nelson, J. (2004). *Leadership, accountability and partnership: Critical trends and issues in corporate social responsibility. Report of the Corporate Responsibility Initiative*. Cambridge, MA: Harvard University.

Newton, L. H., & Ford, M. M. (2008). *Taking sides: Clashing views on controversial issues in business ethics and society*. New York: McGraw-Hill.

Nourick, S. (2001). *Corporate social responsibility: Roundtable conference partners for progress: Towards a new approach*. Washington, DC: Brookings Institution Press.

Orlitzky, M., Schmidt, F. L., & Rynes, S. L. (2003). Corporate social and financial performance: A meta-analysis. *Organization Studies*, *24*(3), 403–441. doi:10.1177/0170840603024003910

Ostrom, E., & Walker, J. (2003). *Trust and reciprocity*. New York: Russel Sage.

Palazzo, G. (2002). *Die Mitte der Demokratie*. Baden-Baden: Nomos.

Porter, M. E. (1991). America's green strategy. *Scientific American, 264*(4), 168.

Porter, M. E., & Kramer, M. R. (2003). *The competitive advantage of corporate philanthropy. Harvard Business Review on Corporate Responsibility*. Cambridge, MA: Harvard Business School.

Powell, B. (2008). *Making poor nations rich: Entrepreneurship and the process of economic development*. Stanford, CA: Stanford Economics and Finance and the Independent.

Prahalad, C. K., & Hammond, A. (2003). *Serving the world's poor profitably. Harvard Business Review on Corporate Responsibility*. Cambridge, MA: Harvard Business School.

Puaschunder, J. M. (2006). *Vom symbolischen Markennutzen: Interkulturelle Darstellung der Markenwahl als Beziehung von Persönlichkeiten* (Unpublished doctoral dissertation). Vienna University of Economics and Business.

Puaschunder, J. M. (2015). *Intergenerational transfer model*. New York: The New School Working Paper.

Puaschunder, J. M. (2017a). Global Alliance for Information and Communication Technologies and Development (GAID) as an International Platform for Cross-Sectoral Solution Finding and Policy Dialogue on Information and Communication Technologies for Development. In M. Gudic, T. K. Tan, & P. M. Flynn (Eds.), *Beyond the Bottom Line: Integrating the UN Global Compact into Management Practices* (pp. 32–46). New York, NY: Greenleaf. doi:10.9774/GLEAF.9781783535606_5

Puaschunder, J. M. (2017b). Socio-psychological motives of socially responsible investors. *Advances in Financial Economics, 19*, 209–247. doi:10.1108/S1569-373220160000019008

Puaschunder, J. M. (2018). Intergenerational leadership: An extension of contemporary corporate social responsibility models. *Corporate Governance & Organizational Behavior Review, 2*(1), 7-17.

Putnam, R. D. (2000). *Bowling alone: The collapse and revival of American community*. New York: Simon & Schuster. doi:10.1145/358916.361990

Putnam, R. D., Leonardi, R., & Nanetti, R. Y. (1993). *Making democracy work: Civic traditions in modern Italy*. Princeton, NJ: Princeton University Press.

Reese-Schäfer, W. (1995). *Was ist Kommunitarismus?* Frankfurt am Main: Campus.

Reinhardt, F. L. (2000). Sustainability and the firm. *Interfaces, 30*(3), 26–41. doi:10.1287/inte.30.3.26.11667

Reinhardt, F. L., Stavins, R. N., & Vietor, R. H. (2008). *Corporate social responsibility through an economic lens*. Working paper, Harvard Kennedy School.

Renneboog, L. D. R., Horst, J. R. T., & Zhang, C. (2007). *Socially responsible investments: Methodology, risk and performance*. Tilburg University Center for Economic Research Discussion Paper 2007-2031, Tilburg, The Netherlands.

Rivoli, P. (2003). Making a difference or making a statement? Finance research and socially responsible investment. *Business Ethics Quarterly, 13*(3), 271–288. doi:10.5840/beq200313323

Roberts, A. S. (2010). *Disciplined democracies: Global capitalism and the new architecture of government*. Oxford: Oxford University Press. doi:10.1093/acprof:oso/9780195374988.001.0001

Rockness, J., Schlachter, P., & Rockness, H. O. (1986). Hazardous waste disposal, corporate disclosure and financial performance in the chemical industry. In M. Neimark (Ed.), *Advances in Public Interest Accounting* (pp. 167–199). Greenwich, CT: JAI.

Rodrik, D. (2007). *One economics, many recipes*. Princeton, NJ: Princeton University Press.

Ruggie, J. (2008). *Promotion and protection of all human rights, civil, political, economic, social and cultural rights, including the right to development: Protect, respect and remedy: A framework for business and human rights.* Report of the Special Representative of the Secretary-General on the issue of human rights and transnational corporations and other business enterprises. Presented at the Eighth Session of the Human Rights Council. Retrieved from http://www.businesshumanrights.org/Documents/RuggieHRC2008

Russo, M. V., & Fouts, P. A. (1997). A resource-based perspective on corporate environmental performance and profitability. *Academy of Management Journal, 40*, 534–559.

Sachs, J. (2007). *Common wealth: Economics for a crowded planet.* London: Penguin.

Sennett, R. (1998). Der flexible Mensch: Die Kultur des Kapitalismus. Berlin: Berlin.

Sheehy, B. (2005). Screening the reluctant stakeholder: Theoretical problems in the shareholder-stakeholder debate. *University of Miami Business Law Review, 14*(3), 193.

Sheehy, B. (2015). Defining CSR: Problems and solutions. *Journal of Business Ethics, 131*(3), 625–648. doi:10.100710551-014-2281-x

Sichler, R. (2003). Neue Arbeitswelt und Autonomie. Aspekte menschlicher Selbstbestimmung im flexibilisierten Kapitalismus. In A. Birnbaumer & G. Steinhardt (Eds.), *Der flexibilisierte Mensch: Subjektivität und Solidarität im Wandel* (pp. 139–149). Heidelberg: Asanger.

Sichler, R. (2004). Autonomie. Ihre Konstitution und Ambivalenz im Kontext von Arbeit und Lebensführung. In W. G. Weber, P. Pasqualoni, & Ch. Burtscher (Eds.), *Wirtschaft, Demokratie und soziale Verantwortung: Psychologie und Beruf* (pp. 104–126). Göttingen: Vandenhoeck & Ruprecht.

Sichler, R. (2006). *Autonomie in der Arbeitswelt: Psychologie und Beruf.* Göttingen: Vandenhoeck & Ruprecht.

Simon, H. A. (1957). *Models of man: Social and rational.* New York: Wiley.

Simon, T. (2004). *Gute Policey: Ordnungsbilder und Zielvorstellungen politischen Handelns in der Frühen Neuzeit.* Frankfurt am Main: Klostermann.

Simons, J. G., Powers, Ch. W., & Gunnemann, J. P. (1972). *The ethical investor: Universities and corporate responsibility*. New Haven, CT: Yale University Press.

Smith, C. (2003). *The new corporate philanthropy. Harvard Business Review on Corporate Responsibility*. Cambridge, MA: Harvard Business School.

Soros, G. (2000). *Open society: Reforming global capitalism*. New York: Public Affairs.

Sparkes, R. (2002). *Socially responsible investment: A global revolution. Cronwall*. Wiley.

Spicer, B. H. (1978). Investors, corporate social performance and information disclosure: An empirical study. *The Accounting Review*, *53*, 94–111.

Springer, J. (1999). Corporate law, corporate constituency statues: Hollow hopes and false fears. *New York University School of Law Annual survey of American Law*.

Steurer, R. (2010). The role of governments in corporate social responsibility: Characterising public policies on CSR in Europe. *Policy Sciences*, *43*(1), 49–72. doi:10.100711077-009-9084-4

Steurer, R., Margula, S., & Martinuzzi, A. (2008). *Socially responsible investment in EU member states: Overview of government initiatives and SRI experts' expectations towards governments. Analysis of national policies on CSR, in support of a structured exchange of information on national CSR policies and initiatives. Final report to the EU High-Level Group on CSR provided by the Research Institute for Managing Sustainability*. Vienna University of Economics and Business.

Stiglitz, J. E. (2003). *Globalization and its discontents*. New York: Norton.

Stone, B. K., Guerard, J. B., Gületkin, M. N., & Adams, G. (2001). *Socially responsible investment screening: Strong evidence of no significant cost for actively managed portfolios*. Working paper. Retrieved from the internet at http://www.socialinvest.org/pdf/research/Moskowitz/2001%20Honorable%20 Mention %20-%20Moskowitz.pdf

Strebel, H. (1980). *Umwelt und Betriebswirtschaft: Die natürliche Umwelt als Gegenstand der Unternehmenspolitik*. Berlin: Schmidt.

Taylor, C. (1988). *Negative Freiheit? Zur Kritik des neuzeitlichen Individualismus*. Frankfurt am Main: Suhrkamp.

Thaler, R. H., & Sunstein, C. R. (2008). *Nudge: Improving decisions about health, wealth, and happiness*. New Haven, CT: Yale University Press.

Thomson, J., & Wheeler, D. (2004). *Human capital based investment criteria for total shareholder returns: A Canadian and international perspective. Phase I Report to SSHRC*. Toronto: York University.

Tippet, J. (2001). Performance of Australia's ethical funds. *The Australian Economic Review*, *34*(2), 170–178. doi:10.1111/1467-8462.00186

Trivers, R. (1971). The evolution of reciprocal altruism. *The Quarterly Review of Biology*, *46*(1), 35–57. doi:10.1086/406755

Tumpel-Gugerell, G. (2009, June 15). *Monetary policy challenges in the light of the current financial market development*. Notes to the speech delivered at the Vienna Alpbach Talks.

Tversky, A., & Kahneman, D. (1974). Judgment under uncertainty: Heuristics and biases. *Science*, *185*(4157), 1124–1131. doi:10.1126cience.185.4157.1124 PMID:17835457

Van Maanen, J., & Laurent, A. (1993). The flow of culture: Some notes on globalization and the multinational corporation. In S. Ghoshal & D. E. Westney (Eds.), *Organization Theory and the Multinational Corporation* (pp. 275–312). New York: St. Martin's. doi:10.1007/978-1-349-22557-6_12

Van Slyke, D. M. (2003). The mythology of privatization in contracting for social services. *Public Administration Review*, *63*(3), 296–315. doi:10.1111/1540-6210.00291

Waddock, S. A., & Graves, S. B. (1997). The corporate social performance-financial performance link. *Strategic Management Journal*, *18*(4), 303–319. doi:10.1002/(SICI)1097-0266(199704)18:4<303::AID-SMJ869>3.0.CO;2-G

Weber, W. G. (1997). *Analyse von Gruppenarbeit: Kollektive Handlungsregulation in soziotechnischen Systemen*. Bern: Huber.

Weber, W. G., Pasqualoni, P., & Burtscher, Ch. (2004). *Wirtschaft, Demokratie und soziale Verantwortung. Psychologie und Beruf*. Göttingen: Vandenhoeck & Ruprecht.

Weinreb, E. (2004, March 22). Top talent looks beyond bottom line. Letter to the editor. *Financial Times*.

Werther, W. B., & Chandler, D. (2006). *Strategic corporate social responsibility: Stakeholders in a global environment*. Thousand Oaks, CA: Sage.

Whitley, R. (1997). Business systems. In A. Sorge & M. Warner (Eds.), *The IEBM Handbook of Organizational Behaviour*. London: Thomson Business Press.

Williams, C. A., & Aguilera, R. V. (2006). *Corporate Social Responsibility in a comparative perspective*. Working paper. Retrieved from http://www.business.uiuc.edu/aguilera/pdf/Williams%20Aguilera%20OUPfinal%20dec%202006.pdf

Windsor, D. (2001). Corporate citizenship: Evolution and interpretation. In J. Andriof & M. McIntosh (Eds.), *Perspectives on Corporate Citizenship*. Sheffield: Greenleaf. doi:10.9774/GLEAF.978-1-909493-19-3_4

Winship, C., & Rein, M. (1999). The dangers of 'strong' causal reasoning in social policy. *Society*, *36*(5), 38–46. doi:10.1007/BF02686150

Wolff, M. (2002). Response to "Confronting the critics.". *New Academy Review*, *1*, 230–237.

World Development Report. (2005). *A better investment climate for everyone*. Washington, DC: The World Bank.

Yamagishi, T., & Yamagishi, M. (1994). Trust and commitment in the United States and Japan. *Motivation and Emotion*, *18*(2), 129–166. doi:10.1007/BF02249397

Young, L., Cushman, F., Hauser, M., & Saxe, R. (2007). The neural basis of the interaction between theory of mind and moral judgment. *Proceedings of the National Academy of Sciences of the United States of America*, *104*(20), 8235–8240. doi:10.1073/pnas.0701408104 PMID:17485679

Zak, P. J. (2008). *Moral markets: The critical role of values in the economy*. Princeton, NJ: Princeton University Press.

Zak, P. J., & Knack, S. (2001). Trust and growth. *Economic Journal (London)*, *111*(470), 295–321. doi:10.1111/1468-0297.00609

Chapter 2
Global Governance

ABSTRACT

Global governance advances societies by enhancing social responsibility in market systems and improving governmental efficiency. CSR becomes a feature of global governance when corporations provide social welfare, but also when CSR serves a multi-stakeholder conflict resolution means in public private partnerships (PPPs). Governments foster corporate social service provision as this flexible, soft-law approach benefits from comparatively low resistance. Under the lead of international organizations, the contributions of CSR to global governance have foremost been institutionalized by the UN Global Compact (UNGC). The United Nations Global Alliance for Information and Communication Technologies and Development (UN GAID) is a currently-launched global governance PPP. This chapter explores global governance.

INTRODUCTION

Derived from governmental public management, global governance strengthens international societal progress by enhancing social responsibility in market systems, improving governmental efficiency and complementing governmental social service endeavors.

CSR contributes to global governance in social service provision and as a multistakeholder conflict resolution means in public private partnership (PPP) solutions. PPPs incorporate social responsibility into the business agenda and combine public and private forces in providing social services as an innovative and flexible global governance form. Partnering endeavors

DOI: 10.4018/978-1-5225-7619-8.ch002

build on different constituents' interest in pursuing shared social objectives by mutual resource exchange (Steurer, 2010). PPPs feature voluntary information sharing and regulatory flexibility, which are key for solving transnational social constraints. Rising economic and institutional cross linking let PPPs appear as a viable means of flexible social service provision.

Throughout recent decades, corporate executives increasingly paid attention to tackle international problems out of reach for national entities. Various political and societal trends have increased corporate contributions to global governance. The decline of nation state social service provision in the wake of the reinventing government idea gave market actors a greater role in social welfare provision. Innovative public management concepts – such as outsourcing, networked governance and multi-stakeholder partnerships – have leveraged social responsibility into corporate obligations and let CSR become part of corporate conduct.

As corporations gained ground in global governance, nowadays corporate and governments attribute social responsibility in PPPs. CSR has become an essential component of international social service provision and leveraged international corporations into global governance entities. Global governance provided by CSR opened a new frame of reference on which to evaluate corporate impacts on society. Corporate goal setting became an opportunity to address societal concerns and promote CSR to quasi-democratic constituents.

In response to the CSR trend, governments have become interested in flexible corporate social service provision as these voluntary business efforts redistribute corporate resources to public causes. From the governmental perspective, CSR complements hard-regulations with a visionary soft-law approach benefitting from comparatively low resistance (Moon, 2007 in Steurer, 2010). For the public sector, PPPs offer flexible and efficient social responsibility provision. PPPs address governance gaps and foster international development. Governments therefore assist and stimulate corporations to raise the voluntarily social performance beyond minimum legal requirements (Liston-Heyes & Ceton, 2007 in Steurer, 2010). Governmental CSR initiatives form a cross-sectoral policy field that is based on voluntariness and collaboration of public and private sector entities.

The novelty of PPPs brings along an absence of standardized legislative or regulatory frameworks that guideline disparate entities administering global governance. Multistakeholder constituents feature conflicts of interest hindering agreements on policy ratifications and implementations. Expertise imbalances can counterweight effective dialogues and multi-stakeholder solution finding (Ruggie, 2008). As a remedy CSR serves for multi-stakeholder management and conflict resolution between multiple PPP constituents that contribute to global governance.

Under the guidance of international organizations, CSR in PPPs fosters the harmonization of cooperative regulatory reforms and trust between multiple stakeholders (Ruckelshaus, 1996). Since the 1950s, PPPs have been institutionalized under the guidance of international organizations. International organizations bring together multiple constituents in addressing global governance. In a multi-stakeholder approach, public-private multi-stakeholder partnerships create flexible networks for addressing social deficiencies and providing social welfare. Bringing together national representatives to constitute international agreements, international organizations promote the standardization of social and environmental policies. International organizations foster transnational consortia advocating for global social policies and provide a framework for implementation strategies to nation states with respect for national interests and corporate endeavors. International organizations guide the harmonization of national endeavors and contribute to global governance by PPP on-ground capacity-building and technical assistance.

Seeking institutionalized solutions, the UN provides legislative or regulatory frameworks to govern the activities of multiple public and private representatives in addressing global governance. Foremost the United Nations Global Compact (UNGC) guides CSR enhancing PPPs and multi-stakeholder global governance. As an example of a global governance PPP, the United Nations Global Alliance for Information and Communication Technologies and Development (GAID) is currently set up to promote information and communication technologies (ICT) for development.

PUBLIC PRIVATE PARTNERSHIPS (PPPs)

Globalization has leveraged the demand for global governance. As of today, international deficiencies out of reach for nation states have risen due to industrialization, global trade, international corporate expansions, environmental challenges and economic frictions of interconnected financial markets (Mathiason, 2007). An emerging trend in global governance provision features the combination of public and private sectors forces in public private partnerships (PPPs). With the rise of international problems and global crises beyond the scope of nation states, PPPs have developed into innovative and flexible means to tackle societal deficiencies, avert global crises and foster societal welfare (Hart, 1995).

For global governance the combination of public and private sector forces in PPPs builds political, economic and judicial infrastructures in addressing societal challenges. PPPs bring together the leaders of business and government for mutual knowledge exchange and expertise enhancement on social welfare provision and crises prevention. In multistakeholder approaches, governmental agencies and business practitioners attribute social responsibility with the greater goal of improving societal progress. Innovative hybrid partnership models feature expanded partnering with trade unions, academia, financial institutions, philanthropists and the civil society.

The establishment of Bretton Woods Institutions such as the United Nations (UN), the World Bank, the International Monetary Fund, but also the World Trade Organization has increased the administration of global governance by PPPs (Mathiason, 2007). International organizations promote PPPs as for supporting international development throughout the world. International organizations provide a combination of regulatory frameworks, technical assistance, training, mentoring and evaluation of contributions to partnerships. With continuing globalization and worldwide corporate expansions of corporations, international organizations are believed to increasingly foster PPPs for development (Beck, 1998; Levitt, 1983; Livesey, 2002; Scholte, 2000).

In connecting the forces of business, society and government, PPP create multiple values for society. In the public sector, PPP improve public management by knowledge transfer. As multi-stakeholder attempts, partnerships offer flexible access to key resources and strengthen public institutions in their regional, national and international management and public administration endeavors.

In the corporate world, PPPs imbue social responsibility into the corporate agenda and align CSR with corporate goals (Bekefi, 2006). PPPs build a stable business climate by bringing together various constituents to reflect upon the corporate role in society. Partnerships with governments, donors, NGOs and community organizations strengthen multi-stakeholder relations (Nelson, 2004). In the integration of overseas markets, partnerships broaden corporate value chains and corporate distribution networks. PPPs build relations with public sector entities and engage corporate officials in public policy dialogues.

As for the early attention to future regulations and adoption of innovative corporate practices, PPPs grant first mover advantages to corporations (Prahalad & Hammond, 2003).

For society, PPPs solve long-term societal problems out of reach for national entities. Partnerships build flexible framework conditions for good governance and responsible corporate conduct around the world. In the developing world, PPPs spread the benefits of open market societies and drive economic growth with respect for posterity. As for long-term business opportunities, corporate partners make sustainable development contributions to communities such as basic infrastructure and access to social welfare (Bekefi, 2006; Kanter, 2003). Innovative PPPs expand economic opportunities to un(der)served segments and provide financial services in an economically viable manner (e.g., Grameen banking).

Downsides of PPPs are transaction costs of the establishment and maintenance of partnership relations. Multiple stakeholders administering global governance can imply conflicting interests. In the international arena, intercultural differences, expertise imbalances and differing access to resources can counterweight an effective dialogue of multiple stakeholders (Ruggie, 2008). The relative novelty of multi-stakeholder global governance provision brings along an absence of legislative frameworks for administering partnerships and no regulation on standardized PPP conduct. As a remedy, CSR serves as an innovative PPP management approach. As a multi-stakeholder participation framework, CSR brings together diverse constituents in their attempts to address global governance. As a co-regulatory arrangement, CSR guidelines corporations and governments in their pro-social endeavors (Moon, 2002). As a management practice, CSR reduces the complexity imposed onto various PPP constituents and alleviates conflicts between multiple public private partners contributing to global governance. By providing tools, standards and means for corporate social conduct, CSR – as a multi-stakeholder management means – harmoniously coordinates the multiple partners' views on social service provision (Ruckelshaus, 1996).

CSR AS MULTI-STAKEHOLDER MANAGEMENT MEANS

Originally the word 'company' derives from the Latin *cum panis* – meaning to break bread together – which attributes the role corporations play in society (Werther & Chandler, 2006). In recent decades, corporate endeavors have leveraged from a primary shareholder-value focus to a broader variety of stakeholders. Corporations engage in mutually beneficial ways with society and touch on multiple actors. As "any group or individual who can affect, or are affected by, the achievement of the organisation's objectives," corporate stakeholders comprise *economic* (e.g., shareholders, customers, creditors, suppliers, competitors), *organizational* (e.g., CEOs, managers, executives, employees) and *public* stakeholders (e.g., representatives of international organizations, governments, trade unions, NGOs, nonprofits) (Freeman, 1984, p. 46).

The recent trend towards PPPs has widened the spectrum of corporate constituents. Tackling social, economic and societal deficiencies in multi-stakeholder approaches, PPPs comprise various constituents and engage corporate entities with multiple stakeholders. Multistakeholder partnerships are complex combinations of diverse actors that may hold differing interests, goals and perspectives as well as represent counterweighing power regimes.

- **Primary Stakeholders:** Such as CEOs, managers, employees – are prone to focus on profit maximization, enhance competitive advantages and corporate growth. *Corporate owners* demand return on investments by efficient and profitable corporate conduct in line with legislative and regulatory obligations. *Employees* are interested in remuneration and care for safety, health standards and human rights. *Suppliers* attribute fair trade and continued business relations.
- **Secondary Stakeholders:** Are *institutional representatives* that shape corporate conduct and set best practice standards. *Governmental agencies* emphasize anti-corruption and compliance with legal and regulatory boundaries. *NGOs and activists* advocate for corporate social performance in triple-bottom-line reporting. *Related communities* want corporate conduct to be in line with societal norms and environmental protection. *Customers* demand products and services in sync with their preferences and values.

In general, multi-stakeholderism raises the likelihood of goal ambiguity and dissenting views on goal achievement strategies. Multiple stakeholders may feature power differences – for example, international organizations have a different standing than NGOs within the international arena. Varying cultural contexts imply differing social, political, historical and economic circumstances impacting on PPPs that accentuate conflicting interests and communication barriers between constituents (Meyer & Höllerer, 2005; Van Maanen & Laurent, 1993; Whitley, 1997). Countries, in which governments traditionally have assigned corporations to take over a significant amount of social responsibility by mandatory regulations, feature a relative low attention to CSR, which draws attention from decreasing partnership challenges.

To balance the needs and interests of multiple constituents of PPPs, corporations feature total responsibility management (TRM) (Waddock & Graves, 1997). TRM stakeholder approaches address a wide range of constituents. TRM multi-stakeholder analyses depict partner contributions and differing standpoints on multiple goal settings to overcome principal-agent predicaments (Freeman, 1984). In this feature, TRM implicitly protects corporate stakeholders from contributing to negative externalities of corporate conduct.

As a feature of TRM, CSR brings together various constituents on social responsibility matters. Enhancing the relationship between corporations and stakeholders, CSR aligns corporate activities with constituents' demands. In harmoniously according multiple stakeholders, CSR serves as an implicit stakeholder management and conflict prevention means (Risse-Kappen, 1995). In addition, CSR signals interest in stakeholder demands and corporate engagement in public matters. CSR pays attention to the needs and wants of multiple constituents with the greater goal of increasing the social value of corporations and lowering the downsides of corporate conduct within society.

As for the novelty of TRM, there is no standardized framework of best practice to implement CSR, which impacts on the effectiveness of PPPs. The most sophisticated institutional attempt to standardize disparate CSR endeavors is provided by the United Nations Global Compact (UNGC).

The United Nations Global Compact (UNGC)

Globalization, the rise of international corporations and global governance trends connected the corporate sector with society. In recent decades, corporations have steadily become key actors in the provision of global governance administered through CSR and PPPs. Institutionalized CSR was first promoted by the International Chamber of Commerce and advanced in the Organization for Economic Cooperation and Development (OECD) Guidelines for Multinational Enterprises as well as the International Labour Organisation (ILO)'s Tripartite Declaration of the Multinational Enterprises and Social Policy. The UN Declaration of Rights addressed corporate social and environmental responsibility for the achievement of the UN Millennium Development Goals (UNMDs) outlined in Table 1 (Kettl, 2006).

In 1999 UN Secretary General Kofi Annan presented the United Nations Global Compact (UNGC) to define the relationship between the UN and the corporate world, regulate CSR endeavors and strengthen partnerships for the

Table 1. The United Nations Millennium Development Goals (UNMDGs)

United Nations Millennium Development Goals (UNMDGs)
▪ Eradicate extreme poverty and hunger ▪ Achieve universal primary education ▪ Promote gender equality and empower women ▪ Reduce child mortality ▪ Improve maternal health ▪ Combat HIV/AIDS, malaria and other diseases ▪ Ensure environmental sustainability ▪ Develop a global partnership for development

achievement of UN goals. The UNGC advocates for corporate contributions to global governance and provides a framework for voluntary social engagement.

As of today, the UNGC has become the world's largest and most renowned PPP global governance initiative by featuring over 3,500 corporations and more than 700 civil society partners.[1] In a multi-stakeholder approach, the UNGC embraces a growing network of corporations and international stakeholders with the binding goal of fostering a more sustainable and inclusive world economy. The UNGC comprises representatives of the UN, governments, corporations, labor unions, civil society and academia.

The *UN* is the main UNGC umbrella organization.

- Within the UN, the UNGC is a network of the following agencies:
  - The Office of the High Commissioner for Human Rights
  - The United Nations Environment Programme
  - The International Labour Organization
  - The United Nations Development Programme
  - The United Nations Industrial Development Organization – The United Nations Office of Drugs and Crime
- The UNGC is represented by:
  - **The GC Leader Summit:** A triennial gathering of participants and stakeholders to derive future strategies of the initiative. The Summit targets at deepening the commitment of leaders in business, the labor force and civil society.
  - **The GC Board:** The multi-stakeholder advisory body touches on the corporate world, civil society, labor unions and the UN. The UNGC Board meets annually to provide a strategic outlook and policy advice for the initiative. The Board enhances synergies between the global and local levels by promoting program ownership, integrity management and quality assurance in the implementation of the UNGC principles.

  - **The GC Office:** Supports the management of the UNGC as a coordinating entity. Holding the system-wide responsibility for sharing best practices in networks, the GC Office facilitates dialogues between corporate actors, the UN and stakeholders. The GC Office advances the partnership agenda across the UN system, manages the UNGC brand and oversees integrity measures.
  - **Local Networks:** In the implementation of the UNGC, corporate units around the world engage in local networks to pursue UN goals. Country and regional networks translate the UNGC principles into local action whilst facilitating learning among stakeholders.
  - **Inter-Agency Teams:** Focus on the internalization of principles within the UN and among global constituents. These advisory teams measure corporate integrity and manage complaints.
- *Governments* provide legislative, regulatory and financial frameworks that define UNGC principles.
  - Governmental frameworks grant long-term stability in promoting corporate social practices, corporate conduct transparency and innovation.
  - Governments launch events that support public policy making and international organizations' global governance.
- By CSR *corporations* contribute to PPPs that foster the UN vision of a more sustainable and inclusive marketplace.
  - Corporations are expected to align their operations, work practices and codes of conduct with the UNGC principles.
  - Corporations should operate in sync with UNGC principles that are ingrained in the corporate strategy, culture and day-by-day operations. Corporate executives are invited and trained to consider environmental, social and governance goals in corporate decision-making.
  - CSR best practice transfer in networking, dialogue, learning and partnering mainstreams CSR to replicate the UNGC principles within the corporate world. – PPPs engage corporate stakeholders to accomplish the UNMDGs.
  - Corporate executives are advised to publicly advocate for the UNGC in press releases, speeches and annual reports.
  - For corporations the UNGC is an entry point to the UN agenda, a means to benefit from public sector outlooks and innovative stakeholder management tool. Corporations that engage in the

UNGC experience social and environmental governance as long-term strategies.[2]

- Paying attention to the UNGC and demonstrating active participation in societal issues provide best practice leadership advantages.
- Corporate conduct in line with the UN principle attracts a loyal workforce and enhances consumer identification.
- Embracing the UNGC improves the corporate reputation and lowers stakeholder pressure.

- *Civil society & Labor organizations* represent stakeholder communities.
    - The *civil society* implicitly sets the social standards on corporate social conduct.
    - *Labor organizations* are driving forces in the implementation of the UNGC and provide accountability control.
- *Academia* strengthens the theoretical advancement of business ethics and disseminates information about the UNGC.
    - Academics influence corporate leaders through research, business education, management development, trainings and advocacy.
    - Academics independently monitor the effectiveness of UNGC partnerships, measure their impact and provide accountability control.
    - Academic teaching educates in business ethics.

The UNGC raises awareness for the corporate role in global governance. As a platform for exchange, the UNGC motivates corporations to connect with society. The UNGC Learning Forum offers a network of experts and practitioners to exchange knowledge on CSR best practices. In disseminating CSR case studies, the UNGC fosters interdisciplinary learning on business ethics. In regularly conferences and summits, leaders from the business and governmental world are brought together to align in the alleviation of global governance problems.

In an attempt to regulate CSR, the UNGC sets specific rules, norms and conventions to be implemented by the corporate sector with respect for legal foundations, ethics standards and moral values. As a frame of reference, the UNGC provides universal corporate principles with respect for human rights, labor standards, environmental protection and anti-corruption to create sustainable benefits for corporations and society (see Table 2).[3]

Table 2. The Ten Principles of the UNGC

The United Nations Global Compact Ten Principles
Human Rights[4]
Based on the UN Universal Declaration of Human Rights signed by member states in 1948, corporate actors should promote ▪ Human rights ▪ Freedom from discrimination ▪ The right to life, liberty and security ▪ The right to not be held in slavery or subjected to inhuman or degrading treatment ▪ The right to rest and leisure ▪ The right to education ▪ The right to an adequate standard of living ▪ Protection from corporate crime and contract breaches
Principle 1: Corporations should support and respect the protection of internationally proclaimed human rights.
End state: Corporations support and respect the protection of internationally proclaimed human rights.
Principle 2: Corporations must not be complicit in human rights abuses.
End state: Corporations do not engage in any form of human rights violations.
Activities
• Human rights and related values are embedded in corporate mission statements, codes of conduct and procedural manuals. • Corporate legal councils oversee human rights standards implementation and address deficiencies. • Corporate departments implement human rights in corporate conduct. • Managers are trained in business ethics to conduct business with respect for human rights.
Performance indicators
• Human rights violations are detected and reported by internal councils and external stakeholders. • Internal and external audits of corporate human rights standards in headquarters and subsidiaries. • Qualitative and quantitative reports on human rights violations.
Labor Standards[5]
The International Labour Organization (ILO) Declaration on Fundamental Principles and Rights at Work that was adopted by governments, corporations and labor organizations of 177 countries in 1998 defines: ▪ The right to equal opportunity and treatment in employment and occupation ▪ The right to a safe and healthy work environment ▪ The prohibition of forced and child labor ▪ Freedom of Association and the right to collective bargaining
Principle 3: Corporations should uphold the freedom of association and the effective recognition of the right to collective bargaining.
End state: Corporations uphold the freedom of association and the right to collective bargaining.
Principle 4: The elimination of all forms of forced and compulsory labor.
End state: All forms of forced and compulsory labor are eliminated.
Principle 5: The effective abolition of child labor.
End state: Child labor is eliminated.
Principle 6: The elimination of discrimination in respect of employment and occupation.
End state: All forms of discrimination in employment and occupation are eliminated.

continued on following page

Table 2. Continued

The United Nations Global Compact Ten Principles
Activities
• Labor association standards are incorporated in corporate practices. • Labor associations are supported and the right to collective bargaining is respected by corporate management. • Child and forced labor is excluded from any corporate activities with special attention to subsidiaries. • Safety and quality standards are ensured throughout the corporate world. • Discrimination is diminished by a well-tempered quota system comprising all corporate levels. • Employees are trained to detect, report and target explicit and implicit forms of discrimination. • Intra- and interorganizational touch points for discrimination reporting are established. • Change and diversity management empowers minorities.
Performance indicators
• The absence of infringements of the freedom of association and the right to collective bargaining. • Quantitative and qualitative reduction of reports on forced, compulsory and child labor. • The absence of reported forced, compulsory and child labor in internal and external audits on an international basis. • Stakeholder monitoring on corporate activities in headquarters and subsidiaries. • Minorities entering all corporate levels throughout the corporate world.
Environment[3]
Environmental protection is based on the Declaration and International Plan of Action (Agenda 21) that was adopted at the Rio Conference on Environmental and Development in 1992 as well as the Brundtland Commission Report that requires corporations to avoid large-scale environmental decay. The Rio Declaration defines sustainable development as: ▪ A precautionary and pro-active approach to environmental protection and employment of preventive measures. ▪ The incorporation of environmental considerations into policies, decisions and actions. ▪ The adoption of environmentally friendly technologies leading to resource savings. ▪ The development and diffusion of environmentally friendly technologies, products and processes ▪ The enhanced communication on the advantages of environmental improvements.
Principle 7: Corporations should support a precautionary approach to environmental challenges.
End state: Corporations are precautionary in terms of environmental challenges and conduct business in an environmentally responsible way.
Principle 8: Corporations should undertake initiatives to promote greater environmental responsibility.
End state: Corporate activities are geared towards the proactive promotion of environmental responsibility.
Principle 9: Corporations should encourage the development and diffusion of environmentally friendly technologies.
End state: Businesses encourage the development and diffusion of environmentally friendly technologies.
Activities
• Corporate executives pro-actively seek environmentally friendly products, services and corporate conduct. • Sustainability and environmentally friendly corporate practices are promoted by the corporate management. • Incorporation of sustainability in corporate cultures, business practices and codes of conduct. • Corporations initiate and engage in stakeholder dialogues on environmental responsibility. • Environmentally harmful technologies are replaced by alternative energy sources. • Corporate conducts' impact and externalities on the environment are made transparent in CSR and sustainability reports. • Environmentally conscientious resource consumption is promoted by the corporate culture throughout the entire value chain.

continued on following page

Table 2. Continued

The United Nations Global Compact Ten Principles
Performance indicators
• Qualitative and quantitative reduction of negative externalities of corporate conduct negatively impacting on the environment. • Enhancement of environmentally friendly codes of conduct. • Qualitative and quantitative increase of the development and diffusion of environmentally friendly innovations and technologies. • Qualitative and quantitative rise in CSR assessments as well as sustainability reports and audits.
Anti-Corruption[4]
The UNGC 10th principle against corruption is based on the 2003 UN Convention Against Corruption for the: ▪ Promotion of corporate work against corruption through policies and actions ▪ Promotion of the rule of the law as a prosecution for criminal defence ▪ Avoidance of corporate bribery, extortion and other forms of corruption ▪ Extortion as an illegal means of enriching oneself by coercion, violence and threats ▪ Avoidance of favoritism and nepotism ▪ Divestiture of markets that are not clear of bribery
Principle 10: Corporations should work against corruption in all its forms, including extortion and bribery.
End state: Well-functioning corporate anti-corruption systems are established.
Activities
• Corporations launch and promote anti-corruption policies throughout headquarters, subsidiaries, partners, contractors and stakeholders. • Install policies and procedures encouraging employees to report bribery, extortion, corruption, favoritism and nepotism. • Promote whistle-blowing reporting mechanisms.
Performance indicators
• Reduction of reported corporate corruption, extortion and bribery incidents.

The UNGC raises awareness for the corporate role in global governance. As a platform for exchange, the UNGC motivates corporations to connect with society. The UNGC Learning Forum offers a network of experts and practitioners to exchange knowledge on CSR best practices. In disseminating CSR case studies, the UNGC fosters interdisciplinary learning on business ethics. In regularly conferences and summits, leaders from the business and governmental world are brought together to align in the alleviation of global governance problems.

The UNGC principles provide a leadership model of CSR corporate conduct. The UNGC participating parties are meant to align their policies and work practices according to the Ten Principles. The UN endeavors should be attributed in corporate policies, stakeholder dialogues, corporate learning and networking partnership projects.

To ensure a quality control, the UNGC features systematic impact assessments and evaluations of corporate performance. Quality control is made transparent by UNGC statements of continued support, in Communication on Progress in the achievement of the UNGC principles as well as public commitment statements.[5] Corporate CSR and partnership commitments are also monitored in periodic letters of support. In addition, an UN ombudsperson and contact points for complaints on social and environmental violations are in place. The UNGC output indication metrics serve as leadership best practice models and public accountability control for pro-social engagement of the corporate sector. The UNGC paves the way for CSR as a successful contribution to PPPs in the accomplishment of the UNMDGs – as in the case of the currently launched United Nations Global Alliance for Information and Communication Technologies (ICT) and Development (UN GAID).

The Global Alliance for Information and Communication Technologies (ICT) and Development (GAID)

The importance of Information and Communication Technologies (ICT) in achieving the United Nations Millennium Development Goals (UNMDGs) has risen in recent decades. With the greater goals of achieving international civil society progress, global crises prevention and societal deficiencies alleviation, the UN launched the Global Alliance for Information and Communication Technologies and Development (GAID) as an international platform for cross-sectoral solution finding and policy dialogue on ICT for development in 2006.[6] The UNGAID is an international forum on ICT use in partnerships for development (Puaschunder, 2017b).

Within the private sector, GAID represents workers associations, producers and suppliers of ICT and the media community. In the public sphere, governmental representatives institutionalize ICT for development. Within the civil society, GAID addresses NGOs, private foundations and consumers. Scientific and academic ICT advocates, but also individuals and institutions providing oversight on information issues are part of the GAID network. Agencies implementing ICT programs for development contribute to GAID.

Within the UN system, GAID is a think tank on ICT for development-related issues and advisory group to the UN Secretary-General. GAID comprises a *Steering Committee*, Strategy Council, High-level Panel of Advisers and a Network of Champions.[7]

The *Steering Committee* is composed of 14 Members designated by the UN SecretaryGeneral. The Steering Committee

- Gives executive direction to the Secretariat via the approval of the Business Plan.
- Establishes and reviews mandates of Communities of Expertise, stakeholder and regional networks as well as regional centers of excellence to carry out specific tasks within the focus areas of the Alliance.
- Exercises a leadership role in high-level advocacy and policy advice in the field of ICT for development.
- Seeks partnerships and liaises with global entities in the field of ICT for development.
- Reviews and approves recommendations of the Secretariat in regards to additional partnerships, fundraising, sponsorship of events and in-kind contributions.
- Spearheads activities to raise contributions by members, partners and other organizations.
- Identifies emerging issues on ICT for development.

The *Strategy Council* provides an overall vision, guidance and priority setting to the Alliance by identifying themes and priorities to be addressed. The Council comprises 74 members – 30 representing governments, 15 the private sector, 17 the civil society and 12 executives of international organizations. The Council

- Reviews the annual and the financial reports on the activities of the Alliance.
- Features high-level expertise and leadership to facilitate ICT outreach.
- Contributes to the formulation of advice to the Secretary-General and to the UN system on issues related to ICT for development.
- Serves as a think tank to disseminate knowledge to policy-makers, practitioners and the wider stakeholder constituents.
- Develops an action plan and policy platform to promote the scalability, replicability and sustainability of Alliance activities.
- Raises awareness in advocacy campaigns for ICT for development.
- Promotes multi-stakeholder partnerships and initiatives by innovative networking and information-sharing approaches.
- Raises funds for GAID activities, partnerships and events.

The GAID *High-level Panel of Advisers* is composed of practitioners, policy-makers and other experts who support the mission of the Global Alliance. The High-level Panel of Advisers

- Brings attention to the Alliance development in theory and practice.
- Provides policy and expert advice to the Strategy Council and Steering Committee based on research and practical experience in reports, papers, presentations and faceto-face dialogue.

The *Network of Champions* combines practitioners, activists and experts promoting development through ICT. The Network of Champions

- Fosters ICT for development at the grass-roots and community level.
- Facilitates the diffusion of knowledge and experience in innovative uses of ICT for the achievement of development goals.
- Promotes a bottom-up flow of information on the implementation of GAID activities and ICT endeavors in the field.
- Fosters the formation of on-site partnerships for ICT on development.

GAID enhances intercultural and cross-sectoral dialogues among stakeholders to globally address and facilitate the transfer of knowledge on ICT for development. As an umbrella organization, GAID promotes the use of ICT for the achievement of the UNMDGs. GAID is composed of representatives from various stakeholders who contribute to advocacy and the policy debate on the role of the information society in international development.

In a multi-stakeholder attempt, GAID facilitates PPPs to foster the dissemination of technological solutions for the achievement of development. As a networking governance platform, GAID steers the dissemination of innovations on ICT for development. The partners of the Alliance have the overarching goal of tackling societal challenges in a knowledge-based information society. Partners demonstrate leadership on ICT and mainstream the global ICT agenda for the accomplishment of UN endeavors. Best practices knowledge on ICT is shared in policy dialogues and presentations of innovative business models for pro-poor investment, economic growth through access to new media technologies and the ICT empowerment of people living in poverty.

As of July 2009 the Networking Partners[8] comprised the

- *Development Gateway Foundation (DGF)* as an international nonprofit organization with the mission to reduce poverty in IT and web-based platforms. In a multistakeholder approach, DGF features local partner programs in nearly 50 countries targeted at connecting the developing world through IT.
- The *Egyptian Ministry of Communications and Information Technology* representing a public sector entity focusing on ICT for development.
- *Global Knowledge Partnership* as an international network of over 100 public and private sector entities and civil society who share knowledge on the advancements of ICT for development.
- The *ICT4Peace Foundation* aims at crisis management by the application of ICT as a means of effective and sustained communication on international development, humanitarian aid and peacebuilding.
- The *IT4ALL Network* is a decentralized cooperation network of local authorities reaching out for an inclusive information society.
- The *RIOS Institute* is dedicated to design social and technological development projects to achieve ICT collaborations for development in line with the UNMDGs.
- The *Suzanne Mubarak Women's International Peace Movement* is a non-profit, nongovernmental international association focusing on cooperations for sustainable peace and human security.
- The *UNITAR Webinar Series on ICT Policy Issues for Development* provides UN delegates with a discussion and learning forum on ICT for development.
- The *UN Office of the High Representative for Least Developed Countries, Landlocked Developing Countries and Small Island Developing States (UN-ORHLLS)* monitors and reviews the implementation of the Programme of Action for the decade 20012010 with a special emphasis on ICT.
- *Word Summit Award (WSA)* is a global initiative under the guidance of the UN World Summit on the Information Society. WSA promotes the improvement of e-contents and innovative ICT applications to bridge content gaps in the developing world. WSA works for a global information society that enables individuals to share knowledge for societal progress. As a networking platform, WSA events bring together governmental leaders, business executives and civil society.
- *Global Huddle* outlines strategies for the use of ICT in creating global awareness of the UNMDGs by enhancing e-contents.

- *WSYA Amphitheatre* promotes creative ICT products fostering the accomplishment of the UNMDGs.

The GAID Partnering Network comprises *Flagship Partnership Initiatives*, *Stakeholder* and *Regional Networks* as well as *Communities of Expertise* (CoE), which address ICT for development issues and disseminate ICT best practices. CoEs feature the areas of Education, Entrepreneurship, Governance, Health and Cross-cutting themes.[9] An overview of the GAID partnership initiatives as of July 2009 is provided by Figure 1.

Descriptions the endeavors of the GAID partnership initiatives[10] are outlined in Tables 3-6.

As of today ICT has strengthened global governance by improving the performance and efficiency of markets and governments. ICT revolutionized the availability and access to information. In the wake of the IT revolution, ICT has gained importance as a means of information dissemination in e-newsletters, blogs and e-forums. ICT has leveraged the potential and engagement opportunities of multiple stakeholders to communicate, facilitate access to information and coordinate in the advancement towards the UNMDGs. As a multidimensional knowledge brokerage tool, ICT enhances information synthesis and transparency. New media sources grant unprecedented accountability and benchmarking opportunities to stakeholders.

Regarding the UNMDGs, ICT has become an essential tool for the alleviation of societal deficiencies. As for the *eradication of hunger*, the IT revolution has perpetuated the efficiency in the information flow on drought,

Figure 1. GAID partnership initiatives

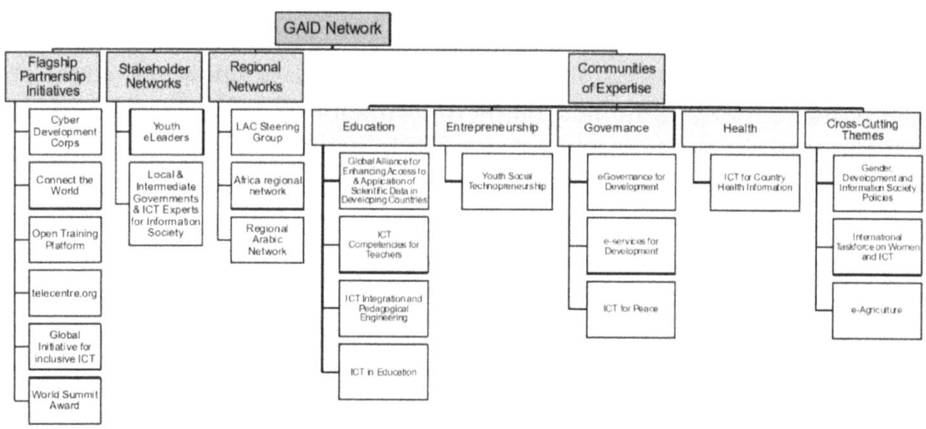

Table 3. GAID partnership initiatives: Flagship partnership initiatives

Cyber Development Corps	Connect the World (Better connectivity with broadband Africa)	UNESCO Open Training Platform (OTP)	telecentre.org	G3ict (Global Initiative for inclusive information and communication technologies)	World Summit Award (WSA)
• Systemic platform to accelerate the development and advancement of global ICT for development programs. • Creates partnership channels for governments, corporations, civil society organizations, community leaders, professionals and civil society. • Combines bottom-up application initiatives with topdown policy strategies for advancing ICT for development. • Long-term focus on bridging the ICT development gap and promoting more inclusive global ICT for development policies, strategies, programs and institutions. • Builds upon existing ICT for development programs for scaling and coordination of community programs. • Establishes community centers to provide awareness-raising on the potential of ICT and the application of ICT for socioeconomic development. • Global outreach for volunteering to help lesser-developed communities benefiting from a global ICT infrastructure and resources. • Capacity-building to create a voluntary corps of young ICT teachers.	• The International Telecommunication Union (ITU) engages governments, industries, financial institutions, civil society and other partners to connect the developing world through ICT. • Understands ICT as a means of spurring investments, social and economic development. • Fosters networks and projects to expand information and communication for access to ICT for development. • Sets up conferences and regional summits to bring together ICT constituents	• In collaboration with nine UN agencies and 1600 members, OTP matches existing access centers, learning resources, development agencies and initiatives advocating for open source ICT education. • Knowledge-brokerage information centers provide trainings and access to ICT for development. • OTP offers web-space and internet learning opportunities to enhance knowledge and skill acquisition in developing countries. • Responding to local e-learning needs, OTP gives access to free quality trainings. • Capacity-building resources provide training-on-demand services target at local learning. • Technology watch and mobilization of development stakeholders is accompanied by networking activities such as conferences and workshops.	• Promotes an inclusive digital world by fostering telecenters. • Telecenters feature knowledge societies and the integration of ICT in social and economic development with applications in health care, local economic development, livelihood rural ecommerce, education and egovernance. • Telecenter growth is stimulated by investments, institution building and partnerships that enhance capacity building and promote sustainability. • Community engagement is fostered in international networks and trainings, certifications and mentoring. • Telecenters of excellence and leadership forum events serve as a source for documentation of best practices. • By testing new technologies, telecenters advance community computing initiatives.	• As a means of empowerment for about 18 percent of the world's population living with disabilities, ICT provides access to information and societal participation. • Promotes ICT solutions for people with disabilities and related best policy practices among governments. • G3ict tackles economic and social development challenges related to disabilities by seeking the involvement of the world's leading ICT providers in disability empowerment. • Brings together civil society organizations that represent disabled as well as governmental officials, academia and the private sector to contribute to developing ICT solutions for disabled. • Accelerates the standardization and economic efficiency of ICT to make technology solutions more affordable for disabled. • Derives guidelines and regulatory frameworks for access to ICT to disabled. • Sets up multi-stakeholder global and regional forums, meetings and working groups that engage in respective research, development and best practices promotion.	• The WSA stimulates entrepreneurship and creativity in the e-industry that support the UNMDGs. • Increases access to knowledge with attention to education, culture, health, science, entrepreneurship, business, governance and public administration. • WSA serves as a global hub to bridge the ICT for development community in creative contests and events. • Provides and sustains inclusive multi-stakeholder activities for the selection and promotion of best practice in e-content with the greater goal of bridging information gaps. • Organizes and executes a global contest on best practices in e-content. • Invites member states, the business community and civil society organizations in forward-looking multistakeholder partnerships. • Seeks cooperation with UN organizations and agencies as well as private sector sponsors. • Initiates and supports WSA global e-content summits to bring together speakers, experts and e-content producers.

Table 4. GAID partnership initiatives: Stakeholder networks

Youth eLeaders (Committee of e-Leaders for ICT and Youth)	Network of Local and Intermediate Governments and ICT Experts for the Information Society (LRAEIS)
• Spearheads regional programs working on the UNMDG agenda for ICT related to youth. • Helps create youth networks for the regional development of ICT. • Coordinates initiatives of the Global Youth Coalition on ICT for development. • Brings together multiple ICT constituents for advocacy and oversight on information issues • Fosters exchange of knowledge and experience with ICT for development on youth issues. • Promotes awareness and advocacy campaigns on regional ICT for development. • Raises funds and mobilizes resources by outreach to young individuals.	• Network of local and regional authorities including cities, intermediate governments, associations of regions and groups of local communities comprising ICT experts from all over the world. • Promotes cooperation among local and intermediate governments and ICT experts as for the exchange of best practices and the development of ICT programs. • Promotes collaboration on initiative aspects related to ICT for development. • Ensures local voices and intermediate governments to be incorporated into the policy dialogue on ICT for development. • Sets up networks in Africa, the Asian Pacific Region, Latin America and Europe.

Table 5. GAID partnership initiatives: Regional networks

LAC Steering Group	Africa	Regional Arabic Network
• Promotes the objectives of GAID through outreach to governments, business leaders, civil society, academic institutions and technology communities. • Coordinates the work and initiatives of the GAID LAC network and mobilizes resources for the initiative. • Facilitates and creates platforms for better coordination among existing programs and initiatives. • Promotes awareness and advocacy campaigns on regional ICT for development. • Organizes stakeholder activities and events.	• Frameworks mechanisms, modalities and structures for ensuring Africa's effective participation in the GAID process. • Identifies and implements Africa-specific GAID flagship initiatives, advocacy groups and stakeholder activities. • Implements mainstream GAID activities during the on-going ICT for development build-up in Africa. • Contributes to the overall GAID policy-dialogue on advancing the global ICT for development agenda.	• Brings together knowledge, expertise and best practices on ICT for development in the Arabic countries. • Promotes the exchange of strategies, plans and experiences in order to maximize the effectiveness of the initiatives in the achievement of the UNMDG. • Fosters ICT for development collaborations among stakeholders at all levels of policy making and public administration in the Arabic world. • Seeks contributions from stakeholders including governments, international organizations, businesses, NGOs and academia. • Coordinates activities and encourages communication between stakeholders.

hunger and crises. As an innovative avenue for fighting *poverty*, ICT provides access to capital online and by mobile phones. Information flow is key to *medical assistance* of underserved communities and an essential prerequisite for effective epidemiology. As an essential feature of preventive medical assistance, ICT helps educating on maternal health and combating child mortality, HIV, malaria and other diseases.

Table 6. GAID partnership initiatives: Communities of expertise

Education
eSDDC (Global Alliance for Enhancing Access to and Application of Scientific Data in Developing Countries) • Fosters open and sustainable access to ICT. • Provides an interdisciplinary forum and mechanisms for exchanging information about scientific data sharing strategies, policies and activities in developing countries. • Develops a web-based information network, holds workshops and disseminates community expertise in working papers by the help of newmedia technologies.
ICT Competencies for Teachers • Engages global stakeholders to improve the quality and consistency of teacher education by the help of ICT. • Accelerates teacher training by the use of new technologies and technologysupported learning opportunities for students. • Delivers an online environment for teacher training. • Fosters information exchange among stakeholders in the field of ICT teaching. • Provides ICT guidelines and curricula recommendations for teachers. • Serves as an international supervisory board for mentoring of ICT teaching.
ICT Integration and Pedagogical Engineering • Promotes open access to information and distance learning by integrated international ICT education. • Organizes wide-scale events and on-site workshops for empowerment and capacity building through ICT.
ICT in Education • Creates a dialogue on ICT education and coordination among stakeholders to advance and detect barriers to using ICT in education. • Increases the use of ICT for education through infrastructure, policies, regulations, standards and best practice dissemination. • Develops policies as legal and regulatory frameworks for the advancement of ICT in education. • Supports academic activities to improve research, teaching and learning processes on ICT. • Empowers educational communities with ICT and ICT-driving teaching and learning skills. • Promotes information sharing on ICT for education in forums, publications and e-space for stakeholder. • Promotes ICT usage among stakeholder communities for the advancement of education and learning.
Entrepreneurship
Youth Social Technopreneurship • Builds capacities of rural, economically disadvantaged young people aspiring to become social technopreneurs. • Broadens network memberships among youth and youth-serving organizations engaged in social technopreneurship in developing countries. • Creates opportunities for IT society policy engagement of young people in rural areas and impoverished communities of developing countries. • Expands community memberships to include donor agencies, like-minded networks and socially responsible investors. • Fosters capacity-building networks, work programs and workshops.
Governance
e-Governance for Development • Integrates ICT at the local, national and regional levels by development strategies and programs. Promotes ICT as a means to improve good governance by fostering the effectiveness and efficiency of governments, granting citizen access to information, enhancing participation in democratic processes and embracing stakeholders. • Includes a number of representatives ranging from governments, business, international organizations, civil society, technical and academic communities. • Brings together existing and emerging local, national, regional and global networks that work on e-governance and a common knowledge platform for information sharing. • Enhances outreach and promotes partnerships for action within the global multi-stakeholder community engaged in e-governance for development.
e-services for Development • Foster the cooperation of interrelated systems of development through a platform of e-services for development. • Studies the feasibility of e-services for development in ICT village test markets under the guidance of the UN Public Private Alliance on Rural Development.

continued on following page

Table 6. Continued

ICT for Peace • Fosters exchange of best practices and multi-stakeholder processes in the field of ICT. • Establishes best practice principles and multi-stakeholder input to enhance the performance of the international ICT community. • Raise awareness about the contribution and potential of ICT in crises management. • Derives training modules for peace building by the help of ICT. • Launches an e-database on the use of ICT in crises management and peacebuilding.
Health
ICT for Country Health Information • e-health is a fundament in health care delivery and public health practices in countries that are vulnerable to threats from diseases, disasters and poverty. • Develops and validates a joint planning process to support the implementation of ICT for public health. • Defines public infrastructure requirements. • Facilitates policies and governance principles required for investments and the implementation initiatives.
Cross-Cutting Themes
Gender, Development and Information Society Policies (GDISP) • Explores the complex relationship between gender, development and IT policies. Provides online and face-to-face platforms for a sustained dialogue on the development of analytic frameworks and policy recommendations. • Fosters policy processes at local, national and global levels with respect for gender and development. • Develops linkages to policy-making mechanisms at national and global levels. • Extends linkages at local and implementation levels for ICT development projects working on female empowerment. Strengthens women's organizations to engage in IT policy advocacy. • Undertakes research and other forms of knowledge and expertise building.
International Taskforce on Women and ICT • Ignites new initiatives and strengthens current efforts to provide economic, social and educational ICT opportunities for women. • Coordinates networks and international projects and events for the dissemination of information on the use of ICT for female empowerment. • Derives policy recommendations and programs contributions to ICT • Generates metric benchmarking indicators and conducts monitoring.
e-Agriculture • Contributes to the development of policies, guidelines, strategies and priorities related to e-agriculture. • Engages global stakeholders to improve communication and virtual learning forums and web-portals on eagriculture. • Guides to planning, monitoring and coordination of action on e-agriculture. • Fosters the share of knowledge, know-how on ICT implementation, monitoring and evaluation of eagriculture policies and best practices. • Facilitates the development of partnerships involving respective eagriculture stakeholders. • Identifies stakeholder organizations, groups and individuals who endeavor take part in e-agriculture.

ICT has led to groundbreaking insights on the decay of natural resources and climate change. Information and communication foster *environmental protection* and sustainability. New media technologies are pivotal to preventing environmental crises and managing risk in the domain of climate change.

Access to information and the reduction of information transfer costs have helped *educating* underserved groups as an essential ingredient for societal development and the empowerment of minorities. Web-based communication has developed into an innovative teaching and learning method that features fast interactivity, cooperative learning arrangements and richness in content.

As a communication and information tool for education, ICT is also key for minority advocacy and *empowerment*. Within corporations ICT develops competencies necessary for lifelong learning and employee empowerment. In the implementation of policies, ICT links minorities and local project bodies with global umbrella organizations.

Overall, ICT strengthens policy-making bodies on a national and global level in collaboration with the UN. ICT steers societal progress throughout the world (Reinfried, Schleicher & Rempfler, 2007).

Future endeavors for the GAID initiative comprise the exploration of innovative information transfer possibilities. GAID aims at spreading ICT throughout the world with a special focus on developing countries and sector extensions. In the year of 2009, GAID concentrated on extensions to Africa and Arabic countries and the use of IT in the public sector.

Overall the importance of ICT in international development is predicted to rise. ICT is attributed to foster international cooperations on development among global constituents (Reinfried et al., 2007). Digital media education, ICT medical assistance and new media supported crises management tools are perceived as future ingredients for the accomplishment of the UNMDGs. Internet banking and banking for the poor via mobile phones account for the most innovative features of ICT for international development and financial social responsibility.

REFERENCES

Beck, U. (1998). Wie wird Demokratie im Zeitalter der Globalisierung möglich? In U. Beck (Ed.), *Politik der Globalisierung* (pp. 7–67). Frankfurt am Main: Suhrkamp.

Bekefi, T. (2006). *Business as a partner in tackling micronutrient deficiency: Lessons in multisector partnership. Report of the Corporate Responsibility Initiative*. Cambridge, MA: Harvard University Press.

Freeman, R. E. (1984). *Strategic management: A stakeholder approach.* Mashfield, MA: Pitman.

Hart, S. L. (1995). A natural resource-based view of the firm. *Academy of Management Review, 20*(4), 986–1014. doi:10.5465/amr.1995.9512280033

Kanter, R. M. (2003). *From spare change to real change. Harvard Business Review on Corporate Responsibility.* Cambridge, MA: Harvard Business School.

Kettl, D. F. (2006). *The global public management revolution.* Washington, DC: The Brookings Institution.

Levitt, T. (1983). The globalization of markets. *Harvard Business Review, 61*, 2–11.

Liston-Heyes, C., & Ceton, G. C. (2007). Corporate social performance and politics. *Journal of Corporate Citizenship, 25*(25), 95–108. doi:10.9774/GLEAF.4700.2007.sp.00010

Livesey, S. (2002). The discourse of the middle ground: Citizen Shell commits to sustainable development. *Management Communication Quarterly, 15*(3), 313–349. doi:10.1177/0893318902153001

Mathiason, J. (2007). *Invisible governance: International secretariats in global politics.* Bloomfield, CT: Kumarian.

Meyer, R. E., & Höllerer, M. A. (2005, August). *From value management to values management: Contrasting views or just two sides of the same coin: Shareholder value and corporate social responsibility in Austrian publicly listed corporations. 18th NFF Meeting*, Aarhus School of Business, Aarhus, Denmark.

Moon, J. (2002). The social responsibility of business and new governance. *Government and Opposition, 37*(3), 385–408. doi:10.1111/1477-7053.00106

Moon, J. (2007). The contribution of corporate social responsibility to sustainable development. *Sustainable Development, 15*(5), 296–306. doi:10.1002d.346

Nelson, J. (2004). *Leadership, accountability and partnership: Critical trends and issues in corporate social responsibility. Report of the Corporate Responsibility Initiative*. Cambridge, MA: Harvard University.

Prahalad, C. K., & Hammond, A. (2003). *Serving the world's poor profitably. Harvard Business Review on Corporate Responsibility*. Cambridge, MA: Harvard Business School.

Reinfried, Y., Schleicher, A., & Rempfler, A. (2007). Geographical views on education for sustainable development. *Geographiedidaktische Forschungen*, *42*, 243–250.

Risse-Kappen, T. (1995). *International relations: Theory and the end of the cold war*. New York: Columbia University.

Ruckelshaus, W. (1996). *Trust in government: A prescription for restoration. Webb lecture series*. Washington, DC: National Academy of Public Administration.

Ruggie, J. (2008). *Promotion and protection of all human rights, civil, political, economic, social and cultural rights, including the right to development: Protect, respect and remedy: A framework for business and human rights*. Report of the Special Representative of the Secretary-General on the issue of human rights and transnational corporations and other business enterprises. Presented at the Eighth Session of the Human Rights Council. Retrieved from http://www.businesshumanrights.org/Documents/RuggieHRC2008

Scholte, J. A. (2000). *Globalization: A critical introduction*. Basingstoke: Palgrave.

Steurer, R. (2010). The role of governments in corporate social responsibility: Characterising public policies on CSR in Europe. *Policy Sciences*, *43*(1), 49–72. doi:10.100711077-009-9084-4

Van Maanen, J., & Laurent, A. (1993). The flow of culture: Some notes on globalization and the multinational corporation. In S. Ghoshal & D. E. Westney (Eds.), *Organization Theory and the Multinational Corporation* (pp. 275–312). New York: St. Martin's. doi:10.1007/978-1-349-22557-6_12

Waddock, S. A., & Graves, S. B. (1997). The corporate social performance-financial performance link. *Strategic Management Journal*, *18*(4), 303–319. doi:10.1002/(SICI)1097-0266(199704)18:4<303::AID-SMJ869>3.0.CO;2-G

Werther, W. B., & Chandler, D. (2006). *Strategic corporate social responsibility: Stakeholders in a global environment*. Thousand Oaks: Sage.

Whitley, R. (1997). Business systems. In A. Sorge & M. Warner (Eds.), *The IEBM Handbook of Organizational Behaviour*. London: Thomson Business Press.

ENDNOTES

1 Enhancing partnership value: A tool for assessing sustainability and impact. The United Nations Global Compact office. Retrieved from the internet in June 2007 at http://www.unglobalcompact.org/docs/news_events/8.1/Partnership_value.pdf.

2 The Global Compact. Annual Review. 2007 Leaders Summit. The United Nations Global Compact office. Retrieved from the internet in July 2007 at http://www.unglobalcompact.org/docs/news_events/8.1/GCAnnualReview2007.pdf.

3 based on The Rio Declaration on Environment and Development.

4 Business against corruption: Case stories and examples. Implementation of the 10th United Nations Global Compact Principle against corruption. The United Nations Global Compact office. Retrieved from the internet in June 2007 at http://www.unglobalcompact.org/AboutTheGC/publications.html.

5 The UN Global Compact operational guide for medium-scale enterprises. The United Nations Global Compact office. Retrieved from the internet in July 2007 at http://www.unglobalcompact.org/docs/news_events/8.1/Operational_guide_ME.pdf.

6 Retrieved from the internet in February 2008 at http://www.un-gaid.org/.

7 Retrieved from the internet in February 2008 at http://www.un-gaid.org/.

8 Latest update retrieved from the internet in August 2009 at http://www.un-gaid.org/.

9 Latest update retrieved from the internet in August 2009 at http://www.un-gaid.org/.

10 Latest update retrieved from the internet in August 2009 at http://www.un-gaid.org/.

Chapter 3
Socially Responsible Investment (SRI)

ABSTRACT

The most common forms to align financial investments with ethical, moral, and social considerations are screenings, shareholder advocacy, community investing, and social venture capital funding. Screenings integrate the evaluation of corporate financial and social performances into portfolio selections. Positive screenings target corporations with sound social and environmental responsibility. Negative screenings exclude entities featuring morally and ethically irresponsible corporate conduct. Shareholder advocacy is the active engagement of shareholders in the corporate management by voting, activism, and dialogue. The majority of shareholders exercise their voting rights by proxy resolutions, in which a third party has the right to advocate for the shareholders before the corporate board. Negative shareholder activism comprises political lobbying, consumer boycotts, stakeholder confrontation, and negative publicity. Community investing describe ear-marks of investment funds for community development, but also features access to financial products and services to un(der)served communities. Social venture capital supports pro-social start-ups and social entrepreneurs for the greater goal of increasing the social impact of financial markets. This chapter explores socially responsible investment.

DOI: 10.4018/978-1-5225-7619-8.ch003

INTRODUCTION

SRI features various forms and foci to align financial considerations with ethical, moral and social endeavors. The most common are ***socially responsible screenings***, ***shareholder advocacy***, ***community investing*** and ***social venture capital funding*** (Steurer et al., 2008).

Socially responsible screenings are 'double bottom line analyses' of corporate economic performance and social responsibility. In screenings financial market options are evaluated based on economic fundamentals as well as social features and corporate conduct externalities (Schueth, 2003). In addition to the traditional scanning of expected utility and volatility, screenings include qualitative examinations of intra- (e.g., corporate policies and practices, employee relations) and extra-organizational (e.g., externalities on current and future constituents) features of corporate conduct (Schueth, 2003). In general screenings are based on corporate track records of societal impacts, environmental performance, human rights attribution and fair workplace policies as well as health and safety standards outlined in CSR reports. Consequentially screening leads to the in- or exclusion of corporations from portfolios based on social, environmental and political criteria.

Positive screenings feature the selection of corporations with sound social and environmental records and socially responsible corporate governance (Renneboog et al., 2007). Areas of positive corporate conduct are human rights, the environment, health, safety and labor standards as well as customer and stakeholder relations. Corporations that pass positive screenings meet value requirements expressed in their social standards, environmental policies, labor relations and community-related corporate governance.

Negative screenings exclude corporations that engage in morally, ethically and socially irresponsible activities. Pro-active negative screenings refrain from entities with corporate conduct counter-parting from international legal standards and/or implying negative social externalities (Renneboog et al., 2007). Negative screenings may address addictive products (e.g., liquor, tobacco, gambling), defense (e.g., weapons, firearms), environmentally hazardous production (e.g., pollution, nuclear power production), but also social, political and humanitarian deficiencies (e.g., minority discrimination, human rights violations). Specialty screens feature extraordinary executive compensations, abortion, birth control, animal testing and international labor standard infringements (Dupré et al., 2008). In 2005 the most common screenings in the US targeted at tobacco (US $ 159 billion in total net assets; approximately 28%); liquor (US $ 134 billion; 25%); gambling (US $ 41 billion; 7%); defense/weapons (US $ 34 billion; 6%); community impact (US $ 32 billion; 5%); labor concerns (US $ 31 billion; 5%); environmental issues (US $ 31 billion; 5%); consumer safety (US $ 28 billion; 5%); workplace diversity and equal employment opportunity (US $ 27 billion; 5%); faith-based objections (US $ 12 billion; 2%); adult entertainment (US $ 12 billion; 2%); human rights (US $ 11 billion; 2%); animal testing (US $ 10 billion; 2%); abortion, healthcare, biotechnology, medical ethics, youth concerns, anti-family entertainment and excessive executive compensation (US $ 5 billion; 1%). The proportions of screening techniques are outlined by Figure 1 (Social Investment Forum Report, 2006).

Post-hoc negative screening implies divestiture as the removal of investment capital from corporations and/or markets. Divestiture is common to steer change in politically incorrect regimes, but also used to promote environmental protection, human rights, working conditions, animal protection, safety and health standards (Broadhurst, Watson & Marshall, 2003; Harvey, 2008; McWilliams & Siegel, 2000). *Political divestiture* describes foreign investment flight from politically incorrect markets based on CSR information (Steurer, 2010). Political divestiture targets at forcing political change by imposing

Figure 1. Distribution of SRI screening topics in the US in 2005

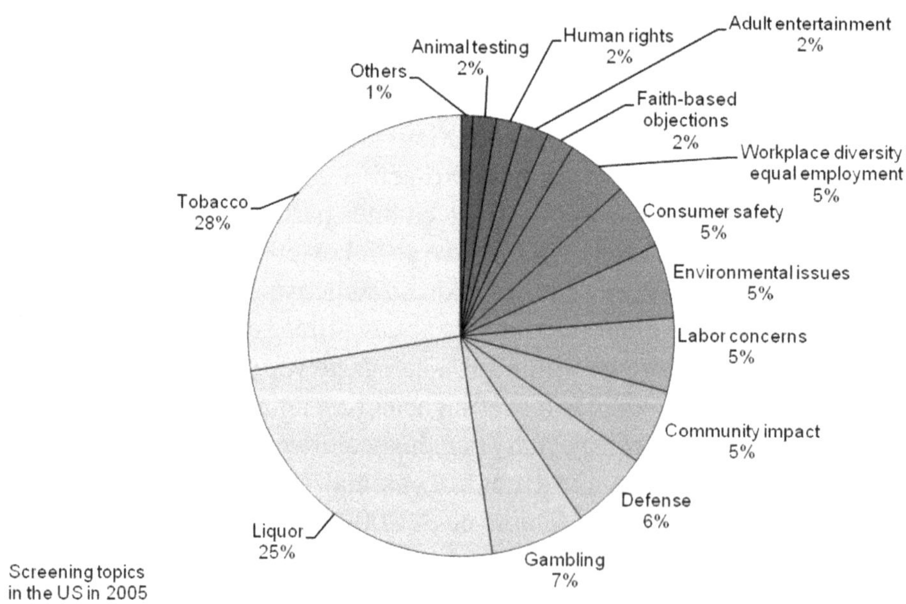

financial constraints onto politically incorrect regimes that counterpart from international law resulting in war, social conflict, terrorism and human rights violations. Prominent cases are South Africa during the Apartheid regime; governmental human rights violations in Burma as well as the current humanitarian crises in Sudan's Darfur region.

Up to now the effects of negative screenings on corporations and whether divestment is associated with an in- or decrease of shareholder value are unclear. Unanswered remains the question if political divestiture grants first-mover advantages for early withdrawing entities as politically fractionate markets lead to long-term economic decline (Posnikoff, 1997). Empirical investigations of political divestiture are primarily based on event studies. This methodology is limited as for refraining to take externalities on the wider constituent group into consideration, relative short time frames under scrutiny, small sample sizes and the irreplicability of unique political events (McWilliams, Siegel & Teoh, 1999; Teoh, Welch & Wazzan, 1999).

The majority of socially screened funds use multiple screens and sometimes complement screening with shareholder advocacy, community investing and political interests.

Based on transparent and accountable corporate policies and procedures, ***shareholder advocacy*** is the active engagement of shareholders in corporate policy making, managerial practices and corporate social conduct (Little, 2008). Shareholder advocacy comprises *shareholder activism* and *dialogues* as well as *active endowments*.

In their role as corporate owners, socially conscientious investors target at positively influencing corporate conduct in *shareholder activism* (Schueth, 2003). Shareholder activism refers to shareholder groups engaging in "coordinated action to utilize their unique rights to facilitate corporate change" (Sparkes & Cowton, 2004, p. 51). Positive shareholder activism implies advocating for socially responsible corporate conduct in shareholder meetings. Shareholder resolutions provide formal communication channels on corporate governance among shareholders, management and the board of directors. Resolutions can request information from the management and ask for changes in corporate policies and practices. In resolutions shareholders use their voting right as a means to influence corporate behavior and steer corporate conduct in a more socially responsible direction (Little, 2008). In the US shareholder resolutions are managed by the US Securities and Exchange Commission. Shareholders who wish to file a resolution must own at least US $ 2,000 in shares in a given corporation or one percent of the corporate shares one year prior to filing proposals. Resolutions appear on the corporate proxy ballot, where they can be voted on by all shareholders or their representatives either electronically, by mail or in person at the annual meeting. The vast majority of shareholders exercise their voting rights by proxy. Proxy resolutions grant third parties rights to vote for shareholders on matters before the corporation (Little, 2008). Proxy resolutions on social issues and corporate governance generally aim at improving corporate policies and practices as well as encourage management to exercise good corporate citizenship with the goal of long-term shareholder value increase. Current trends comprise transparent and accountable proxy voting policies to support social and environmental responsibility. For example, mutual fund proxy disclosure regulations target at making corporate records publicly available. Negative shareholder activism exerts activist influence and ranges from political lobbying, consumer boycotts and confrontations geared by negative publicity to pressure corporations into socially responsible corporate conduct (Sparkes & Cowton, 2004). In light of climate change, the most recent trends include sustainable finance for raising funds for climate stabilization in climate change mitigation and adaptation efforts (Puaschunder, 2017c; 2018a).

Parties engaging in *shareholder dialogues* seek to influence corporate policies and practices without introducing a formal resolution on their concerns. The corporate management is attentive to shareholder dialogues as for avoiding formal proxy resolutions and investment withdrawal.

Active endowments emerged from academics establishing procedures for integrating social responsibility in university endowments. SRI campus advisory committees issue proxy-voting guidelines as recommendations on proxy ballot votings.

Community investing started in the 1970s with direct investment for unserved communities. Community investing involves investor set-asides and ear-marks of investment funds for community development, but also features access to traditional financial products and services ranging from credits, equity and banking products to low-income and at-risk communities (Schueth, 2003). Community development banks focus on lending and rebuilding lower-income segments. Community development credit unions grant access to credits to unserved communities. Community development loans provide credit for small businesses with focus on sustainable development and resource conservation, but also sponsor community services. For individuals, community loans open avenues to affordable housing, education, child and health care (Little, 2008; Schueth, 2003). Financial empowerment of micro-enterprises helps disadvantaged minorities by financial education, mentoring and technical assistance.

Social venture capital funding finances socially responsible start-ups and social entrepreneurs to foster the positive social impact of capital markets. Community development venture capital funds provide capital for small start-ups with growth potential in traditionally un(der)developed regions. The very many forms of financial social responsibility expression embrace a wide range of SRI stakeholders and entities.

STAKEHOLDERS

Due to various forms of expression, SRI is a multi-stakeholder phenomenon. Building the relationship between the financial world and society, SRI comprises multiple stakeholders. Corporate, financial and public constituents are *economic* (e.g., institutional and private investors), *organizational* (e.g., labor union representatives, banking executives, fiduciaries) and *societal* (e.g., representatives of international organizations and non-governmental organizations, governmental officials, public servants, nonprofits, media representatives, academics) actors.

1. ***Banking executives*** at the managerial level are promoting SRI options to clients. In this function, bankers are the key information agents on SRI to financial decision makers.
2. The largest segment of screened accounts comprises private and institutional portfolios managed by fiduciaries. ***Fiduciaries*** (e.g., private equity executives, fund managers, investment managers) are financial professionals. As opinion leaders in the field, fiduciaries are key players in promoting financial options and advocating for SRI.
3. ***Institutional investors*** (e.g., universities, governments) range from public pension funds to small nonprofit organizations and can include corporations, state and municipal governments, religious organizations, hospitals and healthcare plans, college and university endowments, foundations, trade unions and other entities with social and environmental endeavors.
4. ***Private investors*** (e.g., shareholders) are individuals who choose SRI as for efficiency considerations in combination with altruistic and social responsibility notions. For private investors, SRI can be connected to the need for innovation, self-enhancement and self-expression. Private investors may view SRI as a long-term competitive leadership advantage.

5. ***International organizations*** play an important role in promoting responsible investment. The UNGC and the UN Environment Programme (UNEP) Finance Initiative launched the Principles for Responsible Investment (PRI) in April 2006 at the New York Stock Exchange (NYSE) to ingrain social responsibility in investment decision making of asset owners and financial managers. The UN Conference on Trade and Development spearheaded the 'Responsible Investment in Emerging Markets Initiative' in 2008.
6. Public pressure and governmental control to enhance financial accountability and market transparency trigger SRI. ***Governmental policy makers*** craft regulations that foster accountability and transparency of financial assets and operations – for example, the freedom of information legislature. Governmental regulations fortify institutional investors to adopt socially responsible criteria in their investment decisions.
7. ***Non-governmental organizations (NGOs)*** promote transparency and accountability within the financial sector. NGOs have become vital forces to monitor corporate conduct and sophisticate shareholder activism – all of which are important prerequisites for SRI (Mohr et al., 2001; Williams, 2005).
8. In recent decades, ***labor unions*** have paid attention to SRI as a means to imbue social responsibility into financial markets – foremost in the areas of human rights, labor conditions and minorities empowerment.
9. Within recent decades, SRI has emerged into a prominent investment option. From the beginnings, the ascent of SRI was backed up by the ***academic community***. Foremost academic financial experts, behavioral economists, sociologists and social psychologists have increasingly paid attention to social responsibility within economic market systems.
10. The public opinion on SRI is partially created by ***media representatives*** who gather, select, process and disseminate information on socially responsible corporate conduct and financial social responsibility.

As a novel multi-stakeholder phenomenon, SRI is driven by a variety of internal and external forces. Financial social responsibility touches on diverse interests of the various stakeholders. Diverting stakeholders' SRI notions and differing, underlying interest and motives of SRI constituents imply multi-stakeholder predicaments. As a means to reduce the complexity of the phenomenon, stakeholder management concepts depict the various engaged groups and study their view on SRI (Freeman, 1984). To overcome socio-economic losses implied by various SRI notions and stakeholder approaches to administer financial social responsibility, stakeholder dialogues create common goals by integrating adverse opinions that have evolved in the wake of the rise of SRI over the last decades.

EMERGENCE

SRI originally emerged from a niche market option that was offered by a small number of specialist retailers. In the wake of the rising trend towards financial social responsibility, SRI grew qualitatively and quantitatively (McCann, Solomon & Solomon, 2003; Solomon, Solomon & Norton, 2002; Sparkes, 2002).

In recent decades, SRI options have increased in size, number and scope (McCann et al., 2003; Solomon et al., 2002; Sparkes, 2002). Over the last ten years, assets involved in social investing have risen four percent faster than all professionally managed investment options in the US. As outlined by Figure 2, SRI funds grew from US $ 40 billion in 1984 to US $ 162 billion in 1995, to US $ 1.19 trillion in 1997, to US $ 2.16 trillion in 2001 reaching US $ 2.71 trillion in 2006 (Cui, 2008; Knoll, 2008; Social Investment Forum Report, 2006).

Figure 2. SRI growth in the US from 1984 to 2006

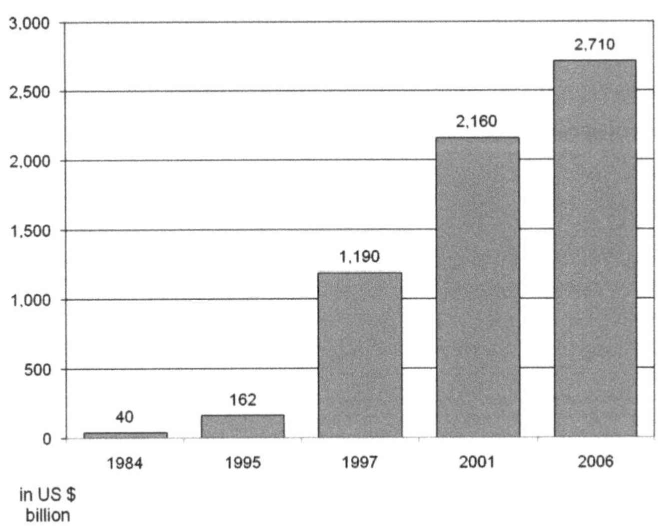

Based on data presented in the Social Investment Forum Report 2006, the overall emergence of financial social responsibility options for the decade from 1995 to 2005 in the US is exhibited in Table 1.

In 2005 SRI was a growing segment of the US financial services industry that controlled around US $ 2.5 trillion dollars – accounting for about 20.7% of the US market – in professionally managed assets (Schueth, 2003; Williams, 2005). Screenings were the dominate SRI form (with US $ 1,802 billion in assets), followed by shareholder advocacy (US $ 703 billion) and community investing valuing for US $ 20 billion. Over the years, screenings were accompanied by a rise in community investing and shareholder advocacy.

In the US ***screened funds*** were available in more than 370 classes that represented US $ 1.8 billion in net total assets in 2005. The majority of SRI assets comprise socially screened separate accounts that are managed for individual and institutional clients. SRI separate accounts have increased more than twenty-fold from US $ 40 billion to US $ 1.79 trillion in the decade from 1995 to 2005. Assets in socially screened mutual funds and other pooled products rose from US $ 151 billion in 2003 to US $ 179 billion in 2005.

Institutional Investors: The largest segment of screened assets comprises the combined publicly – on behalf of institutions – or privately managed institutional portfolios with around US $ 1.49 trillion in investment assets in 2005. Institutional investors feature corporations, state and municipal governments, religious entities, hospitals and healthcare facilities, college and university endowments, foundations, trade unions and other institutions that are engaged in financial markets. Institutional investors of insurance corporations, depository institutions and investment entities issue pension, mutual and endowment funds (Harvey, 2008). In the US institutional investors range from public pension funds with more than US $ 100 billion in socially screened assets to small nonprofit organizations with less than US $ 100,000

Table 1. Ten-year development of SRI from 1995 to 2005 in the US

SRI Options (in US $ billions)	1995	1997	1999	2001	2003	2005
Screening	$162	$613	$1,762	$2,602	$2,584	$1,802
Shareholder Advocacy	$473	$736	$922	$897	$448	$703
Community Investing	$4	$4	$5	$8	$14	$20
Total	$639	$1,353	$2,689	$3,507	$3,046	$2,525

in screened assets under management. From 2003 to 2005, assets controlled by institutional investors increased from US $ 448 billion to US $ 703 billion (Social Investment Forum Report, 2006).

Shareholder Advocacy: In 1995 US $ 473 billion in institutional assets involved shareholder advocacy expressed in resolutions or formal proxy-voting guidelines on social issues (Social Investment Forum Report, 2006). From 2003 to 2005, shareholder resolutions on social and environmental issues increased from 299 to 348 shareholder proposals, of which 177 reached a proxy vote (Social Investment Forum Report, 2006). In addition, shareholders are increasingly entering into corporate dialogues.

Commercial SRI Funds: Several commercial SRI funds account for financial social innovations in products, measurement indices and accountability control. The market leader KLD Research & Analytics hold the oldest SRI performance measurement index. As one of the largest social responsibility indices, the US Domini 400 Social Equity Fund started in May 1990 and recently launched the Domini European Social Equity Fund (Little, 2008). The large-cap growth fund Calvert offers the Calvert Social Index comprising 641 corporations that have been screened for social, economic, and environmental purposes (Farzad, 2007). As a large-cap growth fund, Vanguard features the FTSE4Good US Select Index, which holds 425 screened options.

In terms of sector-specific distributions (Table 2), overall SRI is geared towards finance products, information technology, consumer goods and health care. Vanguard offers innovative finance options, while Calvert primarily comprises finance and information technology entities (Little, 2008). Calvert and Vanguard hold more than two-thirds of their investment in the health care, finance and information technology sectors. In comparison to the general S&P 500 Index, SRI options tend to refrain from the energy sector (e.g., petroleum).

The ascent SRI has been accompanied by a change in the qualitative nature of social investments. The current SRI notion is very different from the earlier 'ethical investment' based on negative screenings (McCann et al., 2003). Although a moral touch remains, the establishment of SRI retail funds and the adoption of SRI by institutional investors have leveraged SRI into a pro-active positive screening option.

Today the SRI market has reached unprecedented diversity featuring a wide range of sophisticated SRI activities and a variety of stakeholder engagement possibilities. Financial social responsibility comprises commercial SRI retail to the public in socially screened separate accounts, mutual and pension funds, bonds and community development as well as hybrid instruments that undergo

Table 2. Industry distribution of SRI funds

Sectors	Calvert Social (%)	Vanguard FTSE (%)	S&P 500 Index (%)
Energy	2	2	11
Materials	1	1	3
Industry	7	4	11
Consumer Goods	17	20	19
Healthcare	13	17	12
Finance	27	39	21
Information Technology	27	15	15
Telecommunication Services	5	2	4
Utilities	1	1	4

financial and ethical value tests (Mathieu, 2000; Rosen, Sandler & Shani, 1991; Sparkes & Cowton, 2004). The establishment and advancement of SRI retail and the adoption of SRI by major institutional investors has matured SRI from a margin to a more mainstreamed asset allocation style (Mathieu, 2000; Rosen et al., 1991; Sparkes & Cowton, 2004).

The growth of financial social responsibility expressions has leveraged SRI into an investment philosophy adopted by a growing proportion of investment firms and governmental agencies around the world (Knoll, 2008; Mohr et al., 2001; Sparkes & Cowton, 2004). The sophistication of socially responsible shareholder engagement has triggered an upcoming of social and environmental stock exchange rating agencies, SRI impact measurement tools, corporate social and environmental reporting and certifications (Steurer et al., 2008). SRI has proliferated as a prominent term in the financial literature with business professionals and analysts monitoring and reporting on social, ethical and environmental corporate performance (e.g., Dow Jones Sustainability Index, FTSE4Good Index, OeSFX). This trend goes hand in hand with practitioners and academia documenting financial social responsibility.

The most recent SRI innovations comprise improved disclosure standards, benchmarking of CSR and SRI codes of conduct, screening for biotechnology as well as environmental funds paying attention to climate change. Future forecast trends are the growth in screened funds, active SRI ownership models and community investing innovations in combination with a focus on ICT for development (Little, 2008; Social Investment Forum Report, 2006). The variety and ascent of SRI options can be traced back to the historic roots of financial social responsibility.

HISTORICAL BACKGROUND

Historically SRI can be traced back to ethical investing of religious institutions (Puaschunder, 2016a). Already in medieval times, Christianity imposed financial restrictions based on the Old Testament. The Catholic Church prohibited usury as early as 1139. Judaist writings praised ethical monetary policies. Methodism urged people to refrain from 'sinful' trade and profit maximization from exploitation (Cuesta & Valor, 2007). In the 17th century, the Quaker Society of Friends refrained from weapons and slave trade. The UK Methodist Church advocated for avoidance of unethical corporate conduct. The Christian Pioneer Fund was the first official exclusion of 'sin stocks.' Until today, Islamic banking restricts adult entertainment and gambling (Renneboog et al., 2007).

The early beginnings of modern SRI are attributed to social responsibility concerns emerging from an attention to social, environmental and political market deficiencies. The demand for financial social responsibility became blatant in the wake of humanitarian, social and environmental crises (Williams, 2005).

Until the end of WWII, the financial industry was strictly regulated with very few financial shares being traded over the counter and the range of financial options being limited (Soros, 1998). The post-war years featured a gradual lifting of financial market restrictions, which gave leeway for an individualization of financial asset allocations. During the post-war period, SRI was propelled by stakeholder pressure in connection with legislative and policy compulsion. Legislative information disclosure reforms coupled with governmental encouragement of trustees to develop social responsibility drove SRI (Solomon et al., 2002; Sparkes & Cowton, 2004).

In the late 1960s, modern SRI evolved in the wake of shareholder activism (Puaschunder, 2018b). Civil rights campaigns and social justice movements opposed college endowments to fund warfare. Minority empowerment, consumer rights activism and environmentalist movements leveraged the sensitivity for financial social responsibility (Renneboog et al., 2007; Sparkes, 2002). Since 1969 the Council on Economic Priorities rated corporate social and environmental performance. In 1970 SRI was introduced to academic discourse at a conference at Yale University. Subsequently many universities established committees to advise trustees on social investment. In the 1970s the Investor Responsibility Research Center (IRRC) and the Interfaith Center on Corporate Responsibility (ICCR) were launched to promote shareholder advocacy and proxy resolutions (Social Investment Forum Report, 2006). In the 1960s anti-Vietnam War institutional investors sold Dow Chemical shares as for producing napalm (Biller, 2007). In 1971 the first modern SRI mutual fund – the PAX World Fund – was created by a group of US Methodist clergy that aimed at divestiture from Vietnam War supporting corporations (Broadhurst et al., 2003; Renneboog et al., 2007). The Dreyfus Third Century Fund opened the following year to avoid 'sin stocks' and raise labor standards. The subsequent Domini 400 Social Index screened corporations for environmental and social performance. In 1972 activists criticized Harvard University for owning shares in petroleum corporations. Around the same time, political divestiture was firstly discussed in the case of the Angolan repressive government (Alperson, Tepper-Marlin, Schorsch & Wil, 1991). By the mid-1970s, a significant number of governments had enacted shareholder rights to address corporate activities that caused 'social injury' and many universities had established committees to advise trustees on SRI and shareholder rights. In 1976 Reverend Leon Sullivan – a civil rights activist and director of General Motors – developed the Sullivan Principles to foster equal remuneration and workplace opportunities to empower minorities (Voorhes, 1999). During the 1980s political divestiture became prominent in the case of the South African Apartheid regime featuring racial segregation and economic discrimination against non-European groups (Merriam Webster Dictionary, 2008). By 1979 a majority of universities had established advisory committees on South Africa investments followed by a widespread divestiture trend of socially concerned investors, churches, cities and states to end Apartheid in South Africa (Schueth, 2003; Voorhes, 1999). By the end of the 1980s, billions of dollars had been divested South Africa backed by governmental statutes – such as the 1986 US Comprehensive Anti-Apartheid Act – which impacted on the South African economy. In the 1980s catastrophes in Chernobyl, Bhopal and the Exxon Valdez oil spill triggered antinuclear and environmental concerns of stakeholders. Political libertarian movements rose ethical considerations in financial investment decisions (Soros, 2008). With the desire to set standards for corporate social and environmentally conscientious conduct, social investors started to use positive screenings to identify and support corporations that pay attention to human rights standards, equal opportunities, labor relations, environmental protection, consumer safety and community concerns. Positive screenings outlined corporations that meet or exceed certain social and environmental standards based on information of social and environmental records. In 1981 the American Social Investment Forum was formed as a professional body for individual and institutional SRI constituents (Broadhurst et al., 2003). In the beginning of 1990s, the Domini 400 Social Index was created as the first socially screened index of corporations listed by the Standard & Poor's 500 (S&P) Index. In the 1990s SRI was perpetuated by the micro-finance revolution and the co-operative banking system (Brenner, 2001).

Since the turn of the century, financial markets were attributed a rising share of global governance. Institutional investors increasingly used their clout to influence corporate conduct (Solomon et al., 2002; Sparkes & Cowton, 2004). Socially conscientious investors became active in demanding corporate governance reforms impacting on societal causes. SRI emerged in the wake of heightened information disclosure on corporate social conduct in combination with governmental encouragement of trustees to develop SRI. As for all these trends, the UNGC division launched the 'Principles for Responsible Investment' (PRI) in collaboration with the NYSE in 2006. This PPP initiative was set up to increase the number of socially responsible investors and steer SRI by creating models for positive change within the investment community.

In the beginning of 2008, CEO's of world-leading corporations agreed on the diminishing power and influence of nation states in providing global governance. Globalized capitalism was praised as the triumphing market system and an upcoming financial market hegemony was forecast (Ahmad, 2008). Rising levels of social venture capital in international development led to predictions about the emerging influence of financial markets in providing social welfare. Given the world-wide outreach of financial markets in social and political affairs, financial social responsibility was attributed as an innovative means of global governance. However, the 2008/09 World Financial Recession put a new perspective on the role of financial markets in addressing global governance.

SRI in the Light of the 2008/09 World Financial Recession

The impact and influence of the 2008/09 World Financial Recession on economic markets, global policy making and society is undoubtable. The crisis has caused what Alan Greenspan recently called a 'once in a century credit tsunami' featuring governmental takeovers and bailouts, a 'lock-up' of credit markets and inter-bank lending, a 25 percent drop in financial market indices per month and two almost bankrupt European countries (Duchac, 2008).

Multi-faceted contributing factors ranging from demographics, political influences, financial exuberance and over-confidence in innovative and deregulatory financial markets are believed to have caused the crises: *Demographic trends* of the baby boom generation's peak in purchasing power fuelled financial market and real estate bubbles. September 11, 2001 in combination with other *political events* created collective uncertainty that was met by the US Federal Reserve's aggressive interest rate cutting, which increased the amount of circulating capital to nurture bubbles and triggered a refinancing boom with sub-prime borrowers. *Financial lending practices* of securitizations propelled capital flows from investors to subprime borrowers creating an illusion of wealth, which attracted speculators who further fuelled bubbles. *Deregulation* in the wake of the 1999 Financial Service Reform Act repealed the Glass-Steagall Act, which removed legal separations of commercial and investment banks and exposed an interconnected market system to higher risk levels. In *principal-agent dilemmas*, mortgage brokers focused on short-term self-interests. In addition, trust in *financial modelling techniques* caused irrationally low default estimates. Credit rating agencies publishing optimistic ratings lead to overconfidence causing financial turmoil (Duchac, 2008).

In the light of social, political and economic deficiencies having propelled SRI in the past, the current challenges of the financial sector are believed to perpetuate SRI (Trevino & Nelson, 2004). As an implication of the crisis, citizens have become more attentive to social responsibility within market systems. Media coverage of financial fraud, fiduciary responsibility breaches, astronomic CEO remunerations and financial managers' exuberance are increasing stakeholder calls for the inclusion of transparency and accountability control in financial markets. To avoid a recurrent scenario in the future, enhanced transparency and accountability of investment options and ethicality of responsible market participants have become blatant demands. Corporate governance, information disclosure and monitoring within the corporate and financial world have become central issues of concern of shareholders, policy makers and civilians.

As implications of the crisis, corporate executives are increasingly forced by stakeholders to pay attention to financial social responsibility. SRI featuring direct attention to corporate accountability and transparency in screenings, resolutions and stakeholder dialogues seems as a remedy to re-establish trust in corporate and financial market conduct (Social Investment Forum Report, 2006). Therefore the 2008/09 World Financial Recession is likely to leverage SRI into a more common financial investment option.[1]

Accompanied with the rise of SRI is the current academic and public debate on the influence of public and private actors in administering social responsibilities within market systems. In the wake of the crisis, stakeholders re-discuss the role of economic and financial markets in providing and administering global governance (Little, 2008). The manifold expressions of the interplay of governmental, corporate and financial market forces in addressing social responsibility and attributing global governance becomes apparent when comparing various SRI conduct throughout the international arena.

INTERNATIONAL DIFFERENCES

SRI is a context and culture-dependent phenomenon. International differences in SRI conduct stem from differing market practices, governmental and institutional frameworks, societal values and moral obligations that impact on financial market behavior. While Anglo-Saxon capital market systems (such as the US and UK) feature private share- and stockholder investments, European financial markets are significant for governmental and institutional banking (Puaschunder, 2017b).

Today financial social responsibility is booming in the Western World. SRI has foremost been adopted in Central Europe and Anglo-Saxon countries (Sparkes & Cowton, 2004). North America, Europe (especially the UK) and Australia account for the most vital SRI markets.

North America

The US: Prior to the 2008/09 World Financial Recession, the US was home to half of the world's capital and publicly traded corporations. Hosting 7,000 self-made millionaires and 170 billionaires, the US political and legal systems disproportionately reward capital allocation talent. The US features the most liberal market economy in the world coupled with a comprehensive set of market transparency rules, a vigorous, free media and highly educated market actors (Roberts, 2006). The US Constitutional Law endows with substantive rights of freedom of speech, assembly or association, press and religious exercise as well as property securitization. The US is renowned for explicit CSR combined with a competitive market system and low governmental social welfare.

Having grown out of niche market options for value-led investors, SRI is attributed to have prospered in the US due to shareholder activism, shareholder participation and independent financial entities' efforts. In recent decades, US shareholders have increasingly gained access to proxy statements for the sake of disclosure on social and environmental externalities of corporate conduct. Since 2004 various corporate scandals led to legislations addressing funds disclosure of proxy votes, which leveraged shareholder resolutions to become the mainstream track record for socially responsible corporate conduct (Little, 2008). The so-called 'Wall Street Rule' implicitly captures the role of shareholder activism as a soft-law market regulation (Lydenberg, 2002).

Today the US features the widest variety of SRI options and socially responsible performance measurement indices. In 2005 US $ 2.5 trillion assets were attributed as socially responsible funds accounting for growing 20.7 percent of total US investments (Williams, 2005).

In ***Canada*** SRI was officially introduced by the Ethical Growth Fund in 1986 (Williams, 2005). Since 2001 the Canadian shareholder resolution rules were based on the respective US model leading to a rise in SRI (Sparkes & Cowton, 2004). The Canadian Institute of Chartered Accountants introduced disclosure guidelines in 2001 combined with a mandatory disclosure obligation since 2004 (William, 2005). Since 2006 the Canadian Securities Administrators have mandated mutual funds to publicly disclose their proxy voting records and policies. SRI is foremost organized by the Social Investment Organization (SIO) which is renowned for regular SRI surveys and conferences (Williams, 2005). Recently SRI and foremost community investing have grown significantly in Canada (Social Investment Forum Report, 2006).

Europe

The ***European Union*** features institutionalized and governmentally administered SRI. From 2003 to 2006, the European SRI market grew by 36 percent (Steurer et al., 2008).[2] In 2005, 375 green, social and ethical European funds were identified with € 24.1 billion. According to Eurosif, responsible investments by European institutional investors (excluding the Nordic region) comprised € 1.138 billion in 2006. In 2008 SRI funds accounted for up to 18 percent of the market share.[3] As exhibited in Figure 3 the UK lead the SRI movement with € 8.0 billion in total assets, followed by Germany with € 6.7 billion, Austria with € 5.3 billion, France with € 3.1 billion, Switzerland with € 2.9 billion, Italy with € 2.7 billion and Sweden with € 2.5 billion in 2005 (Social Investment Forum Report, 2006).

Figure 3. Value of SRI throughout Western European countries in 2005

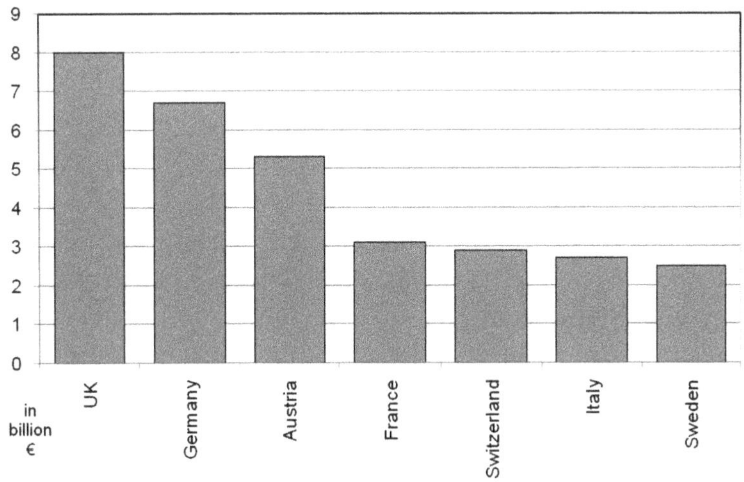

While SRI booms in Northern and Central European countries, the movement is slower to take off in Southern Europe. Community investing is more frequent in Latin countries – foremost Italy, France or Spain – than in Nordic regions.[4]

Within Europe, the *UK* leads in socially responsible assets under management (Sparkes, 2002). First UK Victorian concerns about employment conditions shed light on corporate social conduct. Ethical banking was established by the Mercury Provident in 1974 and introduced to retail banking in 1992. In 1997, a group of university affiliates launched a campaign for ethical and environmental investment of pension funds, which led to Sustainable and Responsible Investment policies in 2000 (Williams, 2005). Since 2000 the UK law requires all occupational pension funds to formally consult the adoption of social, ethical and environmental policies (Sparkes & Cowton, 2004; Williams, 2005). The UK government regulations reassure pension funds to declare the extent to which environmental, social or ethical considerations are taken into account in the selection, retention and realization of investments (Steurer et al., 2008; Sparkes, 2002). Similar regulations have been passed in Germany and Sweden and are currently considered by the European Parliament.

Political divestiture was enacted by the *Belgian government* in 2007 by forbidding Belgian investors to finance anti-personnel mines and cluster munitions (Steurer, 2010). The enforcement of the law, however, is problematic as disclosure requirements for professional investors are low and sanctions are not foreseen (Steurer, 2010).

Sweden's 2000 Public Pension Fund Act required all Swedish National Pension Funds to address environmental and social topics in the report of investment activities and management of the funds (Steurer, 2010). While the law gives leeway to what extent funds comply with the law, it helped providing access to information and raising awareness for SRI. In addition, a Joint Ethical Council offers investment recommendations for stakeholders (Steurer, 2010).

The *Dutch Green Funds Scheme* grants information on tax exemptions for SRI (Steurer, 2010). The *French* Pension Research Fund offers insurance plans in line with SRI principles.

In *German*-speaking countries, SRI was propelled in the wake of the 1970s green wave that focused on environment protection and peace movements. The 'Gemeinschaftsbank' as well as the 'Ökobank' became the first SRI traders (Williams, 2005). Major influences are attributed to Green Parties, the 1991 Renewable Energy Act as well as tax exemptions and information campaigns for green funds (Williams, 2005).

The Pacific Rim and Asia

In ***Australia*** direct share ownership leads to a heightened number of pro-active SRI screenings of individual investors (Williams, 2005). The first Australian ethical investment movement began in the early 1980s, which formulated the Australian Ethical Investment Trust in 1989 (Cummings, 2000). The Ethical Investment Association (EIA) emerged throughout the 1990s to launch first SRI benchmarking reports in 2001 and create a SRI symbol as a seal of approval for SRI products (Williams, 2005). The Financial Service Reform Act 2002 introduced ethical product disclosure statements for financial services. In 2003 the Australian Securities and Investment Commission (ASIC) issued SRI disclosure guidelines (Williams, 2005). From 2001 to 2004, SRI activities raised by over 100 percent from AUS $ 10.5 billion to AUS $ 21.5 in 2004 (Williams, 2005). From 2004 to 2005, managed SRI portfolios increased by around 70 percent from AUS $ 4.5 billion to AUS $ 7.7 billion – making SRI the fastest growing investment segment (Jones, van der Laan, Frost & Loftus, 2008).

Emerging Markets

In ***emerging markets*** SRI promotes international development. Even in countries where screening and shareholder advocacy are relatively limited, the impacts of community investing, microfinance and enterprise development have been substantial (Social Investment Forum Report, 2006). Newly emerging and rapidly growing SRI markets are Latin America (foremost Brazil), South Africa and Asia reaching US $ 2.7 billion in total SRI assets. Japan remains Asia's leading market for SRI with more than 100 billion yen in over ten SRI funds. More than twelve screened funds are available in the Islamic banking territories of Malaysia, Taiwan and Singapore. Hong Kong has been identified as a ripe market for an Asian SRI expansion. Microfinance and community investing continue to play a significant role for Asian low-income social entrepreneurs and developing communities. Barriers to social investors in emerging markets are the lack of accountable CSR practices, standardized SRI market options and access to financial markets.

Cross-culturally operating institutions may face challenges for CSR implementation stemming from local differences in corporate practices and social ethical norms as well as differing thresholds to sustainable behavior. For instance, challenges arise if corporations or even nation states of the industrialized world outsource intergenerational practices (e.g., environmental pollution) into territories with weaker law enforcement and public scrutiny. These findings emphasize the need for sensitivity to local conditions, transparency along the production and value chains as well as stakeholder expectations monitoring when conducting business in different contexts. In the international arena, international organizations' global governance sets the institutional framework for SRI.

INSTITUTIONAL FRAMEWORK

From a global governance perspective, the UN plays a pivotal role in promoting SRI. In January 2004, the UN attributed the key role of the financial sector in meeting the UNGC's objectives. Subsequently a group of leading financial institutions were invited to form a joint financial sector initiative under the guidance of the UNGC Board. This forum was set up to discuss ways in which financial investment banks and fiduciaries can consider and implement social responsibility as a risk management tool.[5] In associated research units, the initiative developed guidelines and recommendations on how to integrate environmental, social and corporate governance in asset management and securities brokerage services.

To advance financial social responsibility, the UN launched 'The Principles for Responsible Investment' (PRI) at the NYSE in April 2006. The PRI are supported by the UNGC Conference Board, the chief executive officers of 20 global corporations, the International Finance Corporation of the World Bank Group, the Swiss Government, Columbia University and the UNEP Finance Initiative. Under the auspice of the UNGC and the UNEP Finance Initiative, the PRI invite institutional investors to consider SRI and mobilize chief executive officers of the world's largest pension funds to advance SRI on an international level. The principles are designed to place financial social responsibility into the core of investment decision making of financial managers and asset owners of pension funds, foundation assets and institutional endowments. At the one-year anniversary of the PRI, more than 170 institutions representing approximately US $ eight trillion in assets had committed to the PRI.

Corporations that join the PRI report concomitant tangible (profit gain, efficiency, product innovations, market segmentation) and intangible (reputation, employee morale) benefits.

In February 2008 the UN Conference on Trade and Development (UNCTAD) launched the 'Responsible Investment in Emerging Markets' initiative at the Geneva PRI office. This PPP targets at fostering transparency and disclosure of emerging financial markets. The key constituents are stock exchange and financial analyst communities as future SRI drivers to support the UNGC goals. In addition, NGOs are invited to advance financial market transparency and accountability.

For the future the world's leading Stock Exchange Commissions seek to further support the PRI and to consider innovative ways how to partner with the UNGC. The influence of financial markets in global governance becomes apparent in political divestiture.

POLITICAL DIVESTITURE

Divestiture is an act of removing stocks from a portfolio to screen out socially irresponsible corporations based on social, ethical and religious objections (McWilliams & Siegel, 2000). In the case of political divestiture, investments are withdrawn from politically incorrect markets in the wake of stakeholder pressure and global governance sanctions. Sanctions are economic or military coercive measures to put pressure on governments that depart from international law. By cultural neglect and economic trade restrictions such as tariffs, sanctions yield to adjudication with the greater goal of triggering positive political and societal change (Merriam Webster Dictionary, 2008).

Divestiture became a global governance means in the case of the South African Apartheid regime during the 1980s. Current political divestiture sanctions have been imposed to the Sudanese government as for implying a humanitarian crisis in Darfur (Puaschunder, 2015).

South Africa

One of the most prominent cases for political divestiture has been the capital flight from South Africa during the Apartheid regime. The Apartheid system came into effect in South Africa in 1948 when the National Party gained parliamentary majority leading to repression, censorship, majority disenfranchisement and racial separation. Apartheid refers to political and social policies of racial segregation connected to economic discrimination against nonEuropean groups in the Republic of South Africa (Merriam Webster Dictionary, 2008).

India became the first country to take action against South Africa by imposing an export embargo followed by a range of economic, social and political sanctions. The first wave of US anti-Apartheid activism began in 1965, when members of 'Students for a Democratic Society' protested at the Wall Street Chase Bank headquarter against loans to the South African government (Crawford & Klotz, 1999). Throughout the late 1960s and early 1970s, students urged university endowment administrators to divest South African holdings. The Sullivan Principles became a basis for political divestiture advocating for investors' social responsibility (Voorhes, 1999). By the late 1970s, it became apparent that the National Party would not abandon the Apartheid system in fear of losing political power to the African National Community (Zeff & Pirro, 1999). In the international arena, social and political pressures on public pension funds to restrict or eliminate investments in corporations engaging in business and trade with South Africa grew. Coordinated divestiture of US corporations from South Africa began in 1978. Political divestiture became legally backed up by the enactment of the US Comprehensive Anti-Apartheid Act in November 1986 (Ngassam, 1992). In the decade 1978 to 1988, the number of US publicly traded firms with operations in South Africa fell from 274 to 175 – featuring prominent multi-nationals such as Exxon, Xerox, Coca-Cola, General Motors, Honeywell and Citicorp. In 1986 South African trade plummet by 15 percent with Britain, by 25 percent with Germany and by 40 percent with the US in 1987. By the mid-1990s more than 200 US corporations had either totally or partially disinvested from South Africa on a voluntary basis and new investments in South Africa were scarce (Alperson et al., 1991). All these activities impacted on the South African economy, led to an overall decline in the living standard of South Africans and triggered emigrations from South Africa (Alperson et al., 1991). Attempts of the National Party to tighten its hold on South Africa resulted in racial killings, religious bombings and steering so-called 'black on black' violence. These atrocities triggered waves of anti-Apartheid activism in the international arena (Zeff & Pirro, 1999). The student-led 'South African Catalyst Project' coordinated anti-Apartheid action across the US and investment communities adopted total divestment policies (Voorhes, 1999).

However, during the 1970s and 1980s, high gold, diamond, metal and mineral prices let some traders turn a blind eye to South Africa's Apartheid policies (Zeff & Pirro, 1999). South Africa was often successful in replacing trade partners, to whom it sold raw materials for an 'Apartheid discount' (Zeff & Pirro, 1999). For example, whilst the US, Denmark and France prohibited imports of South African coal in 1985, South Africa became the major supplier of coal imports to the European Economic Community in 1986. As trade never completely stopped with South Africa, the anti-Apartheid movement became criticized as a patchwork of voluntary and mandatory prohibitions undertaken by only some market actors.

By the mid-1980s, increasing international social, political pressure to end Apartheid was backed up by UN trade sanctions. By the end of the 1980s, a multitude of international corporations had pulled out of South Africa and the end of the Cold War eased the strategic need for minerals, which lead to falling commodities prices. South Africa was unable to trade in the international markets and had become a pariah nation, cast out of the UN and the Commonwealth and isolated from international sporting activities (Zeff & Pirro, 1999).

The end of Apartheid is dated in February 1990, when President FW de Klerk announced Nelson Mandela's release and slowly began to dismantle the Apartheid system. In 1992 a referendum approved the Apartheid reform process. On April 27, 1994 the first democratic elections in South Africa, wherein all races were allowed to vote, led to Nelson Mandela becoming the first native president of South Africa. Political divestiture in combination with respective cultural and economic sanctions is attributed as a contributing factor to the end of Apartheid in South Africa (Zeff & Pirro, 1999).

A timeline of the actions against Apartheid from 1946 to 1998 is provided by Table 3 (after Crawford & Klotz, 1999).

Table 3. Political divestiture from South Africa

Chronology of political divestiture and sanctions against South Africa
1946
The newly founded UN addresses South African domestic discrimination.
India withdraws its ambassador from South Africa as for racial discrimination.
1948
The South African Malan National Party defeats the Smuts United Party and institutes Apartheid policies
The UN adopts the Universal Declaration of Human Rights as an international legal basis against Apartheid.
1954
India formally severs diplomatic ties with South Africa and other countries – especially newly independent African states – follow.
Father Trevor Huddleston pleads the international community to boycott South Africa in the wake of political constraints and human rights infringements.
1958
The African National Congress (ANC) president Albert Luthuli calls for sanctions against South Africa in the wake of racial discrimination.
1959
A number of South African ANC members go into exile and launch the *Boycott South Africa* movement in Great Britain.
1960
The Sharpeville killings lead to international outrage. African states call for sanctions against South Africa because of genocide.
The *Anti-Apartheid Movement* is founded in London.
The American Committee on Africa begins a sanctions campaign in the US.
South Africa installs the financial rand system in an attempt to control the capital outflow as a result of economic sanctions. The financial rand system features two exchange rates – one for current account transactions, and one for capital account transactions for non-residents. Investments made in South Africa by non-residents can only be sold for financial rand and the convertibility of financial rand into foreign currencies is limited as a means of protectionism.
1961
Many Apartheid-opposition leaders are banned, jailed or go into exile.
South Africa withdraws from the Commonwealth in the face of anti-Apartheid pressure.
Albert John Luthuli, a South African politician opposed to the Apartheid system, receives the Nobel Peace Prize.

continued on following page

Table 3. Continued

Chronology of political divestiture and sanctions against South Africa
1962
The UN General Assembly calls for diplomatic, economic and military sanctions against South Africa in the wake of Apartheid.
The South African Non-Racial Olympic Committee is formed.
1963
The UN Security Council adopts an arms embargo for South Africa.
The US announces the end of military supply trade with South Africa.
At its founding, the African Union excludes South Africa and supports sanctions against South Africa.
International organizations reject South Africa as a member.
1964
Great Britain bans arms exports to South Africa.
Japan freezes foreign direct investment to South Africa.
South Africa is excluded from the Tokyo Olympics.
1965
The UN establishes a Trust Fund and education programs for South African.
Artists and actors sign the *We Say No to Apartheid* pledge.
US students protest at Manhattan's Chase Bank headquarters against loans to South Africa, which starts a first wave of controlled divestiture.
The Rhodesian Unilateral Declaration of Independence and resulting sanctions increase pressure on South Africa.
1968
South Africa is excluded from the Olympic Games in Mexico.
1970
South Africa is expelled from the overall Olympic movement.
Throughout the 1970s major banks and governments ban investments and loans to South Africa.
1971
Reverend Leon Sullivan advocates for General Motors' withdrawal from South Africa.
1972
The book *The Ethical Investor* promotes political divestiture leading to numerous universities divesting.
1973
The UN General Assembly recognizes the South African liberation movements as 'authentic representatives' of the South African majority.
The Arab oil embargo adds to South Africa's energy problems, spurring coal-to-oil trade developments.
South African plays are boycotted in New York City.
1974
The UN General Assembly suspends South Africa.

continued on following page

Table 3. Continued

Chronology of political divestiture and sanctions against South Africa
1976
The Soweto uprising feature a series of clashes between the black youths and South African authorities.
The number of South African political activists in exile rises.
International banks and governments raise loan restrictions on South Africa.
South Africa boycotts the Montreal Olympics.
The South African region *Transkei* declares independence, but is not recognized as independent – neither within South Africa nor internationally. The regions *Bophuthatswana*, *Venda* and *Ciskei* follow, but face similar responses.
1977
The US restricts nuclear technology transfer with South Africa. In August states and corporations are urged at the World Conference for Action Against Apartheid to cease all assistance and cooperation enabling South Africa's nuclear proliferation.
South Africa is removed from the International Atomic Energy Agency (IAEA) governing board.
The Commonwealth adopts the *Glen Eagles Declaration* against Apartheid.
In the wake of a second wave of US student protests against Apartheid, more universities and colleges set out divestment policies.
The Sullivan Principles guide multi-nationals' corporate conduct with South Africa.
New York performances of South African musicals are boycotted.
The UN Security Council adopts a mandatory arms embargo with South Africa.
1978
European and Canadian corporate codes of conduct oppose operations in South Africa.
The US tightens restrictions on military support of South Africa.
1979
The UN General Assembly calls on the Security Council to consider preventing South Africa from developing nuclear weapons.
The Southern African Development Community is established to counter South African destabilization and economic dominance in the region.
Iran halts petroleum exports to South Africa.
The US announces the suspicion of South African nuclear activities; South Africa denies conducting nuclear tests.
1980
The UN General Assembly calls for a cultural boycott of South Africa.
1981
The US announces the policy of 'constructive engagement' including the relaxation of previously imposed sanctions to South Africa.
The UN conference on Sanctions Against South Africa calls for action against South Africa's acquisition of nuclear weapons.
South African activists in exile advocate for boycotts of South African art and international artists who performed in South Africa.

continued on following page

Table 3. Continued

Chronology of political divestiture and sanctions against South Africa
1982
Connecticut becomes the first US state to legislate a South Africa divestment policy for pension funds.
1983
The US Congress passes the *Gramm Amendment*, blocking IMF loans to Apartheid-practicing states.
The director of the film *Gandhi* cancels plans to attend the showing of his movie in South Africa in support of the cultural boycott.
The UN General Assembly adopts a *Programme of Action against Apartheid* that halts nuclear technology transfer, nuclear cooperation as well as the delivery of reactors and fissile material to South Africa.
1984
The New South African constitution establishes a tricameral parliament with separate chambers for so-attributed 'coloreds' and 'Indians' but leaves out blacks, which leads to widespread violent protests.
The South African anti-Apartheid campaigner Bishop Desmond Tutu is awarded the Nobel Peace Prize.
The *Free South Africa Movement* is launched at the South African embassy in Washington DC.
The UN Security Council expands the military boycott to ban South African imports.
1985
As the Chase Bank and other international banks refuse to roll over their loans, the South African government declares a partial moratorium on repayments of commercial debt.
In response to township violence, South Africa declares a state of emergency and rules out political power-sharing with blacks.
The UN Security Council resolution 569 urges all member states to prohibit nuclear-related contracts with South Africa.
Australia bans trade of South African arms, weapons and computer equipment.
The Commonwealth passes economic sanctions against South Africa in October, including a ban on purchases of South African uranium and Commonwealth exports of enriched uranium and nuclear technology.
The US Corporate Council on South Africa is formed to oppose Apartheid.
The third and most intensive wave of US student anti-Apartheid activism features groups of university presidents to promote sanctions against South Africa and to increase divestment activities.
Several US cities adopt selective contracting provisions to foster sanctions.
The US, the European community and other countries implement additional sanctions on South Africa.
1986
France bans weapons trade with South African.
The Commonwealth adopts additional economic sanctions.
The European community votes to ban imports of iron, gold and South African goods.
Japan bans imports of South African iron and steel.
General Motors divestiture is followed by a flood of US corporations leaving South Africa.
A first interim agreement between South Africa and its creditors is reached in March, covering repayments through June 1987.
Barclay's Bank ends loans to South Africa in response to customer pressure in May and withdraws from South African operations in November. Other banks follow.

continued on following page

Table 3. Continued

Chronology of political divestiture and sanctions against South Africa
The US Congress enacts the Comprehensive Anti-Apartheid Act in October.
South African students protest abrogation of the academic boycott by Conor Cruise O'Brien – a leading member of the Irish anti-Apartheid Movement at the University of Cape Town.
1987
US retirement funds' shareholder resolutions target at withdrawing South Africa.
Reverend Sullivan calls for economic sanctions against South Africa, which spurs university and municipal divestment policies.
Second Interim Agreements on South African debt repayment are reached in February, covering through June 1990.
ANC President Oliver Tambo proposes a selective boycott of South African culture and academics.
The US removes the tax exempt status from corporations operating in South Africa.
1988
The Commonwealth reports on the positive potential of sanctions and political divestiture in the case of South Africa.
1989
Exxon Mobil and Goodyear – the largest remaining corporations – withdraw from South Africa.
The Third Interim Agreement on South African debt repayment is reached in October, covering through December 1993.
President Frederik Willem De Klerk succeeds Pieter Willem Botha and announces intentions to repeal Apartheid laws, release anti-Apartheid prisoners and unban some political organizations in opposition to Apartheid.
1990
Nelson Mandela is released after 27 years in prison.
The ANC and other opposition groups are unbanned; the process of returns from exile begins.
South Africa ends its nuclear weapons program and starts dismantling of existing weapons.
1991
The International Olympic Committee recognizes the first (non-racial) National Olympic Committee of South Africa.
The US, Great Britain and European lift South Africa sanctions.
South Africa signs the Nuclear Non-Proliferation Treaty (NPT) and allows the first IAEA inspection in years.
1992
A Whites-only referendum validates president de Klerk's reforms.
South Africa participates in the Cricket World Cup and returns to the Olympic games in Barcelona.
South Africa is selected as the host of the 1995 Rugby World Cup.
The UN provides educational opportunities for South Africans.
The South African government destroys 12,000 sensitive Apartheid documents.
1993
In March president de Klerk publicly admits that South Africa acquired nuclear weapons.
Nelson Mandela calls to end economic sanctions against South Africa.
In October, the UN General Assembly lifts most anti-Apartheid sanctions.

continued on following page

Table 3. Continued

Chronology of political divestiture and sanctions against South Africa
1994
Nelson Mandela becomes the first democratically-elected president of South Africa, who calls for the end of remaining sanctions on South Africa.
US colleges and universities repeal divestment policies against South Africa.
South Africa begins the process of rejoining international organizations and re-establishing diplomatic ties throughout the world.
1998
The US arms and trade embargo on South Africa ends.

Sudan

First international trade restrictions on the Sudanese government originated as a response to alleged support of international terrorist organizations. Since 1997 the US imposed sanctions against Sudan prohibiting import and export of goods and technology exempt humanitarian aid. In addition, financial support of the Sudanese government projects was limited. Multiple US states, local entities, universities and institutional investors pursuing a divestment strategy against Sudan triggered an international foreign direct investment drain from Sudan.

In 2003 atrocities and genocide committed against the population of the Darfur region by the Sudanese government raised an international call for political divestiture. Since July 2004 the international community recognized the fighting in the Darfur region as a response to genocide and humanitarian infringements. In the absence of direct military intervention, financial activists and socially responsible investors seek an end to the politically incorrect regime in Sudan. Key political events that put pressure on international corporations to divest Sudan as well as reactions in favor of investments in Sudan are outlined by Table 4.

Some of the outlined events caused US universities, cities and states to divest Sudan. As of today US state and local entities as well as numerous universities and institutional investors have divested Sudan. To date "over two dozen US states, fifty-nine universities, and sixteen cities have placed restrictions on their Sudan-linked investments…and at least ten major corporations have either ceased operations in Sudan or significantly changed their behavior in the country."[17] A timeline of institutional divestiture of US universities and cities from Sudan as well as governmental divestiture legislations passed is provided by Table 5.

Table 4. Political events triggering divestiture from Sudan

Chronology of political events triggering divestiture from Sudan
September 13, 2004[6]
Political pressure on European corporations operating in Sudan increases as German Development Minister Heidemarie Wieczorek-Zeul speaks in favor of sanctions against Sudan. The German Minister reports that contradictory promises from the Sudanese government had counterweight ending the genocide and humanitarian infringements in Sudan's troubled Darfur region. Wieczorek-Zeul recommends an arms and oil embargo along with freezing Sudanese foreign financial assets.
July, 2005[7]
New Jersey's divestment law, adopted in July 2005, requires all state pensions and annuity funds to phase out investments in corporations supporting the Sudanese government exempt from humanitarian aid.
November 1, 2005[21]
The 1997-imposed US sanctions against corporations that operate in Khartoum are renewed by President Bush.
Public pension fund holders are informed to re-consider shares of corporations conducting operations in Sudan that may indirectly support a genocide regime.
March 27, 2006[8]
As divestiture from Sudan unfolds, the Sudanese Government pays close to US $ one million for an eight-page supplement New York Times Advertisement advocating for investments praising for a "peaceful, prosperous and democratic future." In response, Sudan activists flooded the New York Times with demands for an apology.
April 5, 2006[9]
Seeking to counter divestment campaigns, Khidir Haroun Ahmed – Sudan's ambassador to the US – calls on American corporations and universities to invest in Sudan by saying: ''If your goal is to send a message of disapproval, divestment is not the correct tactic. If your
goal is to promote peace, unity and development in Sudan, engagement is the correct course.''
September 28, 2006[10]
US Governor Arnold Schwarzenegger signs a bill banning California's state pension funds from investing in corporations with interests in operating in Sudan.
The move comes a day after the US Congress passed a bill imposing sanctions on the Sudanese government.
The new California law provokes protests and suits by trade organizations who claim that individual states do not have authority to intervene in international diplomacy.
Schwarzenegger declares that the bill sends a message to Darfur that California does not stand for murder and genocide. "We cannot watch from the sidelines and be content to mourn this atrocity as it passes into history," Schwarzenegger says with actor and political activist George Clooney at his side. "We must act and that is exactly why we will divest Sudan. Divesting will show our defiance against the murderers and their inhumanity."
May 16, 2007[11]
Fidelity Out of Sudan is set up as a non-profit, public campaign to pressure the investment corporation Fidelity to change its investment strategy with Sudan. The group advocates for Fidelity to divest holdings of PetroChina and Sinopec – two Chinese oil corporations that are indirectly funding military actions in Sudan. The campaign works with individuals, corporations, organizations, financial institutions, the media, Fidelity employees and government agencies to build awareness and create financial, public stakeholder and regulatory pressure for Fidelity to change its investment strategy with Sudan. The ultimate goal is to force Fidelity and other financial institutions to adopt moral investment policies.
Divestiture of retirement funds from Fidelity Investments over Sudan takes place on May 16, 2007.
Social(k) – a socially responsible retirement plan – announces 29 major corporations to divest Fidelity retirement plans as for involvement with Sudan and advocates for other corporations to divest retirement assets from institutions involved in immoral practices.

continued on following page

Table 4. Continued

Chronology of political events triggering divestiture from Sudan
In response, Fidelity seeks stakeholder contact to reconsider and attune its investment strategy (Pozen, in conversation, September 2008).
July 26, 2007[12]
The House Financial Services Committee eases divestiture from Sudan and proposes legislations that protect divesting mutual funds corporations from shareholder lawsuits.
August 2007[13]
In August 2007, the Genocide Intervention Network, Amnesty International and Calvert hold a
workshop on the crisis in Sudan and the appropriate role of shareholder activism in addressing the conflict.
A coalition of investors passes shareholder resolutions with major financial institutions (Citibank, JP Morgan Chase, Merrill Lynch, Morgan Stanley, T. Rowe Price, Wells Fargo) to adopt divestment policies and procedures "when a company, in which the financial institution is invested, or its subsidiaries or affiliates, is identified as contributing to human rights violations through their businesses or operations in a country with a clear pattern of mass atrocities or genocide."
December 20, 2007[14]
On December 20, 2007 Human rights groups and value-based investors advocate on Wall Street for divestiture from Sudan.
A coalition of leading human rights organizations, six major banks and financial institutions as well as other corporations announce the filling of shareholder resolutions on divestiture from Sudan with a special attention to petroleum corporations. The overarching goal is to promote divestiture from Sudan on Wall Street in order to end the violence in Darfur.
January 1, 2008[15]
The Sudan Divestment Task Force (SDTF) announces the first Sudan-free index and provides tools to calculate indices that exclude Sudan investments from standard ratings.
March 11, 2008[16]
A Sudan shareholder resolution campaign takes off on March 11, 2008.

In general, divestment campaigns target at industries that fund or indirectly support the Sudanese government. Corporate divestment strategies comprise international corporations operating in the petroleum (70 percent of petroleum revenues are used to fund military action), energy and defense industries. Other divestment strategies aim for corporate activities that fund or support the Sudanese government or refrain from providing goods and services to the disadvantaged populations of Sudan.[19] A list of publicly traded corporations that meet divestment criteria is exhibited in Table 6.[20]

Major corporations that have divested Sudan by 2007 are provided in Table 7:

Once enough financial pressure has been exerted by corporations refraining from operations in Sudan, divestiture is believed to force the Sudanese government into change. Unlike in South Africa, where an established

Table 5. US academic, governmental, and municipal divestiture from Sudan

Divestiture activities from Sudan of US academic institutions, states and cities[18]			
Month	**Academic divestiture**	**Governmental divestiture**	**Municipal divestiture**
2005			
April	Harvard University		
June	Stanford University	Illinois	
July		New Jersey	
August		Oregon	
October	Northwestern University		
November	Dartmouth University		
2006			
January	Amherst University		
February	Yale University		
March	University of California Brown University		
April	Brandeis University Columbia University Middlebury College	Maine	Providence New Haven Connecticut
May	Boston University Trinity College University of Vermont	Connecticut	
June	Oberlin College University of Maryland University of Pennsylvania Williams College University of Washington		
August	Cornell University University of Wisconsin		
September	Princeton University American University Seton Hall University		California Philadelphia
October	Colby University University of Rochester Vassar College		
November	Bowdoin College Drew University University of Virginia	North Carolina	San Francisco
December	Andover Theological School University of Colorado		

continued on following page

Table 5. Continued

Divestiture activities from Sudan of US academic institutions, states and cities[18]			
Month	**Academic divestiture**	**Governmental divestiture**	**Municipal divestiture**
2007			
February	Hendrix College	Vermont	Los Angeles
March	University of Connecticut Emory University Regis University Wellesley College	Arkansas	
April	Howard University Hampton University Duke University University of Denver University of Minnesota University of Massachusetts	Iowa Colorado Maryland	Denver
May	Smith College Nazareth College University of Illinois Wheaton College Connecticut College	Indiana Kansas Minnesota	
June		Florida New York Hawaii Texas Rhode Island	
August		North Carolina	

financial infrastructure could somewhat insulate the ruling party; Sudan lacks the capacity to sustain itself financially. Financial constraints and foreign investment dependence let political divestiture appear as for having a major impact on the Sudanese government. The Sudanese Divestment Task Force outlined Sudan's dependence on foreign direct investment and political divestiture weakening the Sudanese government.[22] As a direct consequence to the capital flight, Sudanese officials published a US $ one million advertisement in the New York Times in 2006 to promote re-investing in Sudanese governmental bonds and condemning political divestiture from Sudan.[23] To this day, political divestiture from Sudan is prominent as for several socio-psychological motives of socially responsible investors. Most recently the role of political divestiture for sustainable development has been thematized foremost regarding climate change and fossil fuel divestment (Puaschunder, 2016c).

Table 6. Publicly traded corporations meeting divestment criteria in 2008

Publicly traded corporations listed to meet divestment criteria[21]			
Corporation	**Industry**	**Country**	**Market listing**
PetroChina CNPC	Petroleum	China	NYSE
Petronas Gas	Petroleum	Malaysia	Kuala Lumpur
ONGC	Petroleum	India	Bombay
SINOPEC Group	Petroleum	China	NYSE
Lundin Petroleum	Petroleum	Sweden	Stockholm
Ranhill Berhad	Petroleum	Malaysia	Kuala Lumpur
Dietswell Engineering	Petroleum	France	Paris
Muhibbah Eng.	Petroleum	Malaysia	Kuala Lumpur
Kencana Petroleum	Petroleum	Malaysia	Kuala Lumpur
KSTB	Petroleum	Malaysia	Kuala Lumpur
AVICHINA	Defense	China	Hong Kong
ALSTOM	Energy	France	Paris
Petrofac	Petroleum	UK	London
WÄRTSILÄ OYJ	Energy	Finland	Helsinki
Bharat Heavy Elec.	Energy	India	Bombay
Dogfeng Auto	Defense	China	Berlin
Indian Oil Corp Ltd.	Petroleum	India	Bombay
SCOMI Group	Petroleum	Malaysia	Kuala Lumpur
PECD Berhard	Petroleum	Malaysia	Kuala Lumpur
SUEZ SA	Energy	France	Paris

Table 7. Corporations that divested Sudan by 2007

Corporations that divested Sudan by 2007		
Corporation	**Industry**	**Divestiture**
3M	Consumer Goods	March 2006
Xerox	Industry / Consumer goods	March 2006
Baker Hughes	Petroleum	December 2006
Siemens AG	Transportation / Electronics	January 2007
Berkshire Hathaway	Insurance	July 2007
Weatherford International	Petroleum	November 2007
Marathon Oil	Petroleum	April 2008

SOCIO-PSYCHOLOGICAL MOTIVES OF RESPONSIBLE INVESTORS

Traditional financial market theory holds investment decisions being based on rationality (Baron, 2000; Carswell, 2002; Michelson, Wailes, van der Laan & Frost, 2004). Classical portfolio theory depicts investment allocations dependent on profit maximization of expected utility and volatility (Carswell, 2002; Dupré et al., 2008; Harvey, 2008; Michelson et al., 2004). Contrary modern experimental economics describes human decision making being "more global in nature" by addressing irrational socio-psychological motives of investment behavior (Becker, 1976, p. 147).

In first attempts to analyze the reasons for socially responsible market behavior, demographic correlates revealed socially responsible investors to be well-educated and more likely to be female (Hayes, 2001; Rosen et al., 1991; Tippet, 2001; Tippet & Leung, 2001). As outlined by Figure 4, the majority of ethical investors is young to middle-aged with about 13 percent being below 36 years of age, 30 percent between 36 and 45 years and 29 percent between 46 and 55 years old (Sparkes, 2002). Socially responsible investors are described as perfectionists serving in caring professions such as medicine, education or social work.

Figure 4. Age distribution of socially responsible investors in the US

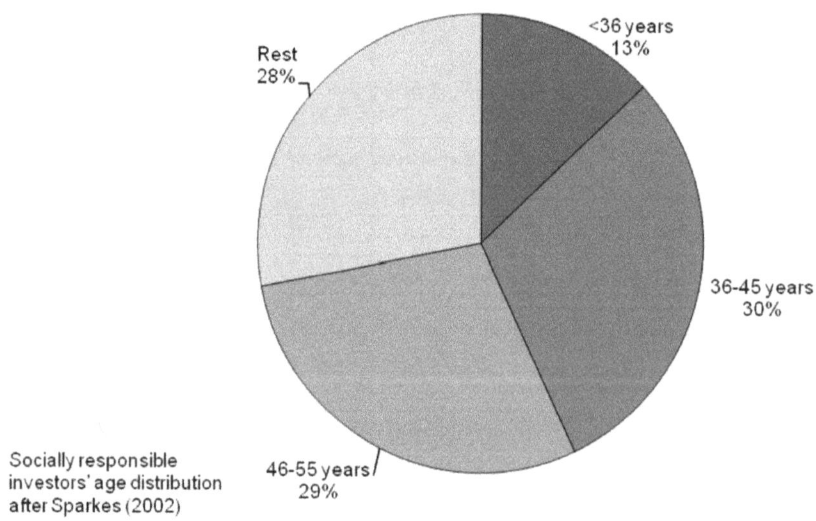

As for investment distributions, 80 percent of socially responsible investors have mixed portfolios and only 20 percent exclusively hold onto SRI options (Dupré et al., 2008). No significant levels of materialism, risk propensity and investment performance concerns are found for socially responsible investors, who tend to believe that SRI implies lower returns than ordinary market options (Sparkes, 2002).

A survey of over 1,100 individual investors showed correlations between SRI and sociopsychological lifestyle factors such as post-materialism, self-image enhancement and social attitudes (Lewis, 2001 in Sparkes, 2002). Socially responsible investors are described as liberal pro-environmentalist who are open to exotic cultures. As idealistic altruists, socially conscientious investors are less likely to be self-centered and hold onto traditional gender roles (Ray & Anderson, 2000). At the same time, SRI is connected to religious and moral thoughts (O'Neil & Pienta, 1994; Sproles, 1985; Sproles & Kendall, 1986).

Investors consider SRI options for economic, psychological and social reasons. SRI grants multifarious utilities to investors – some of them rational, others less in sync with classic homo oeconomicus assumptions. When it comes to SRI, monetary gratification is accompanied by socio-psychological pay-offs and intangible social values (Waldman, Siegel & Javidian, 2004).

With the current body of SRI studies focusing on the supply side and financial performance, scarce is the understanding of socio-psychological motives for SRI (Cuesta & Valor, 2007; Mohr et al., 2001). Overall, the reasons for investors exhibiting social responsibility and underlying investor motives to integrate ethicality in their portfolio choice are yet opaque. Exploratory findings on the objectives of socially responsible investors are primarily based on anecdotal evidence (Rosen et al., 1991). As classic finance theories have blacked out moral and ethical dimensions, a descriptive framework for financial social responsibility has yet to be built (Dupré et al., 2008). In a first attempt to shed light on socio-psychological SRI facets, the following investor motives are proposed (Puaschunder, 2016b, 2017c):

1. The intention to maximize profits
2. Altruism as the concern for the societal well-being
3. Need for innovation and entrepreneurship
4. Strategic leadership advantages
5. Need for transparency and information disclosure
6. Self-enhancement through identification and self-consistency
7. Expression of social values
8. Long-term considerations

The Intention to Maximize Profits

Empirical investigations of the relationship between SRI and profitability offer no stringent, generalizable pattern (Butz, 2003; Hamilton et al., 1993). Up to date no clear answer on the performance and efficiency of SRI has been identified (Dixon, 2002; Jones et al., 2008; Little, 2008; Mackey, Mackey & Barney, 2004). While some evidence holds SRI out- (e.g., Kempf & Osthoff, 2007), others underperforming the market (e.g., Fowler & Hope, 2007) and some studies report no difference of SRI to conventional market indices at all (e.g., Abramson & Chung, 2000; Boutin-Dufresne & Savaria, 2004).

Since 1992 the Domini 400 Social Index has outperformed the S&P 500 (Harvey, 2008). Data of the 100 'Best Corporate Citizens' corporations underlined the SRI profitability to outperform the Standard & Poor's 500 Index (S&P 500) – an index of 500 widely-held stocks to measures the general market performance (Kotler & Lee, 2005). In addition, a pool of 277 corporations listed at the Toronto Stock Exchange exhibited a positive relation of social responsibility, positive financial return and low volatility from 1996 to 1999.

Sector-specific investigations related corporate environmental responsibility to higher riskadjusted returns (Cohen, Fenn & Konar, 1997; Posnikoff, 1997).

In contrast, stocks of 451 UK corporations with sound social performance were depicted to significantly under-, while corporations with low corporate social performance to considerably outperform the market (Brammer et al., 2006). Within the Australian market, ethical funds were significantly undervalued in the market from 2002 to 2005 (Jones et al., 2008). In sync, Wright and Ferris (1997), McWilliams et al. (1999), Meznar, Nigh & Kwok (1994) and Ngassam (1992) reported political divestiture to be associated with shareholder wealth loss.

No difference in the financial performance or volatility rates of SRI to the rest of the market was outlined by Abramson and Chung (2000) as well as Boutin-Dufresne and Savaria (2004).

In closing, there is no stringent answer as to whether SRI is associated with an in- or decrease in shareholder return and volatility (Berman, Wicks, Kotha & Jones, 1999). Sometimes socially responsible financial market options increase shareholder value, in some cases SRI reduces shareholder profits and sometimes SRI does not deviate from ordinary financial options (Little, 2008; Maux & Saout, 2004).

The inconsistency of findings is attributed to manifold SRI expression forms and measurement deficiencies.

Positively screened SRI funds are more likely to feature IT-technology and alternative energy industries that attract innovative venture capital providers. Positively screened SRI options tend to be more volatile, yet if successful, grant high profitability – e.g., solar energy funds have significantly outperformed the market in recent years and remained relatively stable during the 2008/09 World Financial Recession.

As for excluding high-return, high-volatility industries such as petroleum, defense and addictive substances, negatively screened options are more likely to underperform the market, at the same time are robust to overall market changes. Negative screening asset holders are more loyal to their choice in times of crises, which contributes to the stability of these funds. Data on the profitability of political divestiture indicates a potential first mover advantage for early divestiture.

In a cost and benefit analysis, SRI implies short-term expenditures, but grants long-term sustainable investment streams.

In the short run, screened funds have a higher expense ratio in comparison to unscreened ones – that is social responsibility imposes an instantaneous 'ethical penalty' of decreased immediate shareholder revenue (Mohr & Webb, 2005; Tippet, 2001). In addition, for investors the search for information and learning about CSR is associated with cognitive costs. Screening requires an extra analytical step in decision making, whereby positive screens are believed to be more cognitively intensive than negative ones (Little, 2008). Screening out financial options lowers the degrees of freedom of a full-choice market spectrum and risk diversification possibilities (Biller, 2007; Mohr & Webb, 2005; Williams, 2005).

On the long run, SRI options offer higher stability, lower turnover and failure rates compared to general assets (Dhrymes, 1998; Geczy, Stambaugh & Levin, 2003; Guenster, Derwall, Bauer & Koedijk, 2005; Schroeder, 2003; Stone et al., 2001). Being based on more elaborate decision making processes, once investors have made their socially responsible decision, they are more likely to stay with their choice (Little, 2008). As a matter of fact, SRI options are less volatile and more robust during cyclical changes (Bollen & Cohen, 2004).

SRI measurement deficiencies stem from intangible and time-inconsistent pay-offs as well as measurement errors. SRI studies are methodologically limited as for small sample sizes due to the relative novelty of financial social responsibility, inconsistencies in the short time frames under scrutiny and differing modelling techniques used to estimate investment returns (Jones et al., 2008; McWilliams & Siegel, 1996; Mohr et al., 2001; Ngassam, 1992; Teoh et al., 1999). Most SRI studies do not take externalities on the wider constituency group into consideration, which lowers the external validity of the results and calls for a more wholerounded examination of SRI (McWilliams et al., 1999).

Altruism as the Concern for the Societal Well-Being

A mixture of egoistic and altruistic acts constitutes all human behavior as both are features of human nature (Becker, 1976). Contrary to classical economic assumptions of pure selfinterest driving all human beings, behavioral economics attributes altruism as a part of economic decision making (Frank, 2007).

The duality of altruism and egoism in human behavior is addressed as early as in ancient Greek writings. Already Socrates is believed to have connected egoistic individual responsibility to altruism (Sichler in Weber et al., 2004). The predicament of altruism versus egoism is also blatant in Adam Smith's writings (Beinhocker, 2007). In *An Inquiry into the Nature and Causes of the Wealth of the Nations*, Smith (1776/1976) proposes self-interest as the motivating force for any economic activity to enhance societal well-being (Jones & Pollitt, 1998). In *The Theory of Moral Sentiments*, Smith (1759/1976) argues that all human beings are selfishly interested in the well-being of others as for altruistic moral sentiments (Zak, 2008).

Altruism is a state, by which individuals increase the fitness of others at the expense of their own (Wilson, 1975). As one of the most enduring human traits, altruism is evolutionary explained by the increased survival likelihood of those who are supported by others (Becker, 1976). As a source of value for those who give, altruism is associated with selfish pleasure (Brooks, 2008). Granting meaning to the individual beyond the self, altruism contributes to the positive self-perception and well-being of the giver. Short-term intangible gratification of altruism is related to the warm glow – an internally rewarding positive feeling derived from the giver being aware of their pro-social behavior (Brammer, Williams & Zinkin, 2005; Frey & Stutzer, 2007; Heyman & Ariely, 2004).

Today classic market fundamentalism is challenged by findings of the roles of altruism in decision making as well as trust and cooperation in market transactions (Osnabrugge & Robinson, 2000). Contrary to classic portfolio theory that holds investments being based on rationality, business ethics describe affluent societies to exhibit altruism in investment choices, which deviate from pure profit maximization (Becker, 2008; Brooks, 2008; Frey & Stutzer, 2007). Market behavior is found to not only be based on striving for competitive fitness, but also to feature pro-social, altruistic endeavors. Within society, altruism breeds cooperation and creates long-term beneficial societal ties. Altruism contributes to collective trust and social capital as implicit prerequisites for any economic market activity and societal prosperity (Brooks, 2005; Frey, 2008).

Behavioral economists introduce altruism and pro-social behavior in financial decision making analyses. The economic psychology paradigm portrays altruism as a pivotal motivation factor for investment allocations (Brooks, 2008; Csikszentmihalyi, 2003). Investors are attributed altruistic investment motives as for their pro-social concerns (Kirchler, 2001). As socially conscientious investors are found to be willing to sacrifice profits for the sake of altruism, SRI is portrayed as an investment strategy that combines profit intentions with social considerations (Little, 2008).

Extended investors' altruism is expressed in investor philanthropy, which is believed to stem from a utility decline of marginal profits (Holman et al., 1985). Investor philanthropy is most common in the US due to a combination of financial wealth accumulation, cultural values of giving and tax exemptions for charity. Prominent US investor philanthropists are Warren Buffett – who recently donated over 85 percent of his fortune to charity – and George Soros, who couples economic investments with philanthropy by holding the Soros Fund Management alongside the non-profit Open Society Institute and Soros Foundation (Bernstein & Swan, 2007; Soros, 1997, 2003).

Need for Innovation and Entrepreneurship

The concept of innovation is as old as mankind. Innovations emerge from entrepreneurial traits and related behavior in advantageous settings (Drucker, 1985).

Since industrialization innovations are attributed as the mainspring of societal progress and economic prosperity (Schumpeter, 1951/1989). Already Karl Marx described the constant revolution of means of production and diffusion of innovations to spur capitalism. Joseph Schumpeter (1934) attributed profit creation to stem from innovations of entrepreneurs who uniquely combine means of production to generate new products for innovation-seeking market participants. In uniquely and efficiently using resources in an unprecedented, productive way, entrepreneurs spur innovative change. Creative entrepreneurs feature dynamic energy, an extraordinary striving for innovative progress and high levels of risk acceptance (Drucker, 1985; Goleman, 2006; Kirchler, 2001). For entrepreneurs, innovative activities grant excitement. Innovation is related to altruism in the case of social entrepreneurship (Schumpeter, 1951/1989). Social entrepreneurs seek innovative opportunities to alleviate social deficiencies about which they care.

Entrepreneurs are in need of a supportive environment and advantageous societal settings that support their innovative endeavors. While entrepreneurial activities are reported in various historical contexts and exist in almost all cultures, the success of innovative entrepreneurship is dependent on external, culture-related factors such as institutional and regulatory frameworks, investment capital and societal values (Brooks, 2008; De Woot, 2005). As incubators for entrepreneurship, innovative milieus attract entrepreneurs and bring innovations to prosper (Aydalot & Keeble, 1988). Libertarian, open market societies foster innovative milieus as for featuring high levels of economic freedom, a constant investment climate, private property securitization and high levels of social capital (Camagni 1991; De Woot, 2005; Fromhold-Eisebith, 2004; Rodrik, 2007). Within innovative milieus, knowledge dissemination in sync with collective learning processes and expertise platforms stimulate entrepreneurial activities. In open market societies, entrepreneurial innovations are attributed to drive productivity, create and extend markets and steer economic development (Handy, 2006).

Within financial market, SRI is an innovative and entrepreneurial investment option (Waldman et al., 2004). As a means of stakeholder activism, SRI allows investors to reward societal progress and innovatively tackle social and environmental concerns. Especially positively screened SRI funds feature innovative corporations that pro-actively administer social responsibility beyond the legal requirements (Aiken & Hage, 1971; Little, 2008). Positively screened environmentally friendly corporations contribute to future-oriented funds that attract innovative and entrepreneurial investors (Blank & Carty, 2002; Coulson, 2002; Meyers & Nakamura, 1980; Russo & Fouts, 1997; Ziegler, Rennings & Schröder, 2002). In shareholder advocacy, SRI becomes a platform to steer entrepreneurial activities, unprecedentedly influence corporate conduct and address social entrepreneurship within the corporate context (Little, 2008).

As an innovative capital allocation form that attracts entrepreneurial spirits, SRI is preferred by venture capitalists and business angel investors. These future-oriented investors have an interest in innovative market options that instigate societal change and sustainably improve the societal conditions (Schueth, 2003).

Social venture capitalists are prone to screen financial options for entrepreneurial opportunities. Venture capitalists seek to finance social entrepreneurs and early-stage businesses innovations. Venture funds feature relatively high levels of risk in combination with extraordinary return expectations. Venture capital-backed corporations are prone to astronomic growth of highly valuable market shares. Venture capital serves as an important source for innovative economic growth and international development (Gompers, Kovner, Lerner & Scharfstein, 2005).

Business angel investors are the oldest, major external entrepreneurial start-up funding source. In the US close to three million business angles invest more than US $ 50 billion in entrepreneurial corporations per year (Little, 2008). Business angels fund 30-40 times as many entrepreneurial start-ups than venture capitalists (Little, 2008). As innovative investors, business angels are attracted to entrepreneurial ideas, willing to take high risks and accept lower returns. Angel investors primarily finance early-stage projects that may require handson managerial involvement. As for interests in start-up corporations and early-stage ventures, business angels are less likely to make follow-up investments in the same entities. In the US individual angel investors are predominantly male, 35 to 40 years old – which is significantly older than the average venture capitalist – while their European counterparts are slightly older (Wetzel & Freear, 1996). Business angels are well-educated with 60 percent holding postgraduate degrees and 13 percent PhDs in various disciplines. Having more corporate exposure than venture capitalists, around 90 percent of business angels have prior corporate experience. Business angels tend to be more flexible than venture capitalists and make industry-wide investments. In recent decades, the overall market for business angels has grown quantitatively and qualitatively.

Strategic Leadership Advantages

SRI implies leadership advantages for investors, when being perceived as distinct, innovative market option related to altruism.

Leaders express and distinguish themselves from others by their possessions and in their prosocial activities.

Sociologists outline conspicuous consumption as a means of leadership distinction (Becker & Murphy, 2000; Coleman, 1990; Veblen, 1899/1994). In general, leaders are willing to pay premium prices for trademarked high-end goods and innovative first editions to differentiate themselves from others (Becker & Murphy, 2000).

Related to advantageous power and wealth distributions, leaders are in the position to give to others and those who give distinguish themselves as leaders. Altruistic social responsibility and charitable giving are leadership features. Pro-social behavior of leaders is accompanied by positive feedback and a benevolent climate of subordinates (Brooks, 2008). Giving grants leaders control over their social environment and discourages others from causing harm to givers. In pro-social activities, leaders thereby create strong interpersonal networks that lift their position in hierarchies (Brooks, 2008). As altruism contributes to the social reputation of the altruist, social responsibility serves as a means of status enhancement for leaders (Becker, 1976; Brooks, 2008; Hermann, 2008; Sichler in Weber et al., 2004). Prosocial behavior thereby becomes a source of value for those who give and leads to higher personal standing, leadership effectiveness and ultimately greater success.

SRI implies leadership advantages as for being an innovative, high-end market option that allows investors to distinguish themselves from others and establish and maintain leadership positions. As an innovative entrepreneurial financial market option, SRI implies first mover advantages and a competitive edge over others. Screenings leverage SRI into high-end, branded products that are related to altruism. Positive image transfer portrays socially responsible investors as pro-social leaders (Ait-Sahalia, 2004). For their charitable giving, socially responsible investors enjoy a positive reputation and related status gains (Ait-Sahalia, 2004; Wright & Ferris, 1997). In this light, SRI serves personal and social interests alike (McWilliam et al., 1999).

Need for Transparency and Information Disclosure

When making consumption choices, individuals seek information. Information about products and corporate performance diminishes uncertainty in purchase situations.

Transparency of corporation conduct impacts on consumption choices.

Investment decision making depends on information about corporate conduct. Information on corporate social conduct is a prerequisite for investors' trust in corporations, lowered stakeholder pressure and litigation risks. Information on CSR impacts on investors' behavior and triggers financial social responsibility (Gill, 2001; Mohr et al., 2001; Myers, 1984; Siegel & Vitaliano, 2006; Williams, 2005).

Investors' access to information about CSR is a prerequisite for SRI. SRI is based on disclosure of corporate social conduct (Crane & Livesey, 2002; Little, 2008; Mohr et al., 2001). In general, consumers' knowledge about the CSR performance heightens the positive perception of corporations and triggers investment endeavors.

The basis for shareholder activism is transparency and information disclosure, monitoring of corporate conduct, accountability of the implementation of corporate codes of social conduct as well as internal and external CSR monitoring systems. In the search for trustworthy information on CSR and corporate conduct externalities, socially conscientious investors primarily use corporate track records and shareholder resolutions on social and environmental performances (Graves, Rehbeim & Waddock, 2001; Little, 2008). Apart from social scrutiny, SRI selections are influenced by information-sharing networks, word-of-mouth knowledge transfer and facial emotional display (Thaler & Sustein, 2008). Information provision on corporate conduct is triggered by stakeholder pressure and spearheaded by respective security and transparency legislations. Shareholders react positively to governmental transparency demands of CSR conduct and a lack of information on CSR causes investors to refrain from SRI options (Cuesta & Valor, 2007; Williams, 2005). Publicity disclosed unethical corporate behavior leads to divestment and lowered stock prices for a minimum of six months (Dasgupta, Laplante & Mamingi, 1998).

In the wake of the 2008/09 World Financial Recession, corporate governance failures and responsibility deficiencies of market actors have pushed investor calls for transparency of corporate conduct, accountability of shareholder meetings, standardized tracking of proxy votings and accessibility of shareholder meetings. Access to information is believed to lower economic default risks of socially irresponsible corporate conduct and contribute to SRI trends. Financial market disclosure regulations are currently installed to prevent future economic turmoil due to financial fraud and principal-agent defaults. As a positive externality of the 2008/09 World Financial Recession, the drive towards transparency and accountability within financial markets is likely to foster SRI in the future.

Self-Enhancement Through Identification and Self-Consistency

While socially responsible investors are interested in financial profitability, at the same time they want their portfolio choice to conform to personal opinions and societal norms (Little, 2008; Statman, 2007; Williams, 2005). Socially responsible investors are willing to sacrifice financial returns in order to base their investment allocations on personal and societal values (Statman, 2008).

Financial social responsibility is linked to deontological ethics, which comprise internal obligations to uphold protected values of prescriptive moral rules. When paying attention to protected ethicality, decision makers depart from rationality. Emotional connections to protected values make individuals resistant to economic utility considerations. Forced tradeoffs from deontological ethics result in resistance, anger and denial by wishful thinking. Protected values of ethicality are relatively stable across cultures and hold for public and private conditions (Baron & Spranca, 1997).

Financial social responsibility allows investors to attribute causes that are in line with their beliefs and societal values. SRI combines financial investments with personal values based on societal ethicality (Alperson et al., 1991; Frey & Irle, 2002; Sparkes & Cowton, 2004). As a means to integrate ethicality in economic decision making, SRI enables investors to address protected ethicality notions that are in line with their personally held, culturally established social values (Knoll, 2008).

Socially responsible investors fund ethical causes about which they personally care and refrain from ethical infringements. The integration of personal ethics in their portfolio decision making and the perception of the investment decisions being in sync with personal protected values lets investors identifying themselves with their choice (Mohr & Webb, 2005). The alignment of beliefs and actions evokes identification with investments that grants investors the notion of self-consistency. Self-consistency triggers positive feelings and contributes to the self-enhancement of socially responsible investors (Frey & Irle, 2002; Schueth, 2003).

Expression of Social Values

Everyday economic decisions are influenced by social considerations. Social motives underlie financial decision making (Frey & Stutzer, 2007; Hong & Kacperczyk, 2006). Social norms are a prerequisite for financial social responsibility, which enables investors to align personal economic endeavors with social obligations and societal concerns (Hitsch, Hortaçsu & Ariely, 2005).

In the case of SRI, socially responsible economic activities can leverage into a form of expression of social conformity (Soros, 1995; Statman, 2000). SRI signals culturally endorsed protected values. Socially responsible asset allocations connect the individuals with social reference groups. Thereby SRI becomes a means of expression of accordance of personal values with societal norms and the wider society. The expression of personal values by SRI is attributed to stem from an internal need for conformity of words and deeds with social norms and societal values (Hofmann, Hoelzl & Kirchler, 2008).

Expressing social norms in their investment behavior empowers socially responsible investors as for the social gratification of their pro-social choice and as an implicit form of influence.

Individuals who care about their pro-social images signal their conformity with societal norms in socially responsible investment choices (Huberman, Loch & Önçüler, 2002). The accordance of market interactions with social norms expresses positive, meaningful social identities. Stemming from the positive image of socially responsible corporations and the social gratification of pro-social behavior, socially responsible investors benefit from reputation and prestige gains (Derwall & Koedijk, 2006; Hong & Kacperczyk, 2006; Schroeder, 2003; Simons et al., 1972; Stone et al., 2001; Webster, 1975). When paying attention to SRI in their decision making, investors can thus improve their societal status.

SRI is a means of expression for self-determination in the wake of rising levels of autonomy (Sichler, 2006). In quasi-political processes, socially responsible investors use their investments as for expressing their value system by influencing corporate conduct (Dupré et al., 2008; Frey, 2008; Kashyap & Iyer, 2006; Lewis & Mackenzie, 2000). Corporate shares give investors the right to vote at the shareholders' general assembly as well as the possibility to put forward resolutions on corporate governance. Shareholder advocacy allows influencing corporate policies targeted at positive societal implications (Mohr et al., 2001). As a positive externality, the expression of personal values in SRI positively contributes to the overall long-term societal progress.

Long-Term Considerations

Investment decisions are based on reflections about future prospects. Investment strategies can build on intentions to maximize sustainable financial returns as well as considerations of long-term societal implications of investments (Crowther & Rayman-Bacchus, 2004).

Socially responsible corporate conduct attributes long-term perspectives. Socially attentive corporate conduct features sustainability considerations of corporate executives who are mindful of future risks and social impacts of their decision making. Long-term viability of corporate conduct is ingrained in CSR practices. CSR grants long-term stability of corporate conduct as for creating a supportive business environment and decreasing the likelihood of stakeholder pressure and litigations risks (Little, 2008; Posnikoff, 1997; Sparkes, 2002).

When taking rising CSR trends into consideration, SRI offers long-term financial prospects (Dupré et al., 2008; Little, 2008; McWilliams et al., 1999).

SRI allows investors to support corporations that have a lasting impact on society. Investors interested in 'social change' put their investments to work in ways that sustainably improve the overall quality of life. Socially conscientious investors thereby use SRI as a long-term strategy to contribute to society (Knoll, 2008; Schueth, 2003).

From a multi-stakeholder perspective, SRI implies long-term positive societal outcomes (Sparkes, 2002). SRI ensures that corporations are held accountable for any social and environmental impacts and investments are in line with societal values (Sparkes, 2002). By shifting capital from socially disapproved to socially conscientious corporations, SRI fosters corporate social performances. As for being incentivized by first mover leadership advantages, more and more corporations may pay attention to social responsibility in the future. Accompanied by followers, the rising supply of SRI in combination with a heightened demand for the integration of personal values and societal concerns into financial decision making may prospectively leverage social conscientiousness to become a standard feature of investment markets. On the long run, the integration of SRI into the overall competitive model will further sophisticate social responsibility in corporate conduct (Schueth, 2003; Starr, 2008; Stiglitz, 2003). Financial market demand and supply geared towards SRI will stretch the option range in a more socially responsible direction. In addition if the majority of investors are socially conscientious, socially responsible corporations will continuously benefit from increasing investment streams. Directed capital flows to socially responsible market options will sustainably contribute to CSR and SRI trends (Dupré et al., 2008). Overall, financial markets attuned to social responsibility will lift entire industries onto a more socially conscientious level (Trevino & Nelson, 2004). As such SRI is attributed the potential to positively impact on the financial markets and create socially attentive market systems that improve the overall standard of living and quality of life for this generation and the following.

THE ROLE OF LEADERSHIP AND TRUST

Globalization converged the concept of nation states (Held & McGrew, 2007). Nowadays the range of opportunities of what contemporary states can autonomously do is ultimately limited by their dependence on each other (Panitch & Gindin, 2012). The role of states in maintaining property rights, overseeing contracts, stabilizing currencies and reproducing class relations has gradually deteriorated in the age of internationalization. Due to global capitalism, the power and political authority have been diffused away from local state ruling to global governance. The classic ideal of the command and control state was displaced by a philosophy of economic hegemony (Held & McGrew, 2007). As multilayered economic system are structured by the strategic coordination of international corporate entities, corporate multinationals nowadays have turned to solve global societal crisis beyond the control of singular nation states and entities to breed trust in the overall economy.

While the trend of internationalization has weakened the power of local governance and national control, globalization has also lead to unprecedented problems of climate change, overindebtedness in the aftermath of the 2008/09 World Financial Crisis and pension reform needs of an aging Western world population. In the light of growing socio-political and environmental challenges, heightened stakeholder concern has risen attention of global stakeholders on corporate ethical conduct. In the aftermath of the 2008/09 World Financial Crisis, corporations are under scrutiny for societal contributions and corporate board managers increasingly respected for corporate social conduct with stakeholders playing a conspicuous role in influencing the interaction between governments and business. The corporate world is nowadays more than ever urged to consider the needs of a wider range of stakeholders in their decision-making, go beyond ethical requirements and outperform responsibility expectations within the surge of a positive organizational scholarship movement. Trust through responsible corporate leadership and wide-spread stakeholder consideration and engagement, seems to be a vital prerequisits for a functioning economy.

In the age of heightened shareholder and stakeholder activism towards corporate social endeavors, the time has come for trust to be seen as a vital governmental and corporate leadership advantage. With growing socio-political and environmental challenges around the world in the domains of financial social irresponsibility, environmental resource consumption and growing costs for an aging populace, there is increasing pressure from stakeholders – among them governments, local communities, NGOs, and society at large – that corporations and their leaders contribute to societally-attentive business practices. Access to information law revolutions in the Western world have steered attention to corporate ethicality. Corporate social reporting and the engagement of stakeholders have led to the adoption of a variety of global ethical standards, which may directly affect the propensity to engage in intergenerational equity implementations. Local communities, customers, employees, and NGOs as well as shareholders are increasingly monitoring ethical behavior in the digital age featuring greater transparency, accessibility and reachability of corporate conduct. All these features are prerequisites for trust as a vital corporate asset derived from responsible leadership. Trust thereby becomes a novel extension of contemporary CSR models. Responsible leadership is built on the idea that corporate executives have an obligation to incorporate needs of far-ranging constituent.

As a case study on trust as a governance factor in the public sector, carbon tax ethics are discussed. In the sustainability domain, research may set out to investigate how to bear the burden of climate taxation in a fair and just way in the climate change burden-sharing context. Finding the optimum balance between consumption tax adjusted for income levels through a progressive tax scheme will unravel drivers of tax compliance in the sustainability domain. If climate taxation is perceived as fair and just allocation of the climate burden, this should help convince taxpayers to pay one's share to avert global warming. A novel 'service-and-client' atmosphere could promote taxpayers as cooperative citizens that would be willing to comply voluntarily if they perceive their share as fair contribution to a collectively enjoyed stable environment. This strategy of taxpayer collaboration promotion could ultimately enhance tax morale in the environmental domain. Contemporary climate taxation schemes should be studied descriptively coupled with economic cost-benefit analyses. Information is advised to be collected on taxation aiding climate change risk mitigation and adaptation strategies with a special emphasis on the finance sector.

In order to finance climate change mitigation and adaptation efforts, a diversified taxation scheme is proposed. Climate justice *within* a country acknowledges adjusting climate taxation for consumption and income levels as well as past environmental damaging behavior to find a fair distribution of the burden of climate change. The idea is to share the burden of climate taxation in a mix of (1) consumption tax, (2) progressive tax and (3) inheritance tax.

A carbon tax on top of the existing tax system could reduce the burden of climate change and ultimately allow clean economic growth through subsidies for clean energy. Carbon emission consumption tax appears just in light of placing a heavier burden on those who engage in activities that offset climate change. Consumption tax can also curb harmful emissions and directly nudge behavior towards sustainability. Yet to place a fair share of the burden of climate change mitigation upon society, these taxes have to be adjusted to the income level of individuals in order to not charge low-income heavier than deep pocket households.

Besides progressive taxation schemes to imbue a sense of fairness in climate change burden sharing, inheritance taxation is a creative means to reap past wealth accumulation, which potentially offset and caused past environmental damage. Allocating the burden of climate change mitigation and adaptation in a fair way within society will therefore also feature research on contemporary inheritance tax structures in place and their role of financing the climate stability agenda. Retroactive taxation of past wealth accumulation at the expense of environmental damage through inheritance tax will be legally justified.

Empirically, future research should comprise of a macroeconomic tax revenue cost-benefit analysis to find the optimum solution on how to distribute the taxation burden within society. The analysis should cover consumption tax, progressive tax and inheritance taxation and aim at estimating the optimum taxation mix to ensure the burden of climate abatement and adaptation costs are distributed in a fair manner within society.

FINANCIAL REPORTING AND FRAUD PREVENTION

Torgler (2003b) stressed the importance of trust in the political and legal system to enhance tax compliance and as fraud prevention (Kramer & Tyler, 1996; Tyler, 2001a, b). Citizens have been found to claim that tax authorities fail to communicate respect and trust to the taxpayer (Kirchler, 2007). Torgler (2003c) analyzed Canadian data from the World Values Survey and found evidence that trust in government has a systematic positive influence on tax morale (Schwartz & Orleans, 1967). Based on these descriptive results, citizens' trust in authorities is argued to determine voluntarily tax compliance apart from conventional tax compliance enforcement. As such, trust in the corporate sector and responsible leadership may serve as fraud prevention.

Trust in governmental institutions may build social norms that positively affect tax morale and responsible corporate conduct (Puaschunder, 2015). Trusting citizens may be more willing and compliant to contribute to common goods and so may corporate actors be steered towards responsible behavior by trust in the management and corporate leadership. Trustful relations breed a culture of reciprocity. Attitudes toward the government based on experience shape social ethics (Kirchler, 2007). Respectful, polite and dignified treatment of taxpayers was found to enhance voluntary compliance and may therefore be elicit in the corporate sector as fraud prevention. If the societal climate is friendly and taxpayers trust authorities, compliance occurs (Bergman, 2002; Feld & Frey, 2005; Frey, 2003). If taxpayers agree with the government activities and fiscal policies, taxpayers are cooperative and so may corporate actors if operating guided by trust (Puaschunder, 2015).

Given the importance of a favorable social environment to develop social tax ethics norms, an investigation of the concrete antecedents of tax morality and the relation of social interactions and tax compliance is recommended. In an innovative attempt, tax compliance could be seen as a product of favorable social experiences with the community and the government. Reciprocity may enhance a sense of moral obligation to be honest and strengthen social norms' compliance (Gintis, Bowles, Boyd & Fehr, 2003).

Efficient performance of the state and tax authorities also depends on the individuals' feelings of obligation towards the community (Kramer, 1999). Tax morale and civic duty aggregate citizens' beliefs and evaluations of other citizens and their behavior. A mutual understanding of taxpayers and corporate actors raises their willingness to cooperate (Cialdini, 1996).

A climate of cooperation is likely if government policy is accepted and trusted, personal and social norms are favorable to cooperation and tax burden and tax procedures are perceived as fair. When investigating tax systems, fairness and the relative treatment in comparison to others are the most frequently mentioned topics (Antonides & Robben, 1995; Braithwaite, 2003a, b; Brooks & Doob, 1990; Jackson & Milliron, 1986; Mason & Calvin, 1978; Thorndike & Ventry, 2002). Extensions of neoclassical economic assumptions capture the choice of a taxpayer to evade taxes depending upon the perceived fairness of the tax system (Kirchler, 2007). Willingness to comply with the laws is determined by the perceived fairness. Citizens are motivated to pay tax when taxes are perceived to be fair and just (Schmölders, 1960). Exchange equity considers fair distributions of the results of exchanges between partners within the social reference group and institutional conditions (Adams, 1965). If taxpayers are treated as equal partners, they are more cooperative. Distribute justice is measured by the individual horizontal fairness of distributed resources and burdens between taxpayers of comparable income groups.

Fairness depends on the object of comparison and taxpayers' identification with a social reference group. Fairness judgments are not stable but influenced by comparison and taxpayers' identification with a social group or category to which justice refers (Taylor, 2003). Taxpayers weight their exchange equity with the government and equity of one's contributions relative to the contributions of other taxpayers as a framework for fairness (Wenzel, 2003). If an individual's perceived tax burden is heavier than that of comparable others or if taxpayers perceive the exchange with the government as unjust, tax evasion increases.

Justice concerns seem to have an especially strong impact if taxpayers identify with their reference group and national government (Wenzel, 2002). Procedural fairness plays a key role in shaping the legitimacy that citizens grant to government authority. On the individual level, procedural justice refers to the quality of treatment in interactions between taxpayers and authorities (Frey, 2003). According to social categorization theory and the group value model (Lind & Tyler, 1988), taxpayers are more concerned about fairness and less about personal outcomes and egoistic advantages when they identify strongly with the group to which procedures and distributions apply.

Equity and fair treatment are believed to build trust and lead to the development of a psychological contract and compliance due to binding social norms. Fairness perceptions are related to trust and trustworthiness derived from dignified and respectful treatment (Tyler & Lind, 1992). When authorities are perceived to behave fairly and respectful, greater compliance results. Taxpayers seek procedural justice in terms of neutrality, trustworthiness and reciprocity. At the individual level, fair treatment of individual taxpayers and the culture of interaction based on reciprocity are relevant aspects of fairness and building trust. A relation of voluntary trust and reciprocity may lead to voluntary cooperation. Preliminary findings on fairness are inconsistent as heterogeneous aspects of fairness have been investigated and the operationalization varied. Social exchange is a prerequisite of peoples' judgments of fairness (Güth & Sausgruber, 2004).

MANAGERIAL ETHICS

Socially responsible leadership steers intentional corporate executive actions to benefit the stakeholders of the company as well as the larger society including future generations. Socially responsible corporate leadership imbues *should-do* care for future generations alongside concerns about future society. Not simply considering avoiding unethical behavior, such as bribery, fraud and employmen discrimination, but also adopting a positive and proactive ethics lens, responsible leadership is an Überethical drive to consider the interests of a wider range of stakeholders (Puaschunder, 2017a, d, e). Intergenerational justice concerns of the corporate world thereby directly reach out to future world inhabitants.

There are several advantages of TC&MEs implementing intergenerational equity as a CSR means. TC&MEs hold enormous economic potential, with the largest multi-national corporations having revenues larger than many nation states. In their corporate governance, TC&MEs leadership decision-making quickly adapts to market demands without having to reach international consensus – contrary to stakeholder engagement and international consensus negation demands of classic global governance entities such as the United National International Monetary Fund and the World Bank. TC&MEs are not dependent on voters – such as governmental officials – and can thus address societal concerns faster and more flexibly than governmental technocrats. In addition, TC&ME leadership may be more stable than governmental officials enacted through voting cycles – that is global corporate leaders are likely to stay longer in 'office' than their governmental counterparts.

If the corporate world adopts CSR endeavors, it could help governmental officials in very many different ways ranging from tax ethics to first-aid global governance support. For society, acknowledging CSR practices promises to alleviate current pressing societal predicaments of overindebtedness, social welfare reform needs and environmental threats in the wake of climate change. Investigating the possibilities to integrate a temporal dimension in contemporary CSR work innovatively guides the implementation of financial social responsibility, environmental protection education and social welfare. For academia, applying the notion of CSR in corporate governance models fills an up-to-date undiscovered research gap that spearheads interdisciplinary behavioral law and economic models to aid in the global corporate arena.

Increasing and expanding CSR initiatives indicate that more and more business leaders commit their companies to contribute to the "triple bottom line" to harmoniously considers social, environmental, and economic sustainability in every day corporate decision-making (Elkington, 1998). Respect for 'people, planet, and profits' has become a corporate necessity and industrial imperative. Corporate sustainability and social responsibility has thus emerged to unprecedented momentum in academia and practitioners' discourse. In the international arena, the UN Global Compact has raised over 10,000 members 2000, including over 7,000 businesses in 145 countries around the world. Today business leaders tend to contribute to the creation of economic and societal progress in a globally responsible and sustainable way by means as never before experienced.

Surpassing state-of-the-art ethical corporate leadership quests on ethically compliant behavior and avoidance of unethical corporate conduct, incorporating CSR models may extend the idea of 'positive CSR' – that is outdoing legal and ethical expectations – with respect for future constituents. Going beyond mere compliance involves actions that pro-actively promote social good, beyond what is required by law, intergenerational corporate responsibility extends CSR as a broader social contract between business and society over time. Intergenerational equity leadership of the corporate sector defines social responsibility beyond compliance and encompasses the wider obligation to contribute to societal progress in a responsible and sustainable way. Stretching the constituency attention to future generations is based on a voluntary sustainability with respect for future generations' needs to ensure the long-term viability of society.

Corporate leaders thereby pro-actively outperform legal and ethical expectations regarding the rights and needs of future generations. This positive CSR drive refers to an Überethical enhancement of societal welfare beyond the narrow scope of the current generation. As a broader definition of corporate responsibility beyond avoidance of negative downfalls, the call for intergenerational responsible leadership in the corporate world encompasses the obligation to contribute to societal progress with respect for the needs of future generations. Defining novel responsibilities with a broader social contract between business and society embraces discretionary activities that contribute to sustainable societal welfare and thereby provides a broad range of corporate, social and societal advantages.

In the given literature on global responsible leadership in the corporate sector and contemporary CSR models, intergenerational equity appears to have widely been neglected. While the notion of sustainability has been integrated in CSR models, intergenerational equity has hardly been touched on as intergenerational fairness differs from sustainability as for being a more legal case for codifying the triple bottom line, which pays attention to a balance of social, economic and environmental obligations of corporations to the wider constituency.

Integrating CSR models in academia and practice appears as advantageous alternative given the enormous untapped potential of corporations to implement equity. Nowadays, international trade is driven by transnational corporations. As corporate entities with economic influence beyond the borders of nation states holding subsidiaries in various nations of the world (Binder et al., 2014), TC&MEs are acknowledged as international legal entities and must therefore abide by international law standards and fulfill international court laws (e.g., ICSID and UNCITRAL). Therefore, TC&MEs should, like nation states, consider adopting concern for CSR.

Knowledge of contextual factors that promote intergenerational managerial decision-making with regard to corporate sustainability and social responsibility could include favorable characteristics of the organization and aspects of the broader institutional and cultural contexts in which firms are embedded that automatically trigger intergenerational concern. Thereby the antecedents of sustainable and responsible management touch on multiple levels (individual, group, organization, national context, supranational bodies) but also the interlinkages among variables should be investigated. Institutional contexts within which companies and their managers operate determine executives' responsible choices. Differences in corporate governance and legal contexts but also the nature of regulation and the likelihood of enforcement shape business ethics as well as expectations of what is considered good governance and ethical conduct in a country. Managers' responsible leadership may therefore vary across institutional contexts in the international arena. What may be considered as social practice in one part of the world may not be ethical state-of-the-art in another. As a consequence, corporate leaders embedded in different national systems may exhibit different intergenerational ethics. Cross-national variations in socially responsible practices could be captured in order to derive implications for organizational decision makers on how their corporate responsibility. Adopted CSR strategies may be scrutinized for globally standardized, locally adapted, and transnational factors to delineate globally consistent as well as locally-oriented intergenerational equity CSR approaches with attention to intergenerational equity.

Cross-culturally operating institutions may face challenges for CSR implementation stemming from local differences in corporate practices and social ethical norms as well as differing thresholds to sustainable behavior. For instance, challenges arise if corporations or even nation states of the industrialized world outsource intergenerational practices (e.g., environmental pollution) into territories with weaker law enforcement and public scrutiny. These findings emphasize the need for sensitivity to local conditions, transparency along the production and value chains as well as stakeholder expectations monitoring when conducting business in different contexts.

Future research may also address ethical dilemmas facing managers in the global arena and their coping strategies in order to enhance research outcomes are leaders' potential operating in the global arena to balance global and local considerations in making responsible decisions. As an implication, CSR practices should be locally oriented and emphasize sensitivity to local conditions when conducting business in different cultural contexts.

Corporate executives with foreign subsidiaries should gain training to adapt to specific needs and circumstances of local CSR customs. The role of supranational factors that influence responsible leader behavior provide further insight into the propensity to engage in intergenerational equity. With supranational institutions – such as the UN – having turned to the codification of the triple bottom line in the UN Global Compact, managers are increasingly respected for their accountability and responsibility. Insights on the influence of supranational regulatory measures and institutions (e.g., NGO activism and the enactment of the UN Global Compact) on responsible managerial behavior may shed light on success factors in the adoption of socially responsible corporate practices in the global arena. International institutions should set priorities on the corporate intergenerational equity implementation agenda. Quantitative metrics based on standardized evaluation frameworks will coordinate a global monitoring and impact assessment of the role of corporations in the CSR implementation. Indices of local, national, regional and global corporate endeavors will help build public private partnership synergies but also shed light on positive and negative externalities and trade-offs. Independent governance institutional evaluation frameworks will help streamline social, economic and environment goals through cost benefit analysis, life cycle cost discounting and social equality programs. Public private partnerships will aid adaptability and flexibility in collaborations between governments, the private sector and academia. International organizations' emergent risk and crises prevention frameworks will help reform CSR endeavors.

The organizational-, situational-, societal, and supranational-level determinants of responsible managerial behavior can be influenced by top management teams, policy makers, educators, and external regulators. Best practice studies in this area could shed light on how companies can systematically design and utilize human resource management practices and leadership development programs to promote responsible managerial behavior. Prospective findings may thus enhance our understanding of how companies and other stakeholders can effectively prevent, manage and control the corporate risks associated with unethical conduct of leaders. Capturing the impact of external factors on intergenerational equitable decision-making and coping with the ethical dilemmas in leadership challenges may serve as a basis for training and development activities. The implementation of intergenerational equity could further be solicited through building corporate cultures that enhance an ethical climate.

On the corporate incentive level, CSR may be implemented through performance management and reward systems to hold managers accountable for irresponsible behavior as well as creating psychological incentives to think about future consequences of current corporate conduct. Best practices studies on intergenerational equity in the corporate world will serve as corporate risk management tool to help build a culture of intergenerational CSR and foster a corporate design that pays tribute to social concerns. In building a cadre of responsible corporate leaders through corporate trainings and team building development but also corporate social performance measurement and CSR reward systems, intergenerational leadership in the corporate sector will be advanced.

At the organizational level, when recruiting, selecting and promoting managers, it is essential for organizations to understand how individual-level variables such as personality traits, motives and values may predict managers' propensity to engage in ethical behavior. For example, firms can use personality tests and integrity tests, along with interviews and assessment centers, to help determine which employees might be more likely to act irresponsibly. They can also assess applicants' attitudes and values to decide whether they will match the corporate culture, with the assumption that candidates' formal qualifications and job-related skills may not be the best predictors of responsible behavior on the job. Studying personality traits but also motives and values that steer managers' propensity to engage in CSR will allow setting up assessment centers that reveal which individuals are more likely to act irresponsibly and if the managerial ethics will likely match the corporate culture on the intergenerational equity scale.

CSR can also be imbued in corporate activities by creating and enforcing company policies and codes of conduct, supporting training and development initiatives, which are aimed at increasing moral awareness regarding future generations. Once the individual has joined the organization, induction programs, individual coaching by the supervisor, training and development programs, and other socialization practices could ensure that newcomers learn values, expected behaviors, and social knowledge that are necessary to become socially conscientious managerial leaders. In terms of communication and control systems, top management teams and governmental officials may actively promote responsible behavior and discourage irresponsible behavior by communicating ethical integrity messages. Implementing performance management and reward systems to hold managers accountable for irresponsible behavior could in addition create a psychologically favorable situation for corporate social conduct (Matten & Crane, 2005).

Future research should connect the individual experience to social responsibility in order to unravel ethicality nudges. Common goal compliance is hoped to be modeled by contexts that automatically nudge corporate decision makers in an intergenerational equitable direction. Public and private sector discourse on intergenerational imbalances will help fortify the codification of intergenerational fairness on a global scale. Internationally validated CSR models will elucidate intercultural, national and regional differences on social responsibility in the intergenerational domain. The prospective findings will help imbue efficiency measures on intergenerational equity implementation through real-world relevant means. CSR advocates advanced with intergenerational conscientiousness will lead to fruitful corporate contributions for a sustainable humankind alongside fostering a harmonious corporate-citizen relation.

With the underlying premises of exhibited behavior being a function of both the person and the environment in which that behavior takes place, future research may also unravel ethical decision-making under situational constraints that the broader cultural and institutional environment impose on the adoption of sustainable and socially responsible practices. Overall, enhancing social conscientiousness in the corporate world is an innovative way to unprecedentedly leverage untapped potentials to implement social welfare and environmental protection through future-oriented and socially responsible economic market approaches. Thereby averting future predictable economic, social and environmental crises serves the greater goal to ensure a future sustainable and temporally harmonious humankind. Cross-national sustainability solutions and interculturally sensitive intergenerationally equitable business practices may help imbue social conscientiousness and intergenerational equity in corporate conduct in the global arena with direct implications for today's and tomorrow's society.

FROM IMAGE RISK TO GLOBAL RISK MANAGEMENT

Globalization converged the concept of nation states (Held & McGrew, 2007). Nowadays the range of opportunities of what contemporary nation states can autonomously do is ultimately limited by their dependence on each other (Panitch & Gindin, 2012). The role of states in maintaining property rights, overseeing contracts, stabilizing currencies and reproducing class relations has gradually deteriorated since the beginning of internationalization. International interdependence limits national sovereignty and economic autonomy (Held & McGrew, 2007). In the wake of global capitalism, the power and political authority have been diffused away from local state ruling to global governance. The classic ideal of the command and control state was displaced by a philosophy of global economic hegemony (Held & McGrew, 2007). While industrialization has weakened the power of local governance and national control, globalization has also lead to unprecedented problems of climate change and overindebtedness in the aftermath of the 2008/09 World Financial Crisis. Globalization also shifted national governments' responsibility implementation to international governance solutions in the corporate world (Panitch & Gindin, 2012).

Nowadays pressing dilemmas beyond the control of singular nation states call for attention for corporate social activities to back governmental crisis mitigation (Centeno, Cinlar, Cloud, Creager, DiMaggio, Dixit, Elga, Felten, James, Katz, Keohane, Leonard, Massey, Mian, Mian, Oppenheimer, Shafir & Shapiro, 2013). In the light of growing sociopolitical and environmental challenges, heightened stakeholder concerns have risen attention of global stakeholders on corporate ethical conduct. Today's responsible leadership has become blatant through information provided to stakeholders by heightened transparency in the digital age that makes corporate conduct and governmental actions visible to a broad range of constituents. Local communities, customers, employees, and NGOs as well as shareholders are increasingly monitoring ethical behavior in the digital age featuring greater transparency, accessibility and reachability of corporate conduct.

In a climate of corporate governance and global challenges beyond the control of singular nation states, the idea of promoting social responsibility in the corporate world as crises prevention has reached unprecedented momentum. Departing from narrow-minded, outdated views of responsibilities of corporations only adherent to making profit for shareholders and abiding by the law (Friedman, 1970); corporate executives nowadays are more prone to act responsibly in meeting the needs of a wide range of constituents. Apart from avoiding unethical societally harmful behavior, such as bribery, fraud and employment discrimination, corporate executives currently pro-actively engage in corporate governance practice with a wider constituency outlook.

Especially in the aftermath of the 2008/09 World Financial Crisis, corporations have become under scrutiny for societal contributions and corporate board managers increasingly respected for corporate social conduct with stakeholders playing a conspicuous role in influencing the interaction between governments and business. The corporate world is nowadays more than ever urged to consider the needs of a wider range of stakeholders in their decision-making, go beyond ethical requirements and outperform responsibility expectations within the surge of a positive organizational scholarship movement.

With growing socio-political and environmental challenges around the world in the domains of financial social irresponsibility, environmental resource consumption and growing costs for an aging populace, there is increasing pressure from stakeholders – among them governments, local communities, NGOs, and society at large – that corporations and their leaders contribute to societally attentive business practices. Access to information law revolutions in the Western world have steered attention to corporate ethicality. Corporate social reporting and the engagement of stakeholders have led to the adoption of a variety of global ethical standards, which may directly affect the propensity to engage responsibility implementations. In the age of heightened shareholder and stakeholder activism towards corporate social endeavors, the time is ripe to investigate the potential of corporate activities to engage in responsibility in the aftermath of the 2008/09 World Financial Crisis.

As multi-layered economic system are structured by the strategic coordination of international corporate entities, corporate multinationals nowadays have turned to solve global societal crisis beyond the control of singular nation states. International trade, global capitalism and economic hegemony of corporations have led to a strategic coordination of public and private actors' awareness of intergenerational imbalances (Binder, Kriebaum, Marboe, Nowak, Reinisch & Wittich, 2014).

The future conceptualization of sustainable and responsible managerial behavior may therefore embrace the wider constituency range and stretch the concept of corporate responsibility to voluntary sustainability for future generations. An extended stakeholder view considers a broader set of constituencies, including future generations, in corporate decision-making with impact on the social performance and long-term viability of their organizations. A broader, social contract between business and future society may be enacted by discretionary activities that are not expected of corporations and their leaders in a moral or legal sense but directly contribute to societal welfare and the wellbeing of future generations. This suggests that there is a need for a broader definition of corporate responsibility that goes beyond compliance and encompasses the obligation to contribute to societal progress in a responsible and sustainable way.

As we can learn from the historic case of Political Divestiture during Apartheid in South Africa, governments and intergovernmental entities play a major role in being first movers in divestiture activities. As in the case with South Africa, the UN is expected to play a key role in instigating action by clear leadership and international outreach of multi-faceted stakeholders. As with the South African Apartheid divestiture, human rights declarations and the connection of climate justice to human rights on an international legal basis appear as most important first steps to gain momentum and credibility. France prohibited imports of South African coal in 1985, South Africa became the major supplier of coal imports to the European Economic Community in 1986. As trade never completely stopped with South Africa, the anti-Apartheid movement became criticized as a patchwork of voluntary and mandatory prohibitions undertaken by only some market actors.

In the case of carbon divestiture, a broad based support is therefore recommended to be back by UN sanctions, which played a major role in implementing divestiture from Apartheid. Religious and renowned public and artistic leaders can foster the outreach on an international scale. The stark impact of international corporations to pull out of unethical markets but also the predicted prices of unethical commodities losing value over time give hints about carbon industries' decline in the future. South Africa was unable to trade in the international markets and had become a pariah nation, cast out of the UN and the Commonwealth and isolated from international sporting activities (Zeff & Pirro, 1999).

In closing the theoretical part, we have outlined that responsibility is ingrained in human nature and learned within the societal context. As a prerequisite for the functioning of market, social responsibility complements corporate activities and is considered in financial investments. As a multistakeholder phenomenon, CSR is of value to various constituents. CSR emerged in the Western World and is a culture-dependent phenomenon. CSR becomes a feature of global governance in PPPs addressing social service provision and as a multi-stakeholder management means. The United Nations Global Compact (UNGC) provides CSR best practices principles and fosters CSR in PPPs. The United Nations Global Alliance for Information and Communication Technology (UN GAID) is a currently launched PPP initiative advancing Information and Communication Technologies (ICT) for development.

Financial Social Responsibility is based on considerations of CSR in investment behavior. CSR is the basis for Socially Responsible Investment (SRI) in screenings, shareholder advocacy, community investing and social venture capital funding. As a multi-stakeholder phenomenon, SRI comprises economic, organizational and societal constituents. The emergence of SRI within the Western World can be traced back to a combination of historical incidents, legislative compulsion and stakeholder pressure. SRI is a context and culture-dependent phenomenon. The UN provides an institutional framework to promote SRI and align multiple stakeholders' view on SRI. As a special case of SRI, political divestiture refers to the investment withdrawal from socially irresponsible market regimes with the greater goal of accomplishing socio-psychological changes. SRI is proposed to stem from socio-psychological motives complementing rational profit maximization considerations.

REFERENCES

Abramson, L., & Chung, D. (2000). Socially responsible investing: Viable for value investors? *Journal of Investing*, *9*(3), 73–81. doi:10.3905/joi.2000.319381

Adams, J. S. (1965). Inequity in social exchange. In L. Berkowitz (Ed.), Advances in Experimental and Social Psychology (pp. 267–299). New York: Academic Press.

Ahmad, M. (2008, January 24). Global CEOs at World Economic Forum cite sovereign wealth funds as the new power broker. *BI-ME*.

Aiken, M., & Hage, J. (1971). The organic organization and innovation. *Sociology*, *5*(1), 63–82. doi:10.1177/003803857100500105

Ait-Sahalia, Y. (2004). Disentangling diffusion from jumps. *Journal of Financial Economics, 74*(3), 487–528. doi:10.1016/j.jfineco.2003.09.005

Alperson, M., Tepper-Marlin, A. T., Schorsch, J., & Wil, R. (1991). *The better world investment guide: One hundred companies whose policies you should know about before you invest your money*. New York: Prentice Hall.

Antonides, G., & Robben, H. S. J. (1995). True positives and false alarms in the detection of tax evasion. *Journal of Economic Psychology, 16*(4), 617–640. doi:10.1016/0167-4870(95)00027-4

Aydalot, Ph., & Keeble, D. (1988). *High technology industry and innovative environments: The European experience*. London: Routledge.

Baron, J. (2000). *Thinking and deciding*. Cambridge, MA: Cambridge University Press.

Baron, J., & Spranca, M. (1997). Protected values. *Organizational Behavior and Human Decision Processes, 70*(1), 1–16. doi:10.1006/obhd.1997.2690 PMID:9236161

Becker, G. S. (1976). *The economic approach to human behavior*. Chicago: The University of Chicago Press.

Becker, G. S., & Murphy, K. M. (2000). *Social economics: Market behavior in a social environment*. Cambridge, MA: Harvard University Press. doi:10.4159/9780674020641

Beinhocker, E. D. (2007). *The origin of wealth: The radical remaking of economics and what it means for business and society*. Cambridge, MA: Harvard Business School.

Bergmann, M. S. (2002). Who pays for social policy? A study on taxes and trust. *Journal of Social Policy, 31*(2), 289–305. doi:10.1017/S0047279401006614

Berman, S. L., Wicks, A. C., Kotha, S., & Jones, T. M. (1999). Does stakeholder orientation matter? The relationship between stakeholder management models and firm financial performance. *Academy of Management Journal, 42*(5), 488–506.

Bernstein, P. W., & Swan, A. (2007). *All the money in the world: How the Forbes 400 make – and spend – their fortunes*. New York: Knopf.

Biller, A. (2007). Socially responsible investing now part of the landscape. *Benefits & Compensation Digest, 44*, 12.

Binder, C., Kriebaum, U., Marboe, I., Nowak, M., Reinisch, A., & Wittich, St. (2014). *Völkerrecht*. Vienna: University of Vienna Faculty of Law Juridicum.

Blank, H. D., & Carty, C. M. (2002). *The eco-efficiency anomaly*. Innovest working paper. Retrieved from http://www.sristudies.org/Blank+and+Carty+(2002)?

Bollen, N. P. B., & Cohen, M. A. (2004). *Mutual fund attributes and investor behavior*. Unpublished working paper, Vanderbilt University.

Boutin-Dufresne, F., & Savaria, P. (2004). Corporate social responsibility and financial risk. *Journal of Investing*, *13*(1), 57–66. doi:10.3905/joi.2004.391042

Braithwaite, V. (2003a). Dancing with tax authorities: Motivational postures and non-compliant actions. In V. Braithwaite (Ed.), *Taxing Democracy: Understanding Tax Avoidance and Tax Evasion* (pp. 15–39). Aldershot: Ashgate.

Braithwaite, V. (2003b). Perceptions of who's not paying their fair share. *The Australian Journal of Social Issues*, *38*(3), 335–362. doi:10.1002/j.1839-4655.2003.tb01149.x

Brammer, S., Williams, G. A., & Zinkin, J. (2005). *Religion and attitudes to corporate social responsibility in a large cross-country sample*. Nottingham University Business School.

Brenner, R. (2001). *The force of finance: Triumph of the capital markets*. New York: Texere.

Brooks, A. (2005). *Gifts of time and money: The role of charity in America's communities*. New York: Rowman & Littlefield.

Brooks, A. (2008). *Social entrepreneurship. Course Reader, Spring 2008*. Maxwell School of Citizenship and Public Affairs, Syracuse University.

Brooks, N., & Doob, A. N. (1990). Tax evasion: Searching for a theory of compliant behaviour. In M. L. Friedland (Ed.), *Securing Compliance: Seven Case Studies* (pp. 122–164). Toronto: University of Toronto Press. doi:10.3138/9781442679696-006

Butz, Ch. (2003, September). Decomposing SRI performance: Extracting value through factor analysis. *Pictet Quants*.

Camagni, R. (1991). *Innovation networks*. London: Routledge.

Carswell, A. (2002). Crisis of conscience. *Australian CPA*, *72*, 26–27.

Centeno, M. A., Cinlar, E., Cloud, D., Creager, A. N., DiMaggio, P. J., Dixit, A. K., . . . Shapiro, J. N. (2013). *Global systemic risk. Unpublished manuscript for research community*. Princeton Institute for International and Regional Studies, Princeton University.

Cialdini, R. B. (1996). Social influence and the triple tumor structure of organizational dishonesty. In D. M. Messick & A. E. Tenbrunsel (Eds.), *Codes of Conduct* (pp. 44–58). New York: Sage.

Cohen, M., Fenn, S. A., & Konar, S. (1997). *Environmental and financial performance: Are they related?* Unpublished working paper, Vanderbilt University.

Coleman, J. (1990). *Foundations of social theory*. Cambridge, MA: Harvard University Press.

Coulson, A. (2002). *A benchmarking study: Environmental credit risk factor in the panEuropean banking sector*. London: ISIS Asset Management.

Crane, A., & Livesey, S. (2002). Are you talking to me? Stakeholder communication and the risks and rewards of dialogue. In J. Andriof, S. Waddock, S. Rahman, & B. Husted (Eds.), *Unfolding Stakeholder Thinking* (pp. 39–52). Sheffield: Greenleaf.

Crawford, N., & Klotz, A. (1999). *How sanctions work: A framework for analysis: Lessons from South Africa*. New York: St. Martin's.

Crowther, D., & Rayman-Bacchus, L. (2004). *Perspectives on corporate social responsibility*. Burlington, VT: Ashgate.

Csikszentmihalyi, M. (2003). *Good business: Leadership, flow, and the making of meaning. New Baskerville*. Penguin.

Cuesta de la, G. M. & Valor, C. (2007). Fostering corporate social responsibility through public initiative: From the EU to the Spanish case. *Journal of Business Ethics*, *55*(3), 275–293.

Cui, C. (2008, March 6). Social investing soars amid more options. *The Wall Street Journal*.

Cummings, L. A. (2000). The financial performance of ethical investment trusts: An Australian perspective. *Journal of Business Ethics*, *25*(3), 167–177.

Dasgupta, S., Laplante, B., & Mamingi, N. (1998). *Capital markets responses to environmental performance in developing countries*. Policy Research Working Paper 1909. Washington, DC: The World Bank.

De Woot, A. (2005). *Should Prometheus be bound? Corporate Social Responsibility*. London: Palgrave Macmillan. doi:10.1057/9780230502062

Derwall, J., & Koedijk, K. (2006). *Socially responsible fixed-income funds*. Unpublished working paper, Erasmus University.

Dhrymes, P. J. (1998). *Socially responsible investment: Is it profitable? The investment research guide to socially responsible investing*. The Colloquium on Socially Responsible Investing. Retrieved from http://www.columbia.edu/~pjd1/

Dixon, F. (2002). *Financial markets and corporate environmental results*. Unpublished working paper, Innovest.

Drucker, P. F. (1985). *Innovation and entrepreneurship: Practice and principles*. New York: Harper Business.

Duchac, J. (2008, December 15). The perfect storm: A look inside the 2008 financial crisis. WU talks special notes. Vienna, Austria.

Dupré, D., Girerd-Potin, I., & Kassoua, R. (2008). *Adding an ethical dimension to portfolio management*. Working paper. Retrieved from the internet at www.ssrn.com

Elkington, J. (1998). *Cannibals with forks: The triple bottom line of 21st century business. Gabriola Island*. New Society.

Farzad, R. (2007). Article. *Business Week*, (January): 22.

Feld, L. P., & Frey, B. S. (2005). Illegal, immoral, fattening or what? How deterrence and responsive regulation shape tax morale. In C. Bajada & F. Schneider (Eds.), *Size, Causes and Consequences of the Underground Economy* (pp. 16–37). Aldershot: Ashgate.

Fowler, S. J., & Hope, C. (2007). A critical review of sustainable business indices and their impact. *Journal of Business Ethics*, *76*(3), 243–252. doi:10.100710551-007-9590-2

Frank, R. H. (2007). *The economic naturalist: In search of explanations for everyday enigmas*. New York: Perseus.

Freeman, R. E. (1984). *Strategic management: A stakeholder approach*. Mashfield, MA: Pitman.

Frey, B. S. (2003). Deterrence and tax morale in the European Union. *European Review (Chichester, England)*, *11*(3), 385–406. doi:10.1017/S1062798703000346

Frey, B. S. (2008). *Happiness: A revolution in economics*. Cambridge, MA: MIT Press. doi:10.7551/mitpress/9780262062770.001.0001

Frey, B. S., & Stutzer, A. (2007). *Economics and psychology: A promising new crossdisciplinary field*. Cambridge, MA: MIT Press.

Frey, D., & Irle, M. (2002). *Theorien der Sozialpsychologie*. Bern: Hans Huber.

Friedman, M. (1970). The social responsibility of business is to increase its profits. *New York Times Magazine, 13*, 33-38.

Fromhold-Eisebith, M. (2004). Innovative milieu and social capital: Complementary or redundant concepts of collaboration-based regional development? *European Planning Studies*, *12*(6), 747–765. doi:10.1080/0965431042000251846

Geczy, C. C., Stambaugh, R. F., & Levin, D. (2003). *Investing in socially responsible mutual funds*. Philadelphia, PA: The Wharton School.

Gill, A. (2001). *Saints and sinners: Who's got religion?* Hong Kong: Credit Lyonnais Securities Asia Report.

Gintin, H., Bowles, S., Boyd, R., & Fehr, E. (2003). Explaining altruistic behavior in humans. *Evolution and Human Behavior*, *24*(3), 153–172. doi:10.1016/S1090-5138(02)00157-5

Goleman, D. (2006). *Social intelligence: The new science of human relationships*. New York: Bantam.

Gompers, P., Kovner, A., Lerner, J., & Scharfstein, D. (2005). *Venture capital investment cycles: The impact of public markets*. NBER Working Papers, 11385. Cambridge, MA: National Bureau of Economic Research.

Graves, S. B., Rehbeim, K., & Waddock, S. (2001). Fad and fashion in shareholder activism: The landscape of shareholder resolutions 1988-1998. *Business and Society Review*, *106*(4), 293–314. doi:10.1111/0045-3609.00117

Guenster, N., Derwall, J., Bauer, R., & Koedijk, K. (2005). *The economic value of corporate eco-efficiency*. Unpublished working paper, Erasmus University.

Güth, W., & Sausgruber, R. (2004). *Tax morale and optimal taxation.* CESifo Working Paper No. 1284. CESifo GmbH.

Hamilton, S., Hoje, J., & Statman, M. (1993). Doing well while doing good? The investment performance of socially responsible mutual funds. *Financial Analysts Journal, 49*(6), 62–66. doi:10.2469/faj.v49.n6.62

Handy, Ch. (2006). *What's a business for? Harvard Business Review on Corporate Responsibility*. Cambridge, MA: Harvard Business School.

Harvey, C. (2008). *Campbell R. Harvey's hypertextual finance glossary*. Retrieved from the internet at http://www.duke.edu/~charvey/Classes/wpg/bfglosa.htm

Hayes, J. (2001). The greater good: How ethical investment pays off. *Australian Financial Review, 26*(8), 29–31.

Held, D., & McGrew, A. G. (2007). *A new world economic order? Global markets and state power: Beyond globalization/anti-globalization: Beyond the great divide*. New York: Polity.

Hermann, M. (2008). *Political leadership. Course Reader, Spring 2008*. Maxwell School of Citizenship and Public Affairs, Syracuse University.

Heyman, J., & Ariely, D. (2004). Effort for payment: A tale of two markets. *Psychological Science, 15*(11), 787–793. doi:10.1111/j.0956-7976.2004.00757.x PMID:15482452

Hitsch, G. J., Hortaçsu, A., & Ariely, D. (2005). *What makes you click: An empirical analysis on online dating*. Retrieved from the internet at www.ssrn.com

Hofmann, E., Hoelzl, E., & Kirchler, E. (2007). A comparison of models describing the impact of moral decision making on investment decision. *Journal of Business Ethics, 82*(1), 171–187. doi:10.100710551-007-9570-6

Holman, W. R., New, J. R., & Singer, D. (1985). The impact of corporate social responsiveness on shareholder wealth. In L. Preston (Ed.), *Research in Corporate Social Performance and Policy* (pp. 137–152). Greenwich, CT: JAI.

Hong, H., & Kacperczyk, M. (2006). *The price of sin: The effects on social norms on markets*. Unpublished working paper, Princeton University.

Huberman, B. A., Loch, Ch. H., & Önçüler, A. (2002). *Status as a valued resource*. Unpublished working paper. Retrieved from the internet at www.ssrn.com

Jackson, B. R., & Milliron, V. (1986). Tax compliance research: Findings, problems, and prospects. *Journal of Accounting Literature*, *5*(1), 125–165.

Jones, I., & Pollitt, M. (1998). *The role of business ethics in economic performance*. London: Macmillan. doi:10.1057/9780230379794

Jones, S., van der Laan, S., Frost, G., & Loftus, J. (2008). The investment performance of socially responsible investment funds in Australia. *Journal of Business Ethics*, *80*(2), 181–203. doi:10.100710551-007-9412-6

Kashyap, R. K., & Iyer, S. I. (2006). *Who are socially responsible investors?* Unpublished working paper, University of Massachusetts at Amherst.

Kempf, A., & Osthoff, P. (2007). The effect of socially responsible investing on portfolio performance. *European Financial Management*, *13*(5), 908–922. doi:10.1111/j.1468-036X.2007.00402.x

Kirchler, E. M. (2001). *Wirtschaftspsychologie*. Göttingen: Hogrefe.

Kirchler, E. M. (2007). *The economic psychology of tax behaviour*. Cambridge, UK: Cambridge University Press. doi:10.1017/CBO9780511628238

Knoll, M. S. (2008). *Socially responsible investment and modern financial markets*. Unpublished working paper, University of Pennsylvania Law School.

Konrad, A., Martinuzzi, A., & Steurer, R. (2008). When business associations and a Federal Ministry jointly consult civil society: A CSR policy case study on the development of the CSR Austria guiding vision. *Corporate Social Responsibility and Environmental Management*, *15*(5), 270–280. doi:10.1002/csr.152

Kotler, P., & Lee, N. (2005). *Corporate social responsibility: Doing the most good for your company and your cause*. Wiley.

Kramer, R. (1999). Trust and distrust in organizations: Emerging perspectives, enduring questions. *Annual Review of Psychology*, *50*(1), 569–598. doi:10.1146/annurev.psych.50.1.569 PMID:15012464

Kramer, R., & Tyler, T. (1996). *Trust in organizations*. Thousand Oaks, CA: Sage.

Lewis, A. (2001). A focus group study of the motivation to invest: Ethical, green and ordinary investors compared. *Journal of Socio-Economics*, *30*(4), 331–341. doi:10.1016/S1053-5357(01)00103-2

Lewis, A., & Mackenzie, C. (2000). Morals, money, ethical investing and economic psychology. *Human Relations*, *53*(2), 179–191. doi:10.1177/a010699

Lind, E. A., & Tyler, T. R. (1988). *The social psychology of procedural justice*. New York: Plenum. doi:10.1007/978-1-4899-2115-4

Little, K. (2008). *Socially responsible investing: Put your money where your values are*. New York: Penguin.

Lydenberg, S. (2002). Envisioning socially responsible investing: A model for 2006. *Journal of Corporate Citizenship*, *7*(7), 57–77. doi:10.9774/GLEAF.4700.2002.au.00007

Mackey, A., Mackey, T., & Barney, J. (2004). *Corporate social responsibility and firm performance: Investor preferences and corporate strategies*. Working paper. Retrieved from http://www.sristudies.org/Mackey+et+al+(2004)

Mathieu, E. (2000). *Response of UK pension funds to the SRI disclosure regulation*. London: UK Social Investment Forum.

Matten, D., & Crane, A. (2005). Corporate citizenship: Toward an extended theoretical conceptualization. *Academy of Management Review*, *30*(1), 166–179. doi:10.5465/amr.2005.15281448

Maux, J. & Saout, E. (2004, April 1). The performance of sustainability indexes. *Finance India*.

McCann, L., Solomon, A., & Solomon, J. F. (2003). Explaining the growth in U.K. socially responsible investment. *Journal of General Management*, *28*(4), 15–36. doi:10.1177/030630700302800402

McWilliams, A., & Siegel, D. (2000). Corporate social responsibility and financial performance: Correlation or mis-specification? *Strategic Management Journal*, *21*(5), 603–609. doi:10.1002/(SICI)1097-0266(200005)21:5<603::AID-SMJ101>3.0.CO;2-3

McWilliams, A., Siegel, D., & Teoh, S. W. (1999). Issues in the use of the event study methodology: A critical analysis of corporate social responsibility studies. *Organizational Research Methods*, *2*(4), 340–365. doi:10.1177/109442819924002

Merriam Webster Dictionary. (2008). Retrieved http://merriam-webster

Meyers, J. G., & Nakamura, L. (1980). Energy and pollution effects on productivity: A PuttyClay approach. In J. Kendrick (Ed.), *New Developments in Productivity Measurement and Analysis* (pp. 391–442). Chicago: University of Chicago Press.

Meznar, M. B., Nigh, D., & Kwok, C. C. (1994). Effect of announcements of withdrawal from South Africa on stockholder wealth. *Academy of Management Journal*, *37*, 1633–1648.

Michelson, G., Wailes, N., van der Laan, S., & Frost, G. (2004). Ethical investment processes and outcomes. *Journal of Business Ethics*, *52*(1), 1–10. doi:10.1023/B:BUSI.0000033103.12560.be

Mohr, L. A., & Webb, D. J. (2005). The effects of corporate social responsibility and price on consumer responses. *The Journal of Consumer Affairs*, *39*(1), 121–147. doi:10.1111/j.1745-6606.2005.00006.x

Mohr, L. A., Webb, D. J., & Harris, K. E. (2001). Do consumers expect companies to be socially responsible? The impact of corporate social responsibility on buying behavior. *The Journal of Consumer Affairs*, *35*(1), 45–72. doi:10.1111/j.1745-6606.2001.tb00102.x

Myers, St. (1984). The capital structure puzzle. *The Journal of Finance*, *39*(3), 575–592. doi:10.2307/2327916

Ngassam, C. (1992). *An examination of stock market reactions to U.S. corporate divestitures in South Africa*. Newark, DE: University of Delaware.

O'Neil, R. F., & Pienta, D. A. (1994). Economic criteria versus ethical criteria toward resolving a basic dilemma in business. *Journal of Business Ethics*, *13*(1), 71–78. doi:10.1007/BF00877157

Osnabrugge, M. V., & Robinson, R. J. (2000). *Angel investing: Matching start-up funds with start-up companies: The guide for entrepreneurs, individual investors, and venture capitalists*. San Francisco, CA: Jossey-Bass.

Panitch, L., & Gindin, S. (2012). *The making of global capitalism: The political economy of American empire*. New York: Verso.

Posnikoff, J. F. (1997). Disinvestment from South Africa: They did well by doing good. *Contemporary Economic Policy*, *15*(1), 76–86. doi:10.1111/j.1465-7287.1997.tb00456.x

Puaschunder, J. M. (2015). Trust and reciprocity drive social common goods allocation norms. In *Proceedings of the Cambridge Business & Economics Conference*. Cambridge, UK: Cambridge University.

Puaschunder, J. M. (2016a). On the emergence, current state and future perspectives of Socially Responsible Investment (SRI). Consilience: The Columbia University. *Journal of Sustainable Development*, *16*(1), 38–63.

Puaschunder, J. M. (2016b). Socially Responsible Investment as emergent risk prevention and means to imbue trust in the post-2008/2009 world financial crisis economy. In O. Lehner (Ed.), *Routledge Handbook of Social and Sustainable Finance* (pp. 222–238). London: Taylor & Francis.

Puaschunder, J. M. (2016c). The role of political divestiture for sustainable development. *Journal of Management and Sustainability*, *6*(1), 76–91. doi:10.5539/jms.v6n1p76

Puaschunder, J. M. (2017a). Ethical decision making under social uncertainty: An introduction to Überethicality. *Sustainable Production and Consumption*, *12*, 78–89. doi:10.1016/j.spc.2017.05.005

Puaschunder, J. M. (2017b). Ethical, environmental, social and governance-oriented investments. *Archives of Business Research*, *5*(8), 151–159. doi:10.14738/abr.58.3622

Puaschunder, J. M. (2017c). *Global Responsible Intergenerational Leadership*. Wilmington, DE: Vernon Art & Science.

Puaschunder, J. M. (2017d). Socio-psychological motives of socially responsible investors. *Advances in Financial Economics*, *19*, 209–247. doi:10.1108/S1569-373220160000019008

Puaschunder, J. M. (2018a). Nachhaltigkeit und Investment: Psychologische Aspekte von nachhaltigkeitsorientiertem Investitionsverhalten. In C. T. Schmitt & E. Bamberg (Eds.), *Psychologie und Nachhaltigkeit: Konzeptionelle Grundlagen, Anwendungsbeispiele und Zukunftsperspektiven* (pp. 127–134). Wiesbaden: Springer Nature. doi:10.1007/978-3-658-19965-4_11

Puaschunder, J. M. (2018b). The history of Ethical, Environmental, Social and Governance-oriented investments as a key to sustainable prosperity in the finance world. *Public Integrity*, *1*, 1–21. doi:10.1080/10999922.2018.1439563

Ray, P., & Anderson, S. R. (2000). *The cultural creatives: How 50 million people are changing the world*. New York: Three Rivers Press.

Renneboog, L. D. R., Horst, J. R. T. & Zhang, C. (2007). *Socially responsible investments: Methodology, risk and performance*. Tilburg University Center for Economic Research Discussion Paper 2007-2031.

Rodrik, D. (2007). *One economics, many recipes*. Princeton: Princeton University Press.

Rosen, B. N., Sandler, D. M., & Shani, D. (1991). Social issues and socially responsibility investment behavior: Preliminary empirical investigation. *The Journal of Consumer Affairs*, *25*(2), 221–234. doi:10.1111/j.1745-6606.1991.tb00003.x

Russo, M. V., & Fouts, P. A. (1997). A resource-based perspective on corporate environmental performance and profitability. *Academy of Management Journal*, *40*, 534–559.

Schmölders, G. (1960). *Das Irrationale in der öffentlichen Finanzwirtschaft*. Frankfurt am Main: Suhrkamp.

Schroeder, M. (2003). *Socially responsible investments in Germany, Switzerland, and the United States*. Centre for European Economic Research Discussion Paper 03-10, March 2003.

Schueth, S. (2003). Socially responsible investing in the United States. *Journal of Business Ethics*, *43*(3), 189–194. doi:10.1023/A:1022981828869

Schumpeter, J. A. (1934). *The theory of economic development*. Cambridge, MA: Harvard University.

Schumpeter, J. A. (1951/1989). *Essays on entrepreneurs, innovations, business cycles, and the evolution of capitalism*. Transaction.

Schwartz, R., & Orleans, S. (1967). On legal sanctions. *The University of Chicago Law Review. University of Chicago. Law School*, *34*(Winter), 274–300. doi:10.2307/1598934

Sichler, R. (2004). Autonomie. Ihre Konstitution und Ambivalenz im Kontext von Arbeit und Lebensführung. In W. G. Weber, P. Pasqualoni, & Ch. Burtscher (Eds.), *Wirtschaft, Demokratie und soziale Verantwortung: Psychologie und Beruf* (pp. 104–126). Göttingen: Vandenhoeck & Ruprecht.

Siegel, D. S., & Vitaliano, D. F. (2006). *An empirical analysis of the strategic use of corporate social responsibility*. Working paper, Rensselaer Polytechnic Institute.

Simons, J. G., Powers, Ch. W., & Gunnemann, J. P. (1972). *The ethical investor: Universities and corporate responsibility*. New Haven, CT: Yale University Press.

Social Investment Forum Report. (2006). *Report on socially responsible investing trends in the United States*. Social Investment Forum Industry Research Program 10-year review.

Solomon, J. F., Solomon, A., & Norton, S. D. (2002). Socially responsible investment in the UK: Drivers and current issues. *Journal of General Management*, *27*(3), 1–13.

Soros, G. (1995). *Jan Patocka memorial lecture: A failed philosopher tries again. Unpublished notes*. New York: The Open Society Institute.

Soros, G. (1997). *The capitalist threat*. Tbilisi: Open Society Georgia Foundation.

Soros, G. (1998). *The crisis of global capitalism: Open society endangered*. New York: Public Affairs.

Soros, G. (2000). *Open society: Reforming global capitalism*. New York: Public Affairs.

Soros, G. (2003). *The alchemy of finance*. New York: Wiley.

Soros, G. (2008). *The new paradigm for financial markets: The credit crisis of 2008 and what it means*. New York: Public Affairs.

Sparkes, R. (2002). *Socially responsible investment: A global revolution. Cronwall*. Wiley.

Sparkes, R., & Cowton, Ch. J. (2004). The maturing of socially responsible investment: A review of the developing link with corporate social responsibility. *Journal of Business Ethics*, *52*(1), 45–57. doi:10.1023/B:BUSI.0000033106.43260.99

Sproles, G. B. (1985). From perfectionism to faddism: Measuring consumers' decision making styles. *Proceedings of the American Council on Consumer Issues*, 79-85.

Sproles, G. B., & Kendall, E. L. (1986). A methodology for profiling consumers' decisionmaking styles. *The Journal of Consumer Affairs*, *20*(2), 267–279. doi:10.1111/j.1745-6606.1986.tb00382.x

Starr, M. (2008). Socially responsible investment and pro-social change. *Journal of Economic Issues*, *42*(1), 51–73. doi:10.1080/00213624.2008.11507114

Statman, M. (2000). Socially responsible mutual funds. *Financial Analysts Journal, 56*(3), 3039.

Statman, M. (2007). *Socially responsible investors and their advisors*. Working paper, Santa Clara University. Retrieved from the internet at www.ssrn.com

Statman, M. (2008). *The expressive nature of socially responsible investors*. Working paper, Santa Clara University. Retrieved from the internet at www.ssrn.com

Steurer, R. (2010). The role of governments in corporate social responsibility: Characterising public policies on CSR in Europe. *Policy Sciences*, *43*(1), 49–72. doi:10.100711077-009-9084-4

Stiglitz, J. E. (2003). *Globalization and its discontents*. New York: Norton.

Stone, B. K., Guerard, J. B., Gületkin, M. N., & Adams, G. (2001). *Socially responsible investment screening: Strong evidence of no significant cost for actively managed portfolios*. Working paper. Retrieved from the internet at http://www.socialinvest.org/pdf/research/Moskowitz/2001%20Honorable%20Mention %20-%20Moskowitz.pdf

Taylor, N. (2003). Understanding taxpayer attitudes through understanding taxpayer identities. In V. Braithwaite (Ed.), *Taxing Democracy. Understanding Tax Avoidance and Evasion* (pp. 71–92). Aldershot: Ashgate.

Teoh, S. H., Welch, I., & Wazzan, C. P. (1999). The effect of socially activist investment politics on the financial markets: Evidence from the South African boycott. *The Journal of Business*, *72*(1), 35–89. doi:10.1086/209602

Thaler, R. H., & Sunstein, C. R. (2008). *Nudge: Improving decisions about health, wealth, and happiness*. New Haven, CT: Yale University Press.

Thorndike, J. J., & Ventry, D. J. J. (2002). *Tax justice: The ongoing debate*. Washington, DC: The Urban Institute Press.

Tippet, J. (2001). Performance of Australia's ethical funds. *The Australian Economic Review*, *34*(2), 170–178. doi:10.1111/1467-8462.00186

Tippet, J., & Leung, P. (2001). Defining ethical investment and its demography in Australia. *Australian Accounting Review*, *11*(3), 44–55. doi:10.1111/j.1835-2561.2002.tb00389.x

Torgler, B. (2003a). Tax morale in transition countries. *Post-Communist Economies*, *15*(3), 357–381. doi:10.1080/1463137032000139052

Torgler, B. (2003b). Tax morale, rule-governed behavior and trust. *Constitutional Political Economy*, *14*(2), 119–140. doi:10.1023/A:1023643622283

Torgler, B. (2003c). To evade taxes or not to evade: That is the question. *Journal of Socio-Economics*, *32*(3), 283–302. doi:10.1016/S1053-5357(03)00040-4

Trevino, L. K., & Nelson, K. A. (2004). *Managing business ethics: Straight talk about how to do right*. Hoboken, NJ: Wiley.

Tyler, T. R. (2001a). Public trust and confidence in legal authorities: What do majority and minority group members want from the law and legal institutions? *Behavioral Sciences & the Law*, *19*(2), 215–235. doi:10.1002/bsl.438 PMID:11385699

Tyler, T. R. (2001b). Trust and law abidingness: A proactive model of social regulation. *Boston University Law Review. Boston University. School of Law*, *81*(2), 361–406.

Tyler, T. R., & Lind, E. A. (1992). A relational model of authority in groups. In M. P. Zanna (Ed.), Advances in Experimental Social Psychology (pp. 115–191). San Diego, CA: Academic Press. doi:10.1016/S0065-2601(08)60283-X

Veblen, T. (1994). *The theory of the leisure class: An economic study of institutions*. New York: Dover. (Original work published 1899)

Voorhes, M. (1999). *The US divestment movement: How sanctions work: Lessons from South Africa*. New York: St. Martin's.

Waldman, D. A., Siegel, D., & Javidian, M. (2004). *Transformational leadership and corporate social responsibility*. Working paper, January 2004. Retrieved from the internet at http://www.sristudies.org/Waldman+et+al+(2004)

Webster, F. E. Jr. (1975). Determining the characteristics of the socially conscious consumer. *The Journal of Consumer Research*, *12*(2), 188–196. doi:10.1086/208631

Wenzel, M. (2002). The impact of outcome orientation and justice concerns on tax compliance: The role of taxpayers' identity. *The Journal of Applied Psychology*, *87*(4), 629–645. doi:10.1037/0021-9010.87.4.629 PMID:12184568

Wenzel, M. (2003). Tax compliance and the psychology of justice: Mapping the field. In V. Braithwaite (Ed.), *Taxing democracy: Understanding tax avoidance and evasion* (pp. 41–69). Aldershot: Ashgate.

Wetzel, W. E., & Freear, J. (1996). Promoting informal venture capital in the United States: Reflections on the history of the venture capital network. In R. T. Harrison & C. M. Mason (Eds.), *Informal Venture Capital: Evaluating the Impact of Business Introduction Services* (pp. 61–74). Hemel Hempstead: Woodhead-Faulkner.

Williams, G. (2005). *Are socially responsible investors different from conventional investors? A comparison across six countries*. Unpublished working paper, University of Bath.

Wilson, E. O. (1975). *Sociobiology*. Cambridge, MA: Harvard University Press.

Wright, P., & Ferris, S. (1997). Agency conflict and corporate strategy: The effect of divestment on corporate value. *Strategic Management Journal*, *18*(1), 77–83. doi:10.1002/(SICI)1097-0266(199701)18:1<77::AID-SMJ810>3.0.CO;2-R

Zak, P. J. (2008). *Moral markets: The critical role of values in the economy*. Princeton: Princeton University Press.

Zeff, E., & Pirro, E. (1999). *Redistribution of authority: The South African case*. Washington, D.C.: International Studies Association.

Ziegler, A., Rennings, K. & Schröder, M. (2002). *Der Einfluss ökologischer und sozialer Nachhaltigkeit auf den Shareholder Value europäischer Aktiengesellschaften*. Diskussionspapier 02-32, Zentrum für Europäische Wirtschaftsforschung.

ENDNOTES

1 Spiegel online retrieved from the internet in January 2009 at http://www.spiegel.de/spiegel/0,1518,589895,00.html

2 European Social Investment Forum report retrieved from the internet in January 2009 at http://www.eurosif.org/

3 European Social Investment Forum retrieved from the internet in January 2009 at http://www.eurosif.com/publications/sri_studies

4 European Social Investment Forum report retrieved from the internet in January 2009 at http://www.eurosif.org/

5 Who cares wins: Connecting financial markets to a changing world: Recommendations by the financial industry to better integrate environmental, social and governance issues in analysis, asset management and securities brokerage. The United Nations Global Compact office. Retrieved from the internet in November 2007 at http://www.unglobalcompact.org/docs/news_events/8.1/WhoCaresWins.pdf

6 Deutsche Welle, September 13, 2004.

7 Retrieved from the internet in March 2008 at http://www.sudanreeves.org/Article14.html 21 Retrieved from the internet in March 2008 at http://www.sudanreeves.org/Article14.html

8 Retrieved from the internet in March 2008 at http://www.democracynow.org/2006/3/27/blood_money_as_divestiture_movement_heats

9 Retrieved from the internet in March 2008 at http://georgemiller.house.gov/Darfurdivestment4-26-06.html

10 Retrieved from the internet in March 2008 at http://sudanwatch.blogspot.com/2006/09/uss-schwarzenegger-signs-pensionfund.html

11 Retrieved from the internet in March 2008 at http://fidelityoutofsudan.googlepages.com/fidelity'smay15secfiling

12 Retrieved from the internet in March 2008 at http://www.wbur.org/news/2007/69046_20070726.asp

13 Retrieved from the internet in March 2008 at http://www.sudandivestment.org/home.asp

14 Retrieved from the internet in March 2008 at http://www.amnestyusa.org/document.php?id=ENGUSA20071220001&lang=e

15 Retrieved from the internet in March 2008 at http://www.sudandivestment.org/docs/msci_indices_press_release_1_7_07.pdf

16 Retrieved from the internet in March 2008 at http://www.sudandivestment.org/home.asp

17 Retrieved from the internet in March 2008 at http://www.sudandivestment.org/divestment.asp

18 Retrieved from the internet in March 2008 at http://fidelityoutofsudan.blogspot.com/

19 Retrieved from the internet in March 2008 at http://www.sudandivestment.org/divestment.asp

20 Retrieved from the internet in March 2008 at http://www.sudandivestment.org/home.asp

21 Retrieved from the internet in March 2008 at http://www.sudandivestment.org/home.asp

22 Sudan Divestment Trust Fund report retrieved from the internet in March 2008 at http://www.sudandivestment.org/divestment.asp

23 Sudan Divestment Trust Fund report retrieved from the internet in March 2008 at http://www.sudandivestment.org/divestment.asp

Section 2
Empirical Part

Chapter 4
Empirical Part

ABSTRACT

The empirical investigation is targeted at describing corporate and financial social responsibilities within market systems with a special attention to global governance provision under the auspice of international organizations. Expert interviews on CSR and SRI aim at understanding social welfare notions of public and private actors. The innovative combination of corporate and government in PPP social service provision will be analyzed with a focus on the network start-up phase. The impact of political divestiture as a means of financial social responsibility, but also measurement impediments will be subject to scrutiny. The exploration of social and psychological SRI motives will complement classic finance theories by behavioral economics insights.

INTRODUCTION

As of today social responsibility has emerged into an *en vogue* topic for corporate executives, governmental officials, international public servants and stakeholder representatives. Due to globalization, worldwide business mergers, but also as for international deficiencies beyond the scope of nation states; the call for CSR and SRI has reached unprecedented momentum (Ahmad, 2008; Beck, 1998; Levitt, 1983; Livesey, 2002, Scholte, 2000). In the wake of the 2008/09 World Financial Recession, corporate social misconduct and financial fraud have steered consumers and investors to increasingly pay attention to democracy and social responsibility within market systems. Current stakeholder pressure addresses social responsibility of market actors

DOI: 10.4018/978-1-5225-7619-8.ch004

and information disclosure of corporate and financial conduct. Legislative reforms enhance the accountability of financial market operations. With the era of liberalization being halted by the 2008/09 World Financial Recession, the reinterpretation of the public-private sector roles in providing social services has leveraged social responsibility into a pressing topic of debate. The renaissance of attention to responsibility as a prerequisite for the functioning of economic systems portrays CSR and SRI as windows of opportunity to re-establish trust in fallible market systems (Little, 2008; Livesey, 2002; Matten & Crane, 2005; Trevino & Nelson, 2004). As for all these trends, the research explores up-to-date issues of concern.

The empirical investigation targets at describing corporate and financial social responsibilities within market systems. The role of responsibility within market systems will be studied in CSR and SRI as well as global governance provision in PPPs and political divestiture.

As a newly emerging multi-stakeholder phenomenon, **CSR** is challenged by a plethora of concurrent social responsibility notions that imply communication barriers among various constituents in their pursuit of multiple goals (Mohr et al., 2001; Pandey & Wright, 2006).

Featuring a counter-parting role in providing societal welfare, corporate executives and governmental officials are likely to hold onto differing standpoints on social responsibility. Conflicting interests of public and private actors in the administration of social responsibility imply economic and societal losses.

As a first step towards a unified CSR approach, civil servants' attributions of the role of corporations in social welfare provision will become subject to scrutiny. In the corporate domain, public officials are key constituents to promote CSR. Public servants play a pivotal role in crafting respective social policies, raising awareness among corporate executives and incentivizing corporate decision makers for societal responsibility. However, the current CSR body of knowledge and research are scarce on governmental officials' opinion on social responsibility.

The empirical research will survey civil servants' understanding of social responsibility to contrast corporate and governmental perspectives on social responsibility. Investigating the perceived motives for exhibiting social conscientiousness of corporate actors will delineate circumstances under which CSR is likely to occur and by which corporate social conduct can be triggered. Featuring a symbiotic yet counter-parting role in providing societal welfare, the relation of governments and corporations in contributing to societal obligations is attributed. Governmental officials' perception of the chances and risks of corporations administering social responsibility will outline the advantages and disadvantages of the corporate sector taking over governmental social responsibilities. Analyzing corporations' role as 'governmental step-ins' in social service provision will help diminishing downfalls of CSR and conflicts embedded in the multiple parties evolved.

Overall, expert interviews with public administrators on social responsibility of corporations will complement primarily corporate-focused CSR research. Being knowledgeable about public administrators' view of CSR will foster an effecting social responsibility implementation by the productive interplay of public and private sector forces. Depicting governmental representatives' view of CSR will help lowering constraints for a successful corporate social conduct. Public officials' perceptions of advantages and risks of corporations taking over social responsibility will help aligning the interests and goals of corporate executives and public sector officials in social service provision. Adding information to the current discussion on public and private sector social responsibility will allow predicting future societal trends on global governance.

In addition, the empirical investigation will attribute **PPPs** as an emerging global governance phenomenon. By combining public and private sector forces for addressing civil society calls, PPPs enhance societal responsibility. On a global scale, international organizations administer partnerships by bringing together corporations with civil society to ingrain responsibility in public and private endeavors.

Multi-stakeholder PPP relationships can be bound by the diversity of various parties involved. PPP constituents may hold onto differing views, conflicting interests and counter-parting objectives. This is foremost the case in hybrid partnerships that can comprise governmental officials, donors, NGOs and community organizations. Especially during the start-up phase, partners are challenged by aligning disparate views on the creation of sustainable partnership structures. As the scientific discourse on the establishment of multi-stakeholder PPPs by the help of international organizations is scarce, a partnership set-up process will become subject to scrutiny with a special attention to the guidelining role of umbrella organizations.

The following research will shed light on the launch of the GAID PPP under the auspice of the UN. The investigation will cover the degree to which partners and flagship initiatives have begun their activities on ICT for development. The start-up progress of the GAID PPP network will be descriptively analyzed for its effectiveness in bringing together key constituents, raising public awareness for ICT, facilitating identification with ICT and creating an enabling environment for the implementation of ICT for development. Overall, the analysis is targeted at capturing the extent to which GAID has geared the global ICT agenda towards the accomplishment of the UNMDGs.

The evaluation of the GAID alliance may pave the ground for recommendations on how to launch PPPs and intensify the cooperation of the public and private sectors in administering social responsibility. Research on the implementation and management of PPPs under the auspice of international organizations will generate long-term success factors of international partnerships. The qualitative description of the network building will increase the insight on positive input factors during the establishment of PPPs, but also shed light on set-up deficiencies in order to derive implications for the planning and development of partnerships. All these endeavors serve the greater goal of efficiently mobilizing harmoniously accorded public and private sector forces for international development.

Concurrent with the rise of CSR, the demand for financial social responsibility has grown, yet the scientific coverage of SRI remains scarce. In the domain of **political divestiture**, empirical evidence is primarily based on historical and anecdotal data that leaves out the impact of divestiture on corporations and markets.

In an attempt to investigate financial markets' potential to steer societal and political change, the current body of knowledge on and state-of-the-art measurement of political divestiture will become subject to scrutiny. An evaluation of political divestiture studies will describe the role of political events and public pressure in triggering political divestiture. A metaanalysis of research on investments in South Africa during the Apartheid era will shed light on whether stakeholder pressure has encouraged political divestiture and impacted on corporate profitability. Generalizing insights on the effectiveness of political divestiture will help deriving success factors of political divestiture and explain the effects of foreign investment drain on corporations and society.

The impact of political divesture is foremost captured by event study designs – a method, which has scarcely been subject to evaluations. A planned meta-analysis of divestiture studies will critically examine the event study design based on standardized methodology evaluation criteria. A qualitative analysis of the methodological measurement of political divestiture will reveal advantages and critical aspects of the description of financial social responsibility. The discussion of the current state-of-the-art methodology will help generating a standardized research design for capturing the effects of financial social responsibility on economic and societal systems. Describing the impact of past political divestiture cases holds the potential to conclude on current political downfalls – such as in the case of the current humanitarian crisis in the Sudanese Darfur region.

In today's finance literature, **SRI** has become a prominent term. The importance of financial markets in international development has been attributed by the 2006 Nobel Peace Price awarded to Muhammad Yunus and the Grameen Bank for creating socially attentive banking systems. In the wake of the micro-finance revolution, SRI has been addressed in the World Economic Forum 2009 and found expression in public advocacy in the UN PRI (Ahmad, 2008). The current financial crisis leveraging the demand for transparency and accountability of financial markets perpetuates the drive towards SRI. For the future, economists and trend analysts attribute the emergence of SRI the potential to lift entire market industries into a more socially conscientious level – if the majority of investors are social responsibility and social conscientiousness becomes a feature of everyday's financial decision making.

Given the rising demand of social responsibility within market systems, the common body of knowledge on SRI is fairly limited. Empirical studies on SRI are rare with the current body of research primarily targeting at efficiency and financial correlates of SRI. The insights on socially responsible investors address demographic variables and lifestyle factors, but mainly neglect socio-psychological motives. While market studies foremost focus on economic fundamentals, the knowledge on socio-psychological components of socially responsible financial decision making is scarce. Mild attention has been paid to financial opinion leaders' view of SRI given their potential to support and advocate for innovative financial options. In addition, until today the contributing factors to the rise of SRI and success factors of financial social responsibility are unexplained.

As a multi-stakeholder phenomenon, various actors impact on the management of financial social responsibility (Cuesta & Valor, 2007; Little, 2008; Rosen et al., 1991; Williams, 2005). As a novel topic under debate, multiple SRI constituents may lack a standardized SRI notion, which limits their understanding of social responsibility within financial market systems and hinders the overall communication on SRI (Bruyn, 1987). As investors differ in their social concerns, priorities and tactics to address financial social responsibility, SRI features a plethora of forms of expression (Cooper & Schlegelmilch, 1993; Frankel, 1984; Pandey & Wright, 2006). In order to promote a successful rise of SRI, an understanding of the essential stakeholders' perception of SRI and their attribution of success factors for financial social responsibility is key.

The following research will therefore examine market agents' perception of SRI. As a first step towards a unified SRI approach, the common consent on SRI of financial experts will be investigated. Expert interviews will focus on social and psychological factors attributing to financial social conscientiousness. In the search for deriving information on SRI as a future means to re-establish trust on financial markets, the interviews will address the optimum interplay of deregulated market systems and governmental control in financial social responsibility. Underlying causes and triggers for SRI will be retrieved with a special attention to socio-psychological motives. In addition, the expert interviews will cover success factors of SRI in the light of the 2008/09 World Financial Recession.

The overarching research goals are to define SRI in its various forms and foci, explore sociopsychological facets of financial social responsibility as well as gather information on success factors for SRI – in the light of the 2008/09 World Financial Recession. Paying attention to the ambiguity and complexity of the phenomenon, exploratory expert interviews on SRI will depict mutually shared contents of financial social investment. Understanding financial leaders' SRI notions serves as a first step to resolve societal losses imbued in the novelty, complexity and ambiguity of the phenomenon. Exploring the multi-faceted influences that attribute the SRI demand will outline success factors of financial social responsibility. Gaining a more sophisticated understanding of financial social responsibility will help finding repeatable patterns and crafting policies to trigger SRI within financial markets. Describing key market agents' views on SRI will lead to managerial implications for the implementation of SRI. Being knowledgeable about socio-psychological facets of financial social responsibility may propel SRI to become a mainstream feature of financial decision making with the greater goal of fostering positive societal change.

In summary, the following empirical investigations focus on (1) how various stakeholders perceive CSR and SRI with a special attention to the 2008/09 World Financial Recession, (2) how social responsibility is implemented in PPPs for international development, (3) what mechanisms enhance the effectiveness of political divestiture and how political divestiture is measured (4) what socio-economic motives underlie SRI. In a nested approach, the empirical part will feature qualitative and quantitative methods comprising free association-based interviews, a methodological meta-analysis as well as

Table 1. Research design

Research Design
CSR
1. Exploratory analysis of public servants' CSR notion
■ In what way is CSR defined and perceived by public administrators?
■ What motives are attributed by public servants as triggers for CSR?
■ What advantages and risks are perceived by public administrators for corporations taking over governmental responsibilities?
→ **Aim:** Derive an understanding of public administrators' notions of CSR, CSR motives, advantages and risks of the corporate sector administering social responsibility.
Methodology: Exploratory free association technique to depict collective social representations on CSR.
Operationalization: Expert survey of 22 public administrators.
2. Exploratory data analysis of the GAID initiative set-up endeavors
■ By which means has the GAID PPP brought together key constituents involved in ICT for development, raised public awareness for ICT and established sustainable partnership structures?
→ **Aim:** Derive implications for the set-up phase of PPPs under the auspice of international organizations.
Methodology: Qualitative data analysis.
Operationalization: Qualitative data analysis, interviews and stakeholder correspondence.
SRI
3. Political divestiture as a means of financial social responsibility
■ Does divestment from politically incorrect market result in a corporate market value changes?
→ **Aim:** Determine the impact of political divestiture on corporations.
Hypothesis 1: Corporations divesting politically incorrect markets will experience a market value decrease (due to losses of degrees of freedom and access to economically profitable market options), increase (due to attracted socially conscientious investors and lifted consumer boycotts) or no change in market value (due to the minor proportion of political divestiture of the overall market).
Hypothesis 2: Corporations that remain in politically incorrect markets are more likely to experiencing a decrease (due to economic downturns of divestiture markets), increase in market value (due to monopolistic advantages) or no change in market value (due to the minor proportion of political divestiture of the overall market).
■ In what way is the event study methodology a valid measurement of the impact of political divestiture on corporate success?
→ **Aim:** Evaluating methodological aspects of the measurement of political divestiture.
Methodology: Meta-analysis of studies on the impact of divestiture on corporate profitability with attention to methodological aspects.
Operationalization: Meta-analysis of six descriptive evaluations of political divestiture studies of historical events triggering publicly traded corporations to leave South Africa and institutional investors to sell their holdings in corporations operating in South Africa.
4. Socio-psychological motives for exhibiting SRI
■ In what way is SRI defined and perceived by market agents?
→ **Aim:** To derive a definition and depict the perception of SRI of financial market agents.
■ What motives trigger financial experts to exhibit SRI?
→ **Aim:** Outline socio-psychological motives of financial experts to exhibit socially responsible investment.
■ What success factors are attributed to SRI in the light of the 2008 financial crisis?
→ **Aim:** Find success factors of SRI in the wake of the 2008 financial crisis.
Methodology: Exploratory expert interviews on the perception of SRI will be qualitatively analyzed.
Operationalization: Expert interviews with 94 financial executives at the NYSE.

a descriptive implementation analysis. An overview of the research design is given in Table 1.

Overall, the research may delineate the dynamics and implementation of social responsibility within markets in the interplay of the public and private sectors as well as financial markets.

The empirical part describes public and private actors' perception of CSR and SRI to overcome information deficiencies within the stakeholder community and lower the complexity of these newly emerging phenomena. CSR and SRI stakeholder perceptions provide a sophisticated understanding of social welfare provision in the interplay of deregulated market systems and governmental control.

Depicting the implementation of corporate and financial social responsibility in global governance PPPs derives triggers, impact and success factors for the establishment of international networks to alleviate social deficiencies and improve societal conditions.

Research on political divestiture holds the potential for governments to reach corporations on political concerns (Steurer, 2010). Evaluating up-to-date research on political divestiture will increase the effectiveness of financial social responsibility and allow promoting SRI within the financial community. Addressing measurement deficiencies of political divestiture will help generating alternative SRI measurement techniques.

Synthesizing the experience of key market actors with SRI will allow attributing success factors of financial social responsibility. Information on socio-psychological motives of socially responsible investors may add behavioral insights to classic financial market theories. Research on SRI during the outbreak of the 2008/09 World Financial Recession helps understanding SRI as a means to re-establish trust in financial global governance to foster financial market stability as a prerequisite for sustainable market economies.

In summary, the proposed research may serve as first step towards resolving conflicts embedded in the ambiguity of relatively newly emerging CSR and SRI phenomena. The research is targeted at a successful rise of social responsibility within modern market economies to become mainstream economic trends. Implications for corporate management, global governance as well as financial decision making theory and practice may foster financial stability and sustainable market economies as future guarantors of sustainable societal progress.

Social responsibility within market systems will be explored in interviews with public servants and financial managers to capture expert opinions on CSR and SRI.

Analyzing CSR through the lenses of public administrators will help identifying governmental actor-specific expectations onto corporate social conduct as well as critically examine opportunities and risks of CSR. Gaining an understanding of social servants' CSR view will reduce the absence of a unified social responsibility notion, which currently puts a stem on a more effective CSR communication and performance.

Socially responsible global governance provision is studied by the case of PPPs and political divestiture. Multiple stakeholders' views and collaborative efforts to set up a partnership will be gathered for recommending successful management efforts at all levels of the partnerships.

The second part attributes recent trends in financial social responsibility in the form of political divestiture and SRI.

Political divestiture will be scrutinized as for providing a stakeholder means for fostering positive societal change. Political divestitures' impact on corporate success will be outlined, which is aimed at deriving practical implications for corporate executives. Conclusions about the state-of-the-art political divestiture study designs will spearhead methodological advancements on measuring financial social responsibility.

In the case of SRI, a deeper understanding of SRI notions and practices will grant insights on how to reduce the current ambiguity of the phenomenon. Outlining current trends of research on SRI is aimed at giving practical advice to financial executives and governance providers for a successful rise of SRI.

Overall addressing multi-stakeholder perspectives on CSR and SRI will allow deriving codes of conduct and international guidelines on corporate and financial social responsibility. This endeavor may further the integration and application of responsibility into current market systems given respective market constraints. The conclusions target at fostering a successful harmonization, implementation and administration of social responsibility within the modern market economies.

PUBLIC SERVANTS' VIEW OF CSR

As a newly emerging multi-stakeholder phenomenon, CSR is challenged by a plethora of concurrent social responsibility notions. Featuring a counter-parting role in providing societal welfare, corporate executives and governmental officials hold onto differing standpoints on social responsibility that imply communication and implementation barriers of social service provision. As a first step towards a unified CSR approach, civil servants' attributions of the role of corporations in social welfare provision have been investigated. Capturing social servants' view of CSR provides information for future corporate social conduct, but also sheds light on chances and risks of the corporate sector taking over governmental social responsibilities. In describing the common body of knowledge on CSR and identifying state actor-specific nuances, a more sophisticated understanding of the overall CSR conduct is sought. Gaining knowledge on social motives and public administrators' view of CSR may serve as a fruitful addition to the primarily corporation-based CSR research. Overall the research may be seen as a first step towards resolving socio-economic losses and conflicts embedded in the ambiguity of the phenomenon and thereby provide a guideline for a successful CSR implementation.

Research Questions and Hypotheses

An exploratory analysis of CSR notions addressed the following questions:

1. In what way is CSR defined and perceived by public administrators?
2. What social motives trigger corporations to exhibit CSR?
3. What advantages and risks do public administrators attribute to corporations taking over governmental responsibilities?

Operationalization

In total, 22 Master of Public Administration candidates of the Maxwell School of Citizenship and Public Affairs, who had substantial working experience in the public sector, were surveyed on their perception of CSR as well as the chances and risks implied in corporations taking over governmental responsibilities (see Questionnaire, Appendix A).

Sample Description: The non-representative sample comprised 22 English-speaking public service experts of the Master of Public Administration program of the Maxwell School of Citizenship and Public Affairs (Syracuse University, NY, US). The respondents had prior education and work experiences in *Business and Finance* (4 individuals accounting for 18.2 percent); *Arts,*

Table 2. Sample description

Sample n = 22		
Former education and professional experience	*n*	**Percent**
Business / Finance	4	18.2
Art / Humanities / Media	5	22.7
Politics / Public Service	13	59.1

Humanities and Media (5 individuals, 22.7 percent) as well as *Politics and Public Service* (13 individuals, 59.1 percent) as exhibited in Table 2.

Material

Questionnaire: The survey was based on a two-page questionnaire. Four open-ended questions targeted at collecting free associations on *CSR, social motives for administering CSR* as well as *opportunities and risks of corporations* being socially responsible (see Table 3).

Data Collection

The study was carried out on October 10, 2007 with Master of Public Administration candidates of the Maxwell School of Citizenship and Public

Table 3. Questionnaire

Questionnaire	
Free associations	**Description**
CSR	**Q1:** What comes to mind when you think of "Corporate Social Responsibility?" Write down the first five associations, notions, and feelings you have. Your answer may contain nouns, verbs, and adjectives and can be formulated in sentences, statements, phrases and/or single words. For each association, indicate if it is positive (+), neutral (~) or negative (–).
Social motives triggering CSR	**Q2:** What **social motives** do you think influence corporations to exhibit social responsibility? Write down the first associations that come to mind and indicate for each if it is positive (+), neutral (~) or negative (–).
Opportunities and risks of CSR	**Q3:** What **opportunities and risks** do you think are implied in corporations providing social responsibility – especially in the light of corporations standing in for state actors? Write down the first five associations that come to mind.
Previous education and/or profession	**Q4:** Choose one field that applies best to your previous education and/or profession: Business / Economics / Finance / Investment Arts / Humanities / Media Politics / Public Service

Affairs at Syracuse University. All 22 respondents of the convenience sample participated on a voluntary basis.

METHOD: SOCIAL REPRESENTATIONS

Theoretical Foundation

Based on Durkheim's (1898) concept of collective representations, Serge Moscovici (1961) studied social perceptions of economic changes and developed the theory of social representations. Social representations mirror individual perceptions of mutually shared and collectively discussed concepts. Social representations contain information presented in the media, transmitted by word-of-mouth and social interactions. As a collective amalgamation of individual perceptions, social representations grant orientation, guide the behavior of market constituents and trigger the diffusion of ideas (DeRosa, 1994; Moscovici, 1984). Social representations describe the societal genesis of collective notions of economic phenomena (Moscovici, 1961). Studying social representations allows describing societal perceptions of economic phenomena and deriving behavioral consequences on a collective basis. Knowledge about the contents of social representations provides an opportunity to predict individual behavior and forecast collective societal trends. Social representations are captured by projective methods such as the free associating technique.

Free Association Technique

In the free association technique, respondents are asked to reflect on topics and write down their notions about it. The associations are categorized to capture their aggregated content. Free associating studies describe the subjective interpretation of collectively held notions. The descriptive and exploratory character depicts the societal common sense of knowledge close to the pulse of its constituents. The free associating technique has become a prominent method in socio-economic research and practice as for helping to predict individual behavioral tendencies, collective notions and societal trends (Roland-Lévy, Kirchler, Penz & Gray, 2001; The Human Relations Movement, 2008). To understand the various nuances of market agents' views, categorizations and Core-and-Periphery analysis are used.

Core-and-Periphery Analysis

Core-and-Periphery analyses divert free associations into a stable common body of knowledge and variable contents of social perceptions (Abric, 1993; Meier, 2000). As a posthoc word association technique, in this method free associations are categorized based on the *relative frequency* and the *rank of words* in the individual word flow. The categorization divides associations into fundamental, prototypical core definitions and more descriptive peripheral elements (Abric, 1993; Moliner, 1995; Vergès & Tyszka, 1994; Wagner, Valencia & Elejabarrieta, 1996). Paying attention to the sequence of associations diverts spontaneous emotional thoughts from more cognitively reflective evaluations. By separating central core values from fluent peripheral viewpoints, the Core-and-Periphery analysis reveals the collective salience and individual components of notions. Methodologically, the categorized associations are summarized in a Pivot-Table based on the relative frequency and the rank of every word. The relative rank is weighted based on frequencies as exhibited in Figure 1.

To divide the associations into core and peripheral elements, cut-off scores comprise:

- The *average frequency of an association* based on the absolute frequency divided by the number of association categories.
- The *average rank* is the sum of total rank weight divided by the number of association categories.

Figure 1. Relative rank weight

$$\text{Relative rank weight (r)} = \frac{\sum (f_1 * 1) + (f_2 * 2) + (f_3 * 3) + (f_4 * 4) + \ldots + (f_n * n)}{f_t}$$

f_1 = absolute frequency of associations in 1st rank

f_n = absolute frequency of association in rank n

f_t = absolute frequency of association

Based on these cut-off scores, the Core-and-Periphery analysis distinguishes associations into core and peripheral elements (see Figure 2).

Frequent and spontaneous associations are located in the core, which comprises the main contents (Abric, 1984). Peripheral associations are more reflective, rational evaluations of objects that are also more prone to be individual assumptions and subject to changes (Vergès & Bastounis, 2001). New contents enter social representations as variable peripheral elements. Only some peripheral notions will maintain through time. Due to sustainable public discourse some peripheral elements may leverage into prototypical core elements of representations, however others may become abandoned over time (Flament, 1987; 1994).

Emotional Character

The emotional valence of respondents towards phenomena is measured by polarity indices. The polarity is based on the respondents' classification of the associations as positive (+), neutral (~), and negative (–). To evaluate the emotional character of the associations, a polarity index per person is generated by the number of positive words minus the number of negative words divided by the number of associations per person. The formula for the emotionality of social representations is exhibited in Figure 3.

Figure 2. Core-and-Periphery analysis

Frequency / Rank	High frequency (>average frequency)	Low frequency (<average frequency)
Low rank (<average rank)	Core	Periphery
High rank (>average rank)	Periphery	Periphery

Figure 3. Polarity index (DeRosa, 1994)

$$\text{Polarity Index (P)} = \frac{\text{Number of positive words} - \text{Number of negative words}}{\text{Total number of associations per person}}$$

RESULTS

Free Associations

The study was carried out on October 10, 2007 with Master of Public Administration candidates of the Maxwell School of Citizenship and Public Affairs at Syracuse University.

CSR: Overall, the 22 respondents named 113 free associations on CSR. On average a person had five English associations (m=5.14; *sd*=.77; md=5; mode=5; Range=[3; 7]). To verify the content of the associations, a category system was created based on theoretical assumptions.

Category System: In discussion with a student of the Newhouse School of Communication at Syracuse University a category system with 13 categories was established in an iterative process. Table 4 contains the extracted 13 categories and the 113 categorized associations.

To verify the reliability of the category system, the associations were rated by two independent individuals. The raters independently placed the associations into the retrieved categories. Statistical analysis revealed an interrater reliability of $K_{(\text{Cohen's Kappa})} = 0.48$ implying a moderate reliability of the generated category system. The final attribution of associations to the individual categories was based on the majority principle among the raters.

Description

How did public administrators experience CSR? Civil servants honored CSR to provide *societal value* (f=18; 15.93%). The respondents recalled *corporate examples* (f=13; 11.5%) and attributed the positive impact of CSR on *employees* (f=13; 11.5%). The *future potential* (f=12; 10.62%) of CSR was mentioned. CSR was described as a value-adding tool in *public relations* (f=10; 8.85%) and *shareholder* management (f=9; 7.96%). Also *negative aspects* (f=9; 7.96%) – such as *corporate expenses* (f=5; 4.42%) and CSR as *false statements* (f=5; 4.42%) of the *corporate policy* (f=4, 3.54%) in order

Table 4. Categories of public servants' associations to CSR

Category system			
Category	**Associations**	**f** [1]	**%** [2]
1. Societal value	a generous return; adding value to society; charity; doing the right thing; donate; giving; giving back to community; giving back to the community; honesty; honesty; improving peoples' lives; integrity; integrity; moving towards behavior of public sector; poverty; process vs. value; professional development for youth; supporting the surrounding community	18	15.93
2. Corporate examples	acronym CSR; Andrew Carnegie; Ben & Jerry's „Homemade"; big business; Bill Gates; corporations have done better or worse at corporate social responsibility during various times in history; Enron; multinational company; Phillip Morris' anti-smoking campaign; private foundation; Starbuck's; United States; Warren Buffett	13	11.50
3. Employees	adequate pay for employees; attracting workers; benefits; employee benefits; employees; fair wages; government to build employee loyalty; health benefits; improving employees' quality of life; lots of employees; maintaining worker trust; one of my friends wants to work on corporate responsibility; reducing turnover	13	11.50
4. Future potential	crisis prevention; decreasing trend; genuinely helpful; growing movement; idealistic; positive externality; potential; progressive; supporting academic research; they should / can do more; think tanks; well-intentioned	12	10.62
5. Public relations	advertising; changes in public perception; fair advertising; image; PR; PR; public relations; public relations; trust; window-dressing	10	8.85
6. Negative aspects	a class I do not want to take; controversy; corruption; discrimination; duty; making difficult decisions; necessity; negative externality; obligation	9	7.96
7. Shareholders	accountability; annual shareholder meetings; impact; independent board members; lobby groups; transparency; transparency; transparency; transparency	9	7.96

Category system			
Category	**Associations**	**f** [1]	%[2]
8. Environmental activism	environment; environment sustainability; environmental concern; environmentally conscience; going green; taking care of the environment	6	5.31
9. Competitive advantage	competing with others; elimination of competition; equal opportunity; increasing customer base; power	5	4.42
10. Expense	added expense; fiscal responsibility; lowered financial returns in exchange for increased "social returns"; tax responsibility; varies greatly	5	4.42
11. Fake	B.S. that companies say to get good PR; façade; fake; green-washing; proxy voting	5	4.42
12. Corporate policy	developing mission statement that expresses responsibility; important that corporations follow environment and other health regulations; optional on the part of corporation; reactive to laws	4	3.54
13. Ethics	being ethical; business ethics; ethics; ethics	4	3.54

n=22; Data collection: October 10, 2007 at The Maxwell School of Citizenship and Public Affairs, Syracuse University

to gain a *competitive advantage* (f=5; 4.42%) – came to mind. Concretely, *environmental activism* (f=6; 5.31%) and *ethics* (f=4; 3.54%) were associated with CSR. The absolute and relative frequencies of the associations on CSR are exhibited in Figure 4 and 5.

Emotional Character

In order to evaluate the emotions of the respondents towards CSR, a polarity index was calculated. The between –1 and +1 ranging words were classified as negative (range [-1; 0.05]), neutral (range [-0.04; 0.04]) and positive (range [0.05; 1]) by the respondents. The mean of the polarity index for n=22 was 0.24 (median=0.2; mode = -0.2; SD=0.51, Range [-1; 1]), which indicates an overall positive attitude towards CSR.

Figure 4. Absolute frequencies of associations on CSR

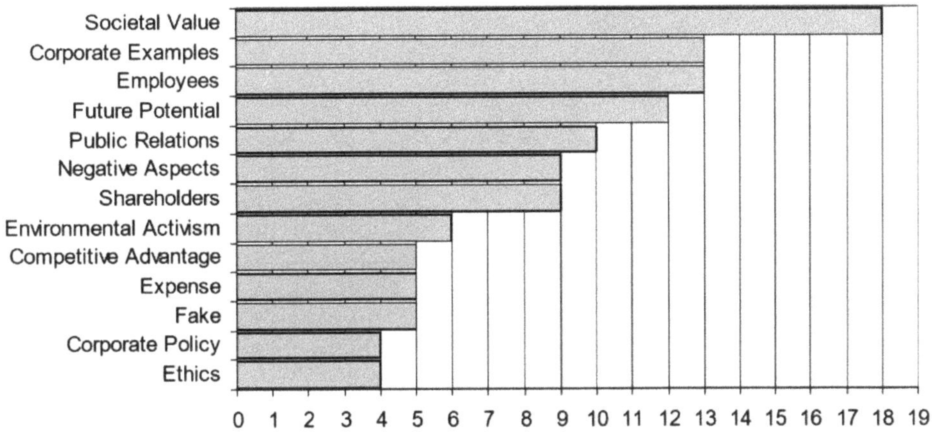

Figure 5. Relative frequencies of associations on CSR

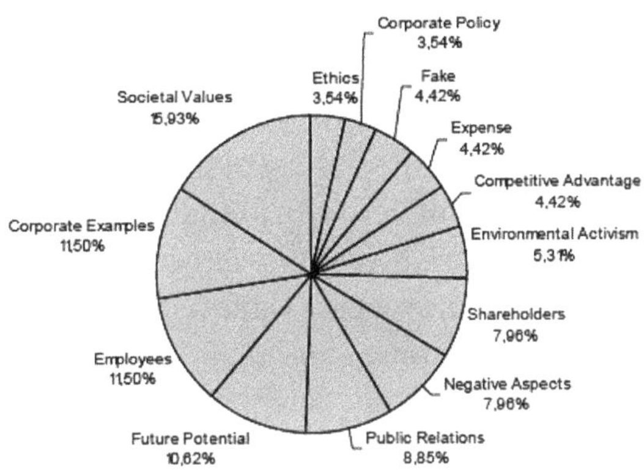

n=22; Data collection: October 10, 2007 at The Maxwell School of Citizenship and Public Affairs, Syracuse University

Core-and-Periphery Analysis

In order to analyze the quality of the associations, a Core-and-Periphery analysis was conducted (Roland-Lévy et al., 2001). The Core-and-Periphery analysis for the associations on CSR revealed distribution of associations into core and peripheral elements outlined in Figure 6.

The respondents' primary associations on CSR honor corporate social conduct as a means to create *societal value*, yet also being used as a *public relations* tool.

Figure 6. Core-and-Periphery analysis for associations on CSR

Frequency / Rank	High frequency (>8.62)	Low frequency (<8.62)
Low rank (<3.89)	Societal Value PR	Negative Aspects Shareholders Environmental Activism Fake Ethics
High rank (>3.89)	Corporate Examples Employees Future Potential	Competitive Advantage Expense Corporate Policy

n=22; Data collection: October 10, 2007 at The Maxwell School of Citizenship and Public Affairs, Syracuse University

CSR Motives: Overall, the 22 respondents named 110 free associations on CSR motives that trigger corporate actors to consider social responsibility. On average, a person had five English associations (m=4.95; sd=1.53; md=5; mode=5; Range=[2; 8]). To verify the content of the associations, a category system was created based on theoretical assumptions.

Category System: In discussion with a student of the Newhouse School of Communication at Syracuse University a category system with 10 categories was generated in an iterative process. Table 5 contains the 10 categories and the 110 categorized associations.

To verify the reliability of the category system, the associations were rated by two independent individuals. The raters independently placed the associations into the given categories. A calculated interrater reliability of $K_{(\text{Cohen's Kappa})} = 0.49$ revealed a moderate reliability of the generated category system.

Description

What motives do public administrators experience as key triggers for social responsibility? CSR was associated with a positive *corporate image* (f=17; 15.45%), that creates *competitive advantages* for corporations (f=7; 6.36%). *Intrinsic motives* (14; 12.73%) and *legal obligations* (14; 12.73%) raise CSR. Positive CSR aspects comprise *public relations* (f=11; 10%), *employee motivation* (14; 12.73%) and *stakeholder communication* advantages (f=13; 11.82%). *Economic factors* (f=11; 10%), *negative aspects* (f=5; 4.55%), but

Table 5. Categories of public servants' associations to social motives of CSR

Category system			
Category	**Associations**	**f** [3]	**%** [4]
1. Image	appearance; corporate image; good media coverage; good reputation; make them look good; marketing; marketing appeal; name recognition; Philipp Morris; prestige; public image; public image; public perception; rehabilitating brand; reputation; they look good; tradition	17	15.45
2. Intrinsic motives	altruistic leader; background; care about service; conscience; environmental activists; must return to poor; out of the goodness of their hearts; past experience; peace of mind; personal motivation of founders; philanthropically; self interest; self interest; sense of responsibility of lenders	14	12.73
3. Legal obligations	attorney advice; being pressured by government; big law firm; court mandated; government policy; governmental regulation; governmental requirements; laws and regulations; laws and taxes; legal; legal compliance; legal obligations; tax incentive?; tax write off?	14	12.73
4. Employees	altruistic employees somewhere in the company; boring work; disinterested; employee concerns; employee will; employees; employees; meant to build employee loyalty; improve HR; labour unions; motivation; satisfy employees; staff unions; unions	14	12.73
5. Stakeholder relation	demand from stakeholders; giving back to the community; good perception in the eyes of stock holders; improve well-being of local community; interest groups; interest groups; need for partnerships; pressure from interest groups, shareholders etc.; shareholder activism; shareholder activism; social pressure; ties to community; to give the appearance that you value stakeholders' opinions	13	11.82
6. Economy	desire for stability; economy; energy efficient; growing trend; lack of sales; private vs. public; profit; public vs. private; recognition of profit center; the business environment; trends in society	11	10.00
7. Public relations	community expectations; demand from public; desiring a good image in the community; gain society's trust; good relations with the community; PR; PR; public health; public relations; public relations; public relations	11	10.00

Category system			
Category	Associations	f[3]	%[4]
8. Competitive advantage	big bucks; competition; competition; Enron; others doing same thing; strong leadership; wanting to stand out (in a good way) among other corporations	7	6.36
9. Negative aspects	duty; expenses; lofty ideals; people exploiting socially responsibility; uncle Jim family member is a CEO of a major private corporation	5	4.55
10. Ethics	civic duty; being ethical; ethics; ethics problems	4	3.64

n=22; Data collection: October 10, 2007 at The Maxwell School of Citizenship and Public Affairs, Syracuse University

also *ethical notions* (f=4; 3.64%) were associated. The absolute frequencies of the associations to CSR motives are exhibited by Figure 7, the relative frequencies of the associations are outlined by Figure 8.

Emotional Character

In order to evaluate the emotions of the respondents towards CSR motives, a polarity index was calculated. The between –1 and +1 ranging words were classified as negative (range [-1; -0.05]), neutral (range [-0.04; 0.04]) and positive (range [0.05; 1]. The mean of the polarity index for n=22 was 0.14

Figure 7. Absolute frequencies of associations on social motives triggering CSR

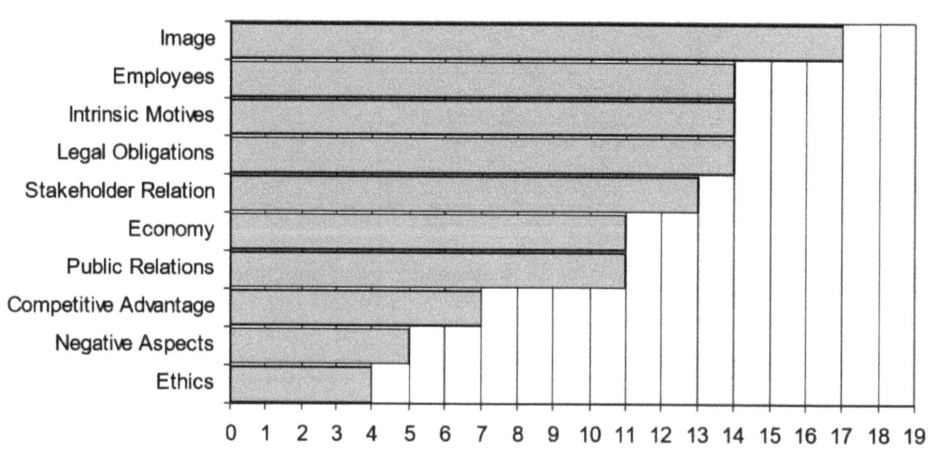

Figure 8. Relative frequencies of association on social motives triggering CSR

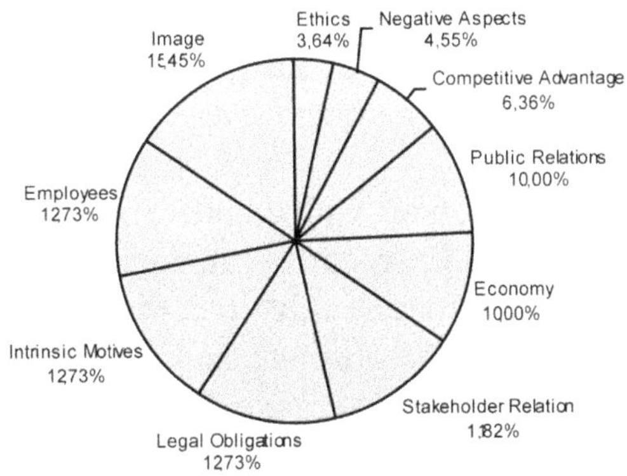

n=22; Data collection: October 10, 2007 at The Maxwell School of Citizenship and Public Affairs, Syracuse University

(median=0.2; mode = 0.6; SD=0.55, Range [-1.33; 2.13]), which indicates a positive attitude towards social motives for CSR.

Core-and-Periphery Analysis

Results: The Core-and-Periphery analysis for the associations on *CSR motives* revealed the following distribution of associations (see Figure 9):

The respondents mention the CSR potential to build a positive *image* with *stakeholders* based on *intrinsic motives* of corporate executives.

Figure 9. Core-and-Periphery analysis for associations on social motives for CSR

Frequency / Rank	High frequency (>11)	Low frequency (<11)
Low rank (<3.22)	Image Intrinsic Motives Stakeholder Relation	Public Relations Competitive Advantage
High rank (>3.22)	Employees Legal Obligations	Economy Negative Aspects Ethics

n=22; Data collection: October 10, 2007 at The Maxwell School of Citizenship and Public Affairs, Syracuse University

Opportunities: Overall, the 22 respondents named 76 free associations to **opportunities** of CSR. On average a person had four English associations (m=3.45; sd=1.82; md=3; mode=5; Range=[1; 7]). To verify the content of the associations, a category system was created based on theoretical assumptions.

Category System: In discussion with a student of the Newhouse School of Communication at Syracuse University a category system with 9 categories was created in an iterative process. Table 6 contains all categories and the 76 attributed associations. The absolute and relative frequencies of the associations on opportunities of CSR are exhibited in Table 6.

Table 6. Categories of public servants' associations to opportunities of CSR

Category system			
Category	**Associations**	**f**[5]	**%**[6]
1. Innovation	become change agents; different opinion; future business; huge impact; increased ability to make change; innovation; investment in underrepresented areas; market-driven change; new attitudes; new sector they are getting into; patents; profit in new areas; progress; to develop new goals for agency	14	18.42
2. Marketing	attracting more customers; big $; business; customer oriented; enhancement of image; good outlook; increased sales; marketing opportunities; media exposure; more loyal customers; positive reputation; reputation; set a standard customers might follow	13	17.11
3. Efficiency	$$ to be reached; big potential; corporations have $; efficiency; greater efficiency; increased efficiency; less bureaucracy; more cost effective; more efficiency; performance based; profits; quick responsiveness	12	15.79
4. Ethics	community outreach; corporations owe to the country and employees not just bottom line and their profits; employees morale; ethics; good to spend money on social needs; morals; more trust; psychological gratification; social perspective; to become socially responsible	10	13.16

Category system			
Category	Associations	f[5]	%[6]
5. Partnerships	better environment; better management; can be more supported by public; less governmental regulation; lower risk of governmental action; partnerships (for profit/non-profit or public/private); public/private partnerships can be win-win for both actors; unity	8	10.53
6. Employees	better employees; better, more loyal workers; better salaries; gain trust of workers; leadership; more jobs; stronger corporate community	7	9.21
7. Stakeholder relation	additional opinion; increased negotiating leverage; social support; stronger general community; the more you give back the more you gain; to integrate more with local/regional community	6	7.89
8. Access to resources	money; more resources; more resources than most non profits; they have lots of money	4	5.26
9. Flexibility	different then governmental or UN $ so can be more flexible; less constitutional obligations	2	2.63

n=22; Data collection: October 10, 2007 at The Maxwell School of Citizenship and Public Affairs, Syracuse University

To verify the reliability of the category system the associations were rated by two independent individuals. The interrater reliability of $K_{(\text{Cohen's Kappa})}=0.5$ reveals a moderate reliability of the generated category system.

Description

CSR is seen as an *innovative opportunity* (f=14; 18.42%) to *conduct business in an ethical way* (f=10; 13.16%), but also as an *efficient* (f=12; 15.79%) *marketing tool* (f=13; 17.11%). Within organizations CSR ensures *employee* satisfaction (f=7; 9.21%). CSR builds strong *partnerships* (f=8; 10.53%) with *stakeholders* (f=6; 7.98%), but also grants *access to resources* (f=4; 5.26%) and *flexibility* (f=2; 2.63%) in tackling social deficiencies. The absolute frequencies of the associations are exhibited in Figure 10, the relative frequencies of the associations in Figure 11.

Figure 10. Absolute frequencies of associations on opportunities of CSR

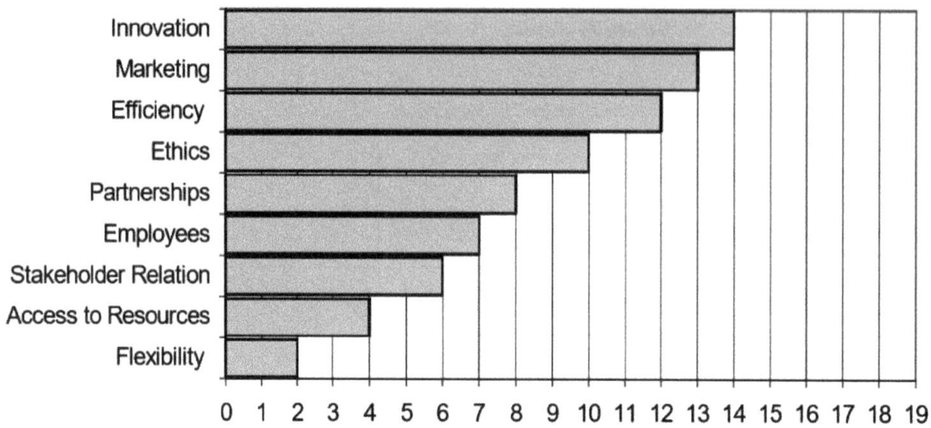

Figure 11. Relative frequencies of associations on opportunities of CSR

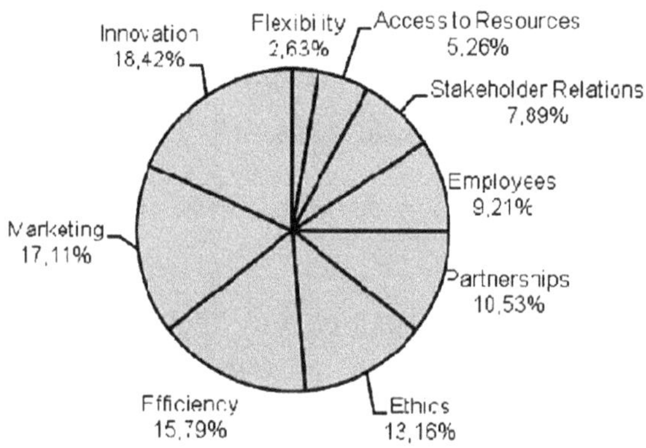

n=22; Data collection: October 10, 2007 at The Maxwell School of Citizenship and Public Affairs, Syracuse University

Core-and-Periphery Analysis

Results: The Core-and-Periphery analysis for the associations on opportunities of CSR exhibits the following distribution of associations (see Figure 12):

The respondents mention CSR *marketing* potentials that increase *efficiency*, build *partnerships* with stakeholders and satisfy *employees*.

Figure 12. Core-and-Periphery analysis for associations on opportunities of CSR

Frequency / Rank	High frequency (>8.33)	Low frequency (<8.33)
Low rank (<3.89)	Marketing Efficiency Partnerships Employees	Stakeholder Relations Access to Resources
High rank (>3.89)	Innovation Ethics	Flexibility

n=22; Data collection: October 10, 2007 at The Maxwell School of Citizenship and Public Affairs, Syracuse University

Risks: Overall, the 22 respondents named 66 free associations to risks embedded in corporations taking over social responsibility. On average a person had three English associations (m=3.00; sd=1.41; md=3; mode=2; Range=[1; 6]). To verify the content of the associations, a category system was created based on theoretical assumptions.

Category System: In discussion with a student of the Newhouse School of Communication at Syracuse University a category system with 9 categories was generated in an iterative process. Table 7 contains the categories and the 66 categorized associations. The absolute and relative frequencies of the associations on risks of CSR are exhibited in Figure 13 and 14.

To verify the reliability of the category system the associations were rated by two independent individuals. The interrater reliability of $K_{(\text{Cohen's Kappa})}=0.32$ reveals a relatively low reliability of the generated category system.

Description

As risks of CSR, public administrators mentioned *democratic deficiencies* (f=14; 20.90%). CSR imposes *expenses* (f=12; 17.91%), *liability problems* (f=8; 11.94%), *general risks* (f=8; 11.94%) and *inefficiency* (f=6; 8.96%), which may result in *diminished competitiveness* of corporations (f=6; 8.96%). *Dishonest corporate social conduct* (f=4; 5.97%) implies potential risks for the *stakeholder relations* (f=5; 7.46%). However, also positive aspects of CSR in terms of its *innovative character* are mentioned (f=4; 5.97%).

The absolute frequencies of the associations are exhibited in Figure 13. The relative frequencies of the associations are exhibited in Figure 14.

Table 7. Categories of public servants' associations to risks of CSR

Category system			
Category	**Associations**	**f**[7]	**%**[8]
1. Democratic failure	decisions are not democratic; democratic ideals violations; diminished social return; ineffective social responsibility policies; less constitutional competence; monopolies; more concerned with the profit line; not really motivated by public service; possibility of redundancy / overlap if not well communicated; selfish gain; they're not elected; they're only concerned with profits; unregulated by democratic guidance could assist preferred needs not all; US courts	14	20.90
2. Costs	added expense; big investment; increased costs; increasing cost; lack of funds; lower revenue (short-term); lowered investment returns; lowered profits; more paperwork!; more responsibility can lead to more hassle; no turning back from social responsibility; profit loss	12	17.91
3. Liability	governmental restrictions; increased liability (new); legal; legal jurisdiction; liabilities; liability as state actor; liability for non-profit agency actions; they can't be impeached	8	11.94
4. Risk	can backfire; engaging without investigating, may make unwise choices where to invest; loss of control; loss of control; might be more implicit focus; not as closely associated with organization; public backlash; risk revealing damaging info	8	11.94
5. Competitive advantage loss	competition; competition gaining on edge; lose sight of mission; loss of competitive advantage; loss of trust; other weaknesses exposed	6	8.96
6. Inefficiency	different priorities; inefficient; lack of control; not really trained to serve; not within area of expertise; value differences	6	8.96
7. Stakeholder Relation	angry shareholders; diminish social action; division; higher expectations; market response (unreceptive)	5	7.46
8. Fake	dishonesty; failure; just for sake of appearance; unproven business	4	5.97
9. Innovation	mechanize; public sector dissolves; removal of investment in typical areas; undermines system	4	5.97

n=22; Data collection: October 10, 2007 at The Maxwell School of Citizenship and Public Affairs, Syracuse University

Core-and-Periphery Analysis

Results: The Core-and-Periphery analysis for the associations on risks of CSR revealed the following distribution of associations (see Figure 15)

The core of the respondents' perception of *CSR risks* comprises *democratic failures*, *liability issues* as well as additional *costs*.

Figure 13. Absolute frequencies of associations on risks of CSR

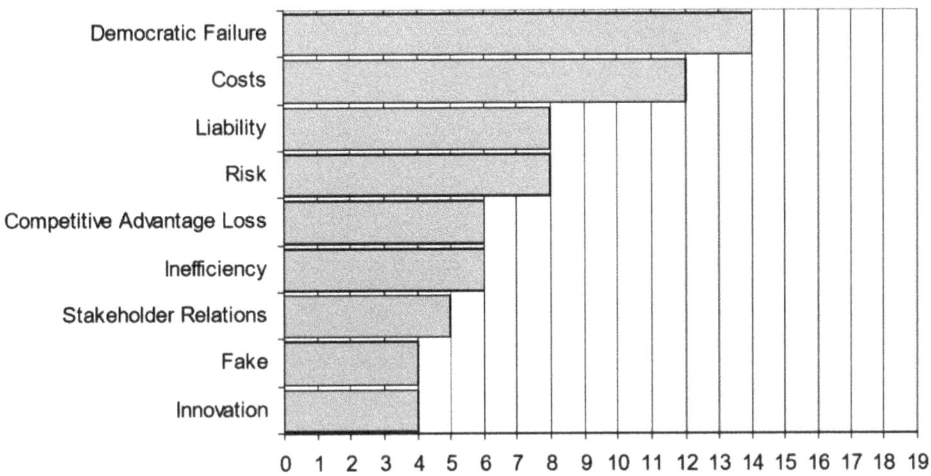

Figure 14. Relative frequencies of associations on risks of CSR

n=22; Data collection: October 10, 2007 at The Maxwell School of Citizenship and Public Affairs, Syracuse University

Correspondence Analysis

As the results lead to the assumption that CSR is a concept that polarizes among social servants, the sample was divided into respondents with positive, neutral or negative attitude towards CSR based on polarity indices. The cut off points were calculated in order to generate the following three groups (displayed in Table 8): Respondents with positive (range [1;.4]), neutral (range [-.1; .4]), and negative (range [-1; -.1]) attitude towards CSR (DeRosa, 1994).

The groups with different attitudes were related to the association categories within a frequency table. The X^2-distance of a correspondence analysis

Figure 15. Core-and-Periphery analysis for associations on risks of CSR

Rank \ Frequency	High frequency (>7.44)	Low frequency (<7.44)
Low rank (<2.34)	Democratic Failure Costs Liability Risk	Fake
High rank (>2.34)	Competitive Advantage Loss Inefficiency	Stakeholder Relations Innovation

n=22; Data collection: October 10, 2007 at The Maxwell School of Citizenship and Public Affairs, Syracuse University

evaluated the deviations of expected and observed values (Strebinger, Otter & Glück, 2002). Table 9 contains information on the extracted dimensions and their contribution to the inertia. The dimensions correlated with -0.17, which indicates their independence.

The contributions of the categories to the inertia of the axis as well as that of the axis to the inertia are displayed in Table 10, Table 11, and Table 12.

The frequency distribution of the association-categories and the attitude groups are displayed in Figure 16 by a correspondence chart that is based on two independent dimensions (r=-0.17).

Table 8. Respondent groups with different polarity towards CSR

n = 22	Polarity index range	n	Percent
Positive Attitude	[1.0; 0.4]	6	27.27
Neutral Attitude	[-0.1; 0.4]	8	36.36
Negative Attitude	[-1.0; -0.1]	8	36.36

Table 9. Dimensions and contribution to inertia

Inertia				
Dimensions	No.	Inertia	Percent	Cumulative Percent
	1	0.534	53.4	53.4
	2	0.466	46.6	100.0

Table 10. Row points of the correspondence analysis

Overview Row Points(a)									
Association	Mass	Score in Dimension		Inertia	Contribution				
		1	2		Of Point to Inertia of Dimension		Of Dimension to Inertia of Point		
					1	2	1	2	Total
Societal Value	.040	.377	.099	.006	.054	.004	.936	.064	1.000
Corporate Examples	.029	.081	.518	.008	.002	.086	.024	.976	1.000
Employees	.049	-.029	.002	.000	.000	.000	.994	.006	1.000
Future Potential	.020	-.616	.832	.021	.070	.147	.354	.646	1.000
Public Relations	.066	.133	.145	.003	.011	.015	.457	.543	1.000
Negative Aspects	.054	-.298	-.168	.006	.045	.017	.758	.242	1.000
Shareholders	.033	-.402	-.591	.017	.051	.125	.316	.684	1.000
Environmental Activism	.013	.107	-.008	.000	.001	.000	.994	.006	1.000
Competitive Advantage	.049	-.252	-.086	.003	.030	.004	.896	.104	1.000
Expense	.027	.107	-.008	.000	.003	.000	.994	.006	1.000
Fake	.022	-.692	-.181	.011	.100	.008	.936	.064	1.000
Corporate Policy	.018	-.122	-.270	.002	.003	.015	.169	.831	1.000
Ethics	.049	.416	.179	.010	.080	.017	.844	.156	1.000
Image	.043	.089	.353	.006	.003	.058	.060	.940	1.000
Intrinsic Motives	.027	.512	.152	.008	.067	.007	.919	.081	1.000
Legal Obligations	.048	-.454	.034	.010	.093	.001	.994	.006	1.000
Stakeholder Relation	.069	.082	-.156	.002	.004	.018	.217	.783	1.000
Economy	.042	.328	-.148	.005	.042	.010	.831	.169	1.000
Innovation	.048	.404	-.353	.014	.074	.065	.567	.433	1.000
Marketing	.027	.107	-.008	.000	.003	.000	.994	.006	1.000
Efficiency	.033	-.072	-.461	.007	.002	.076	.024	.976	1.000
Access to Resources	.015	.732	-.404	.010	.075	.026	.766	.234	1.000
Partnerships	.025	-.643	.467	.015	.096	.058	.654	.346	1.000
Democratic Failure	.036	.226	.128	.002	.017	.006	.758	.242	1.000
Costs	.039	-.127	.141	.001	.006	.008	.450	.550	1.000
Risk	.025	-.198	.644	.011	.009	.110	.086	.914	1.000
Liabilities	.023	-.255	-.422	.006	.014	.045	.267	.733	1.000
Inefficiency	.023	-.255	-.422	.006	.014	.045	.267	.733	1.000
Flexibility	.009	.598	.554	.006	.029	.029	.538	.462	1.000
Active Total	1.000			.198	1.000	1.000			

a Column Principal normalization

Table 11. Column points of the correspondence analysis

Confidence Column Points			
Association	Standard Deviation in Dimension		Correlation
	1	2	1-2
Societal Value	.057	.172	-.954
Corporate Examples	.275	.046	-.800
Employees	.006	.015	.132
Future Potential	.438	.285	.986
Public Relations	.078	.061	-.982
Negative Aspects	.092	.136	-.987
Shareholders	.316	.186	-.985
Environmental Activism	.008	.049	.454
Competitive Advantage	.049	.116	-.969
Expense	.008	.049	.454
Fake	.105	.316	-.960
Corporate Policy	.144	.058	-.966
Ethics	.099	.190	-.981
Image	.187	.045	-.902
Intrinsic Motives	.087	.234	-.965
Legal Obligations	.025	.207	.611
Stakeholder Relation	.083	.038	.964
Economy	.078	.150	.978
Innovation	.186	.185	.989
Marketing	.008	.049	.454
Efficiency	.245	.041	-.809
Access to Resources	.212	.335	.986
Partnerships	.245	.295	.990
Democratic Failure	.070	.103	-.983
Costs	.074	.059	.984
Risk	.340	.097	.937
Liabilities	.226	.119	-.981
Inefficiency	.226	.119	-.981
Flexibility	.298	.274	-.990

Table 12.

Overview Row Points(a)										
Attitude	Mass	Score in Dimension		Inertia	Contribution					
					Of Point to Inertia of Dimension		Of Dimension to Inertia of Point			
		1	2		1	2	1	2	Total	
Negative	.392	-.752	-.992	.059	.222	.386	.397	.603	1.000	
Neutral	.294	-.570	1.440	.066	.096	.610	.152	.848	1.000	
Positive	.314	1.475	-.110	.072	.682	.004	.995	.005	1.000	
Active Total	1.000			.198	1.000	1.000				

a Column Principal normalization

Figure 16. Positive, neutral and negative associations towards CSR

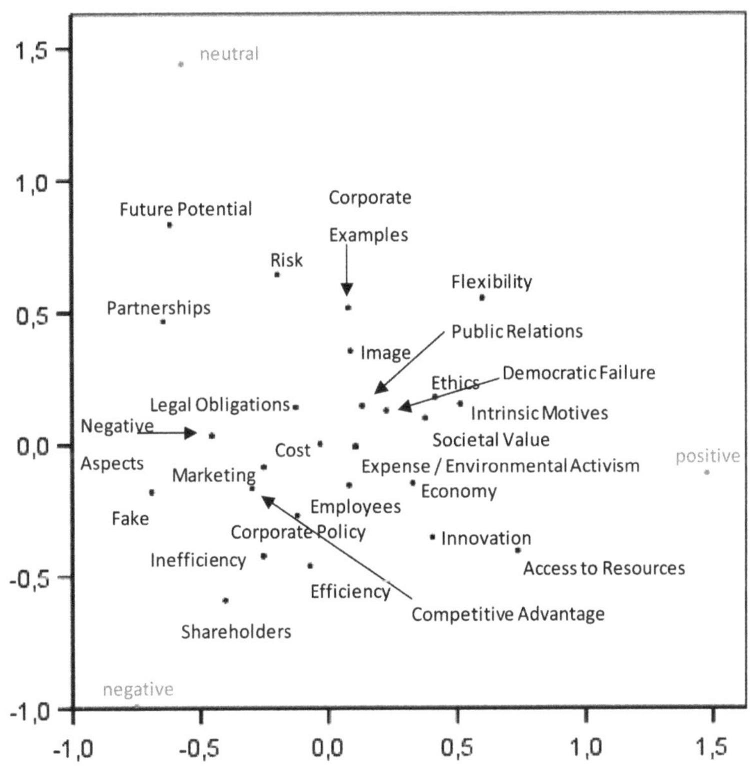

n=22; Data collection: October 10, 2007 at The Maxwell School of Citizenship and Public Affairs, Syracuse University

Interpretation

The first extracted dimension – which contributes 53.4 percent to the inertia – distinguishes between respondents with **positive** and **negative attitudes** towards CSR. Respondents with a **positive attitude towards CSR** honor CSR to grant *access to resources*, allow a high degree of *flexibility* in social service provision, presumably as for an independence from legislature periods. CSR fulfils *intrinsic motives* by contributing to *innovative ethical* and *societal values*. **Individuals with a negative perception of CSR** mentioned the *lack of legal obligations* replaced by *obligation towards shareholders*. Negative aspects comprise *inefficiency* and *honesty deficiencies* in the CSR communication. The second dimension describes the associations of **CSR-neutral individuals**, who associated *corporate examples*, reflected about the *future potential* but also *risks* imbued in CSR.

CONCLUSION

This exploratory survey derived the perception of public servants on CSR. Based on the data of 22 public administrators, CSR can be seen as a polarizing concept. CSR was honored to provide societal value and employee satisfaction; however CSR was also associated with marketing and PR. When it comes to CSR motives, civil servants think of the improvement of the corporate image and stakeholder relations, as well as intrinsic motives and employee satisfaction. Detected downsides of CSR are democratic deficiencies, cost and liability problems. CSR adherents point out access to additional resources provided by the corporate sector as well as the high degree of flexibility in administrating social responsibility. Individuals who are critical of CSR mention the lack of accountability, an obligation towards shareholders as well as inefficiency and dishonesty notions.

Overall, the research serves as a first step towards a comprehensive understanding of public administrators' view on CSR. As for its exploratory character, the study grants an avenue for future research on the symbiotic yet counter-parting relationship of the corporate world and the public sector on social service provision.

REFERENCES

Abric, J. C. (1984). Theoretical and experimental approach to social representations. In R. M. Farr & S. Moscovici (Eds.), *Social Representations* (pp. 169–183). Cambridge, MA: Cambridge University Press.

Abric, J. C. (1993). Central system, peripheral system: Their functions and roles in the dynamic of social representations. *Papers on Social Representations*, *2*(2), 75–78.

Ahmad, M. (2008, January 24). Global CEOs at World Economic Forum cite sovereign wealth funds as the new power broker. *BI-ME.*

Beck, U. (1998). Wie wird Demokratie im Zeitalter der Globalisierung möglich? In U. Beck (Ed.), *Politik der Globalisierung* (pp. 7–67). Frankfurt am Main: Suhrkamp.

Bruyn, S. T. (1987). *The field of social investment.* Cambridge, MA: Cambridge University Press. doi:10.1017/CBO9780511570872

Cooper, C., & Schlegelmilch, B. (1993). *Key issues in ethical investment: Business ethics: A European approach.* Hemel Hempstead: Prentice Hall.

Cuesta de la, G. M. & Martinez, V. C. (2004). Fostering corporate social responsibility through public initiative: From the EU to the Spanish case. *Journal of Business Ethics*, *55*, 275–293. doi:10.100710551-004-0994-y

Cuesta de la, G. M. & Valor, C. (2007). Fostering corporate social responsibility through public initiative: From the EU to the Spanish case. *Journal of Business Ethics*, *55*(3), 275–293.

DeRosa, A. (1994). From theory to metatheory in social representations: The lines of argument of a theoretical-methodological debate. *Social Sciences Information. Information Sur les Sciences Sociales*, *33*(2), 273–304. doi:10.1177/053901894033002008

Durkheim, E. (1898). *Représentations individuelles et répresentations collectives. Sociologie et philosophie.* Paris: Presses Universitaires de France.

Flament, J. C. (1987). Pratiques et représentations sociales. In J. L. Beauvois, R. V. Joule, & J. M. Monteil (Eds.), *Perspectives cognitives et conduites sociales. Cousset: DelVal.*

Flament, J. C. (1994). Consensus, salience and necessity in social representations. *Papers on Social Representations*, *3*, 97–105.

Frankel, T. (1984). Decision making for social investing. In D. M. McGill (Ed.), *Social Investing* (pp. 131–162). Homewood, IL: Irwin.

Levitt, T. (1983). The globalization of markets. *Harvard Business Review*, *61*, 2–11.

Little, K. (2008). *Socially responsible investing: Put your money where your values are*. New York: Penguin.

Livesey, S. (2002). The discourse of the middle ground: Citizen Shell commits to sustainable development. *Management Communication Quarterly*, *15*(3), 313–349. doi:10.1177/0893318902153001

Matten, D., & Crane, A. (2005). Corporate citizenship: Toward an extended theoretical conceptualization. *Academy of Management Review*, *30*(1), 166–179. doi:10.5465/amr.2005.15281448

Meier, K. (2000). *Psychologische Überlegungen zur Währungsumstellung: Bedrohung der österrreichischen Identiät?* (Unpublished doctoral dissertation). University of Vienna.

Mohr, L. A., Webb, D. J., & Harris, K. E. (2001). Do consumers expect companies to be socially responsible? The impact of corporate social responsibility on buying behavior. *The Journal of Consumer Affairs*, *35*(1), 45–72. doi:10.1111/j.1745-6606.2001.tb00102.x

Moliner, P. (1995). A two-dimensional model of social representations. *European Journal of Social Psychology*, *25*(1), 27–40. doi:10.1002/ejsp.2420250104

Moscovici, S. (1961). *La psychoanalyse, son image et son public*. Paris: Presse universitaires de France.

Moscovici, S. (1984). The myth of the lonely paradigm: A rejoinder. *Social Research*, *51*, 939–968.

Pandey, S. K., & Wright, B. E. (2006). Connecting the dots in public management: Political environment, organizational goal ambiguity and public manager's role ambiguity. *Journal of Public Administration: Research and Theory*, *16*(4), 511–532. doi:10.1093/jopart/muj006

Roland-Lévy, C., Kirchler, E., Penz, E., & Gray, C. (2001). *Everyday representations of the economy*. Vienna: WUV.

Rosen, B. N., Sandler, D. M., & Shani, D. (1991). Social issues and socially responsibility investment behavior: Preliminary empirical investigation. *The Journal of Consumer Affairs*, *25*(2), 221–234. doi:10.1111/j.1745-6606.1991.tb00003.x

Scholte, J. A. (2000). *Globalization: A critical introduction*. Basingstoke: Palgrave.

Steurer, R. (2010). The role of governments in corporate social responsibility: Characterising public policies on CSR in Europe. *Policy Sciences*, *43*(1), 49–72. doi:10.100711077-009-9084-4

Strebinger, A., Otter, T., & Glück, J. (2002). *Einführung in die Korrespondenzanalyse*. Wien: Facultas.

The Human Relations Movement. (2008). *Harvard Business School and the Hawthorne experiments (1924-1933)*. Cambridge, MA: Harvard Business School.

Trevino, L. K., & Nelson, K. A. (2004). *Managing business ethics: Straight talk about how to do right*. Hoboken, NJ: Wiley.

Vergès, P., & Bastounis, M. (2001). Towards the investigation of social representations of the economy: Research methods and techniques. In C. Roland-Lévy, E. Kirchler, E. Penz, & C. Gray (Eds.), *Everyday Representations of the Economy* (pp. 19–48). Wien: WUV.

Vergès, P., & Tyszka, T. (1994). Noyau central, saillance et propriétés structurales. L'évocation de l'argent: Une méthode pour la définition du noyau central d'une représentation. *Papers on Social Representations*, *3*, 3–12.

Wagner, W., Valencia, J., & Elejabarrieta, F. (1996). Relevances, discourse and the "hot" stable core of social representations: A structural analysis of word associations. *British Journal of Social Psychology*, *35*(3), 331–351. doi:10.1111/j.2044-8309.1996.tb01101.x

Williams, G. (2005). *Are socially responsible investors different from conventional investors? A comparison across six countries*. Unpublished working paper, University of Bath.

ENDNOTES

1 Absolute frequencies.
2 Relative frequencies.
3 Absolute frequencies.
4 Relative frequencies.
5 Absolute frequencies.
6 Relative frequencies.
7 Absolute frequencies.
8 Relative frequencies.

Chapter 5
Public Private Partnerships (PPPs)

ABSTRACT

The start-up of the global alliance network on ICT for development (GAID) was qualitatively analyzed to derive recommendations for the improvement of PPPs. The evaluation covered web contents, publications, interviews, emails, and blog responses. Since the inception in 2006, GAID has successfully leveraged its position as a UN-related organization that keeps ICT for development on the global agenda. GAID has brought together constituents on ICT for development comprising governmental officials, corporate executives, academia, and civil society. The accessibility and harmonization of ICT best practices standards have been advanced. GAID has secured funding, launched conferences, and extended its network in flagship initiatives, regional networks, and communities of expertise. Some of the partnerships initiatives have successfully linked with the GAID network and facilitated information exchange in conferences, trainings, and workshops. Others had difficulties in integrating with GAID mainly due to resource limitations and a lack of expertise. The current situation of the GAID network implies areas for improvement regarding additional resource mobilization, network establishment and maintenance, as well as business planning, goal achievement strategies, and measurement.

DOI: 10.4018/978-1-5225-7619-8.ch005

UNGC

The UNGC sets basic and transparent principles for the engagement of the private sector in global governance. In a multi-stakeholder approach, the UNGC distinguishes CSR principles of action for the corporate world. In the interaction between the UN and the private sector, the UNGC initiatives help moving towards a universal consensus on the minimum standards of corporate social conduct in the areas of labor standards, human rights, poverty reduction, health and workplace safety, education and community engagement. The participation of corporations in the UNGC is foremost ensured through PPPs. Multi-stakeholder partnerships target at leveraging the quality of corporate commitment to UN principles.

An example of the implementation of the UNGC in PPP practice is GAID. As a newly emerging partnership initiative, GAID fosters future positive outcomes of PPPs in ICT. The following part will shed light on the set-up of the GAID partnerships with a special attention to positive impacts and multi-stakeholder endeavors on ICT for development.

GAID: PPP Implementation Analysis

The following section presents an analysis of the Global Alliance network on ICT for development (GAID). The analysis is based on data on networking GAID partners and their activities in the set-up process. The qualitative analysis of the network structure and outcomes of partnerships during the start-up phase will retrieve recommendations for the improvement of the effectiveness of PPPs. Outlining strengths and challenges of PPPs allows generalizations of best practices for the future implementation of multi-stakeholder partnerships.

Research Questions

The purpose of the evaluation was to identify the initial results obtained by GAID during the set-up in order to generalize recommendations for the future improvement of PPPs. Concretely, the evaluation was targeted at depicting the extent to which GAID initiatives and partners have:

1. Begun their activities on ICT for development.
2. Created partnerships and leveraged a think tank network on ICT for development.

3. Brought together key constituents involved in ICT for development to enhance UN goals.
4. Mainstreamed the global ICT agenda in sync with the UN development goals.
5. Become an advisory group to the Secretary General of the UN.
6. Facilitated an identification of technological solutions for development.
7. Raised public awareness for ICT for development as a policy issue.
8. Enabled environments and innovative business models for the growth of ICT for development.

This procedure was aimed at analyzing success factors that have contributed to the raise of GAID. Lessons learned by the partners in the start-up phase serve as a basis for recommendations and the planning of future PPPs.

DATA COLLECTION

A total of ten partnerships were selected for the analysis including four flagship initiatives, two regional networks and four communities of expertise. Qualitative data on GAID was collected during February to April 2008 by the author and assistants. The analysis focused on the global activities of GAID with a special attention to the endeavors outlined in the 2006 business report. At the global level, events during 2007-2008 were screened. Information was retrieved from web pages, featuring workshop reports and handbook material. Additional knowledge was sought by emails and individual expert interviews with executives who implement GAID. With regard to the ‘think tank’ function of ICT for development, a question on the success of GAID was posed onto the GAID internet discussion list to which considerable responses were received.

Data

Global Level

In February 2002 an inauguration meeting planned the set-up of the GAID initiative to be officially approved by the UN Secretary-General on March 28, 2006. The international focus and distribution of multi-stakeholder participation in the inauguration meeting is outlined in Table 1.

Table 1. Participants of the GAID inauguration meetings

	Shareholder Group					
Stakeholder	**Government**	**Civil Society**	**Private Sector**	**International Organizations**	**Academic**	**Total**
Regional Group						
Africa	17%	9%	0%	17%	11%	10%
Asia and the Pacific	43%	45%	70%	33%	47%	48%
Eastern Europe	6%	2%	0%	0%	0%	1%
Latin America and Caribbean	6%	0%	0%	0%	0%	1%
Western European and Other	29%	45%	30%	50%	42%	41%
Total	10%	26%	19%	20%	26%	100%
Number	35	94	69	72	95	365

GAID comprised multiple partners in the set-up meeting with a bias towards the private sector and academia compared to other UN meetings (Mathiason, in speech, April 2008).

Since the inception, the Global Alliance brings together multiple constituents on ICT for development. Overall, ICT strengthens policy-making bodies on a national and global level in collaboration with the UN. ICT fosters development progress throughout the world through instant communication opportunities and access to information (Reinfried, Schleicher & Rempfler, 2007). During 2006-2008, the Global Alliance organized – mainly in cooperation with other organizations or institutions – a total of 13 UN events. Three of the meetings comprised the GAID Steering Committee and Strategy Council and are considered internal management meetings. The remaining ten meetings were targeted at a wider audience. The meetings were held in conjunction with UN meetings to outline the importance of ICT on development to multiple constituents. The participants ranged from representatives of governments, International Organizations and NGOs that are customarily involved in intergovernmental deliberations. The meetings were organized by GAID with partners to engage a wider stakeholder community. The international representation of stakeholders in the GAID meetings from 2007-2008 is outlined by Table 2.

Table 2. Participants in major GAID meetings 2007-2008

Meeting	Region	TOTAL	Stakeholder Group	TOTAL
Santa Clara (253 participants) February 2007	US	64%	Academic	18%
	Latin America and the Caribbean (LAC)	6%	Civil Society	45%
	Asia and the Pacific	10%	Government	12%
	Africa	4%	Private Sector	25%
	Europe and other	15%		
Geneva (1033 participants) September 2007	US	3%	Academic	21%
	LAC	6%	Civil Society	45%
	Asia and the Pacific	15%	Government	12%
	Africa	66%	Private Sector	23%
	Europe and other	9%		
New York (125 participants) March 2008	US	72%	Academic	2%
	LAC	0%	Civil Society	12%
	Asia and the Pacific	17%	Government	22%
	Africa	6%	Private Sector	63%
	Europe and other	6%		

The events brought together multi-stakeholder participants ranging from governmental civil servants to civil society and the private sector, as well as academia. With the exception of the youth meeting in Geneva in September 2007, the meetings tended to attract participants from the region in which they were held.

Regarding the UN SDGs,[1] which were introduced in September 2015, ICT has become an essential tool for the alleviation of societal deficiencies. As for the eradication of hunger, the IT revolution has perpetuated the efficiency in the information flow on drought, hunger and crises. As an innovative avenue for fighting poverty, ICT provides access to capital online and by mobile phones. Information flow is key to medical assistance of underserved communities and an essential prerequisite for effective epidemiology. As an essential feature of preventive medical assistance, ICT helps educating on maternal health and combating child mortality, HIV, malaria and other diseases. ICT has led to groundbreaking insights on the decay of natural resources and climate change. Information and communication foster environmental protection and sustainability.

To evaluate GAID's establishment as a 'think tank' on ICT for development and advisory role to the UN Secretary-General, the partners' goals and accomplishments in multi-stakeholder network building are outlined as follows.

PARTNERSHIP LEVEL

Flagship Partnership Initiatives, ***Regional Networks*** and ***Communities of Expertise*** promote ICT for development at the national, regional and ground levels. The following part examined the ***Flagship Partnership Initiatives*** of the *Cyber Development Corps*, *Connect the World (Better Connectivity with Broadband to Africa)*, *telecentre.org* and the *Global Initiative for inclusive ICT*. The ***Regional Networks*** investigated comprised the *LAC Steering Group* and the *African regional network*. The ***Communities of Expertise*** analyzed the areas of *Entrepreneurship* featuring *Youth Social Entrepreneurship*; *Governance*; *Health* featuring *ICT for Country Health Information* and *Cross-Cutting Themes* by *e-Agriculture*. The initiatives under scrutiny are exhibited in Figure 1.

Flagship Partnership Initiatives

Cyber Development Corps (CDC)

Source: The evaluation included web contents and interviews with the Cyber Development Corps (CDC) officials.

Figure 1. Analyzed GAID initiatives

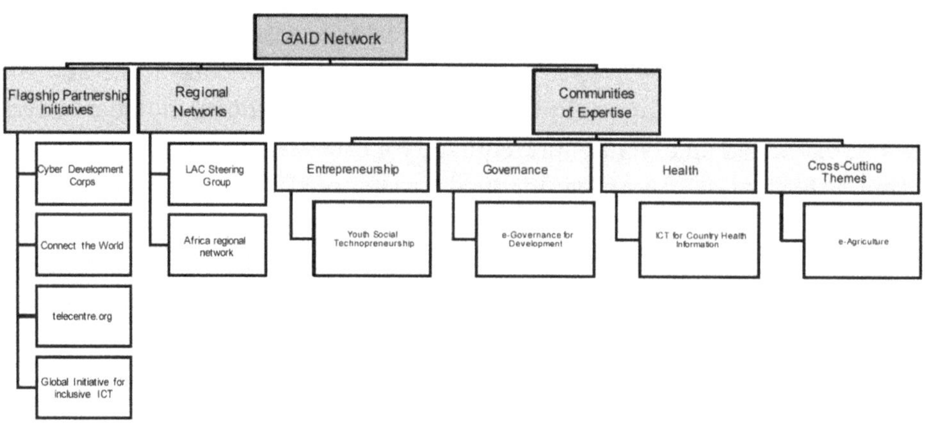

Findings: The CDC is a GAID initiative led by the Government of Malaysia. CDC's goals are to create an internet portal, CDC centers and trainings to promote ICT for development in local communities. The set-up of CDC has been slower than expected and outlined by the business plan. A secretariat has been established to work on the CDC web portal, but website linkages with GAID are not intact. This flagship initiative had made sufficient progress to achieve its outlined objectives. An additional planning meeting is scheduled for May 2008.

Recommendations: CDC forces have to be enhanced to create a web portal, set-up CDC centers and train individuals to promote ICT for development in local communities. The progress should be monitored by accountability control and goal accomplishment checks. The website linkages with GAID have to be intensified to increase the visibility of the connection of the initiative to GAID and the wider UN network.

Connect the World (Better Connectivity With Broadband to Africa)

Sources: Internet-based review of partnership efforts outlined in conference minutes.

Findings: The Connect the World flagship initiative is led by the International Telecommunications Union (ITU) and the World Bank. GAID helped organize the 2007 Connect Africa Summit in Rwanda that served to energize the flagship. The evaluation analyzed the meeting minutes for the Summit and found that 1,036 representatives from 54 countries, 20 industrial partners and 16 financial institutions attended. The World Bank and ITU acknowledged 77 project funding commitments featuring funding of USD 56 billion from 49 partners for the time period from 2008 to 2014. The follow-up summit will be held May 11-13, 2008. The existing network between GAID and ITU primarily features the joint organization of conferences and hyperlinks at the GAID and the ITU websites. In terms of internet linkages with GAID, the flagship showed only a few hyperlinks with the GAID websites and did not feature GAID prominently on the web space maintained by the World Bank.

Recommendations: To this point, the World Bank has not effectively promoted its partnership with GAID concerning African telecommunications projects. As for the novelty of the GAID initiative, GAID needs to develop a strong networking relation with the World Bank and ITU. Thereby the GAID partners are challenged to distinguish themselves from larger member organizations and offer a specialty social service.

Telecentre.org

Sources: For the evaluation the Managing Director of telecentre.org was interviewed and internet documents were reviewed in March and April 2008.

Findings: GAID has successfully facilitated a partnership between the Inter-American Development Bank (IADB) and telecentre.org. Telecentre.org pre-existed GAID and became one of the flagship initiatives with a focus on the creation of telecentre networks. Telecentre.org has irregular and limited communication with GAID, foremost enabled through meetings. No substantial linkages to other GAID initiatives have been established. There are only a few internet references and links to GAID on the telecentre.org webpage, which is in contrast to the numerous references to telecentre.org present on the GAID website. A few new relationships to non-GAID initiatives have been set-up, primarily as innovative funding sources.

In summary, even though there have been some achievements in the telecentre.org and GAID partnership, the results do not fulfil the initial expectation. There is a lack of communication that limits multi-stakeholder opportunities. The linkage between telecentre.org and GAID is hardly visible to the public and is currently suboptimal in promoting telecentre.org's initiatives through the GAID platform.

Recommendations: GAID must identify opportunities for a more pro-active collaboration with telecentre.org. Substantive linkages between telecentre.org and GAID as well as other initiatives should be promoted with consideration of the needs of the individual initiatives. GAID can facilitate access to financial and information resources for network building and training services. ICT for development experts must be engaged to add further value to GAID and the flagship initiatives.

Global Initiative for Inclusive Information and Communication Technologies (G3ICT)

Sources: The evaluation of this initiative was based on an analysis of the websites and publications of the Global Initiative for Inclusive Information and Communication Technologies (G3ICT) as well as an email inquiry. Several G3ICT documents and web resources were reviewed with a special emphasis on the goals of the initiative and resources available to its constituents.

Findings: G3ICT was set-up in the wake of concern for access to ICT for persons with disabilities. G3ICT promotes ICT solutions for people with disabilities and related policies among governments. The G3ICT steering committee is composed of 55 members that include GAID, UN agencies, NGOs, academia and the private sector. The G3ICT is a flagship initiative of GAID that features linkages with the public and private sectors, international organizations and NGOs seeking to foster inclusive IT for individuals living with disabilities. The legal foundation is based in the UN Convention on the Rights of Persons with Disabilities, which target at IT accessibility and integration policies and programs. The G3ICT progress was evaluated on the development of accessible ICT solutions for respective communities.

The evaluation found that the initiative had been active and linked with GAID. There were visible links to GAID on the G3ICT homepage, indicating a commitment to being part of GAID. There had been 30 participants in working groups representing policy makers, NGOs and the private sector attending initial global forums to present findings on ICT for disabled. Attendees at regional forums and plenary sessions in Italy, Ecuador, Paris, Moscow, London, Brussels and China ranged from 150 to 500 policy makers, NGO leaders and government representatives. The minutes of regional forums were made available to the public on the G3ICT website. Related blog entries reflecting the international expertise on ICT represent an unusual level of transparency. G3ICT had obtained sponsorship from several corporations[2] and there was a representation of international experts engaging in the G3ICT. The G3ICT had entered into various PPPs with several public entities such as Cifal Atlanta, GAID, Inter-parliamentary union (IPU), International Telecommunication Union (ITU), Politecnico di Milano, UN Enable and UNITAR. Regional forums had been organized in Ecuador, Chicago, Qatar and Korea hosted by the local partner organizations, academia, governments, NGOs and international institutions. G3ICT has developed a ranking of ICT options and devices that were circulated through presentation panels. Event presentations were available on the web in DAISY format for disabled readers.

Recommendations: G3ICT has successfully leveraged strategic partnerships with multiple stakeholders and thereby fostered the discourse on accessible ICT for the disabled. Partners contributed best practices that have been openly shared through the G3ICT website. G3ICT has successfully partnered with GAID and ITU to develop two global forums on ICT accessibility. G3ICT and its partners have to continuously forge on the harmonization and standardization of ICT for accessibility beyond the requirements as outlined by the Convention on the Rights of the Disabled. A particular focus must be placed in the areas of legislative spearheading, advocacy, training and universal standards creation. The success story of the G3ICT initiative suggests a number of valuable lessons for other partnerships.

Regional Networks

Latin America and the Caribbean Regional Network (LAC)

Sources: The basis for the analysis was information retrieved from contacts with the Latin America and the Caribbean Regional Network (LAC) organizations as well as documents on the internet.

Findings: The LAC is led by the Economic Commission for Latin America and the Caribbean (ECLAC). Partnerships have been built with other organizations, foremost outlined by hyperlinks between the GAID website and LAC partners.

The LAC regional network is successful in engaging a diversity of stakeholders, among whom the LAC network transfers information and initiates networking activities. For example, the San Salvador seminar in February 2008 included 14 individuals from the private sector, 36 from the public sector, 17 from NGOs and 3 from other areas. After the meeting the initiative launched a website. Apart from supporting the GAID Annual Meeting in Kuala Lumpur, LAC has proposed to organize a forum on ICT and education initiatives for the UNESCO. The network continues to identify and tackle regional needs, serve as an information brokerage platform and helps implementing development programs.

While the LAC regional network has made rapid progress, there are a few areas for improvement. The incorporation of GAID and LAC activities into UN resolutions and other documents of other international organizations are not streamlined. In addition, there is ambiguity among respondents in terms of the scope of the LAC regional network. For example, when asked if LAC had developed – or disseminated – any business models to promote usage of ICT in the development in the region, it became apparent that the role of LAC in the knowledge dissemination and creation of new development models was not clear among several constituents. The network executives hold onto ambiguous goals regarding the LAC region development models.

Recommendations: The incorporation of GAID or LAC into UN resolutions and documents of other international organizations must be facilitated by clear strategies and policies negotiated in inter-agency multi-stakeholder meetings. Regional policy makers and administrators have to work closely to implement the respective policies throughout the LAC network. The agreed-upon business models, the network scope and focus must be communicated throughout all layers of administration.

Africa Regional Network

Sources: The evaluation comprised relevant websites, documents and information received from the United Nations Economic Commission for Africa (UNECA).

Findings: The Africa regional network has been built on a pre-existing program managed by the UNECA featuring stakeholders from a variety of sectors. The UNEC's regional Africa network sponsored and promoted the Connect Africa Summit in October 2007 featuring over

1,000 participants from the public and private sectors, international organizations and NGOs. The Connect Africa summit was geared towards building a multi-stakeholder network.

Subsequent to the summit, GAID and UNECA worked jointly to produce a document entitled "Capacity building, applications and services." Since then commitments of USD 55 billion to fund ICT in Africa were made with the Groupe Speciale Mobile (GSM) Association and the World Bank Group being the largest contributors. Further, the GSM Association promised to invest USD 50 billion between March 2007 and 2012 to expand and upgrade the network. The World Bank Group wants to double its commitment to USD two billion to invest in ICT in Africa by 2012. Amidst funding of the African regional network, the plans and goals of the initiative were outlined in a working plan. The implementation of the working plan is challenged in the areas of work-on-progress and communication support. The GAID Africa promotional plan was sent to Africa regional network members for approval, but currently the GAID Africa Secretariat has not received any feedback from those members, which delays the approval of the GAID Africa promotional plan and puts the implementation at stake. While extensive funding has been secured for the African regional network, the implementation faced many difficulties.

In 2008, the Africa network's website was not operational. According to documents prepared by the GAID Steering Committee, the GAID Africa Secretariat is responsible for creating and maintaining the website as a source of information on the network's activities and discussion medium for the network members. Since the website is not intact, there is no internet forum where network members and experts can meet to discuss issues and priorities of the Africa regional network. Also a lack in official network conferences was eminent, which degrades the likelihood and quality of the multi-stakeholder communication.

Although funds have been secured, the Africa regional network faces difficulties in obtaining enough funding for the implementation of all its programs. The UNECA is involved in the Partnership for ICTs in Africa, an informal group of donor and executing agencies committed to improving information exchange and collaboration on ICT in Africa. However, the UNECA is not a very powerful organization within the UN itself, which lowers the possibility of obtaining additional funding for the Africa regional network.

Recommendations: As for the lack of a specified website, other means of information exchange should be explored in the meantime. The homepage has to be set up as soon as possible. Conferences are key for multi-stakeholder initiatives during the start-up phase. Therefore, organizing conferences and summits have to become a key priority for the African regional network. Additional sources of funding must be targeted to leverage and sustainably fund the African regional network. Securing funding itself is not a solution to complex regional problems. On the ground level, operations have to become administered. First results must be evaluated in order to accomplish long-lasting results and foster sustainable development.

Communities of Expertise

These Communities of Expertise bring together multiple constituents to address and solve specific, well-defined ICT for development problems. The thematic Communities of Expertise under scrutiny comprised *entrepreneurship*, *governance*, *health* and *cross-cutting themes*.

Entrepreneurship

Sources: Information on the entrepreneurship community of expertise derived from websites and interviews.

Findings: The entrepreneurship community of expertise features several problems. GAID was successful in getting the partnerships started as outlined by published work plans and goal-setting – however, measurable output criteria have not been defined. Approximately eight months after submitting its inception report to GAID, the entrepreneurial initiatives were in jeopardy – reporting low levels of interest, funding and support from partners. In the "UN Meets Web 2.0" meeting, held in New York City on April 2008, key constituents were brought together from the public and private sectors, of which only a few of the listed partners actually followed up in participating in GAID activities. The entrepreneurship community of expertise indicates problems of maintaining a connection between the partners. In addition, the entrepreneurship initiative has difficulties in connecting the global with the local levels in activities. The lead partners do not feature extensive networks that would be necessary and the expected assistance from the GAID secretariat was mentioned to be missing.

Recommendation: The goals have to be connected to a viable performance control. Meetings should be promoted as for fostering the stakeholder dialogue and vitalizing the connection between the partners to integrate the global with the regional level. Conferences and meetings must facilitate a network extension and engage stakeholders. Stakeholders must commit to transparent goals and make their targets and accomplishments accessible to the public in presentations at meetings as well as periodical reports.

Youth Social Technopreneurship

Sources: The data for the analysis of the Youth Social Technopreneurship consisted of the homepage and email contact with the staff of the leading organization Philippine Resources Sustainable Development (PRSD) and three partner organizations.

Findings: The community of expertise on entrepreneurship is coordinated by PRSD in collaboration with 13 member agencies.[3] As of today, Youth Social Technopreneurship is involved in two networks: 1) an informal network based on the communication among its member channeled through PRSD and 2) the 'Champions Network of GAID' which is a formal way of communication among GAID communities.

The main result of this specific partnership has been training programs organized through a close partnership between PRSD and the Korean Agency for Digital Promotion and Opportunities (KADO). KADO is not a member of GAID, but conducts the IT trainings on the ground by the help of young Korean IT specialists. As of April 2008, three community level training courses have been held in Burundi, Nigeria and Uganda. The community of expertise activities consisted of a series of youth-oriented ICT trainings and workshops such as the 'Global Forum on Youth and ICT for development: Youth and ICT as Agents of Change' which was celebrated in Geneva in September 2007. Two of the community of expertise partners were present at the workshop, in which additional communities of expertise were formed. Since its creation, the Youth Social Technopreneurship has developed a set of ICT trainings in Africa that improved the employability and skills of the rural, impoverished youth. Alone through the community level trainings carried out in 2007, over 100 trainees have improved their ICT capabilities and IT knowledge on Photoshop, flash and webmastering skills. The trainings were targeted at encouraging the African youth to venture into social technopreneurship with the greater goal of reducing poverty.

The major obstacle of the Youth Social Technopreneurship is related to the budget. So far, no funding is secured from GAID; therefore the Youth Social Technopreneurship faces elementary budgetary constraints. As a means for overcoming the financial hindrance, PRSD covers the Youth Social Technopreneurship operations using its own internally generated funds as for fostering the current partnership with KADO. Additionally, due to the lack of funding, the development of a website has been delayed.

There seems to be a weak relationship between the GAID community of expertise board and the current members, who facilitate the ICT trainings for young people in developing countries. The linkages and communication flows between GAID and the Youth Social Technopreneurship are irregular. As a consequence, the activities developed by the partnership between the community of expertise and KADO are taking place without GAID's direct involvement.

Recommendations: To accomplish its objectives, the Youth Social Technopreneurship initiative has to overcome obstacles such as the shortage of funding and weak communications with GAID. A stringent stream of funding for the successful initiative may be ensured by promoting the successes already accomplished. The connection to GAID has to be re-vitalized and strengthened. This can be done by newly defining responsibilities and making current goals and their degree of accomplishment transparent.

Governance

E-Governance for Development

Sources: The governance community of expertise was analyzed by a review of websites and email contact with officials.

Findings: The community of expertise on e-Governance is based on the United Nations Public Administration Network (UNPAN), which pre-existed GAID. This UN effort is meant to promote the use of the internet as a part of substantive activities.

After a somewhat uneven start, during which GAID and UNPAN activities were poorly coordinated, the situation is now improving. As of August 2007, GAID's eGovernance activities are now officially a part of UNPAN. While UNPAN is the lead organization in all e-governance projects, GAID focuses on more concrete products such as capacity building and developing user-friendly e-governance tools. GAID's role at present is the storage and dissemination of the information generated by UNPAN projects.

Recommendations: In accordance with UNPAN goals, GAID has to develop a unique proposition within the UNPAN network. In the communication with UNPAN, GAID can feature an advantageous independent and flexible governance approach. GAID has to establish itself in respective local communities and further advance hands-on grass-roots activities for change.

Health

ICT for Country Health Information

Sources: The evaluation of the health community of expertise was based on the ICT for Country Health Information website and interviews conducted with the program manager of the Country Health Information initiative. The assessments were conducted by the help of the World Health Organization (WHO), which is an e-health partner.

Findings: Led by the WHO, the community of expertise on health pre-dated GAID. While the WHO and GAID are concurrently striving to bring greater emphasis to the potential benefits of ICT in public health, the connection between GAID and ICT for Country Health Information is not solid. In spring 2008, GAID did not have a clear link to the WHO homepage and vice versa. However, it was possible to find information on programs that GAID has been involved with on the WHO's website when using the WHO search engine. The evaluation of GAID – partnering with the WHO – on health issues reveals the need to further push for partnering.

The overall business plan of the community of expertise on health is somewhat vague about the expected outcomes. According to the business plan, the aim for this year was to create and strengthen multi-stakeholder alliances. The findings indicate that although GAID – in partnership with WHO – has taken important steps toward the accomplishment of e-health specific goals, the organization has fallen short of meeting them.

Up to now GAID has reconstituted the information previously available through various WHO and UN reports and publications. In addition, GAID ICT Country Health Information has completed 192 separate national assessments. Within these assessments, GAID evaluated the major health concerns within each nation under scrutiny as well as their current ICT capabilities. The evaluations feature factors that inhibit the spread of the use of ICT – such as for example illiteracy and a decline in the standard of living due to external crises and shocks (e.g., draught, floods etc.). These findings serve as a solid foundation for the planning of later GAID activities and regionally-specific actions.

When discussing e-health with the GAID community of expertise head and WHO Program Manager, it was emphasized that the next goal of the organization would be the creation of a think tank style group of experts. The next step is to ensure that each partner plays to its own strengths and to fulfill the greater goal to maintain these partnerships in the long term.

When analyzing the business plan of the group, their aims have been somewhat vague in terms of the creation and strengthening of the alliance. Although the goal accomplishment is difficult to quantify, it is clear that respective alliances have been formed and the organization is progressing. GAID is still exploring its role and, as evidenced in the interview, formulating and refining its goals for the future.

Recommendations: GAID has entered into several partnerships with organizations in the ehealth sector. In the future, GAID must continuously bring together individuals from disparate backgrounds and organizations on e-health matters. Conferences and regional meetings could engage various constituents on this behalf. The goal attainment has to be specified by clear and transparent goal settings and accomplishment control. Transparency of the goals in business plans and work packages must be facilitated to ensure the further progress of the health initiative.

Cross-Cutting Themes

E-Agriculture

Sources: The evaluation is based on information on the websites maintained by Food and Agriculture Organization (FAO) and information received in response to an e-mail inquiry.

Findings: The e-Agriculture cross-cutting theme is run by the FAO and was created after GAID. The FAO hosted the first e-Agriculture workshop in June 2006. The FAO also conducted an open survey on e-agriculture issues in October 2006 featuring a total of 3,433 participants from 135 countries. The website was created in February 2007 and officially launched in May 2007.

FAO stated that the success of the e-Agriculture movement depends on the active engagement of a wide range of stakeholders, including the UN GAID. FAO considers GAID to be one of its stakeholders and serves as the secretary and facilitator for the community. FAO coordinates between the global bodies, including UNGAID, the World Summit on the Information Society Secretariat, the United Nations Group on the Information Society (UNGIS) and the community-at-large. FAO is also managing the development, editorial content and maintenance of the web-based platform as well as the coordination of face-to-face events. The UN GAID continues to promote the e-Agriculture community activities and to give the e-Agriculture community opportunities to network and engage other UN GAID members and the international community at large.

The cooperation between GAID and FAO has been episodic. FAO members have attended several global events sponsored by GAID. According to FAO officials, GAID has helped ensuring that agriculture and rural development are kept in mind when ICT for development is discussed in UN meetings. Early in the evaluation, no mention of GAID was found on the

FAO website, but by the end of the period links had been added on the FAO partners' pages. FAO reported GAID as one of e-Agriculture's stakeholders on its homepage. This outlined that regular outputs of the e-Agriculture community will be provided to the stakeholders and to relevant global bodies. However, the email correspondence revealed that GAID and FAO have little interaction with each other and the connection between GAID, e-Agriculture and FAO are ineffectual and largely theoretical.

Recommendations: Multi-stakeholder means to create a vital dialogue between all constituents involved such as regular conferences and meetings are recommended. At these gatherings, common goals have to be discussed. Transparent goal setting including all constituents is advised.

A summary of the GAID initiatives' progress, deficiencies and recommendations is exhibited in Table 3.

CONCLUSION

Overall, GAID has shown positive results at the global and partnership levels. At the same time, some areas of improvement were discovered.

Global Level

On the global level, GAID has attracted attention and gained participation from multiple stakeholders on ICT for development, in particular the private sector and academia. GAID has brought ICT considerations into the mainstream of intergovernmental debate. Given the nature of the relative novelty of GAID, the initiatives are sometimes stuck in future opportunity thinking rather than stringent current management planning. The GAID initiative is therefore recommended to advance the current goal attachment on practical functions.

Partnership Level

The individual partner evaluation looked at various networks and found mixed results. Some new partnerships were developed as a consequence of GAID. Several of these have been quite successful and shown strong progress. Other previously existing initiatives were revitalized by the GAID partnering. Some initiatives had successfully organized GAID conferences, summits and meetings. Other accomplishments comprised the advancement of ICT at the ground level by fostering accessibility and technology use.

The evaluation also identified a number of weaknesses. Some partnerships have experienced problems during their start-up phase. Other pre-existing initiatives had difficulties in connecting with GAID. Of the pre-existing initiatives, a few had agreed on partnering with GAID, but had not made their linkages transparent or did not use networking opportunities. Most of these pre-existing partnerships continued to function on their own with little connection to or support by GAID. Several of the partnerships have had

Table 3. Qualitative analysis of the GAID start-up initiatives

GAID start-up process		
Flagship Partnership Initiatives		
Positive progress	**Deficiencies**	**Recommendations**
• Innovative PPPs have been set up, extended and made public • Secretariats have been set up to work on progress • Some flagship partnership initiatives are active and visibly linked with GAID indicating a strong commitment to being a part of GAID • Private sector sponsorships have been established • ICT partners have forged a consensus on the harmonization and standardization of priorities • International conferences and summits fostered information dissemination, networking and funding • Some of the flagship initiatives report working groups representing policy makers, NGOs and the private sector attending initial global forums to present findings • Regional forums and plenary sessions have been organized by the local multi-stakeholder partners that brought together key constituents • Minutes of regional forums were made available to the public via websites featuring blog entries showing a high level of transparency and engaging experts worldwide • Progress has been made accessible to a range of constituents. Global forums on ICT accessibility have been launched. Partnership best practices have been openly shared	• During the start-up period, the set-up has been slower than expected and outlined by the business plan • Website linkages with GAID are not extensive. Missing web-information and internet references hinder the communication and networking of multiple stakeholders	• GAID needs to develop a strong networking relation with international organizations. Thereby GAID faces the challenge to distinguish itself from larger member organizations by offering niche services. • Engage experts that add further value to GAID and the flagship initiatives. • Identify opportunities for pro-active collaboration and substantive linkages between GAID and other initiatives without losing attention to specificities of local constituents • GAID should improve access to financial means and information resources as well as training services • The slower-than-expected progress should be monitored by accountability control and goal accomplishment checks • Create web portals and set-up centers that help promote ICT for development in local communities • Irregular and limited communication with GAID could be overcome by regular and mandatory conferences, summits and meetings. Minutes of the meetings should be made easily accessible in order to enhance best practice advancement among multiple stakeholders • The website linkages with GAID have to be intensified to increase the visibility of the multiple connections of the initiative to the wider GAID network

Regional Networks		
Positive progress	**Deficiencies**	**Recommendations**
• Partnerships have been built with organizations of regional partners • Diverse stakeholders comprising public and private constituents have attended conferences, workshops and seminars. These networking events were staged to identify and tackle regional needs, serve as an information brokerage platform and help implement programs for development. The events were geared towards building and expanding multi-stakeholder networks to better implement policies and raise awareness and funding for respective causes • A variety of stakeholders engage in information transfer and partnering in networking initiatives • Websites were launched to foster partnerships and disseminate information	• Difficulties in obtaining funding for the implementation of the program are apparent • The approval of working plans is delayed, which puts the implementation at stake • The incorporation of resolutions in policies and practices is not streamlined • The network executives appear to hold onto ambiguous goals in terms of the scope of projects. The role of the partners is not clear to several constituents • Some websites are not operational, which limits the information flow on the network's activities and discussion possibility for the network • A lack of official network conferences was apparent, which degrades the likelihood and quality of the multi-stakeholder communication	• Resolutions must be facilitated by clear strategies and policies negotiated in inter-agency meetings • The agreed-upon policy models, network scope and focus must be communicated throughout all layers of the network • Regional policy makers and local administrators have to work closely in the implementation of respective policies • Conferences and summits are key for multi-stakeholder initiatives during the start-up phase. Innovative and new media means of information exchange should be explored • Additional sources of funding should be investigated

Communities of Expertise		
Positive progress	**Deficiencies**	**Recommendations**
• Public and private sector constituents were brought together to address and solve ICT for development problems • Respective websites were launched and web-based networks established. Weblinkages outline networking and collaboration engagements • Official linkages to the UN have fortified the strength of the PPPs • ICT training programs and workshops have been organized and launched through PPPs • Capacity building developed user-friendly e-governance tools • Trainings have improved ICT skills and fostered social development • Open surveys were conducted to identify areas of concern • Additional communities of expertise were formed in workshops • Factors that could inhibit the spread of the use of ICT within areas of expertise were identified • Work plans and goal-setting as well as measurable output criteria have been defined • Future endeavors were planned and outlined • Community and constituent engagement events have served networking purposes • GAID community of expertise have helped ensure that specificities are kept in mind when ICT for development is discussed within the UN and GAID networks	• The lead partners do not feature extensive networks • The initiatives have difficulty in connecting the global with the local level in activities • There seems to be a weak relationship between the GAID community of expertise board and the current members, who facilitate the ICT solutions in developing countries • The connection between GAID and the communities of expertise is partial and irregular. The entrepreneurship community of expertise indicates problems of maintaining a connection between the partners and motivating them to engage in their initiatives • There is a lack of funding and expected assistance from GAID, which imply start up deficiencies • The activities developed by the partners are taking place without GAID's direct involvement • The overall business plan of the community of expertise was reported to be vague about the creation, the strengthening and the expected outcomes of the alliance	• Goals and responsibilities have to be made transparent and accountable. For the outlined goals, respective achievement measurement and performance control must be installed • The connection to GAID has to be strengthened. The communities of expertise have to develop a unique proposition within the wider GAID network. GAID has to establish itself in respective local communities and further advance related activities and grass-roots initiatives • Multi-stakeholder means to create a vital dialogue between all constituents involved have to be considered. Regular conferences and meetings are recommended • At these gatherings, common goals have to be discussed and transparency of goals and goal achievement measurements must be agreed upon • Further meetings, summits and conferences should be launched as for fostering a more vital stakeholder dialogue, extending networks and revitalizing the stakeholder dialogue • To overcome financial constraints, the communities of expertise must continuously look for innovative sources of funding ensured by promoting the successes already accomplished

Summary		
Positive progress	**Deficiencies**	**Recommendations**
• Launch of innovative PPPs • Network extensions • Linkages to the UN • Transparent information sharing worldwide • Private sector sponsorships • Secretariat for work on progress • Harmonization of priorities • Standardization of processes • International forums, conferences and summits for information dissemination, networking and funding • Networking events to identify and tackle regional needs and help implement programs • Surveys to identify areas of concern • Trainings to improve ICT skills to foster development • Goals and accomplishment plans for future endeavors	• Work plan and implementation delays • Multi-stakeholder networking deficiencies • Lack of linkages with GAID • Missing web-information and internet references hinder communication and networking of multiple stakeholders • Funding constraints • Inconsistent policies and practice implementation • Role and goal ambiguity of partners • Vague business plans and undefined outcomes	• Develop a strong networking relation with international organizations and local communities • Identify networking opportunities • Accountability control and goal accomplishment checks • Regular and mandatory conferences, summits and meetings • Transparency on best practices • Promote ICT in local communities • Engage experts • Improve funding • Set clear strategies and policies • Innovate information exchange • Foster a vital dialogue between all constituents

difficulties in establishing networks beyond their current partners, partly due to a lack of knowledge and information about how to expand networks and resource limitations – particularly in developing countries. In some cases, the expectations of the partnerships about the extent to which GAID can mobilize resources or facilitate networking have been unrealistic, given GAID's own resource situation – the GAID secretariat is funded by voluntary sources that are episodic and insecure. This makes longer-term planning and expansion difficult. A few existed but were not well-linked to GAID and at least one had ceased to function.

In summary, GAID has shown some significant results in implementing its mission in its first two years of operation. GAID has launched innovative PPPs and extended its network but also secured funding. GAID's global activities have been particularly successful in leveraging its position as a UN-related organization that focuses on keeping ICT for development on the global agenda. GAID has also been successful in raising and supporting a number of constituent partnerships. Most of the partnerships have demonstrated an ability to achieve first start-up results. For rising partnership initiatives, goals and accomplishment plans have been defined and future endeavors were outlined. Numerous international forums, conferences and summits have strengthened the network. Networking events also have identified and tackled regional needs and helped implementing programs. Information on ICT has been spread worldwide. ICT accessibility and harmonization of best practices standards have been fostered along the progress. Trainings and workshops have improved ICT skills and improved social development on the ground level.

Some problems and areas for improvement have been identified, particularly in terms of the linkages between GAID and the partners. These include time delays, resource limitations, difficulties in establishing and maintaining networks by integrating and linking individual partnerships with GAID due to goal ambiguity and a lack of communication.

Based on the analysis, recommendations include for the network as a whole linking the global with the partnership networks. For GAID and its partners recommendations comprise improving GAID's planning, strengthening resource mobilization and setting up clearer business plans with outcome control mechanisms such as goal accomplishment checks and accountability.

When GAID was analyzed in 2009, its precise direction remained unclear and the added value per stakeholder group was often not obvious (ICT4D Report, 2009). Certain funding streams were lacking for implementing substantial initiatives based on the goals and outlines of the initiative (ICT4D

Report, 2009). A detailed, evidence-based analysis of the status of GAID was performed through scanning online data sources in order to shed light on what had happened since the program began in 2006.

In 2012 a feasibility study of GAID assessed the demand of its services, support for the organizational development, and for its new programming (United Nations Global Alliance for ICT and Development (UNGAID), Feasibility Study & Strategy Development for the United Nation's GAID, 2012).[4] The results helped to retool the program to make it more responsive to its mission in the stakeholder communication at additional conferences and online presence (United Nations Global Alliance for ICT and Development (UNGAID), Feasibility Study & Strategy Development for the United Nation's GAID, 2012).[5] In 2012 the International Solutions Group (ISG)[6] carried out a feasibility check of GAID that provided strategic advice and assistance to UN GAID in assessing its current structure and programming; informed UN GAID about future development strategies; and helped UN GAID to be more responsive to its mission. In particular, the study assessed the demand of UN GAID's services and support for the organizational development of the organization. In addition, it examined new programming that will allow the organization to become more responsive to its mission.[7] A further current search for the GAID program's most recent reports and website updates reveals a stop in new initiatives. This could be a sign of declining interest in ICT for development. For instance, while there seems to have been a fair amount of writings on communication and technology for development about ten years ago (e.g., Heimeriks & Duysters, 2007; Kotlarsky & Oshri, 2005; Leye, 2007); relatively little attention seems to have been paid to the role of ICT for sustainable development. Little seems to be known about the concrete impact of ICT-related programs and the respective PPP efforts for reaching sustainable development. More concrete insights on ICT for development, however, would help better understand the lessons learned from the GAID initiative to overcome similar challenges. The chapter therefore also includes a recent analysis of ICT for development in light of the SDGs that lie at the heart of the UN 2030 Agenda including goals to end extreme poverty, fight inequality and build peaceful societies on a healthy planet (Sustainable Development Goals Report, 2016; Puaschunder, 2017).

The SDGs Report 2016 distributed at the 2016 International Conference on Sustainable Development hosted by Columbia University and The New School New York[8] highlighted ICT playing a key role for the SDG implementation. The technology revolution enabled innovative and cost-effective methods based on mobile phones, mapping, sensors and satellite imagery to collect and improve data for development. But use of these advances was found to require "new partnerships and collaboration between companies, institutions and civil society" (p. 14).

The SDGs Report 2016 also addresses the major challenge of the paucity of data and the poor information on ground work systems that make it difficult to monitor and assess implementation of networking systems. There needs to be a routine of follow ups about the functioning of programs and a vital data collection and analysis over time to ensure the sustainability of long-term ICT for development strategies. The variety of contexts, good investment in information collection and processing requires a broad approach covering all contextual and economic factors relevant to universal ICT for development utilization. Incomplete essential information in the past has hampered development (Puaschunder, 2017).

For the future, GAID is advised to continue to developing a strong networking relation with international organizations and local communities. Further opportunities to network and engage with a wider range of constituents in regular conferences, summits and meetings must be explored. Innovations in ICT for development must be fostered and promoted to constituents.

REFERENCES

Heimeriks, K. H., & Duysters, G. (2007). Alliance capability as a mediator between experience and alliance performance: An empirical investigation into the alliance capability development process. *Journal of Management Studies*, *44*(1), 25–49. doi:10.1111/j.1467-6486.2006.00639.x

ICT4D Report. (2009). *Information and Communication Technology for development*. Cambridge, UK: Cambridge University Press.

International Conference on Sustainable Development. (2016). Columbia University and The New School.

Kotlarsky, J., & Oshri, I. (2005). Social ties, knowledge sharing and successful collaboration in globally distributed system development projects. *European Journal of Information Systems*, *14*(1), 37–48. doi:10.1057/palgrave.ejis.3000520

Leye, V. (2007). UNESCO, ICT corporation and the passion of ICT for development: Modernization resurrected. *Media Culture & Society*, *29*(6), 972–993. doi:10.1177/0163443707081711

Puaschunder, J. M. (2017). Cross-Sectoral Solution-Finding and Policy Dialogue on Information and Communication Technologies for Sustainable Development. In M. Gudic, T. K. Tan, & P. M. Flynn (Eds.), *Beyond the Bottom Line: Integrating the UN Global Compact into Management Practices* (pp. 32–46). New York, NY: Greenleaf Publishing. doi:10.9774/GLEAF.9781783535606_5

Reinfried, Y., Schleicher, A., & Rempfler, A. (2007). Geographical views on education for sustainable development. *Geographiedidaktische Forschungen*, *42*, 243–250.

Sustainable Development Goals Report: The People's Agenda. (2016). UNA-UK.

United Nations Global Alliance for ICT and Development (UNGAID). (2012). *Feasibility Study & Strategy Development for the United Nation's GAID*. Retrieved from http://internationalsolutionsgroup.com/project/feasibility-study-strategy-development-for-the-united-nations-gaid/

World Economic Forum. (2015). *Report*. Davos, Switzerland: World Economic Forum.

ENDNOTES

1 http://www.un.org/sustainabledevelopment/summit/.

2 Samsung, IBM, Internet Speech, Air France, NIIT, Vemics, The Wireless Internet Institute.

3 Youth Action for Change (Italy), United Nations Association of Uganda (UNAU), Prime Resources (Ghana), The Bangladesh Youth Forum on ICT, Burundi Youth Training Center, Commonwealth People's Association of Uganda, Sustainable Development Association (Egypt), Youth and ICTs Mali, Paradigm Initiative (Nigeria), Lagos Digital Village (Nigeria), MadeinKenya.org, Singapore International Youth Council and Africa Youth ICT4D Network.

4 Retrieved October 12, 2016 at http://internationalsolutionsgroup.com/project/feasibility-study-strategy-development-for-the-united-nations-gaid/.

5 Retrieved October 12, 2016 at http://internationalsolutionsgroup.com/project/feasibility-study-strategy-development-for-the-united-nations-gaid/.

6 http://internationalsolutionsgroup.com/project/feasibility-study-strategy-development-for-the-united-nations-gaid/.

7 http://internationalsolutionsgroup.com/project/feasibility-study-strategy-development-for-the-united-nations-gaid/.

8 http://ic-sd.org/.

Chapter 6
Political Divestiture

ABSTRACT

In the wake of historical and political events, stakeholder pressure can trigger divestment from politically incorrect markets. Six evaluation studies of political divestiture from South Africa during Apartheid were meta-analyzed to find a pattern of stakeholder pressure, political divestiture, and corporate endeavors. The meta-analysis covered the question of whether corporations divesting from politically incorrect markets are more likely to experiencing an increase, decrease, or no change in market value, and it found varying results – some studies suggest a positive effect, others a negative impact, and even no overall performance pattern of political divestiture and corporate value was reported. The study also detected a research gap on the impact of political divestiture on corporations operating in politically fractionate markets. Future research may compare values of divesting corporations with those operating in politically incorrect markets. The instringent results are attributed to stem from methodological limitations. Political divestiture is captured by the event study method which was evaluated for validity threats. Internal validity limitations of event study designs stem from confounding and contaminating history occurrences, sample selection biases, and inappropriate time frames. Insider trading information leakage but also industry specificities imply additional validity drawbacks. The external validity is challenged by geographically limited and time-targeted studies as well as non-typical samples that feature a lowered replicability and generalizability of the findings.

DOI: 10.4018/978-1-5225-7619-8.ch006

INTRODUCTION

In the wake of historical and political events, socio-political pressure can evolve that triggers corporations to divest politically incorrect markets. The impact of socio-political events on financial considerations is attributed by political divestiture – the act of removing funds from politically fractionated markets.

Since the start of political divestiture in the 1970s, the connection of politics and investments has been subject to scientific scrutiny, yet comparative results are scarce. This deficiency was attributed in the following meta-analysis. Drawing from the field of SRI, the evaluation analyzed the body of research on political divestiture from South Africa during Apartheid (Puaschunder, 2015).

Most of the studies of political divestiture feature the event study methodology, which describes the effects of socio-political events on markets (Peterson, 1989). Event studies examine how the release of specific information impacts on stock prices and corporate values during a particular time (Harvey, 2008). The event 'time window' under scrutiny comprises the period immediately before, during and after the event of interest (Peterson, 1989). Until today there are hardly any examinations of the strengths and potential weaknesses of the event study methodology. In the following meta-analysis, attention will thus be paid to methodological aspects of the measurement of political divestiture (Puaschunder, 2017).

Research Question

In recent decades ethicality has become subject to scientific scrutiny in the management and business literature (Bazerman & Moore, 2009). Research described CSR codes of conduct and compared social responsibility practices in the international arena (Langlois & Schlegelmilch, 1990; Matten & Moon, 2004; Steurer et al., 2008). CSR business cases outlined success factors of corporate social conscientiousness (Porter & Kramer, 2003). Corporate social engagement was empirically linked to corporate financial performance and related to investments (Choi & Jung, 2008; Epstein, McEwen & Spindle, 1994; Waddock & Graves, 1997).

With the emerging stream of literature on CSR, the finance community concurrently started paying attention to ethical considerations of the asset issuing entities (Little, 2008). Academia promoted SRI and explored socio-psychological motives of ethical investment in expert interviews, questionnaire surveys and experiments (Hofmann, Hoelzl & Kirchler, 2008; Mackenzie & Lewis, 1999). In the political sciences literature, SRI was introduced as a soft-law shareholder activism approach that differs throughout the world (Detomasi, 2007; Steurer, 2010).

Given the emerging prominence of CSR and SRI research literature, political divestiture studies are underrepresented. Anecdotal political sciences studies have foremost captured historical evidence of stakeholder-initiated divestiture. In a financially globalizing world, the investigation of the impacts of foreign investment drain has been limited. In the already scare literature on political divestiture, empirical evidence of the efficiency of political divestiture as a means to foster socio-political change is rare. Understanding the impacts of political divestiture in the international arena, however, is important as foreign direct investment flows hold untapped potentials to complement traditional foreign policy means. Foreign capital drain is a fast way to unconventionally undermine socio-politically incorrect regimes. Limited access to investment capital can unbureaucratically instigating governmental reforms without the necessity of collaterally damaging warfare, long-term foreign affairs engagement or the approval of international agreement on institutionally enforced sanctions – for example through the UN or NATO. Political divestiture therefore appears as a highly efficiently means of global governance, yet many aspects of financial withdrawal to pressure governments have not been clarified sufficiently.

In the primarily politically-focused literature on political divestiture and sociopsychological literature on SRI shareholder activism, the investigation of the impacts of political divestiture on corporate endeavors has been limited (Crampton & Patten, 2008; Patten, 2007). Until now no stringent pattern of political divestiture and corporate performance is at hand (McWilliams, Siegel & Teoh, 1999; Zeff & Pirro, 1999). Exploratory evidence finds variant results, which demand for further comparative studies to nail down specific causes for the inhomogeneous findings.

Understanding the impact of shareholder political activism on corporate values is of interest for business strategists. Revealing SRI as an efficient corporate move will help promoting SRI to corporate executives and financial analysts as a market incentive. Finding evidence for the effectiveness of political divestiture would also offer insights on success factors of political divestiture. While the right timing of divestiture appears as a potential moderator variable, no clear pattern of divestiture time and corporate value has been identified yet. Corporate strategy managers could benefit from recommendations on advantageous divestiture times. In addition, prospectively finding a first-mover advantage for early withdrawing entities could support ethical leadership theory which portrays SRI as a strategic, entrepreneurial move (Surie & Ashley, 2007). Further it is unknown if corporations remaining in politically instable markets suffer long-term losses in the wake of an overall economic market decline that could be avoided by political divestiture.

Structuring the body of knowledge on the impact of political divestiture on corporate values also offers implications for international law. As political divestiture serves many purposes and varies over time and by context, comparative studies will help defining political divestiture in the search for finding an overarching legal framework that unites disparate approaches. A definition of political divestiture will also help drawing inferences about the impact of political divestiture on shareholder wealth. As political divestiture captures transnational foreign investment flows, becoming knowledgeable about the impact of political divestiture on shareholder wealth will help crafting international standards for fiduciaries. Finding evidence for an effect of political divestiture on corporate endeavors will clarify to what degree political divestiture supports or infringes upon shareholder primacy rules and fiduciary responsibilities. As of today there are vast international differences in the legal interpretation of fiduciary responsibility – in Anglo-Saxon fiduciary responsibility is more focused on return on investments, while Western European Roman Law-dominated countries legally grant fiduciaries more leeway in considering the overall societal impact of the asset issuing entities. Prospective insights on the efficiency of political divestiture to serve shareholder goals are a cornerstone in the conceptualization of a standardized international law on fiduciary responsibilities, which appears necessary in a financially globalizing world that demands for ingraining responsibility in market economies in the light of the 2008/09 World Financial Recession. For the international investment community, shedding light on the impact of stakeholder pressure on investment decision is essential as for drawing inferences about the financial market stability.

On the global governance level, the prospective results may help predicting future foreign investment flows and outcomes of contemporary political frictions – such as, for example, humanitarian infringements in Burma, Iran's nuclear proliferation and Sudan's humanitarian crisis in the Darfur region. Insights on the effectiveness of political divestiture will also help generating public policies for international institutional assistance of political divestiture. With the 'US Comprehensive Iran Sanctions, Accountability and Divestment Act' having passed the House vote in April 2010, the downsides of sanctions and political divestiture have been openly debated recently. Critics condemn sanctions as a hostilitybreeding "act of war" and draw attention to unintended consequences of insufficiently understood negative externalities that may eventually backfire. Libertarians critiqued political divestiture as a misuse of financial markets that undermines free trade and shareholder profit maximization goals. To contribute to finding a fact-based solution for this political debate, a more sophisticated in-depth understanding of the corporate implications of political divestiture that is based on comparative results is needed.

Hypotheses

The following study is targeted at capturing the impact of political divestiture on corporate values in order to determine if socio-political pressure upon corporations and investors to leave or to operate in politically incorrect markets offers market incentives.

Two hypotheses will be investigated. The underlying assumption of the *first hypothesis* (see Figure 1) is that socio-political events can pressure institutional and private investors to sell stocks invested in socially fractionate and politically incorrect markets. Hypothesis 1 examines if corporations ceasing operations in politically incorrect markets are more likely to experiencing an *increase* (Hypothesis 1.1), *decrease* (Hypothesis 1.3) or *no change* in market value (Hypothesis 1.2).

Hypothesis 1.1 tests an *increase* in market value for corporations divesting politically incorrect markets. The underlying idea is that corporations that stop operating in politically fractionate areas will attract attention of socially conscientious investors and gain novel finance streams. A positive outcome may also derive from lifted consumer boycotts against products of corporations supporting politically undesirable causes.

Hypothesis 1.2 assumes *no change* in market value for corporations leaving politically incorrect markets. This would indicate that political divestiture does not have any impact on market actors. As a niche market phenomenon, political divestiture may neither resonate in overall market fundamentals nor impact on corporate values.

Hypothesis 1.3 suggests a *decrease* in market value for corporations leaving politically incorrect markets as for a loss of degrees of freedom and access to economically profitable market options.

Figure 1. Hypothesis 1 on political divestiture impact on divesting corporations

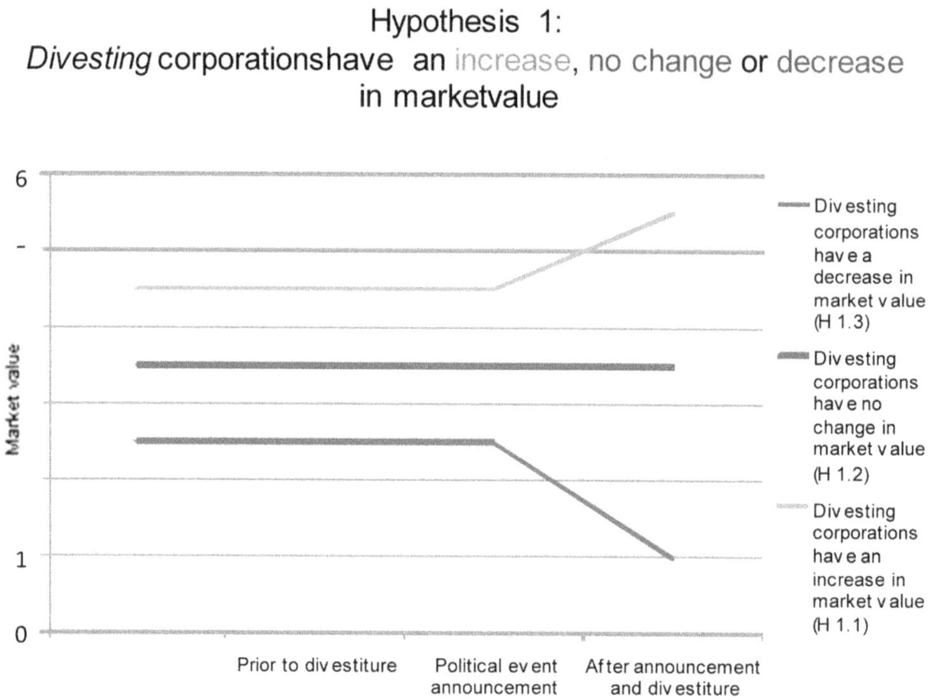

The *second hypothesis* (see Figure 2) investigates if corporations that remain in politically incorrect markets are more likely to experiencing an *increase* (Hypothesis 2.1), *decrease* (Hypothesis 2.3) or *no change* in market value (Hypothesis 2.2).

Hypothesis 2.1 assumes an *increase* in market value for corporations remaining in politically incorrect markets as for benefitting from monopolistic advantages such as lowered competition of dropped out market participants and the ability to operate in an investorfriendly market, in which the supply-side is pressured to offer special discount rates.

As studied by hypothesis 2.2, finding *no change* in market value for corporations remaining in politically incorrect markets would indicate that political divestiture does not have any impact on markets and participants. In combination with Hypothesis 1.2 this would outline that neither staying in nor leaving politically incorrect markets has any influence on corporate value.

Hypothesis 2.3 suggests a *decrease* in market value for corporations remaining in politically incorrect markets. The underlying rationale is that investor herd behavior triggering capital flight from politically-volatiled

Figure 2. Hypothesis 2 on political divestiture impact on remaining corporations

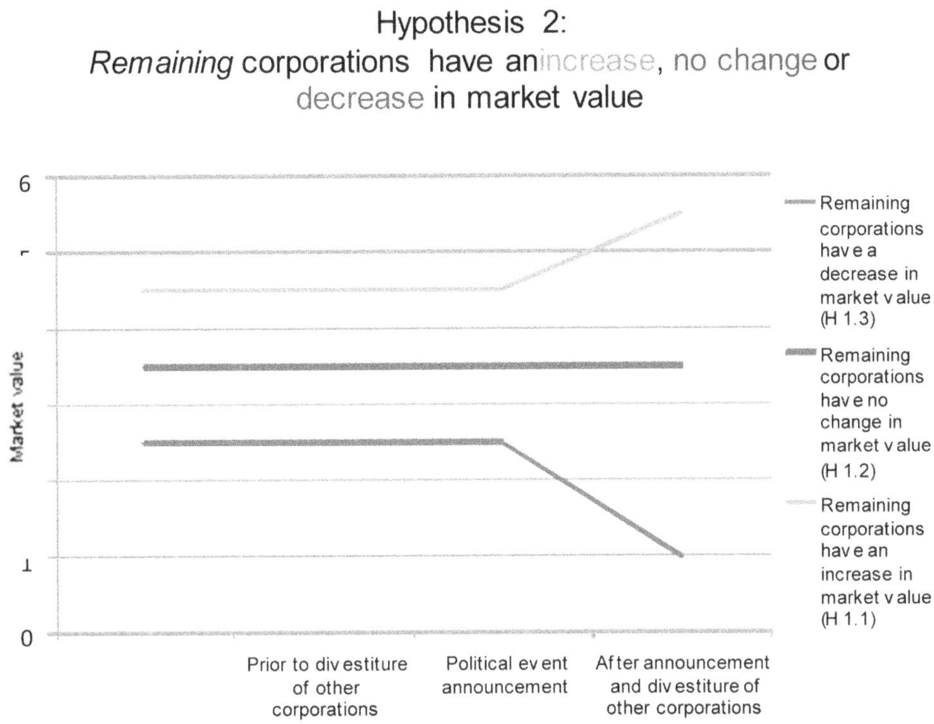

markets and stakeholder pressure causing governmental sanctions lead to an overall economic downturn of economically fragile and politically insecure markets, in which assets drop.

Meta-Analysis of Studies of Divestiture From South Africa During Apartheid

Political divestiture became prominent in the case of divestiture from South Africa during Apartheid. The literature on divestment from South Africa features the effects of media coverage of political atrocities on investment allocations. Stakeholder pressure encouraging publicly traded corporations to leave South Africa and institutional investors to sell holdings in corporations operating in South Africa are hypothesized to be systemically related to corporate value changes. The current body of knowledge on political divestiture from South Africa during the Apartheid era was thus investigated to determine the impact of stakeholderinitiated political divestiture on corporate endeavors.

Material

The analysis included six independent evaluation studies of the impact of divestiture on the corporate financial performance that were retrieved from online scientific databases in February 2008. The meta-analyzed studies investigate the impact of stakeholder pressure events on corporations divesting South Africa (Hypothesis 1) and the trends in institutional ownership of corporations operating in South Africa before, during and after disinvestments (Hypothesis 2).

All studies featured the event study methodology. In the case of political divestiture, event studies examine how the release of information about political events affects stock prices and corporate values (Harvey, 2008). The event study method captures the impact of an impulse on markets and resembles an interrupted time series model. An event study is conceptualized by creating a study group of event dates and study points of corporations. Data from market database sources – such as the Center for Research into Security Prices (CRSP) – offer monthly or daily stock prices and simultaneous market-wide changes. The event time window under scrutiny comprises the time frame immediately before, during and after an event of interest (Peterson, 1989). A projected return is calculated for the event window by using a regression. The results of the projected returns are compared to the actual ones. If graphed, an event study looks similar to an interrupted time series, but with two lines: the projected and the actual return, which would separate on the first day of the event window. The difference between the two lines tests the hypothesis determined by statistically significant deviations. There are variations in the statistical methods used for running these steps (Salinger, 1992). In general, event studies comprise one year's trading data in creating projections for daily returns, while two to five years are common for monthly returns (Peterson, 1989). Including market, industry returns and risk free rates in the statistical models controls for unrelated events.

Past Event Study Evaluations

Evaluation #1: Issues in the use of the event study methodology: A critical analysis of corporate social responsibility studies (McWilliams, Siegel & Teoh, 1999)

The studies of McWilliams et al. (1999) present event study designs as a means to measure CSR impacts on shareholder return. McWilliams et al. (1999) meta-analyzed five studies of divestment from South Africa in the wake of anti-Apartheid movements. Overall, the results stemmed from 1 to 3 day time windows with one exemption of a 41 day time window. The primary goal of the event studies under scrutiny was to assess the effects of unanticipated events on stock prices.

The results on the impact of divestiture on corporate value differ: Two studies found that divestiture had no significant (McWilliams & Siegel, 1997; Teoh et al., 1999), two a negative (Meznar et al., 1994; Wright & Ferris, 1997) and one a positive impact on corporate financial performance (Posnikoff, 1997). The variant results are attributed to methodological specificities of event studies (McWilliams et al., 1999).

Evaluation #2: An examination of stock market reactions to US corporate divestitures in South Africa (Ngassam, 1992)

Ngassam (1992) evaluated the costs and benefits of divestiture from South Africa based on significant price movements around divestiture announcement. Two hypotheses tested whether divestment of assets related to South Africa had an effect on shareholder wealth. A third hypothesis investigated whether shareholder wealth affects of South Africa divestments are positively related to the size of the divested assets.

The sample included 63 US corporations that announced plans to divest South African between 1979 and 1988 published by the Investor Research and Responsibility Center. Stock values from corporations that publicly reported divestiture and completed the asset sales were analyzed. For each corporation daily abnormal returns were computed for a 21 day interval comprising ten days prior and ten days after the announcement t=(-10, +10). Their sum formed the cumulative average abnormal returns. For testing the third hypothesis, large divestitures exceeded one percent of the total corporate values – leading to 20 large and 43 small divestiture cases.

Evidence was found that stocks of corporations that divest South Africa assets experience negative abnormal returns. This is especially the case with corporations that divested after 1985 when the socio-political pressure to divest peaked. There is a positive relationship between the size of the divested assets and shareholder wealth effects.

Overall the findings indicate that divesting South African has a negative effect on shareholder wealth. An inopportune selling time is attributed as the primary cause as in periods of mounting divestment pressure, the majority of withdrawing corporations sell for unfavorable 'fire sale' prices.

Evaluation #3: Divestment from South Africa: They did well by doing good (Posnikoff, 1997)

Posnikoff (1997) evaluated the impact of divestiture from South Africa in response to Apartheid upon publicly-traded corporate stock prices. Data for 40 US corporations with withdrawal announcement between 1980 and 1991 was combined into a single portfolio. In an event study evaluation, the actual stock prices were compared to projected ones during the period immediately surrounding the disinvestment announcement. For each corporation under scrutiny, the date of the announcement was set as date 0. The days before and after the announcement were included in the event window. Separate analyses were run for the event window as (day -1, day 0, day +1), (-1, 0), (0, +1), and (0). A comparison window of the 251st through 3rd trading days prior to the announcement was used along with S&P 500 market data to project the stock prices. Posnikoff (1997) also examined the portfolio with evenly-weighted corporations and corporations weighted by value.

Posnikoff (1997) found statistically significant positive abnormal returns during the periods (1, 0, +1) and (-1, 0) but no statistically significant abnormal returns for (0, +1) or (0). The market return and ordinary least squares methods showed these results for evenly-weighted and value-weighted portfolios. The comparison period return exhibited statistically significant positive returns for the period (-1, 0, +1), but not for (-1, 0). The trading volume was significantly increased for the periods (-1, 0, +1) and (0,+1). Overall, the author's findings indicate an increase in stock prices for corporations leaving politically incorrect markets upon announcing the disinvestment, which is attributed to the economic effects of lifted socio-political pressure.

Evaluation #4: Agency conflict and corporation strategy: The effect of divestment on corporate value (Wright & Ferris, 1997)

In 1997 Wright and Ferris analyzed the impact of disinvestments from South Africa upon US corporate stock prices. The underlying hypothesis was that a negative abnormal return would occur due to a conflict of interests between the principle (shareholders) and agent (senior management). Wright and Ferris (1997) used a portfolio of 31 publicly-traded corporations that divested South Africa between 1984 and 1990. Corporations with poor Sullivan ratings or disinvestments resulting from lawsuits or shareholder resolutions were excluded. Days 260 to -11 were used to calculate expected returns with the Capital Asset Pricing Model (CAPM) including the risk free rate and market returns. Each day of a 21 day time window was analyzed separately, with all corporations viewed as a single unweighted portfolio.

The study revealed a statistically significant negative excess return on the event day. No other statistically significant abnormal returns were found. The researchers interpret this as an evidence for their hypothesis, attributing the negative return to principle-agent problems.

Evaluation #5: The effect of socially activist investment policies on the financial markets: Evidence from the South African boycott (Teoh, Welch & Wazzan, 1999)

Teoh, Welch and Wazzan (1999) covered six distinct questions in an extensive evaluation of political divestiture studies. The authors performed analyses of several separate measures of divestment upon financial markets and corporations. Daily and monthly return data was captured from the CRSP. Market returns, industry returns – based upon The North American Industry Classification System (NAICS)[1] code – and the risk free rates were included in the regressions. The event study methodology featured one month, three day (-1, 0, +1) or one day (0) event windows. Days -205 to -5 were used for the projection equations.

The researchers investigated the impact of ten US legislative and executive event announcements upon US banks with South African investments. A portfolio of nine US banks with loans in South Africa was weighted by the percentage of South Africa loans.

A three day event window showed no support that sanctions would depress and relaxation of sanctions would increase market values. The researchers attribute this to the small proportion of South Africa loans in relation to the overall market.

The impact of US legislative events upon South African financial markets was studied by the reactions of South Africa's largest corporations with Anglo-American roots, two South African stock-based indices and the dollar/rand exchange rate.

The authors found statistically significant evidence for South African financial markets and corporations benefitting from sanctions. The removal of foreign competition may have improved the performance of the large corporations remaining in South Africa. The exchange rate was statistically significant for only one event – the House vote for sanctions – with negative abnormal returns.

The impact of 25 distinct events on 16 pension fund divestments of a portfolio of US corporations operating in South Africa was evaluated. The authors tried four weightings of the portfolio: unweighted, percentage of sales in South Africa, percentage of assets in South Africa and percentage of employees in South Africa. They also normalized the weightings for the percentage of South African subsidiaries owned.

In the study of the impact of pension fund divestment announcements on South African financial markets, none of the methodologies found statistically significant evidence.

For investigating the impact of divestment announcements on institutional investments with CRSP data, the authors analyzed the monthly institutional shareholding of 46 corporations featuring voluntary divestiture.

This analysis found evidence of an increase in institutional investment in corporations after the divestment. The results revealed a negative trend prior to the announcement and positive tendency thereafter. The authors surmise that institutional investors withdrew before and returned after the event.

For the impact of divestment upon returns of individual corporations, the authors used the data of 46 corporations as a single portfolio with four weightings: equal, sales, assets and employees. They included the expected return to compare the abnormal and actual return, with a 33 day time window comprising a 15 days pre-event period, 3 days event period, and 15 days post-event period. No evidence of any reaction was found.

The authors also conducted a time series evaluation of the divestiture period. As this methodology was not explained in detail and differed from the other analyses, it was excluded from the meta-analysis.

Evaluation #6: Effect of announcements of withdrawal from South Africa on stockholder wealth (Meznar, Nigh & Kwok, 1994)

Meznar et al. (1994) analyzed the impact of announcements of corporate withdrawal from South Africa on corporate market values measured by the stock price. An event study design tested if (1) withdrawal announcements are associated with an increase in market value of divesting corporations; (2) announcements of withdrawal are associated with a decrease in market value of divesting corporations and if (3) later announcements of withdrawal are viewed more favorably.

The authors investigated 207 corporations that divested South Africa in the early 1970s and 1990s. This list was ultimately narrowed down to 39 based on the following criteria: (1) the withdrawal was not incidental; (2) the announcement of withdrawal was made in one of seven major newspapers; (3) the corporation was publicly traded on the NYSE or NASDAQ and (4) the event was isolated from other corporate announcements. The event was set as the date of the announcement. The dependent variable was the daily market price collected for several months prior to the event and 10 days after the event. A regression projected the expected stock price for the post-event period. The difference between the actual and the projected stock price represents the effect of the event.

The authors found that a withdrawal announcement lowered the overall corporate market value. Corporations that published withdrawals earlier experienced a more negative effect.

Six evaluations of event studies of divestiture from South Africa were analyzed in order to determine if stakeholder pressure upon corporations and investors to leave politically fractionate market are related to corporate incentives. The analyses comprised: (1) the impact of disinvestment pressure upon stock values of corporations operating in South Africa; (2) the impact upon stock prices of corporations divesting South Africa; and (3) the trends in institutional ownership of corporations operating in South Africa before, during and after divestment.

As outlined by Table 1, the research findings differ. Regarding hypothesis 1 testing the influence of political divestiture on divesting corporations, some studies found a positive effect (Posnikoff, 1997; Teoh et al., 1999; McWilliams et al., 1999), others a negative impact (McWilliams et al., 1999; Meznar et al., 1994; Ngassam, 1992; Wright & Ferris, 1997) and even no overall corporate performance change in the wake of divestiture was reported (McWilliams et al., 1999; Posnikoff, 1997; Teoh et al., 1999).

As for hypothesis 2 on the effect of political divestiture on corporations remaining in politically incorrect markets, the meta-analysis identified an area in which there have been relatively few studies conducted warranting for more research.

Table 1. Evidence for the impact of political divestiture on corporate endeavors

Hypotheses		
Hypothesis 1: Corporations leaving politically incorrect markets experience an increase (Hypothesis 1.1), decrease (Hypothesis 1.3) or no change in market value (Hypothesis 1.2).		
Hypothesis 1.1 Increase in market value	**Hypothesis 1.2** No change in market value	**Hypothesis 1.3** Decrease in market value
• **McWilliams et al. (1999)** meta-analyzed five studies by using 1, 3 and a 41 day time windows that examined divestment from South Africa and found in one study (Posnikoff, 1997) that divestiture had a significant positive impact on corporate financial performance. • **Posnikoff (1997)** based on 40 US corporate values measured by two and three day time windows from 1980 to 1991. • **Teoh et al. (1999)** using divestment announcements on institutional investments of 46 corporations.	• **McWilliams et al. (1999)** meta-analyzed five studies by using 1, 3 and a 41 day time window that examined divestment from South Africa and found in two studies (McWilliams & Siegel, 1997; Teoh et al., 1999) that divestiture had no significant impact on corporate financial performance. • **Posnikoff (1997)** analyzed 40 US corporations' value measured by two and three day time windows from 1980 to 1991. • **Teoh et al. (1999)** investigated ten governmental action announcements and nine US banks with loans in South Africa using a three day time window. • **Teoh et al. (1999)** based on 17 US corporate assets with significant South African operations and 25 distinct events from 16 pension funds divesting. • **Teoh et al. (1999)** studied reactions to divestment announcements of 46 corporations.	• **McWilliams et al. (1999)** meta-analyzed five studies by using 1, 3 and 41 day time windows that examined divestment from South Africa and found in two studies (Meznar et al., 1994; Wright & Ferris, 1997) that divestiture had a significantly negative impact on corporate financial performance. • **Ngassam (1992)** referring to 21 day time window measured price movements of 63 US corporations that publicly reported plans to divest South Africa between 1979 and 1988. • **Wright & Ferris (1997)** viewed at 31 publicly-traded US corporations using a 21 day time window from 1984 to 1990. • **Meznar et al. (1994)** based on 207 reviewed corporations and 39 selected that announced divestments from South Africa in the period of the early 1970s and 1990s.
Explanations: • Economic effects in the wake of lifted socio-political pressure. • Caveat is that institutional investors may have withdrawn before events and returned thereafter.	**Explanation:** • The small fraction of South Africa assets implies minor impacts on overall market prices.	**Explanations:** • Conflicts of interest between the principle (shareholder) and agent (senior management). • In a period of mounting divestment pressure, the negative effect is pronounced as the majority of withdrawing corporations sell at inopportune 'fire sale' prices. • Early divestiture leading to a more negative effect.

Hypothesis 2: Corporations remaining in politically incorrect markets experience an increase (Hypothesis 1.1), decrease (Hypothesis 1.3) or no change in market value (Hypothesis 1.2).		
Hypothesis 1.1 Increase in market value	**Hypothesis 1.2** No change in market value	**Hypothesis 1.3** Decrease in market value
• **Teoh et al. (1999)** based on US legislative events upon South African financial markets impacting on South Africa's largest corporations with Anglo-American roots, two South African stock-based indices and the dollar/rand exchange rate.		
Explanation: • The removal of foreign competition improves the performance of the corporations remaining in South Africa.		

The inconsistent results of South African divestment studies and failed replications with different time-window raise the demand for future comparative research. Reflecting about limitations of the event study methodology will help explaining the instringent results and advance the validity of event study designs.

Event Study Methodology

Over the last decade, the event study methodology was used to investigate the reactions of financial market participants to socio-political events. In the finance and applied economics literature, the event study methodology offers predictions for managerial decisions on financial allocations (Salinger, 1992). As the state-of-the-art means to capture the effects of political divestiture, event study designs feature several advantages. By drawing upon financial market data, the event study method benefits from large sample pools. Almost every security traded on a major stock exchange involves a number of daily transactions far beyond minimum sample sizes of social sciences' standards. The broad base of investment transactions offers the potential for strong statistical evidence.

At the same time, the event study validity is limited by several methodological specificities. As a control of the study design, the **internal validity** examines the causal relationship of the independent and dependent variable (Weiss, 1998). Based on Duncombe's (2008) evaluation framework, the internal validity of event study designs is challenged by ***confounding and contaminating history effects***, ***clustering***, ***maturation leakage***, ***sample selection*** biases, ***attrition*** and the ***regression to the mean*** statistical artefact.

The **external** validity distinguishes the applicability of the results to real-world contexts. Duncombe's (2008) framework comments on the external validity regarding ***geographically-limited***, ***time-targeted studies*** and ***non-typical samples***.

The **internal validity** of event study designs attributes the question whether observed changes in stock prices can be related to socio-political events. Historical incidents have potentially contributed to the overall changes studied and effect the relation of the independent and dependent variables (Dunbombe, 2008). The interconnectedness of several historical events makes it difficult to clearly extract an event and its impact on financial markets. ***Confounding contamination history effects*** stem from concurrent announcements that are inseparable from the studied effect (Barakat & Terry, 2008). If multiple events happen closely to the event under scrutiny, the test has less power to explain the effect (Harvey, 2008; Peterson, 1989). In the light of market-wide influences, the event study design must limit the impact of contaminating history impacts. The length of the time window determines which events are considered. Well-tempered time windows control the event-specific information included in a study. As variantly delayed responses of investors require long event time windows, the likelihood of contamination increases. After the selection of an appropriate time frame, the entire time period must be scanned for confounding market impact factors. When extending the window beyond three days, it becomes difficult to isolate the effect of the event from other stock price changing occurrences. Studies with time windows above 20 days are likely confounded as several other events may have influenced corporate assets. Isolation of such a spill-over is difficult, if not impossible. The selection of a high volume of trading data prevents confounding contamination. A short time window minimizes the spill-over risk but implies a small sample leading to statistical artefacts and a lowered generalizability of the results (Posnikoff, 1997).

All meta-analyzed designs may encounter contaminating history problems if the announcements are not successfully isolated from other news. In order to control for confounding, Meznar et al. (1994) and McWilliams et al. (1999) took overall market trends into consideration. Posnikoff (1997) statistically prevented contamination by separating between the study and the rest of market trading; but mentioned differing reasons for corporate withdrawal from South Africa may have confounded the study. The inclusion of market, industry and risk free factors by Teoh et al. (1999) reduced contamination threats.

In event studies ***clustering*** occurs when conditions disproportionately and systematically effect the industry or a cluster of corporations under investigation (Duncombe, 2008). The clustering bias may be limited by extracting all stock price changes that are expected relative to the market, industry and other corporate-specific factors leaving the residual return solely being associated with the unique event. In addition, financial market price jumps lead to clustering and serial correlations. Teoh et al. (1999) included risk free factors in order to reduce industry-specific clustering biases.

Maturation leakage happens when event-specific information reaches select individuals before it hits the market as a whole – for example if insider trading talks precede an official information release. Information leakage within the investment community causes the announcement date to possibly not coincide with the abnormal returns. Leakage is mitigated by the Security and Exchange Commission (SEC) disclosure requirements that limit insider trading by mandatory public announcements of substantial changes. The length of time windows determines the possibility of information leakage. In the set up of the window it is hard to identify the precise date at which the information about events reached the market and influenced investors. Stretching the time window increases the likelihood of information biases. In the analyzed studies, leakage in the wake of insider trade may have weakened the effects under scrutiny.

Sample selection pays attention to cases that are inherently different from those chosen (Duncombe, 2008). In the event study methodology, critical sample selection issues comprise finding relevant events with sufficient media coverage, drawing an appropriate sample, identifying a well-tempered time frame and controlling for firm-specific and industry effects.

Important political events with sufficient media coverage and precise announcement dates are key in event studies. Implicit sample selection criteria for corporations are the means of information dissemination of political events. An absence of corporate shareholder resolutions on political divestiture implies additional selection biases.

The sample size determines the robustness of results and the error term of a regression. Regarding missing data points, Peterson (1989) favors removing incomplete securities from the sample over drawing an average of prior and succeeding returns to replace information. Other recommendations are using daily returns, time series rather than cross sectional methods and an equally-weighted instead of a value-weighted index (Peterson, 1989).

When balancing the time window an over-extended lengths decreases the power of statistical testing; yet a too short time frame will not capture lagged investor reactions to novel information, which takes time to impact on prices that do not instantaneously reflect all available information. The typical event study design comprises a three day time window (-1, 0, +1) which may omit lagged shareholder reactions. Extensions of the day time window beyond three days make it difficult to isolate the specific event effect from unrelated stock price influences. The problem when events cover many days can be statistically limited by combining days in the event window (Peterson, 1989).

Additional selection biases occur if researchers use an artificial portfolio featuring unrepresentative data of the market sector under scrutiny. Corporate sectors with distinct structural differences may lead to industry-specific results. Corporate specificities are additional potential selection biases.

Regarding the investigated studies, the sample only covered events with media attention and corporations listed on stock exchanges. The exclusion of NASDAQ-traded corporations in the Posnikoff (1997) study and the removal of 81 percent of the total number of scanned corporations in the Meznar et al. (1994) study may have biased the sample. Wright and Ferris (1997) omitted corporations with poor Sullivan ratings and divesting prior to 1984 lead to an unrepresentative portfolio regarding all divesting corporations.

The 1 to 3 day time windows used by McWilliams et al. (1999) may have neglected shareholder reactions. Sample selection biases were mitigated in the Ngassam (1992) study by retrieving data from three different shareholder indices,[2] yet the relatively small sample size increases the regression error term. Posnikoff (1997) using a wide time window increased potential selection biases.

Attrition pays attention to the number of drop-out cases from a selected sample (Duncombe, 2008). In the event study design, attrition applies to data that was excluded from the drawn sample. Posnikoff (1997) refrained from considering one corporation due to becoming privately-held less than one month after its disinvestment announcement. Corporations with multiple announcements were omitted in the Ngassam (1992) study.

Regression to the mean is a statistical phenomenon causing a group's average performance on one measure to regress more than anticipated toward the mean of that measure (Duncombe, 2008). In the event study method, a limited number of days included in a time window impose uncontrollable regression to the mean biases. In addition, stock price jumps imply problems to logarithmic regressions of event studies (Barakat & Terry, 2008).

Regression to the mean is overcome by post-ante designs refraining from pre- and post-tests.

The **external validity** attributes the extent to which studies are reflecting real-world phenomena and if the results have broader implications for similar events. In the case of political divestiture, it is crucial to test if the effects found in one market are generalizable to other populations as for drawing inferences for other political causes and deriving strategies for future corporate endeavors. A decrease generalizability of the results limits the predictability of market reactions to future political events.

The external validity is determined by the geographical and historical focus as well as the sample of a study. Threats to the external validity comprise a narrow ***geographical focus***, ***time-targeted studies*** as well as ***non-typical samples*** (Duncombe, 2008).

The ***geographical focus*** of a study implies the local relevance of the results. Geographically-targeted studies may not represent an overall population and thus trade off from a 'global validity' which allows a world-wide generalization of the findings (Bohnet, in speech, January 2010).

As the analyzed studies focused on South Africa, it remains unclear whether the results can be generalized to other populations. In addition, all studies are geographicallylimited to corporations traded in the US, most of them at the NYSE. The Posnikoff (1997) study excluded the NASDAQ. If there is reason to believe that the foreign exchange and NASDAQ-traded corporations differ, then the results do not apply to those cases.

Time-targeted studies investigate a certain time in history (Duncombe, 2008). Regarding event studies, the question arises if the time window is appropriate to truly capture a general relation of financial trends and societal patterns. The measurement of a specific time window raises questions about the replicability of the findings at variant times in history. The generalizability of the results to other historical events must be investigated by future research. Future comparative studies will help predicting political events' impact on financial markets in order to ingrain stability in economic market systems.

A ***non-typical sample*** limits the applicability of results and thus the external validity. Small sample sizes, short time frames, restrictive portfolios and selection deficiencies create nontypical samples that lower the external validity. All events and samples are insofar nontypical as for covering divestiture cases with media attention and corporations listed on the US stock exchange which limits the generalizability of the results to the overall market. The inclusion of market, industry and risk free factors in the Teoh et al. (1999) study counterweights a potential industry-specific focus.

Overall, the variety of studies investigated demonstrates the wide range of applicability of the event study methodology. While the focus on the South Africa disinvestments limits the direct applicability to other contexts, the methodology and lessons learned will help designing future studies. The breadth of studies provides a resource for generating potential future studies to test the findings' applicability to other socio-political cases. Further investigations of the findings' generalizability will help predicting the overall impact of political divestiture on economic markets and society.

The revealed strengths and weaknesses of event study designs are outlined by Table 2.

Table 2. Evaluation of the event study methodology

Evaluation of Political Divestiture Studies						
Analysis of the event study methodology based on Duncombe's evaluation framework (2008)						
Internal Validity						
Design threat	**Confounding and contaminating history effects**	**Clustering**	**Maturation leakage**	**Sample selection**	**Attrition**	**Regression to the mean**
Description	Concurrent announcements create effects that are inseparable from the event under scrutiny	Conditions disproportionately effect the industry or a cluster of corporations under investigation	When event-specific information reaches select individuals or groups before it hits the market as a whole	Samples selection comprises finding relevant events with sufficient media coverage, drawing an appropriate sample, identifying a well-tempered time frame and controlling for firm-specific and industry effects	Pays attention to the number of drop-outs within a selected sample	Causes a group's average performance on one measure to regress more than anticipated toward the mean of that measure
Strengths	• Well-tempered time windows control the included information. A short time window minimizes spill-over risks but implies statistical artefacts and a lowered generalizability of the results • The selected time period must be scanned for confounding impacts • A high volume of trading data and taking overall market trends into consideration controls for confounding • Separation between the study and the rest of the market trading • Inclusion of market, industry and risk free factors	• The clustering bias is limited by extracting all stock price changes that are expected relative to the market, industry and other firm-specific factors • Inclusion of risk free factors reduces clustering biases	• The Security and Exchange Commission (SEC) disclosure requirements limit leakage-causing insider trading	• Removing incomplete securities from the sample is preferred over drawing an average of prior and succeeding returns to replace missing information. Other recommendations are to use daily returns, time series rather than cross sectional methods and equally weighted instead of a value weighted index • When events cover many days these should be combined in the event window • Sample selection biases are controlled by retrieving data from different shareholder indices		• Post-ante study design with no pre- and post test
Weaknesses	• If multiple events happen closely to the event under scrutiny, the test has less power to explain the effect • Small sample size magnifies confounding • A short time window minimizes spill-over risks but implies statistical artefacts and a lowered generalizability of the results • Variantly delayed responses of investors require long event time windows that increase the likelihood of contamination • Extending time windows beyond three days makes it difficult to isolate the effect of the event from other stock price changing occurrences • Studies with time windows above 20 days are likely confounded as several other events may have spilled over and influenced corporate assets • All designs studied may encounter contaminating history problems if the announcements are not successfully isolated from other corporate news • Corporate withdrawals might have had differing reasons	• Financial market price jumps imply serial correlations	• The length of time windows determines the possibility of information leakage. Stretching the time window increases the likelihood of information biases	• A small sample size can increase the regression error term • An over-extended time window decreases the power of statistical testing, yet a too short time frame will not capture lagged investor reactions to new information • Artificial portfolio choices feature unrepresentative data of the market sector under scrutiny • Corporate sectors with distinct structural differences lead to industry-specific results. Corporate-specific factors are additional selection biases • The investigated samples only covered events with media attention and corporations that are listed on stock exchanges • The exclusion of NASDAQ-traded corporations and the removal of the total number of scanned corporations in the Meznar et al. (1994) study may have biased the sample • Wright and Ferris (1997) omitted corporations with poor Sullivan ratings and divesting corporations prior to 1984 which makes the portfolio unrepresentative of all divesting corporations • Implicit sample selection criteria for corporations are determined by the means of information dissemination and absence of shareholder resolution on divestiture	• Posnikoff (1997) refrained from considering one corporation due to becoming privately-held less than a month after its divestment announcement • Corporations with multiple announcements were omitted by Ngassam (1992)	• Stock market price jumps and small time windows increase the likelihood of regression to the mean

External Validity			
Design threat	**Geographically-focused studies**	**Time- targeted studies**	**Non-typical sample**
Description	Narrowly focused on a geographic area that does not represent the overall population.	Investigate a certain time in history	Limit the generalizability of the results.
Strengths	• Variety of studies under scrutiny demonstrates the wide range of applicability of the event study methodology	• A well tempered time window captures a general relation of financial trends and societal patterns and thus allows an appropriate generalization of the results	• Inclusion of market, industry and risk free factors counterweights a potential industry specific focus
Weaknesses	• Geographical limitations trade off from a 'global validity' that allows a world wide generalization of findings • As the analyzed studies focused on South Africa, it remains unclear whether the results can be generalized onto other populations • Limited to corporations traded in the US, most of them at the NYSE	• Comparative research on the generalizability of the results is needed to predict future political events' impact on financial markets	• Small samples, short time frames and restrictive portfolio selections lower the generalizability of the results • Covering divestiture cases with media attention and corporations listed on the US stock exchange

CONCLUSION

The meta-analysis of event studies of divestiture from South Africa found instringent results for the impact of political divestiture on corporate returns. Some studies revealed a positive effect (McWilliams et al., 1999; Posnikoff, 1997; Teoh et al., 1999), others a negative impact (McWilliams et al., 1999; Meznar et al., 1994; Ngassam, 1992; Wright & Ferris, 1997) and even no overall corporate performance change in the wake of divestiture was reported (McWilliams et al., 1999; Teoh et al., 1999). The meta-analysis helped to identify that the investigation of political divestiture on corporations remaining in politically incorrect markets warrants for more research. Future studies may directly compare the market values of divesting entities with corporations operating in politically fractionate markets.

The instringent results on the impact of political divestiture on corporate endeavors are attributed to methodological specificities of the event study methodology. Critical design issues comprise defining relevant events with reasonable media coverage, drawing an appropriate sample size and finding a well-tempered time window. The major weakness of event study designs stem from inappropriate samples and time frames. Event studies are sensitive to selection biases implying industry- and firm-specific effects. In addition, historical artefacts confound the results. Maturation leakage of information is problematic.

Attrition is a minor issue.

In terms of the external validity, the question remains whether the geographically-focused and time-targeted case of divestiture from South Africa under scrutiny can be generalized. Follow-up studies must determine if political divestiture from South Africa during Apartheid provides a strong parallel for eminent cases. History will not repeat itself, but we must grasp the opportunity to learn from it in order to derive strategies for the future.

REFERENCES

Barakat, M., & Terry, R. (2008). *A re-evaluation of event study methodology*. Retrieved from the internet at http://www.fma.org/SLC/Papers/eventstudypaperrevisedFMA.pdf

Bazerman, M. H., & Moore, D. (2009). *Judgment in managerial decision making*. Hoboken, NJ: Wiley.

Choi, T. H. & Jung, J. (2008). Ethical commitment, financial performance, and valuation: An empirical investigation of Korean companies. *Journal of Business Ethics, 81*(2), 447-463.

Crampton, W., & Patten, D. (2008). Social responsiveness, profitability and catastrophic events: Evidence on the corporate philanthropic response to 9/11. *Journal of Business Ethics, 81*(4), 863–873. doi:10.100710551-007-9553-7

Detomasi, D. A. (2007). The political roots of corporate social responsibility. *Journal of Business Ethics, 82*(4), 807–819. doi:10.100710551-007-9594-y

Duncombe, W. (2008). *Program evaluation. Course Reader, Spring 2008, Maxwell School of Citizenship and Public Affairs*. Syracuse University.

Epstein, M. J., McEwen, R. A., & Spindle, R. M. (1994). Shareholder preferences concerning corporate social performance. *Journal of Business Ethics, 13*(6), 447–453. doi:10.1007/BF00881454

Harvey, C. (2008). *Campbell R. Harvey's hypertextual finance glossary*. Retrieved from the internet at http://www.duke.edu/~charvey/Classes/wpg/bfglosa.htm

Hofmann, E., Hoelzl, E., & Kirchler, E. (2007). A comparison of models describing the impact of moral decision making on investment decision. *Journal of Business Ethics, 82*(1), 171–187. doi:10.100710551-007-9570-6

Langlois, C. C., & Schlegelmilch, B. B. (1990). Do corporate codes of ethics reflect national character? Evidence from Europe and the United States. *Journal of Business Ethics, 11*, 799–808.

Little, K. (2008). *Socially responsible investing: Put your money where your values are*. New York: Penguin.

Mackenzie, C., & Lewis, A. (1999). Morals and markets: The case of ethical investing. *Business Ethics Quarterly, 9*(3), 439–452. doi:10.2307/3857511

Matten, D., & Moon, J. (2004, July). *"Implicit" and "Explicit" CSR: A conceptual framework for understanding CSR in Europe*. 20th EGOS Colloquium, Ljubljana, Slovenia.

McWilliams, A., Siegel, D., & Teoh, S. W. (1999). Issues in the use of the event study methodology: A critical analysis of corporate social responsibility studies. *Organizational Research Methods*, *2*(4), 340–365. doi:10.1177/109442819924002

Meznar, M. B., Nigh, D., & Kwok, C. C. (1994). Effect of announcements of withdrawal from South Africa on stockholder wealth. *Academy of Management Journal*, *37*, 1633–1648.

Ngassam, C. (1992). *An examination of stock market reactions to U.S. corporate divestitures in South Africa*. Newark, DE: University of Delaware.

Patten, D. M. (2007). Does the market value corporate philanthropy? Evidence from the response in the 2004 Tsunami relief effort. *Journal of Business Ethics*, *81*(3), 599–607. doi:10.100710551-007-9534-x

Peterson, P. P. (1989). Event studies: A review of issues and methodology. *Quarterly Journal of Business and Economics*, *28*(3), 37–50.

Porter, M. E., & Kramer, M. R. (2003). *The competitive advantage of corporate philanthropy. Harvard Business Review on Corporate Responsibility*. Cambridge, MA: Harvard Business School.

Posnikoff, J. F. (1997). Disinvestment from South Africa: They did well by doing good. *Contemporary Economic Policy*, *15*(1), 76–86. doi:10.1111/j.1465-7287.1997.tb00456.x

Puaschunder, J. M. (2015). When investors care about politics: A meta-synthesis of political divestiture studies on the capital flight from South Africa during Apartheid. *Business, Peace and Sustainable Development, 5*(24), 29-52.

Puaschunder, J. M. (2017). Ethical, environmental, social and governance-oriented investments. *Archives of Business Research*, *5*(8), 151–159. doi:10.14738/abr.58.3622

Salinger, M. (1992). Value event studies. *The Review of Economics and Statistics, 74*(4), 671681.

Steurer, R. (2010). The role of governments in corporate social responsibility: Characterising public policies on CSR in Europe. *Policy Sciences, 43*(1), 49–72. doi:10.100711077-009-9084-4

Steurer, R., Margula, S., & Martinuzzi, A. (2008). *Socially responsible investment in EU member states: Overview of government initiatives and SRI experts' expectations towards governments. Analysis of national policies on CSR, in support of a structured exchange of information on national CSR policies and initiatives. Final report to the EU High-Level Group on CSR provided by the Research Institute for Managing Sustainability.* Vienna University of Economics and Business.

Surie, G., & Ashley, A. (2007). Integrating pragmatism and ethics in entrepreneurial leadership for sustainable value creation. *Journal of Business Ethics, 81*(1), 235–246. doi:10.100710551-007-9491-4

Teoh, S. H., Welch, I., & Wazzan, C. P. (1999). The effect of socially activist investment politics on the financial markets: Evidence from the South African boycott. *The Journal of Business, 72*(1), 35–89. doi:10.1086/209602

Waddock, S. A., & Graves, S. B. (1997). The corporate social performance-financial performance link. *Strategic Management Journal, 18*(4), 303–319. doi:10.1002/(SICI)1097-0266(199704)18:4<303::AID-SMJ869>3.0.CO;2-G

Weiss, H. (1998). *Evaluation*. Upper Saddle River, NJ: Prentice-Hall.

Wright, P., & Ferris, S. (1997). Agency conflict and corporate strategy: The effect of divestment on corporate value. *Strategic Management Journal, 18*(1), 77–83. doi:10.1002/(SICI)1097-0266(199701)18:1<77::AID-SMJ810>3.0.CO;2-R

Zeff, E., & Pirro, E. (1999). *Redistribution of authority: The South African case*. Washington, DC: International Studies Association.

ENDNOTES

1 NAICS Code: replaced the earlier US Standard Industrial Classification (SIC) system in 1997. This code specifies which industry a corporation is considered to operate within (Census.gov, 2008).

2 Dow Jones News Retrieval Service, The Wall Street Journal Index, The New York Times Index.

Chapter 7
Market Agents' Social Representations of SRI

ABSTRACT

In August 2008, exploratory expert interviews were conducted with 94 financial investors and executives of the New York financial community on their perception of SRI. The semi-structured interviews featuring open-ended questions and collected free associations on SRI. The categorization of the contents sheds light on investors' and fiduciaries' interpretation of SRI. A core-and-periphery analysis depicted the main and emerging contents of the common body of knowledge on SRI. Investors and financial fiduciaries are ambiguous about SRI. While they attribute profitability, long-term perspectives, and innovative future potential with SRI, the majority of respondents also revealed knowledge deficiencies regarding the disparate branches of SRI. At the same time, SRI evoked efficiency considerations, fiduciary responsibility predicaments, and associations about losses of degrees of freedom. SRI is seen as a market-dependent and volatile niche market option. Future improvements for SRI must raise SRI's effectiveness in addressing social deficiencies and create a higher degree of accountability.

DOI: 10.4018/978-1-5225-7619-8.ch007

INTRODUCTION

In order to promote a successful rise of financial social responsibility, one has to understand the key players' view on SRI. The following part is targeted at answering the question: How do actual market agents perceive SRI? Understanding financial leaders' SRI notion may serve as a first step towards resolving socio-economic losses imbued in market agents' hesitance to integrate the concept in everyday financial investment decision making. Overall the following part strives to promote socially conscientious investment and thereby aims at the greater goal of fostering positive societal change.

Research Questions and Hypotheses

An exploratory analysis of different SRI notions will address the following questions:

1. In what way is SRI defined and perceived by **financial executives**?
2. What **motives** trigger corporations to administer and exhibiting SRI?

Operationalization

Sampling: To depict investors' view of SRI, 94 financial investors and financial executives comprising investors, financial managers and mutual fund holders of the NYSE and the World Financial Centers were surveyed on their perception of SRI. A non-representative convenience sample was collected of English speaking financial executives at the NYSE and the World Financial Centers in August 2008 (see Table 1).

Data Collection: The study was carried out during August 2008 at the NYSE as well as the World Financial Centers I, II and III. All respondents of the convenience sample were financial experts and participated on a voluntary basis. The presented exploratory study targeted at market agents' perception of SRI. At first, the respondents had to identify whether they would consider

Table 1. Sample selection

Data Collection
Investors and Financial Managers at the NYSE and World Financial Center I, II and III
Operationalization: Face-to-face exploratory interviews

themselves as Financial market agents. If so, they were asked as an introduction question "What do you think about socially responsible investment?" The openended question was targeted at collecting free associations on SRI. The rest of the unstandardized interviews were based on the response to the first question.

Free Associating of Market Agents: The survey was based on a semi-structured interview (see Table 2). The open-ended questions targeted at collecting free associations on SRI and motives for administering SRI. The collected associations shed light on SRI motives. Shortterm interviews with open-ended questions were pursued as the optimum means for free expression (The Human Relations Movement, 2008). The interviews were targeted at triggering a conversation in which the financial experts were encouraged to express themselves freely about the topic.

In many cases additional information on the SRI concept had to be provided. SRI was thereby described as an investment option that may feature positive and negative screening or political divestiture. These terms were explained and multiple examples provided. The free associations of investors and fiduciaries were collected and taped.

Results

The categorization of the contents sheds light on investors' and fiduciaries' interpretation of SRI. A Core-and-Periphery analysis enabled to depict the main and emerging contents of the common body of knowledge on SRI.

Category System: Overall, the 94 respondents' answers led to 187 English associations on SRI. On average, a person had two associations (m=2.00; sd=.77; md=1; mode=1; Range=[1; 15]). To verify the content of the associations, a category system was created based on theoretical assumptions. In discussion with experts a category system with 25 categories was established in an iterative process (see Table 3).

Table 2. Questionnaire

Questionnaire	
Focus	**Description**
Free associations on "Socially Responsible Investment"	**Q1:** What do you think about "Socially Responsible Investment"?
Follow up question	**Q2:** What **motives** do you think influence corporations to exhibit social responsibility?

Table 3. Financial experts' free associations on SRI

Category System			
Category	**Associations**	**f**[1]	**%**[2]
1. Positive notion	All investment should be socially responsible.	27	14.44
	It's great. It's a good idea. It's good. I'm into it.		
	So socially responsible investing from my perspective is a critically important perspective to take.		
	It's a good idea, because there are a lot of people who want to invest in it.		
	It's good....Everyone should have some social responsibility, they should have it, the companies should have it.		
	It's good, I go with good.		
	It's a fantastic idea, because, in fact, the history, as I understand it, great part in South Africa during the Apartheid era, channelling responsibility with the market is definitively something that has a long history. I see no reason why we would not be embracing this.		
	It's an interesting topic.		
	I think it's a great thing.		
	Sure, I'm all for it.		
	I think it's a very good idea.		
	I am very pro to be honest. I have invested very liberal.		
	I think everybody ought to do that, I think everybody got to have a hand in it.		
	I believe it's a good thing. I mean if you consider screening. It's good to be socially responsible.		
	Socially responsible investing, it's a good idea.		
	Investment should be socially responsible.		
	So the bottom line is, from the individual side it is a good idea that investment should be in sync with socially responsible matters.		
	Yeah, I think it's good.		
	It's a great idea, if you actually get people to invest in it.		
	[I] think it is a decent idea.		
	I think it's a good thing, I wanna know that my money goes to a company that, you know – like Calvert – that does not take my tax money and kill Iraqis with it.		
	I think it's good to be socially responsible.		
	If I think about society, I'm all for it.		
	I think it's a good idea.		
	I think it's a great idea.		
	I think it's a good idea, it's challenging though.		

continued on following page

Table 3. Continued

Category System			
Category	Associations	f[1]	%[2]
	I think socially responsible investment makes sense. You don't want to have positive press?		
2. Lack of knowledge	I don't know, I don't know, I don't have an opinion on that.	16	8.56
	I don't know anything about it.		
	I am not very familiar with the topic unfortunately, I am sorry.		
	I don't know, I've never really thought about it.		
	It's above my head.		
	I don't know.		
	I have no idea what that is.		
	I have no idea.		
	I am not really aware of it.		
	I don't know that much about it.		
	No idea.		
	No idea.		
	I am not in fact active enough to actually comment on it... I don't know if this is socially responsible investing.		
	It does not say so much for me.		
	I have no idea what that is.		
	Socially Responsible Investment, I don't know.		
3. Inefficiency	Really, socially responsible investment. What's the return? That's how I'm interested.	15	8.02
	If it is profitable, it's good to making profits.		
	Is it going to give money? I doubt it. I do not know if that helps.		
	What is a fund? People are looking for investment as far as seeing a return from it, no? How would you see a return from the green funds? It is not an investment, it's actually giving money, no?		
	You can't make any money.		
	Socially responsible investment, it depends if the market pays in that situation. It is a market failure.		
	About socially responsible investment, it's funny, because I did a project on it, I heard it's a European thing, you guys, it's huge in Europe, and I know that, I don't really understand it, because it just gets such a lower rate....The thing is – I don't think it's – the issue is that the World Bank, they wanna lower it to 25, so it's already practically unsalable, and then they want to take it for even lower, you know.		
	It's an investment that is not feasible on the long run. And if it is too good to be true, than it probably won't be good.		

continued on following page

Table 3. Continued

Category System			
Category	**Associations**	**f**[1]	**%**[2]
	It does not necessarily contribute to investment needs.		
	On the other hand, in terms of financial profit, it's probably not the best thing to do.		
	I have not seen one that really makes money.		
	How about the alternative field? There are politicians, who back up the issue and this and that, but we need to realize as a society, to realize in what direction do we go and yet to have a particular idea that gains direction. We need an efficient product. The idea is find an efficient product. And the companies absolutely need to put more money into research and development. There is definitively a need for that….We need to see results first.		
	Right, business does the same thing….Yeah, right, they pollute, they do this, the other thing, it's cheaper to pollute than to not-pollute. But social responsibility is self-imposed and it costs more, right, and unless you can't pass it on to your client, then you can't get it, right, like organically foods, quote-on-quote-whatever-the-hell-that-means-in-this-country, food and they pass the price on….		
	What the majority of portfolio managers do with SRI accounting, is to go about investment banking criteria, and if it looks as a good investment, then they decide and then you put it through a process to see whether it meets the criteria or not. Basically what SRI is, it is an extra step – it is to think for the shareholders and the collective audience – but those without power, they can't do SRI. Only those with a lot of power, they can do it.		
	But from a collective prospective it may not make sense and it may not be the first thing on the agenda as for efficiency reasons.		
4. Refrain from it	Do you mean buying into those stocks – I don't do it.	13	6.95
	We are not interested in it here. I guess none of us would do it.		
	I don't know, it's not my department.		
	We don't really do that too much, as long as we are making money, we don't care if a company is doing wrong.		
	SRI, I mean, I don't think that it personally describes my investing. I don't know if that answers your question….I mean, the market has probably heard about it by now, as far as I know, no one is going with it. As far as I know, I don't know.		
	I think it's insane, because social responsibility has nothing to do with good investments. I will investment in what is going to give me the best return on my money. I could not care less how they are doing that.		
	But I have not seen too much success with it, I don't put my money in it.		
	If I had my own money, I would invest it into oil and gold – commodities is good.		

continued on following page

Table 3. Continued

Category System			
Category	**Associations**	**f**[1]	**%**[2]
	Socially responsible, I mean, you know, I don't know. It's so difficult right now, I have my money in CDs, it's the easiest thing to do right now.		
	Generally speaking it is not something that I consider usually in a day-to-day transaction. I have bought tobacco companies' stocks in the past, and I mean for me it is more of just a calculation, I don't consider the outside implications of doing this or that. And, I mean, I have also sold and shorted the stocks, it's not something that comes into play in generally.		
	Do I use it in my financial decision? I am not a socially responsible investor.		
	Bottom line, do I use it for my financial gain? No, but society should be more important.		
	I know where I work, I mean we invest heavily in emerging markets. I don't know, if there is an opportunity in these markets, we are going to invest there, you know. If there is some kind of critical corruption, we should not invest in it, is that what you are saying that we should not invest in these markets?....We are heavily involved in emerging markets. You make money over there, and we need to make money as we lost a lot of money on the credit crunch, we lost a lot of money over the last year, so we are heavily involved in emerging markets.		
5. Innovative future potential	Some people have made a lot of money going for socially responsible investment and they will have followers.	11	5.88
	It's becoming more and more effective and a key factor in terms of environmental and global warming issues. It is becoming more and more a key factor in decision making processes.		
	If it will make money, it will catch on.		
	I think it seems to be – I mean – a good idea, it seems that there is a lot of advertising moving in that direction, so I mean there are a lot of companies that sort of specialize in specific product lines that are more socially aware. I think that, you know, from what I have seen, you see a curve in the market, not only from the consumers, but from the investors and the press.		
	My personal perspective is, you know, that it is probably the way for the future. Especially with the push towards green. And everybody being more socially conscious, not just about the environment, but – you know – about the world in general. And there are a number of already some socially responsible mutual funds that exist. You know, I think it's the way for the future.		
	Economic Darwinism will take care of it. The best ideas really will take off....I think you are right on, if you get a couple of market leaders, who fund something, then you start seeing profits.		
	Socially responsible investment, people like me are gonna say they want to invest socially conscious in my portfolio, they make the steps in the right direction.		
	I'm probably not the best source, but probably it's an idea that's going to get attraction and gonna move forward.		

continued on following page

Table 3. Continued

Category System			
Category	**Associations**	**f[1]**	**%[2]**
	That's absolutely a direction that we need to go in.		
	I think it can be a catalyst for innovation. I don't know that the concept is innovative in it of itself, perhaps it was at one time, but I don't think it is anymore, that social responsibility and taking care of the environment and one another is a catalyst for innovation. I think it is becoming more and more prevalent…I think it will become an element of the market….Yah, they expect an environmental scorecard, board reports and reviews and all that.		
	But here is opportunity….It makes sense. I think if you appeal to individual investors themselves, like individuals, to make socially responsible investments. If people like me are gonna want to invest and have socially responsible companies in my portfolio, it may be a step into the right direction.		
6. Ignorance	I have not really thought about it, I don't have too much of an opinion about it, I am sorry.	10	5.35
	I never thought about it.		
	It is above my head, I don't believe in it, it is an idea that is not taken up by the market. I do not believe in it, that – for example – the market is not going to change because of corporate social responsibility.		
	I don't put too much thought in it, to be honest.		
	Me, I like bonds and stocks, those are my two investments. Other than that I am not interested.		
	I don't think about it and I invest in my own. I do not look at it if it is not in my own investment. Just do my own.		
	People don't give a shit.		
	I don't know about SRI funds. I have no opinion, right or wrong, about it.		
	There is nothing of interest up here in doing this – not here and even more outside.		
	It's hard, but I work here and there is no insurance in it, it's hard, it's about making your pay check each month, either you make your money or you lose it. It's hard.		
7. Bottom line	There are obviously, you know, sort of affluent implications that come along with those decisions, and same people value those more highly than others. I think a lot of people in this industry are kind of more so just focused on the bottom line and actually focused on getting the highest return possible, so it really does not matter I think to most people. Whereas you select to invest in vested interests – in like the environment and social interests and things like that – but most people will just do what gives the highest return.	9	4.81
	It's a nice idea in theory, but it's all about money making.		

continued on following page

Table 3. Continued

Category System			
Category	**Associations**	**f**[1]	**%**[2]
	Well, I guess there are two ways to look at it. People always want to do the right thing and being green and environmentally conscious is good, you know. But I think when it comes to corporate leadership around the world, when it comes to the bottom line that goes out the window pretty quick. That's my honest opinion….You know, it still boils down to the bottom line, don't forget, your leaders of businesses are judged not by how many tons of carbon they saved, and the footprint, the trees they've saved and stuff like that. They are judged on how their companies do on Wall Street and that's what it boils down to. That's just, that's just my opinion. [Laughs]….It's a nice idea, but at the end of the day, the bottom line is going to be the driving force. That's just my opinion.		
	I would think from a corporation's point of view, they should care about it as far as other stakeholders think about it. From their point of view they can only care whatever's gonna make money. From the individual investor's point of view, I don't care at all, whatever is going to make me money.		
	There are so many socially responsible companies, that it is definitively a market for that, but we need to have – we need to see returns.		
	The issue is not so much the managing of portfolios that are investing in socially responsible quote-on-quote businesses, but businesses first and foremost must be socially responsible and be able to show back to their shareholders – whether its private or public – that there is a return on that investment.		
	For someone who wants to make money, or someone who wants to save the environment?		
	Honestly, I've heard about it, but truthful, I know the industry, they try to exploit as they are just interested in the return on profits….It sounds great, but it will never work in practice, I've seen it on the inside.		
	It depends on if you can make any money.		
8. Market dependency	It depends. I mean, you know, what you are investing, you know. Now is the time to buy. – Everything, you know, our economy is shut, there is no question about it, but, you know that is when the big guys come in and make their money and buy low and the Dow shoots back up, if the Dow shoots up to 13000 you make a lot of money. So I mean, right now, you know, it's definitively not a buy-hold market, more a day trading market.	9	4.81
	The reality is this, I mean, what is their job, it's not about being socially conscious, it's a fact, it may not be a nice fact, it may be a harsh fact, but it is a fact, completely what they do is find solutions to problems. Now, how they go about it to accomplish those two things, there are markets. So the market, and the market is not conscious, so they try to rectify the situation.		
	If there is a market involved, it's very volatile, from one day to the next, for example is, one day the oil price will go up, you can see, such as oil is now 110, you don't know from one day to the next, you don't know.		

continued on following page

Table 3. Continued

Category System			
Category	**Associations**	**f[1]**	**%[2]**
	What the majority of the portfolio managers do with SRI is to go about investment banking and then you put it through a social screening process. It is not angel investment and starting up a company. It has to do with the stage of the company.		
	But at the end, nobody really makes it on their own. See, we wake up everyday, and we put the lights on, we do this and water comes out of the showers, I put my shoes on that somebody else made, I put my socks on that are sought in Italy, my pants they have a zipper, somebody invented the zipper, the people's technology, the button, technology, not me, everyday, all of this – altruistic selfish....Yes, but they can only do it insomuch that it is readily accepted. Of course, people don't make horse buggy whips anymore, do you know why, because there is no market... You can't do it in isolation, there is no me and I, it's me and us.		
	Then those that can find a market – a community of people who value what they do from a socially responsible perspective, when they are equal to others in the market place that are willing to buy or transact with them more than the other one by virtue of the differentiation to social responsibility, they derive a value, but the market has to be there for it. So I can choose to go shopping in a regular grocery store and what not buy biodynamically grown products, this one cost me 1.25 times of that one – I have a choice, my choice might be influenced by my capacity. To observe the extra-costs of my time and energy, it is always personal, it is what do I believe in, am I willing to go the extra distance, to pay the extra price for this fruit, which I think that is better for my body, lower my health costs, health support, you know, growers in the organic fields.		
	You can only be the leader in morality, if you are the economic superpower. You can only set the standards, as long as you stay on top.		
	I think there are plenty of examples where companies do well outside of their line of business, but – of course – there has to be an incentive as well.		
	But, they don't bother too much....Look at them, I don't think that companies should market to children. They don't know, it's not conscious, they do market to children. I am not for that.		
9. Alternative energy	I like going green.	7	3.74
	I am pro alternative energies, you know, I would love to see the research and the US economy going as far.		
	I would argue that companies that are attentive to social issues like the environment are generally better managed and probably do better in time, so I would invest in companies that are environmentally sensitive.		
	I am not against it, you mean in terms of the environment.		
	What do you mean by socially responsible? The alternative fuels and stuff like that?		

continued on following page

Table 3. Continued

Category System			
Category	**Associations**	**f**[1]	**%**[2]
	I don't know. What area are you talking about? Are you talking about hybrid type and carbon, anything in that launch?		
	You mean like green investments?		
10. Fiduciary responsibility	From a fund manager's view, the most important thing is that the shareholders are satisfied and not to be socially responsible.	7	3.74
	I think it's tricky, because the party doing the investing has obligations to the investors, so how do you balance that? Yeah, I mean I want somebody managing my money or investing my money with the highest possible returns.		
	For the portfolio managers what counts, they have two things to keep in mind: The criteria and the mandate. The second thing is I have to make my money for the shareholders. But even though, these may be connected, so we can point them in the right direction in terms of the criteria that we use.		
	People want investment.		
	The need is still to make profits growing and there is the investment idea.		
	But you know what is really important, is it gonna make you and the client money? If it is not making money…		
	I don't know that the American government is catching up, I don't think that the government is catching up, it is private industries. It is people like that gentleman you were talking to, who realizes it, recognizes it, but they are on the racket, his responsibility is to his clients, to get them a return on their investment. The leaders of the business have the responsibility to do the same thing for their shareholders or their clients, right, and the boards and everybody else like that. And if they don't value it, there is no incentive to do it. Again, it's economics.		
11. Disparate branches	There are many definitions…You know, it depends, as there is no definition of socially responsible investing. There is a lack of definition. There is not really one.	6	3.21
	I think it depends what you mean by socially responsible, you mean tobacco, sin or environmental?		
	There is something called Social Investment Forum, which tries to gather all of these various disparate people together and have a common faith to it. As you just said, there are a lot of different forms. No one covers all of them at once.		
	There are so many different SRI funds.		
	But what direction is socially responsible, what is socially responsible? Where are we going with that? How do you see socially responsible investment or socially conscious investment? If it's a particular idea that gains attraction, you have to define socially responsible investment. In some sense it is socially responsible, in other sense it is completely socially irresponsible. It makes sense, but what it is, and what is socially irresponsible investment?		

continued on following page

Table 3. Continued

Category System			
Category	**Associations**	**f**[1]	**%**[2]
	The problem is just that it is such a broad thing. It's personally identifying, what is socially responsible? Is it energy, that's what comes to mind, but it could be anything.		
12. Doubts about solving social deficiencies	But I wonder if any of them is socially responsible. You know, I mean, some of them I think are kind of mixed, you know, for example Apple computers, who does not like Apple computers, right, but, you know, the over-commercialization of the world is, you know, it's creating a lot of land full of whip. So talking about Apple computer, so my computer will be in the trash one day – that is not really good. The markets are passive players in it, like if the stock goes up, then they just apply the standards, yeah I don't believe that.	6	3.21
	It always seems to work a little bit, but it does not solve the whole problem. I think it works to an extent, but it is not the ultimate solution. There should be no social problems. There is a bit of capital going into that direction, but overall it is not solving the actual problems.		
	Especially with SRI, what I say is, use the funds to do socially responsible investments, you would get a lower rate, but you would know that they use it for something else, that's how I understand it. You know, there are other ways to doing something, there are other ways of doing than having someone else doing it for you and getting a lower rate…And in the US, one of the differences is that charity is tax deductible.		
	Yeah, probably, but positive externalities can be vulnerable, I can be very narrow-minded about it and say the only positive externality that I want to extract from a company is positive dividends and a long-term basis that I can count on for my return and I don't give a shit how they do it – cigarettes, booze, oil, any of it, I take it, give me the money, I don't care.		
	Because they also have to look at people who make these investments, usually they invest and then there is a whole bunch of fan care around it, the whole idea is this might not be the bulk of any companies investment, it might be just a little small portion that they're trying to show that they are doing something conscientious, but they are also putting a big PR – public relations – move around it. So they are trying to send a message without really doing too much. So, I guess that is a very jaded opinion about all it, because you are still close down to it, about the bottom line that is what all CEOs are concerned about it, I believe. That's just my opinion….That's just it, a lot of these issues will make your goods and services cost more. So, you know, that's your thing, you know, it's a marketing thing, you know, the company is not going to eat the additional costs without passing it on to the consumer purse. So, it's probably gonna go so far, I can say, when companies do stuff like that, they do a small portion, they get some public relations value out of it and it moves on.		
	It's hard to get corporate investors to buy into it. I feel that people use – for example – the UN Global Compact as a rubber stamp.		

continued on following page

Table 3. Continued

Category System			
Category	**Associations**	**f**[1]	**%**[2]
13. Freedom of choice	So, you mean not being able to invest in those companies, Philip Morris, Budweiser? They are huge money makers. If you take that away, people won't smoke in this country….I think if you do want to invest, you should have the choice, if you take it away, you take away their choice. It is the peoples' choice to smoke. Being able to invest in the majority, it is their choice. Everyone has their own choice. People have bad habits, using that, all those things at the same time are resistant to everything else, the economy, does not matter what, it is resistant, if you take that away, you take away a major aspect of any other investor….It's an addiction, but I guess an addiction is also making money, do you agree?	6	3.21
	Who is to say that – you know – I don't smoke, but, who is to say that you should not be smoking….It's your choice, it's our society, we got to choose what we wanna do.		
	America is especially inefficient on the environmental stuff, a lot of unnecessary efficiencies that should be taken out of the system, but I don't have as much – so I would have a positive inclination towards the environmental stuff, I have less of an inclination towards the sinful – like cigarettes or alcohol or things like that – that to me is more of those religious issues, I mean I don't smoke, but I don't think, you know, I would not ban smokers.		
	But at the same time, you know, the world is terrific, if someone decides to walk on this side of the road, I can advice to not walk on that side of the road, but people have the choice, that's it, you know. For example, I really think it is, you should say yes or no, you know.		
	It's ok, if that's what you like to do.		
	I mean, I am not gonna be saying, hey invest in this and invest in that.		
14. Investor individualism	It's a lifestyle.	6	3.21
	It's like any other investment, it's not different. You will find investors that are interested, and if it works, it's not more complicated and it is not less complicated. It's like saying I believe in oil investment, I believe in real estate investment, fund investments…		
	Every investor is different. You have small investors, you have those who don't work, all they do is invest, you have people who don't invest in those companies at all.		
	So what do I think of it? I think it fills a need.		

continued on following page

Table 3. Continued

Category System			
Category	**Associations**	**f**[1]	**%**[2]
	You will find that people that are over 50 who are in the investment world are much more conscientious about their place in the world, their legacy, and they also become more religious. Because they are getting older and they realizing that despite what they thought that they had full control of in their lives and everything around them, that's not true, and in fact, they can make a difference. And when they reflect on all of what they did and didn't do, they realize how important their singular role in the bigger society is. People who are in investments, they can do a lot; they can really do a lot.		
	Everything is an interpretation....It does not have to be psychological, it's a matter of interpretation, everybody's interpretations are valid, they are equally valid, but not as powerful, but some interpretations are more powerful than others, so, the people that make the interpretation that the value of acting in a socially responsible way, isn't always driven by economics, there is going to be something personal – that's why I was asking you how old is this man – because all economics put aside his personal values have changed....Because people experience and learn about the world that they live in very differently when your body begins to break down. And you're getting a guess. It's biological....Everything is biology. Everything, everything we do is biology....No, you recognize what your place in the world is and that your future is much different than how you viewed your future when you were 20 or 30 years old.		
15. Niche segment	It's still a niche market...So it's where the market is targeted. But it's still not huge, there are a lot of state pensions, especially by the state governments, so it's getting bigger and bigger and at the same time a lot of companies wanna attract those certain investments, so it's gaining steam and it's growing, but whether it actually influences behavior, it's still a marketing toy.	6	3.21
	I think it fills a niche.		
	But once you get to see something that gains attraction, then you will start to see an investment niche gain attraction. It's like the Internet investors. Internet business models were a niche in 1996 and 1997, but once they showed to be business models that actually worked, then they start making money, then they start become feasible investment options.		
	I don't think you get enough people on board for it.		
	I would say, my guess would be that you probably want buy some, not all, but a little bit. I don't even know, it depends, Solar, FDN, that might be something, but I wanna, but not put all your money into it.		
	They probably fulfil a need.		
16. Profitable	I've read some of them do well. Some of them, you know, do well, they have mutual funds. I've read that some of them do well, I mean making money off being socially responsible. It's about making money.	6	3.21

continued on following page

Table 3. Continued

Category System			
Category	Associations	f[1]	%[2]
	I have never been asked that question. [Laughs]. Yeah, socially responsible investment, yeah, I don't know much about it, I am in a different business, I am in interest rate derivatives, so I don't think there is much of a correlation, but I think those funds from what I do know, perform at least as well as other funds, you know, that don't screen for socially conscious firms, so from a profitability perspective they make sense and they are viable, that's all I can tell you.		
	As far as financial concerns, I am positive.		
	There are situations – alternative energy. Companies that invested in the past few years in alternative energy, right now, they are doing well in that sense…hybrid, oil, they are high right now.		
	Socially responsible investment has done really well recently, so, you know, compared to S&P funds.		
	Have you research on the gains in the solar stocks in the last couple of years. Have you seen first solar…solar funds? That's because it improves the environment.		
17. Ambiguity	If you talk about that sort of religious socially responsible investment, I would not be fairly positive about it, but if it is more of the environmental stuff, I would be very positive about it. Interesting, I wrote an article, when I was a law student, I wrote an article on Apartheid, on the US divestiture, obviously it works in some contexts, but for me the key issue would be, do you think it's gonna work?	5	2.67
	You have to balance the needs between the family and the greater community.		
	It's about society. I'm all for it. On the other hand, in terms of financial profit, it's struggling off the best.		
	From the individual investor's perspective it may make sense, but not from the perspective of a fund manager, who is just gonna do what is good for the corporation or what is good for the shareholders.		
	IPO's are a good example, they are a great example for creation of money and standards in progress. I mean I do not have oil stock, but I don't know, the whole world needs oil.		
18. Long-term perspective	There are no sudden moves. No quick changes. It happens naturally, you know, no quick moves and adventurous changes. Gradual changes, no quick changes, you have to be patient.	5	2.67
	My experience with it, down the road, in 10 years it will be more of value, when those companies grow.		
	I would invest maybe in companies that are starting social conduct, for example Wal-Mart, you know, who are extremely coming out of their way, throughout time those are probably better managed and that's a competitive advantage.		

continued on following page

Table 3. Continued

Category System			
Category	**Associations**	**f**[1]	**%**[2]
	Do you study the concept of altruistic selfishness?....So altruism I think is a huge motivator for lots of people and organizations. And those who don't have some element of altruistic outlook or component whether it is conscious or subconscious, spoken or unspoken, probably don't last in the long run, because they become out of touch with the environment that they are in.		
	But I think we all should be investing something in our future.		
19. Governmental action	The problem that we have today is that there is a completely skewed mispricing of what the cost of social responsibility is.... Because there is not enough tax on the ill-effects of what people do – right, like pollute the water, the air, and the earth. Right, that all comes afterwards, or at some time in the very distant future. So there is not enough of a price for it today. If you go to Europe, you are much closer to the impact. Well you're social tax is for the cost of doing business, and having big cars, and being involved in polluting quote-on-quote-industries is your thing now – in this country, four dollars a gallon, 3.5 a gallon, hallo?...[This is] because you realize what the impact is, and it's becoming much more of a closed loop, so what your taxes are being used for is to ameliorate the ills of private industry. The government says, hey wait a minute, you are the one who is causing this and that, we are using tax dollars to fix what you did wrong. It's like, no, no, no. We know, if you do this, it means that we have to do that later, so you pay for it upfront or don't do it. And they will be like, aha, ok. And then it balances it out, you understand...Yeah, the market will price these things out, the problem that the market does not understand what the cost is. And this is where governments are much more conscientious and able to represent the directive costs of the evil than private industry, but that does not always work that way, right. The reason that the road, and waterways and things like that are collectively managed, is because they can do it much more efficient than individual private businesses, I think.	4	2.14
	I think transparency, accountability, which can be exposed externally by government people, at any level, you know, the village, the town, the city, the state or canton as you like or the federal government or much larger supernatural entity – you know – the EU, organizations like the WTO decided to do that as well too, it's not to necessarily people playing field even, but to raise the entire industry.		
	It's in corporation's best interest to care. To do just as much as the government and their competitors make them.		
	I think that governmental policy is the most effective tool for people to invest into social responsibility. Because at the end of the day, investors want return, the issue of risk and return. Governmental policy is more feasible.		
20. Ethical investment	Socially, you mean religious investments?	3	1.60
	One was started by Catholic religion, one was started by Methodist religion, one was started by non-pollutionists...Some of it started as a		

continued on following page

Table 3. Continued

Category System			
Category	Associations	f[1]	%[2]
	Christian fund, some of it is green, there is not one fund that is only socially responsible. It comes from religious roots.		
	There is an obvious line what's right and what's wrong.		
21. Knowledge	I've read about it.	3	1.60
	Essentially, I thought I have read something about it, but I have to apologize, I have not followed it too much, but I have heard about it.		
	I have been at a forum….I have seen a lot of it. I have to deal with many consequences. And I have actually come to the Kennedy School for SRI material.		
22. Shareholder activism	I fact, I have written letters to companies, in which I would say, I've read about this and this and this is not good.	3	1.60
	As sort of different statements or are you better off engaging people?		
	So, you are equating philanthropy with social responsibility? It could be a portion of it, it could be a means by which to engage and be an active member in the larger society. Things like polluting and carbon oxides. I pollute, I pollute, I pollute, yes I'm polluting, but I'm buying the carbon oxides for what I'm doing here, right, it's the same concept, so why not incorporate it into the eco-specific corporation and who they are and making it part of what they are, rather than just pointing at, oh yeah, we give money. Perhaps not [efficient], but that's ok, that's ok. So social responsibility – that's why I am saying – it's much more than philanthropy. You can't, it's like raising your kids, where you can have a nanny, but the responsibility of raising your kids is yours. There is only so much that the nanny will do.		
23. Volatility	I don't know, sounds like kind of risky to me...I try to stay away from anything that I do not oversee.	2	1.07
	So there is a risk.		
24. Accountability	Hopefully I mean I get the Exxon annual report that says that they use their resources for alternative energy. I think that is good. I think part of it is the investor on the street, but then also the companies themselves have to be held accountable for what they do and how they spend their money. For example, put their money into South Africa during Apartheid.	1	.53
25. Intrinsic motivation	Why do you have socially responsible investment? People wanna feel good. If you have a decent standard of living, why won't you do it?	1	.53
Σ		187	100.00

Description

How do market agents experience SRI? Investors and financial fiduciaries are *ambiguous* (f=5; 2.67%) about SRI. If they *know* about SRI (f=3; 1.60%), most notions of SRI are *positive* (f=27; 14.44%) as for associations about *profitability* (f=6; 3.21%), *long-term perspectives* (f=5; 2.67%) and *innovative future potential* (f=11; 5.88%). However, the overall majority of respondents have *knowledge deficiencies* (f=16; 8.56%) as for the various *disparate branches* of SRI (f=6; 3.21%) as well as *inefficiency concerns* (f=15; 8.02%). Therefore, many of the market agents would *refrain from SRI* (f=13; 6.95%) and not be too receptive for the concept. The reason for their *ignorance* (f=10; 5.35%) may be a focus on the overall *bottom line* (f=9; 4.81%), concerns about the *fiduciary responsibility* predicaments (f=7; 3.74%) and the overall *concept of freedom of choice* (f=6; 3.21%) in the light of negative screening activities. SRI is seen as a *market dependent* investment option (f=9; 4.81%), most likely renown for *alternative energy funds* (f=7; 3.74%). SRI is perceived as a *niche market segment* solution (f=6; 3.21%) that attracts only a fraction of *individually differing investors* (f=6; 3.21%), who are *intrinsically motivated* (f=1; .53%). Another downside mentioned is the *doubt about SRI's effectiveness in addressing social deficiencies* (f=6; 3.21%). The investors recommend *governmental action* (f=4; 2.14%) and a higher degree of *accountability* (f=1; .53%) to foster SRI. SRI is also perceived as a *volatile market option* (f=2; 1.07%). In addition, the historical roots of SRI in terms of *shareholder activism* (f=3; 1.60%) and *ethical investment* (f=3; 1.60%) come to mind.

The absolute and relative frequencies of the associations on SRI are exhibited in Figures 1 and 2.

Core-and-Periphery Analysis

In order to analyze the salience and importance of the associations, a Core-and-Periphery analysis was conducted (Roland-Lévy et al., 2001). Based on the relative frequency and rank of the associations within the individual word flow, this analysis diverts notions into central core values and fluent peripheral viewpoints. Methodologically the categorized associations are summarized in a Pivot-Table exhibiting the relative frequency of the categories. The relative rank is weighted by using the formula exhibited in Figure 3 (DeRosa, 1994):

To divide the associations into core and peripheral elements, cut off scores are based on the following two measure points:

Figure 1. Absolute frequencies of associations on SRI

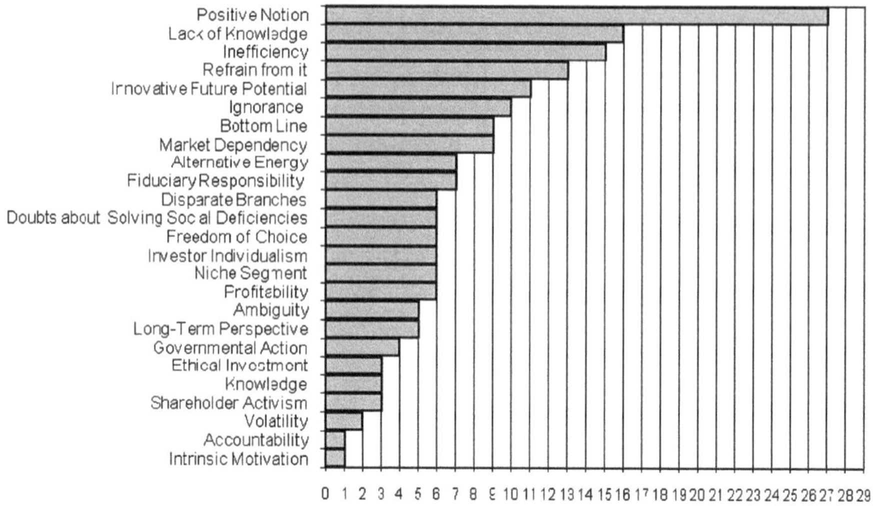

n=94, f=187
Data collection: August 2008 at New York Wall Street World Financial Center I, II, III

Figure 2. Relative frequencies of associations on SRI

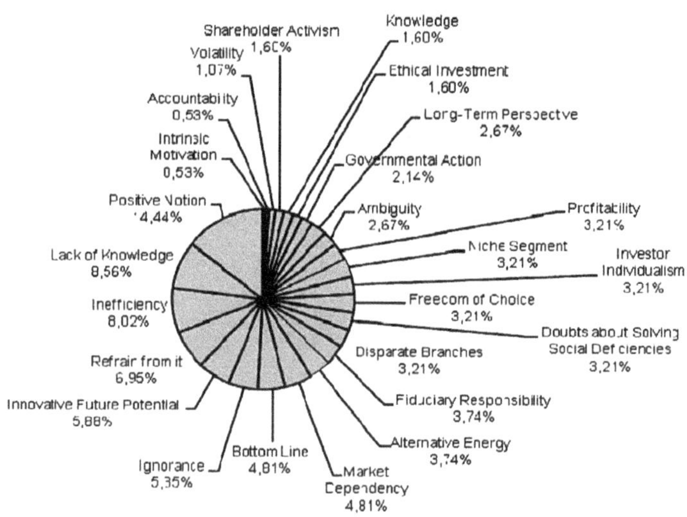

n=94, f=187
Data collection: August 2008 at New York Wall Street, World Financial Center I, II, III

Figure 3. Relative rank weight

$$\text{Relative rank weight (r)} = \frac{\sum (f_1 * 1) + (f_2 * 2) + (f_3 * 3) + (f_4 * 4) + \ldots + (f_n * n)}{f_t}$$

f_1 = absolute frequency of associations in 1st rank

f_n = absolute frequency of association in rank n

f_t = absolute frequency of association

- The *average frequency of an association* is based on the absolute frequency divided by the number of association categories.
- The *average rank* is based on the sum of total rank weight divided by the number of association categories.

The Core-and-Periphery analysis for the associations on SRI reveals the following distribution of associations (see Figure 4):

Results: The core-and-Periphery analysis for the associations on SRI led to the following distinction into core and peripheral elements outlined in Figure 5.

The respondents' primarily associated *positive notions* with SRI. However, the concepts implementation may be hindered by the *lack of knowledge* about the socially responsible financial options.

CONCLUSION

Overall, financial experts and practitioners seem to be ambiguous about SRI – they are optimistic about the idea as for profitability and long-term

Figure 4. Core-and-Periphery analysis

Rank \ Frequency	High frequency (>average frequency)	Low frequency (<average frequency)
Low rank (<average rank)	Core	Periphery
High rank (>average rank)	Periphery	Periphery

Figure 5. Core-and-Periphery analysis for associations on SRI

Rank \ Frequency	High frequency (>8.27)	Low frequency (<8.27)
Low rank (<2.70)	Positive Notion Lack of Knowledge	Refrain from it Ignorance Bottom Line Alternative Energy Freedom of Choice Ambiguity Profitable
High rank (>2.70)		Inefficiency Innovative Future Potential Market Dependency Fiduciary Responsibility Disparate Branches Doubts about Solving Social Deficiencies Investor Individualism Niche Segment Long-Term Perspective Governmental Action Ethical Investment Knowledge Shareholder Activism

perspectives as well as innovative future potential, but lack information on SRI and the various disparate social responsibility forms. Efficiency considerations and fiduciary responsibility concerns in combination with freedom of choice restrictions may cause a hesitancy to choose SRI. The market dependency and volatility of SRI funds let SRI still appear as a niche market solution for intrinsically motivated socially responsible investors. Future improvements for SRI may comprise effectiveness in addressing social deficiencies and a higher degree of accountability.

The free associations reflect all contents of the proposed socio-psychological framework of SRI. Financial experts associate market-dependent profitability and the bottom line as for the intention to maximize profits. Mentioning long-term perspectives and the innovative future potential of SRI addresses the need for innovation and entrepreneurship and implies strategic leadership advantages. The need for transparency and information disclosure is reflected by revealed knowledge deficiencies and the wish for higher accountability but also concerns about possible fiduciary responsibility predicaments. The underlying SRI motive of selfenhancement through identification and self-consistency can be related to associations about the intrinsic motivation of investors. The expression of social values can be found when shareholder activism and ethical investment come to mind. Altruism is referred to by the notion of governmental responsibility.

REFERENCES

DeRosa, A. (1994). From theory to metatheory in social representations: The lines of argument of a theoretical-methodological debate. *Social Sciences Information. Information Sur les Sciences Sociales*, *33*(2), 273–304. doi:10.1177/053901894033002008

Roland-Lévy, C., Kirchler, E., Penz, E., & Gray, C. (2001). *Everyday representations of the economy*. Vienna: WUV.

The Human Relations Movement. (2008). *Harvard Business School and the Hawthorne experiments (1924-1933)*. Cambridge, MA: Harvard Business School.

ENDNOTES

1 Absolute frequencies

2 Relative frequencies

Section 3

Discussion

Chapter 8
Recommendations

ABSTRACT

The recommendations target advancing corporate and financial social responsibility as prerequisites of sustainable financial sucess. The findings of public servant expert interviews about CSR outline the importance of global governance of corporate social conduct. Based on stakeholder consensus, governments may craft CSR frameworks that are backed up by institutional support. Corporations should educate leaders to adopt social responsibility policies in business plans. Accountability and transparency advance CSR.

INTRODUCTION

The analysis of the UNGC initiative lead to recommendations of global governance and stakeholder management on CSR standards in sync with universally agreed upon principles. The implementation of the Ten Principles must be assisted by public and private efforts. The UNGC initiative must incentivize and sanction corporate social performance based on transparent quality control.

The set-up of partnerships requires global governance to foster partnership-enhancing environments. Governments should provide information on societal challenges and advocate for the adoption of socially responsible corporate practices. In networking forums multiple stakeholders must be encouraged to discuss social concerns and find consensus on commonly shared goals. Evaluations must assess and benchmark the transparent social impact of partners.

DOI: 10.4018/978-1-5225-7619-8.ch008

The currently-launched GAID partnership network must secure long-term financial sustainability by strengthening existing alliances and foster extensions. Stakeholder networking activities will help finding consensus and support the network. Regional initiatives must coordinate local action and govern the implementation of ICT for development. Transparent goal accomplishment strategies will monitor the partners' contributions. Benchmarking and impact assessments will derive best practice learning models for future PPPs.

A meta-analysis of South Africa political divestiture studies found inconsistent results which raise questions about the measurement of political divestiture by the event study methodology. Internal validity threats to event studies are recommended to be overcome by well-balanced time windows that minimize confounding, a careful sample selection and transparency about potential study limitations. Threats to the external validity deriving from geographically-focused, time-targeted and non-typical samples challenge the generalizability of the results, which have to be validated in future comparative studies.

Interviews with financial experts revealed a lack of information on SRI that must be reduced by global governance on information disclosure. International financial institutions and governmental policies must work towards providing market actors information on SRI. Financial institutions and experts are encouraged to consider environmental and social responsibility promoted by media reports, social rating criteria as well as social responsibility proxy voting strategies. SRI innovations will ensure concurrent economic market prosperity and societal advancement.

Based on the outlined theoretical background and empirical findings, recommendations are given to advance corporate and financial social responsibility.

CSR

In recent decades, CSR has emerged as for several trends. International organizations have strengthened CSR by providing guidelines and oversight on corporate social conduct. Concurrently governments have fostered social responsibility by legislative reforms and governmental regulations that raised corporate actors' awareness for social deficiencies. With the rise of CSR, governmental entities have started to count in corporate resources and expertise in social welfare provision. At the same time, stakeholder pressure for information disclosure of corporate conduct has propelled CSR and let consumers increasingly pay attention to the social impact of corporate activities. As a consequence, corporations have integrated total responsibility management as an innovative corporate success factor. PPPs have created win-win situations in addressing societal challenges by the combined forces of the public and private sectors. Given these trends corporate social conduct is an *en vogue* phenomenon with the potential to steer entire market systems into a more socially conscientious direction. Based on expert interviews with civil servants as well as qualitative analyses of the UNGC and the setup of the PPP network GAID, recommendations are given to foster CSR with attention to the role of partnership models and the UN.

The empirical part featured expert interviews with public administrators on CSR to shed light on public servants' perception of corporate social conduct. The surveyed public administrators experience CSR as a polarizing concept. While CSR grants access to resources and flexibility in the social service provision, public administrators also associate CSR with marketing purposes and employee satisfaction. Downsides of CSR in comparison to governmentally-administered social welfare are democratic deficiencies, corporate costs and liability risks. Critical is the lack of accountability, shareholder supremacy and dishonest window-dressing by using CSR as a marketing purpose. Based on the findings, CSR is recommended to be enhanced by international governance, governmental assistance and corporate efforts. Transparent corporate social conduct is a prerequisite for accountability control.

International Attention: The UN, World Bank and the Organization for Economic Cooperation and Development but also the European Commission and the US Congress play key roles in advancing social responsibility. International regulatory regimes must set CSR standards that harmonize corporate social endeavors in accordance with global responsibility legislations such as the UNGC, the International Labour Organization (ILO)'s labor regulations or the International Organization for Standardization (ISO) guidelines. At the same time, international initiatives must create supporting environments for the adoption of socially responsible business practices and assist public policy makers in crafting CSR frameworks.

Governmental Assistance: In a plethora of legislative requirements, best practice principles and implementation guidelines; governments must strive for stakeholder consensus on corporate social conduct. By raising awareness for social deficiencies, CSR stakeholders must be encouraged to administer corporate social conduct. Governmental networking forums must engage corporate actors, the media and NGOs to discuss societal concerns and find a common ground on social solution strategies. The invitation to social solution finding will convince corporations to contribute to social goals beyond legal requirements. Based on a universal understanding of CSR, long-term focused governmental regulations and legislations must set social responsibility standards. In a continuing dialogue on CSR standards, governments must promote an authentic adoption of social responsibility practices by outlining the economic, social and environmental impact corporations can have on society. The link between CSR, productivity and innovation will serve as an additional motivating factor for the consideration of social responsibility. Research focused on tangible and intangible CSR assets will portray CSR as a competitive advantage for corporations that mitigate social risks.

To close the gap between the theoretical planning and actual application of CSR, governments must administer the implementation of CSR. Governmental managerial guidelines that pay attention to international legal requirements, national laws and corporate constraints will set best practice standards. The corporate adoption of responsibility codes must be monitored by governmental control. In the implementation assistance of CSR, governments need to move from the qualitative expression of policy objectives to the quantitative measurement of results. Governments must also set up multi-stakeholder collaborative CSR networks as centers of expertise that constantly advance the social responsibility idea.

Governments should incentivize CSR. By steering capital and aid towards social and environmental attention, economic incentives encourage corporations to take on responsibilities. International export opportunities, credits and insurances based on the social performance must be coupled with internationally-renowned accreditations, licenses to operate and CSR certifications. Positive governmental incentives feature tax and fee exemptions, credits, subsidies and loans. Public entities may also fall back on negative sanctions of taxation, penalties, litigations and charges to avert socially irresponsible corporate conduct. Implicit incentives comprise trade controls and outsourcing contracts for corporations that commit to social and environmental standards.

Corporate Social Engagement: Paying attention to strategic opportunities and risks of societal challenges, CSR departments must assign leaders to adopt social responsibility policies, integrate social responsibility in corporate mission plans and assist the implementation of ethical codes of conduct. Corporate leaders must promote a shared CSR vision and provide responsible leadership throughout the corporation and supply chain. At the operational level, the integration of CSR must be guidelined by action plans on day-to-day corporate social practices.

Accountability: Accountability refers to the expectation of having to justify actions to others (Lerner & Tetlock, 1994). Accountability provides an external quality control feedback by public and private actors periodically monitoring corporate social contributions. Civil society must maintain a watch-dog function on corporate social impacts and thereby implicitly supervise the CSR implementation.

Transparency: Transparent corporate conduct is ensured by governmental legal obligations (e.g., freedom of information legislation), the removal of industrial information transfer barriers, economic incentives, stakeholder campaigns and CSR reporting. Information disclosure will help verifying the quality and accuracy of CSR conduct. As the basis for monitoring and benchmarking, transparent CSR information will help identifying areas for improvement and grow the confidence of the stakeholder community and therefore secure investment capital.

Capacity Building: Corporations and governments must educate socially responsible leaders. Academic institutions must ingrain CSR in educational curricular to bestow future leaders with the ability to manifest and implement CSR codes of conduct at all hierarchical levels.

CSR capacity building must be supported by trade unions and NGOs.

UNGC

International CSR standards are the basis for the worldwide spread of corporate social conduct. Universal CSR standards leverage CSR from legal compliance and voluntary philanthropy to a state-of-the-art mainstream corporate practice. Corporate social standards guideline corporate social conduct and are essential for a harmonious CSR implementation. The UNGC offers a framework that sets corporate social standards as an industrial 'level playing field.' The UNGC must be fortified by stakeholder management, implementation assistance and quality control.

Stakeholder Management: As CSR is not only a demand on the current agenda of multinational organizations operating in industrialized countries but also a concern for the developing world, the UNGC must approach global players entering international markets and embrace corporate professionals along the supply chain. In the international arena, inconsistent standards must be harmonized based on the international law. The UNGC framework must extend its range from legal constituents to offering coherent CSR codes of conduct and standardized best practices that are based on internationally agreed principles, formal requirements and contractual agreements. At the same time, the UNGC must remain applicable to national specificities and multi-stakeholder formations. A continued stakeholder dialogue on CSR must ensure that the UNGC implementation remains in accordance with societal demands and meets civic expectations.

The formulation of universal UNGC standards is hindered by differing missions, goal accomplishment time frames and expectations of the constituents who may have diverse motivations to engage in the UNGC. The UNGC global network must mediate conflicts between the UNGC partners by a variety of means. By fostering a mutual understanding of common societal goals, the UNGC should work towards a universal consensus on CSR. Intercultural research projects must target at finding harmonization strategies that strengthen the UNGC's cooperation. To foster the common understanding of CSR, the UNGC initiative must encourage participants to share information within the network and consult responsibility predicaments for the sake of a harmonious CSR conduct. Additional value campaigns must decrease divergences among international constituents. Networking events should engage the corporate world, the public sector and civil society in expertise exchange on CSR. Internet platforms may store data on CSR information to create a common sense and best practice learning platform on corporate social conduct.

Implementation Assistance: The UNGC must be integrated into corporate practices at the operational level. The UNGC participants are advised to change corporate policies in sync with the Ten Principles. By the year 2007, approximately 50 percent of the UNGC members had adopted CSR standards in accordance with the Ten Principles. The principles must further be ingrained in corporate conduct throughout all hierarchical levels. The UNGC and industrial CSR departments must coordinate and oversee the principles' implementation. Corporate executives' adoption of CSR must be assisted by respective action plans in accordance with the Ten Principles. The Ten Principles implementation must be advanced by concrete activities.

In the light of international corporate conduct, the enforcement of international *human rights* standards is challenged by differing national legal frameworks and public policy settings. As some countries have not codified international human rights, these governments are advised to comply with international standards. Transnational legal agreements and contractual CSR requirements must ensure the codification of human rights.

The implementation of basic human rights must be supported and monitored by international and national governance. Gaps in the legal codification and the actual application of human rights must be addressed by the UN and NGOs. International councils and national governments must be encouraged to exchange information and work closely on a joint human rights strategy before multinational corporations.

The improvement of *labor standards* and working conditions contributes to the efficiency of markets, socio-political stability and societal welfare. Governments must therefore promote compliance with labor standards and empower unions. The removal of legal, political and developmental barriers to the exercise of freedom of association will back up labor unions and protect workers' rights. Freedom of association and the right to collective bargaining have to be monitored by the UN – with a special focus on politically unstable countries. Forced and compulsory labor must be detected to overcome human exploitation and discrimination. Citizens must be educated on their rights by governmental and NGO information campaigns. Equal opportunities must be ensured by legal frameworks, quota systems and structural empowerment featuring educational scholarships. In the domain of CSR, interdisciplinary research must attribute the skills needed and motivational factors for socially responsible corporate conduct. UNGC education campaigns must foster CSR learning plans and training facilities advocating for the integration of CSR practices in daily operations. The UNGC's principles must be ingrained in university curricula and business management programs that train employees to consider externalities of corporate conduct.

In terms of social responsibility towards the *environment*, corporate innovations are key. Environmental responsibility must be promoted as an innovative corporate conduct that attracts financial investment. Corporations and investors must be incentivized for aligning corporate conduct with sustainability goals. The UNGC should create a database on environmental responsibility best practices to allow benchmarking and quality control.

The UNGC must engage private and public stakeholders in the set-up of a global governance framework on *anti-corruption*. In the international arena, anti-corruption standards must bundle multi-stakeholder efforts. Backed up by regulatory reforms and legal codifications, anti-corruption codes of conduct must be established. Anti-corruption topics should be addressed by conferences, publications, newsletters and blogs that stress accountability, oversight and public scrutiny on corporate and financial social conduct as prerequisites of economic stability.

Quality Control: A more sophisticated UNGC partner identification and selection based on the real commitment to the UN endeavors will foster the UNGC's credibility. As selfimposed goals and self-reporting on accomplishments give partners leeway to lowering the bar of performance, the compliance with the UNGC standards must be enhanced by transparent goal setting and quality control. The UNGC must provide outcome, output and performance indicators that help monitoring the participants' engagement and the overall effectiveness of the UNGC initiative. CSR auditing will serve as a benchmarking for the improvement of CSR practices and basis for international legislative reforms. Accountability control will nurture the credibility and trust in the UNGC and therefore attract investments. In the international arena, successful UNGC goal accomplishments must be rewarded by governmental and national incentives as well as internationally renowned accreditations and certifications for CSR best practice. Failed CSR goals must be made transparent as for providing learning examples and allowing assistance for improvement. Goal accomplishment deficiencies should be sanctioned. Up to now no immediate actions have been installed against corporations joining the UNGC and not meeting self-imposed goals. Current failures to provide an annual report on progress solely results in mild consequences. Corporations that do not meet self-set targets remain in the UNGC community, which negatively impacts on the overall UNGC's credibility. Transparent and stringent warnings and sanction procedures will counterwork the partners' non-compliance with the UNGC.

PPPs

In the wake of the 2008/09 World Financial Recession, corporate scandals and the recapitalization of the finance sector have raised the demand for restoring public trust and credibility in corporate and financial markets. In the aftermath of the crisis, governmental and corporate actors bear unknown risks and face growing societal expectations of disciplined corporate conduct and responsible financial investments under conditions of heightened levels of public scrutiny. The recent trends have rebalanced social responsibility contributions in partnership models. Currently PPPs feature responsibility restructuring between governance entities, the corporate world and the finance sector. In these challenging times of change, PPPs must meet social responsibility demands by attention to global governance, governmental assistance, stakeholder management and local networks.

Global Governance: In the international arena, PPP administered CSR should be backed up by international organizations. Global governance entities must create a partnershipenhancing institutional, political and judicial infrastructure. Legislative frameworks must be established that aim at corporate social value creation. International public policy makers must ratify social responsibility declarations that are in sync with societal goals and advocate for the adoption of social responsibility policies.

The UN plays a key role in advancing PPPs. The UNGC initiative must become an entry point for corporations to engage in social partnership projects featuring operational flexibility and focus on pragmatic solutions. In addition, the UNGC secretariat should promote CSR to the corporate world as a competitive advantage and PPP-administered social responsibility as a corporate success factor beyond the boundaries of legal compliance and philanthropy. Pro-active CSR reporting should be awarded by UN rewards that gain public recognition.

In networking events, public and private partners must be brought together to find a consensus on social responsibility. A fruitful dialogue of UNGC partners and stakeholders will guideline a successful implementation of CSR partnerships. International conferences must serve as CSR vision councils in which governmental representatives, business executives, financial professionals, NGO representatives and academics share insights on CSR success factors to advance PPPs. Summits will produce a constant stream of literature on PPP best practices that must be made accessible on the internet to further CSR in PPPs.

Governmental Assistance: Apart from the social value created, PPPs engage multiple stakeholders in the policy dialogue and mobilize resources for societal welfare. Governments must create a CSR-fostering environment and assist the coordination of multi-stakeholder CSR partnerships. Based on international regulations, governments must build PPPs frameworks to mitigate social, environmental and political risks in the implementation of CSR. Governmental officials must advocate for the adoption of socially responsible corporate practices and encourage responsible leadership. Thereby governmental initiatives must inform corporate leaders about societal challenges and nurture an understanding of governmental priorities throughout the stakeholder community. Corporate executives' motivation must be enhanced by information on the positive economic, social and environmental advantages of CSR.

Stakeholder Management: Partnerships are networking forums in which multiple stakeholders discuss topics of social concern in an atmosphere of trust and confidentiality. Mutual understanding of public and private partners is challenged by differing goals and time perspectives. Frictions may also stem from industry-specific expectations and individual motivations of the partners. As for these challenges, partners must focus on common goals and determine their roles and responsibilities in their accomplishment. By raising awareness for shared endeavors, the confidence in the UNGC network will be strengthened. Actionable work agendas must feature transparent timetables that pinpoint goal accomplishment strategies. Constant communication on the work in progress will allow monitoring the partners' contributions. Transparency on local goal accomplishment strategies will identify and disseminate best practices for the UNGC implementation. Evaluations must assess the impact of partners and benchmark the partners' CSR practices. As a quality control, external audits will boost the overall efficiency of partnerships.

Local Networks: To manage the UNGC's expansion, networks must facilitate the local progress. As the impact of partnerships depends on coordinated action, local initiatives must foster the implementation of the UNGC principles. Local stakeholder events will bring together CSR administrators for a common solution finding and create multi-stakeholder engagement opportunities. Local ownership of UNGC targets will help rooting CSR in national and cultural contexts. National campaigns in local languages should also comprise seminars and workshops as for providing local learning possibilities. In addition, local meetings will give grass-root feedback opportunities to the UNGC leadership board and allow reflecting about future strategies and challenges for the development of partnerships.

GAID

The UN partnership network GAID was analyzed as an example of a currently-launched international PPP with focus on social development. While the set-up of GAID features positive results, the evaluation also identified areas for improvement.

GAID has been successful in leveraging its position as a UN-related PPP network that advocates for ICT for development on a global basis. GAID introduced ICT for development in the international dialogue. Win-win combinations of the public and private sector expertise have advanced ICT for development. Public and private actors have engaged in advocacy and policy dialogue, corporate social entrepreneurship and philanthropy on ICT for development. On the partnership level, the results are mixed. GAID has supported existing networks and embraced new stakeholders. Novel ICT initiatives developed under GAIDs guidance and several of these have been quite successful. Most of the partners have demonstrated an ability to achieve results, even though GAID is still in its start-up period. As vibrant parts of the GAID network, the successful partners have advanced the use of ICT for development on the regional, national and international levels. Some pre-existing partnerships visibly linked with GAID and have organized meetings to streamline actions for the advancement of common endeavors.

At the same time, the analysis revealed difficulties in establishing the network in terms of integrating individual partnerships with GAID and facilitating information exchange. Some pre-existing partnerships have continued their own endeavors with little attention to GAID. These agencies have merely agreed to be associated with the GAID, but have neither used the network nor contributed extensively to the community's goals. Other partners have experienced problems during the start-up phase – foremost in connecting with GAID and extending the network – mainly due to resource limitations, a lack of stakeholder interest and networking expertise. In some cases the partners overestimated the extent to which GAID can mobilize resources or facilitate networks given GAID's own budget. A few of the preexisting members are still not linked very well with GAID and have become almost inactive or even ceased to function. The current situation of the GAID network implies areas for improvement regarding sustainable development, stakeholder management, regional goal accomplishment strategies and accountability control.

Sustainable Development: GAID's long-term financial sustainability must be ensured by securing multi-year donations. By outlining the progress that has already been accomplished but also drawing attention to future needs, current donors must be motivated to contribute more extensively. In order to tap into new sources of funding, GAID has to build additional alliances with international organizations – foremost the UN and the World Bank – as well as corporate professionals, trade unions, NGOs and academic communities. These entities must be asked for capital, in-kind contributions and collaborative support to develop the initiative. Increasing the visibility of the initiative will help GAID to reach out for novel donors. Providing access to information on GAID by the use of innovative interaction tools – e.g., enewsletters, blogs and facebook – will engage a broad audience. Internet information portals must position GAID as a network hub for information exchange that attracts stakeholders' attention and raises the participants' commitment.

Stakeholder Management: In its 'think tank' function, the GAID secretariat must play an active role in the coordination of the partners' endeavors and fortify the networks' connectivity by launching stakeholder events. As UN-led networking forums, conferences will bring together executives from international organizations and corporations, government officials and the civil society to discuss ICT for development interests. The agreement on common goals will implicitly coordinate the partners' activities and fortify the impact of the entire GAID network. Social gatherings will build a mutual understanding about ICT for development and promote a trust-based, supportive environment throughout the network. For the longer-term planning of the network, stakeholder meetings will also help identifying emerging issues of concern and foster information exchange on future endeavors.

Regional Goal Accomplishment Strategies: The partners must agree on implementation strategies and align activities accordingly. By committing themselves to specific goal accomplishment strategies, the partners must specify how their activities will contribute to the GAID goals. Transparency on goal accomplishment plans will help monitoring the partners' contributions and work in progress. The degree to which partners feature standardized or local ownership of goals must be outlined to all stakeholders at early stages of the partnering process. The GAID constituents must work closely on implementing collectively-shared goals. Corporate partners must incorporate GAID goals into business plans that become the basis for respective training programs. Local meetings must gather participants to coordinate and govern the implementation of ICT for development. Regional campaigns will root ICT for development in the cultural context and thereby support the network extension. Regional seminars and workshops must create learning experiences to foster the overall effectiveness of GAID in local networks. Regional dialogues will foster transfer knowledge on local success patterns and generate applicable problem-solving capabilities. Information share on ICT best practice standards will lead to contemporary ICT solutions and prepare for future challenges.

Accountability Control: Accountability of the partners' commitments will counterbalance a lack of clarity about the purpose of the initiative. Based on transparent activities and monitoring, benchmarking of impact assessments will derive best practice learning models for future PPPs. Accountability control must also feature external goal accomplishment measurement. External audits should become the basis for rewarding positive results and providing assistance in case of defaults. Non-compliance with the goal accomplishment and communication deficiencies of the partners must be sanctioned – e.g., by warnings, de-linking partners from the GAID internet portal or exclusion from the network. As for a long-term development, a reintegration into the GAID must be made possible to steer partner behavior into a favorable direction.

Financial Social Responsibility

The empirical part addressed the financial social responsibility trends of political divestiture and SRI.

In recent decades, stakeholder pressure on corporate and financial institutions has leveraged into a means for spearheading socio-political change. Starting during the 1980s, political divestiture became a way to undermine politically incorrect market systems – such as the South African political regime during the Apartheid era. Since then political divestiture has impacted on economic markets in response to humanitarian crises around the world. After the steady rise of SRI in recent decades, stakeholder concerns for financial social responsibility has reached unprecedented momentum in the wake of the 2008/09 World Financial Recession. In the aftermath of economic downturns, SRI appears as a window of opportunity for fostering social progress whilst re-establishing trust in financial markets. Based on a revitalized demand for transparency and accountability of financial market operations, SRI is believed to sophisticate into a mainstream feature of financial decision making in the years to come (Ahmad, 2008; Brown, in speech). Building on a meta-analysis of political divestiture studies and financial expert interviews on SRI, the following recommendations are targeted at capturing these trends and fostering a successful implementation of financial social responsibility.

Political Divestiture

A meta-analysis of South Africa political divestiture studies aimed at depicting the impact of stakeholder pressure against corporate activities in politically incorrect markets. Six metaanalyzed evaluations of divestiture studies covered a range of stakeholder pressure efforts triggering political divestiture from South Africa during the Apartheid regime.

The findings were instringent. Some studies reported a positive effect, others a negative impact and some showed no effect of divestiture on shareholder values. The results of increasing share prices of divesting corporations and negative returns of corporations operating in politically incorrect markets let political divestiture appear as a viable means for steering socio-political change. In this light, corporate executives are advised to pay attention to political settings and respond to political infringements with ceasing operations in politically incorrect markets. Institutional investors and mutual funds managers should attribute political divestiture as an efficient market behavior. However, the also-reported nonsignificant returns and statistically significant negative returns of divesting corporations let political divestiture seem as irrelevant or even – at least on the short run – inefficient activity. To find a stringent pattern of stakeholder pressure, political divestiture and profit maximization endeavors, follow-up studies are needed.

The inconsistent results of political divestiture studies raise questions about the measurement of political divestiture. As the state-of-the-art measurement of the impact of political divestiture, the event study methodology is challenged by internal and external validity threats. ***Internal validity*** determines the degree of approximate truth of inferences of the causal relationship under scrutiny. In the case of political divestiture event studies, internal validity problems arise if the observed changes in share prices are not linked to the specific political and social events but influenced by unrelated variables. To lower internal validity threats for event study designs, several recommendations are given:

Confounding and contaminating history threats cause difficulties in determining which events and to what degree events effect corporate values. Concurrent announcements that are difficult to separate from the main effect overshadow the relationship under scrutiny. The event study design must include information about the market, industry and risk factors in order to reveal potential history influences. The high volume of share market trading can help overcoming contamination by the use of extensive data sets. Large sample sizes are recommended to avert contamination. Short time windows minimize confounding effects, yet trade off from an advantageously elaborated sample.

Clustering describes conditions that systemically and disproportionately impact on the industry and/or a cluster of corporations. The clustering bias is limited by extracting share price changes that are expected relative to the market, industry and other firm-specific factors.

Maturation leakage occurs when event-specific information reaches select individuals before it hits the market as a whole – such as in the case of insider trading. As event studies are staged as post-hoc analyses of the overall market, leakage is impossible to be controlled for. In order to diminish leakage, using data from markets that restrict insider trading, short time frames and reporting of potential biases are recommended.

The *sample selection* is determined by finding relevant events with media coverage, drawing an appropriate sample, identifying a well-tempered time frame and controlling for firm-specific and industry effects. Unrepresentative portfolio choices with structural differences bias the sample. Above average extensions of the time window make it difficult to isolate the specific event from unrelated influences. Selection considerations must be reported in order to draw conclusions about the generalizability of the results. Missing data should be systemically removed from the entire data pool. Daily returns, precise event dates, time series rather than cross sectional methods as well as equally-weighted rather than valueweighted indices are ways to handle missing data points (Peterson, 1989).

Attrition refers to data that was excluded from the sample. Transparency about the extracted data points must outline study limitations and provide insights for future studies.

Regression to the mean causes a group's average performance on one measure to regress more than anticipated towards the mean of that measure. In the case of the event study methodology, limited days studied impose uncontrollable regression to the mean problems. Regression to the mean biases can be detected if the results derived from different time windows deviate. In this case, the results of additional time windows must be compared.

Threats to the ***external validity*** stem from *geographically-focused*, *time-targeted* and *nontypical samples* that challenge the generalizability of the results. In the case of event studies, the uniqueness of political and historical events limits the external validity. In order to examine if the findings on political divestiture from South Africa during the Apartheid regime provide a strong example for inferences, future comparative studies are recommended.

SRI

In the course of the 2008/09 World Financial Recession, stakeholder pressure on financial social responsibility has reached unprecedented momentum. Corporate social misconduct and fiduciary breaches have geared consumers and investors to increasingly pay attention to social responsibility within financial market. Citizens' attention to social responsibility has fostered information disclosure of financial market conduct. As a consequence legislative reforms and governmental regulations currently promote transparent social responsibility in financial markets. In the light of these occurrences, SRI appears as a window of opportunity for implementing financial social responsibility whilst re-establishing trust in financial markets. Interviews with financial experts and practitioners on financial social responsibility were targeted at gaining insight on the perception of SRI in order to derive recommendations on how to integrate social responsibility in financial markets. The respondents were found to be ambiguous about SRI. Whilst being optimistic about the innovative potential of financial social responsibility, they lack information on SRI. To leverage SRI from a niche market solution to a state-of-the-art financial practice, global governance on financial social responsibility coupled with governmental assistance in providing access to information on SRI are recommended. The interplay of heightened SRI supply of the financial community and demand for SRI options will innovate the financial social responsibility idea.

Global Governance: International organizations must support long-term financial social responsibility. The UN must continue to promote SRI as a means of environmental and social governance. The World Bank Group, the International Monetary Fund, the European Commission and bilateral donors must introduce social responsibility criteria as innovative financial practices. Transnational financial institutions must oversee the implementation of SRI in a systemic way.

Access to Information: The expert interviews on SRI revealed a lack of information about socially conscientious financial practices. Information on SRI builds a shared understanding on social investment within the financial community. In line with the mere exposure effect, access to information on SRI fosters the integration of environmental and social governance in financial decision making and heightens the consumer confident in markets (Frey & Irle, 2002). Information disclosure about the stability and effectiveness of SRI will promote financial social responsibility in times of crises. Information on SRI has the potential to concurrently stimulate the demand for SRI and vitalize the financial industry's efforts to further advance SRI innovations. The combined supply and demand increase will result in a quantitative and qualitative extension of SRI and advance the financial market social responsibility idea. In this light, transparency and accountability of financial social market operations will sophisticate SRI into a mainstream feature of financial decision making. With the rising importance of transparent financial social responsibility and financial institutions integrating social, environmental and governance issues into investment analysis; social investment criteria will become part of the fiduciary duty of trustees, financial advisers, asset managers and intermediary institutions.

International financial institutions and governmental policy makers must therefore provide market actors information on CSR for SRI screenings. International governance bodies must regulate financial social responsibility information disclosure to ensure the widespread availability of accurate, timely and comparable information about SRI. International organizations and governments must launch freedom of information acts that set minimum disclosure standards on environmental and social financial practices. Governance entities must also subsidize media industries and information service providers. New media tools should be used to disseminate material on financial social performance in an easily accessible and standardized form. Web-portals will help promoting social responsibility as a state-of-the-art financial practice and provide internet-based SRI best practice standards.

Governmental Assistance: SRI must be backed up by governmental support. Governmental policy makers must incentivize the integration of social responsibility into the agenda of financial institutions. Governmental control must ensure that financial regulations are balanced with current societal needs, governmental obligations and market demands. Governmental regulatory frameworks must set SRI standards for governmental agencies, financial institutions, self-regulatory bodies, accounting entities, rating agencies, index providers and NGOs. Governments must encourage the integration of social responsibility in financial analyses by regulating fiduciary responsibilities. Concurrently governmental regulations must foster accountability of socially responsible financial conduct by transparency guidelines for the retail of SRI funds. Governmental assistance must provide information on how to adopt SRI-attentive regulations in order to achieve social responsibility goals. As a basis for improvements, governments must reward CSR reporting based on monitoring and benchmarking financial institutions' social performance.

Financial Market Actors: Financial institutions and experts are encouraged to consider environmental and social responsibility in a variety of ways. Information on CSR and SRI must become part of financial market operations. Media reports must inform asset managers and financial analysts about the link between CSR and SRI. Supervisory bodies must promote the inclusion of SRI criteria in financial management. Accounting entities, rating agencies and index providers must adopt environmental and social governance standards as a basis for evaluation criteria that guarantee the concurrent financial and ethical performance. Stock exchange advisors must communicate listed corporations the importance of environmental and social responsibility governance. Asset managers must encourage brokers to conduct SRI screenings. Investors are advised to request information on SRI and develop SRI proxy voting strategies. Pension fund trustees must consider environmental and social criteria in the formulation of investment mandates. Consultants and financial advisers must incorporate environmental and social corporate governance in their portfolio allocation strategies and accept social responsibility as a state-of-the-art of fiduciary obligations. Financial analysts must assess market opportunities with respect for social contributions and actively participate in ongoing voluntary responsibility initiatives.

Innovations: The SRI community must ensure that financial social responsibility is constantly innovated. Analysts must assist policy makers in setting up a SRI framework that reflects practitioners' needs. Financial experts must sophisticate financial social responsibility measurement models and contribute to research on environmental and social investments. Novel SRI options that fulfil unmet responsibility needs will open the market for socially responsible economic growth whilst bringing societal change. Academic institutions must nurture the financial community's ethical sense. Business schools and think tanks must support SRI research and offer financial ethics education. Financial economists must integrate socio-economic factors into standard economic profit maximization models. Concurrently behavioral economists should delve into human decisions making fallibility in responsibility considerations and ethicality perceptions. Profound research findings are the basis for stimulating SRI innovations that lead to the concurrent economic prosperity and societal advancement.

REFERENCES

Ahmad, M. (2008, January 24). Global CEOs at World Economic Forum cite sovereign wealth funds as the new power broker. *BI-ME.*

Peterson, P. P. (1989). Event studies: A review of issues and methodology. *Quarterly Journal of Business and Economics*, *28*(3), 37–50.

Chapter 9
Discussion

ABSTRACT

The discussion features empirical limitations and an outlook for future research. Exploratory expert interviews with public servants served as an exploratory step to understand public administrators' views of CSR. Future research could address social responsibility as a worldwide societal phenomenon. Behavioral economic studies the emergence of responsibility in human beings. Capturing external influences on social responsibility fallibility aids in tackling contemporary responsibility challenges having arisen out of globalization

INTRODUCTION

The set-up of multi-stakeholder partnerships was found to be challenged by institutional, organizational and cultural differences. In the aftermath of the 2008 financial crisis, the optimum interplay of market forces and governmental regulation in an economically transforming world needs to be studied. Global screenings and international comparisons must distinguish PPP-favorable infrastructures to foster the worldwide spread of corporate and financial social responsibility.

Political divestiture is foremost captured by the event study methodology. Event study designs were found to be influenced by the sampling, time windows, lurking variables but also the irreplicability of specific events. Future evaluations may consider the long-term and broader-scale societal impacts of political divestiture. The findings on South Africa could be validated in the

DOI: 10.4018/978-1-5225-7619-8.ch009

case of Sudan's genocide in the Darfur region. Political divestiture should also be attributed in financial market experiments capturing unintentional investment decision making fallibility.

The qualitative interviews with financial experts on SRI at the NYSE during the summer of 2008 should be replicated to measure the perception of SRI in the aftermath of the crisis. Stakeholder interviews may also attribute the potential of SRI to re-establishing trust in financial markets and the optimum interplay of deregulated market systems and governmental control in providing social responsibility. The predicted trend of the rising of SRI should be captured by additional research.

The monograph explored innovative corporate and financial market potentials to create value for society.

The theoretical part described corporate and financial social responsibility. The human foundation of responsibility and decision making fallibility on responsibility were discussed. The international emergence of CSR governance was outlined in the case of the UNGC, which serves as a social responsibility international best practice guideline. CSR was portrayed as a conflict resolution means in multi-stakeholder partnerships.

The rise of SRI was traced back to a combination of historical incidents, legislative compulsion and stakeholder pressure. International comparisons of North American and European legislative frameworks led to conclusions about SRI practices around the globe.

The role of the UN in promoting and implementing financial global governance was discussed. The innovative coupling of stakeholder activism with investment strategies was introduced in the case of political divestiture. A socio-psychological framework of financial social responsibility motives complementing traditional, financial profit maximization investment models was presented.

Empirically the book addressed up-to-date corporate and financial social responsibility conduct. Expert interviews with public servants were staged in the fall of 2007 about the strengths and weaknesses of private sector contributions to social welfare. The exploratory survey found civil servants to be polarized about corporate social endeavors. CSR was honored to grant societal value; but was also associated with stakeholder management. Intrinsic motives and employee satisfaction contribute to CSR. Detected concerns about CSR are democratic deficiencies, costs and liability issues. CSR adherents point out the access to additional resources as well as the high degree of flexibility in administrating social responsibility. Individuals who are skeptic about CSR mention the lack of accountability, shareholder supremacy as well as inefficiency and dishonesty notions.

The study implies several limitations: As the expert interviews featured a limited number of executive university students, the non-representative sample is potentially biased. Although the categorization of the free associations was assisted by independent raters, the moderate interrater-reliability raises methodological concerns. The generalizability of the time- and context-specific results must be validated in future follow-up studies. Overall, the exploratory research remains a first step towards further investigations of public administrators' view on CSR that offers an understanding of the relation of the corporate world and the public sector in attributing social responsibility.

Multi-stakeholder partnerships were analyzed as an innovative combination of public and private sector forces to address international problems. The set-up of PPP networks was found to be challenging. Building partnerships requires time and resources but also the participants' willingness to cooperate on commonly-shared goals. On a global scale, multistakeholder partnerships are prone to be limited by institutional, organizational and cultural differences that must be overcome by governance, stakeholder management and local networking.

The analysis of the current set-up of GAID – a UN multi-stakeholder network – revealed potentials and deficiencies of social responsibility PPP solutions in the international arena. Since its inception GAID has successfully leveraged its position as a UN network that keeps ICT for development on the global agenda. GAID introduced ICT into the mainstream of global governance in stakeholder management. Some of the GAID partners successfully contribute to the network; others have experienced difficulties during the start-up due to resource limitations, goal ambiguity and communication barriers. Securing funding and stakeholder networking coupled with transparent business planning and ICT innovations will advance GAID.

The evaluation included a variety of data – featuring web contents, publications, interviews, email contents and blog responses – that offered a multi-faceted description of GAID. The qualitative interviews allowed the flexible collection of a multitude of information. Open-ended questions granted a high degree of freedom to the respondents. The manifold data collection was targeted at deriving recommendations with practical relevance for the implementation of the GAID network. At the same time, the unstandardized data collection that was conducted by different assistants who – in some cases – reported respondent compliance problems let the sample selection and collection appear to be methodologically noisy. As for the turbulent starting period, some data about partnership initiatives that ceased to function throughout the data analysis and write-up of the book had to be excluded.

Political divestiture was introduced as a financial social responsibility means to foster political change through investment behavior. The meta-analysis of political divestiture cases from South Africa may be insofar biased, as there is a tendency towards publishing positive results whilst neglecting to report attempts with no results in journal publications. While no stringent pattern of stakeholder pressure, political divestiture and corporate success was determined by meta-analyzing South Africa political divestiture studies; areas for the improvement of the event study methodology were identified.

Event studies are the state-of-the-art analysis technique for capturing the impact of political divestiture. The internal validity of the event studies depends on the sample selection, time windows as well as lurking variables. The irreplicability of socio-political events and data specificities trade off from the external validity. While Duncombe's (2008) validated evaluation framework is a standardized tool to determine methodological strengths and weaknesses, the framework is not specifically designed for event studies. Some of the evaluation criteria appear to be inter-related. Future methodological advancements must build on Duncombe's work to draw a clearer distinction between the evaluation criteria. Novel methods that specifically target at analyzing event study designs must be invented and validated.

Although the event study design is the state-of-the-art financial analysis technique for capturing the effects of political divestiture, several limitations are apparent. Future methodological advancements must build on the findings retrieved with Duncombe's (2008) standardized evaluation framework and evaluate the current state-of-the-art literature by more distinct criteria. Novel evaluation methods that specifically target event study designs and additional methodological approaches must capture the impact of stakeholder pressure on investment decisions. Financial market experiments must complementary test microeconomic effects of divestment behavior. While experiments will allow controlling for internal validity threats, however, comparatively smaller sizes and the artificial testing situations may reduce the external validity of experimental findings and thus the applicability to predict real-world phenomena. Experiments must therefore be complemented with macroeconomic models testing the influence of political divestiture on overall market correlates.

In addition, research methods on political divestiture must be extended to capture the long-term, socio-economic impact of foreign investment drain. As event study designs focus on short-run corporate returns, this method leaves lasting and widespread socio-economic effects and socio-political risks without consideration. Future longitudinal political divestiture studies must investigate the long-term impact of foreign capital flight. Socioeconomic models must include stakeholder viewpoints and socio-political externalities of political divestiture in order to conclude about political divestiture's overall and lasting impact.

While market ethics are an internationally prevalent phenomenon, there are context- and time-dependent differences in ethicality perceptions and purposes. In the international arena, political divestiture is a multi-stakeholder phenomenon that serves many disparate purposes. Future investigations must scrutinize the generalizability of the findings on South African divestiture onto other current political cases. In terms of regional specificities, attention must be paid to developing countries which are most dependent on foreign investments and especially vulnerable to political infringements and humanitarian crises. Current attention should be paid to the capital flight from Burma in the wake of democratic infringements, Sudan's humanitarian crisis in the Darfur region and Iran's nuclear proliferation.

As the legal back-up and policy framework for political divestiture varies from country to country, future research must target at providing the basis for an international harmonization of political divestiture policies and conduct. While political divestiture has its clear merits of efficiently acting on socially irresponsible governments, political divestiture is also a novel market approach that imbues political attention in the finance world without stringent global governance assistance – such as for example the IMF's foreign investment aid peg to development conditionalities. International regulations on political divestiture ethics are scarce and currently highly under debate. Problematic appears that political divestiture evokes from media-instigated stakeholder pressure without any democratic justification. As a voluntary expression of world-views, political divestiture lacks – in most cases – international legal back-ups and monitoring control. Missing due-diligence let political divestiture appear as a propaganda-vulnerable, risky proceeding. In addition, the lack of monitoring hinders global governance institutional assistance of political divestiture. As divested social venture capital undermines social development, unassisted political divestiture implies collateral damages. Uncontrolled foreign investment drain can imply drawbacks for emerging communities. As an alternative to transparent physical damages of warfare, political divestiture may result in hindered community improvements that are invisible for monitoring. These downsides of political divestiture were attributed in a 2006 New York Times advertisement of the Sudanese

Government that promoted investing in Sudan. In the international arena, political divestiture may also breed foreign hostility – a potentially unknown, long-term impact of political divestiture that was recently addressed by the US Congress debates in the House vote on sanctions against Sudan. In order for political divestiture to not turn into a mercantilistically back-wardish idea, the capital flight's impacts on civilians must be monitored and institutionally assisted. Coregulatory arrangements of corporations, public administrators and financial executives must act concertedly to pressure politically incorrect governments but at the same time pay attention to avert civilian societal infringements. A well-balanced checks-and-balances political divestiture approach is needed that controls for potentially negative externalities of foreign investment drain. Global governance assistance must support local communities. Concurrent foreign direct aid must alleviate collateral damages and negative externalities for civilians. Long-term international development assistance must built perspectives for future community improvement.

In order to advance the political divestiture idea for corporations, governmental taxation models may compensate corporations for the costs of political divestiture. In addition, funds' readmission criteria for corporations that cease operations in politically irresponsible markets should be established. After a corporation was originally excluded from a portfolio, the possibility of readmission would allow corporations to rejoin if the corporate socially irresponsible conduct has been stopped. Tax benefits and reintegration opportunities will incentivize corporations to exhibit socially responsible conduct and thereby steer the entire market into a more socially conscientious direction. Long-term business strategists must factor in political divestiture as a potential market risk.

In conclusion, the analysis of the event study methodology was meant as a first step towards resolving many questions that emerge from political divestiture. While no stringent pattern of political divestiture and corporate endeavors was determinable from the literature on capital flight from South Africa during Apartheid, the discussion of the current state-of-the-art methodology to measure the impact of political divestiture helped outlining ways how to better capture the effects of financial social responsibility on economic markets and societal systems. The article also drew attention to the necessity of policy advancements and global governance administration of political divestiture. Implications for public and private actors were given to ensure a successful rise of social responsibility within modern market economies as a future guarantor of economic and societal advancement.

Interviews with financial experts on financial social responsibility at the NYSE during the summer and fall of 2008 outlined recent trends but also shed light on current deficiencies of SRI. Financial experts and practitioners are optimistic about the future innovative potential of SRI, but lack information on financial social investment. The novelty of SRI and the range of financial social responsibility contents imply a plethora of SRI notions. Additionally, the overall impact of SRI appears somewhat marginal as only a fraction of the population – less than one percent of the world's inhabitants or roughly two billion people – participates in financial markets as shareholders and/ or investors (Cuesta & Valor, 2007). Within the unrepresentative financial community, SRI remains a niche market solution for wellinformed, intrinsically motivated individuals. As the greatest constraint to invest socially conscientious is the lack of information on SRI, transparency fostering stakeholder confidence in SRI is recommended to be enhanced by regulatory initiatives and accountability control.

The relative vagueness of SRI and unstandardized social screening criteria lowered the response quality of the interviews. The quasi-standardized interviews offered a wealth of information, yet the variant assistance provided by the interviewer biased the responses. The feasibility sample collection was staged at differing places of the New York Financial District during different times of the day in order to accommodate the respondents. Variant trading days and varying group contexts may have impacted on the interviewees' moods and influenced the associations. The time of the data collection paints a unique picture of the perception of responsibility right before and during the outbreak of the 2008/09 World Financial Recession. While capturing this moment in time appears as a valuable historical snapshot, the unconventional occurrences have certainly biased the results. The generalizability of the findings must be tested in future studies.

The theoretical and empirical parts shed light on positive aspects but also critically addressed current downfalls of corporate and financial social responsibility. The presented results lead to recommendations with relevance for public policy makers and public administrators around the world. International governance and multi-stakeholder management appear as essential prerequisites for the ongoing adaptation and adoption of corporate and financial social responsibility in a global economy. Governmental assistance must contribute to the implementation and administration of CSR and SRI with attention to private sector and civil demands. As the basis for stakeholder engagement and monitoring, transparency and accountability are key for advancing corporate and financial social market behavior. The newly emerging CSR and SRI phenomena open avenues for future research with respect for current social responsibility trends.

The beginning of the 21st century has proven to be a time of novel opportunities and unknown risks for corporate innovation, economic stability and human progress. With current trends predicting continuing globalization, heightened environmental concerns in the light of climate change but also socio-economic changes in the aftermath of the 2008/09 World Financial Recession; global governance must create a stable, competitive market economy whilst ensuring sustainable social development. Given this background corporate and financial actors face unfamiliar risks and unprecedented social responsibility demands. In the light of these challenges, future research must address social responsibility as a world-wide societal phenomenon that is construed by human constituents and exogenous influences.

The 2008/09 World Financial Recession underlined the impact of human responsibility on economic market systems. To avoid a recurrent scenario in the future, behavioral economics must study human responsibility. Evolutionary psychologists may explore the emergence of social responsibility in human beings in order to investigate what aspects of responsibility are ingrained in human traits and the constitution of mind and which ones are nurtured by external constituents.

Concurrent research on bounded decision making must reveal implicit irresponsibility. The findings will reduce cognitive barriers of decision making predicaments and lead to educative means for steering behavioral patterns in a more socially conscientious direction.

In addition, capturing external influences on social responsibility fallibility must help managing prudential risks. While globalization has recently attracted scientific attention, until today we have a limited idea of what a globalized world implies onto us in the domain of social responsibility. Interconnected economic, institutional and political networks and a ceasing importance of nation states impose new risks onto corporate and financial actors. Fast-paced information transfer increases the complexity of decisions and the cognitive overload of fallible global leaders. Wading through these challenges has become a formidable task. Research must attribute how a globalizing world moderates individuals' decision making on responsibility. Understanding the impact of globalization on human social responsibility is targeted at averting predictable surprises of future global crises.

Today's global challenges demand for international multi-stakeholder solutions. PPPs offer an effective way to address global deficiencies by the combined forces of governmental regulations and corporate market mechanisms. Multi-stakeholder partnerships mobilize various constituents for the pursuit of commonly-shared goals and foster expertise exchange in the combat of international problems out of reach for a singular entity.

However, the relative novelty of partnerships implies risks. Future research on innovative social responsibility networks and multi-stakeholder conflict resolution is needed to address global challenges. In the aftermath of the 2008/09 World Financial Recession, the optimum interplay of market forces and governmental regulation in a globalizing and economically transforming world must be studied. Global screenings and international comparisons must distinguish favorable political, economic, legislative and institutional infrastructures for the advancement of PPPs and the worldwide spread of corporate and financial social responsibility. As some of the world's most pressing economic and social issues are located in third world countries, special attention must be paid to the developing world.

As a financial social responsibility means, political activism can pressure the investment community to foster societal change. Political divestiture studies featuring the case of the South Africa during the Apartheid regime were meta-analyzed. While no stringent pattern of stakeholder pressure, political divestiture and corporate success was determined; the evaluation identified areas for future research. Follow-up studies must clarify if the findings on political divestiture from South Africa can be generalized for other cases – such as the stakeholder pressure on corporations operating in Sudan in the wake of humanitarian infringements in the Darfur region. Concretely, the follow-up studies may test if stakeholder pressure on corporations operating in Sudan creates positive incentives for corporations to cease operations and shareholders to divest Sudan. The findings will derive political divestment strategies for corporate management, private investors and institutional holdings. Although the event study design is the state-of-the-art financial analysis technique for capturing the effects of political divestiture, several limitations are apparent that demand for methodological advancements. Financial market experiments may measure the microeconomic effect of stakeholder information upon divestment behavior as well as unintentional investment decision making fallibility. Experiments will allow controlling for internal validity threats, yet the small sizes and the artificial testing situation reduce the external validity of experimental findings which limits the applicability to predict real-world phenomena.

While event study designs focus on short-run corporate returns and risks, this method leaves lasting and widespread socio-economic effects and externalities of political divestiture without consideration. Future longitudinal political divestiture studies must investigate the long-term impact of political divestiture and include stakeholder viewpoints to conclude about political divestiture's overall societal value. In terms of regional specific follow-up studies, special attention must be paid to developing countries which are the most dependent on foreign investments and also the most vulnerable to political infringements and humanitarian crises.

Expert interviews on SRI found financial practitioners to be optimistic about the innovative potential of financial social responsibility but lacking knowledge on social investment possibilities. The open-ended interviews provided a wealth of information. The unconstrained free associating authentically captured the momentary zeitgeist of the financial community in the summer of 2008. As for portraying the perception of social responsibility right before and during the outbreak of the 2008/09 World Financial Recession, the results are of historic value. At the same time, collective representations underlie a constant flux, which limits the generalizability of the findings. The NYSE data collection demands for follow-up studies during another time and/or at differing stock exchanges.

Future research may study SRI in a qualitatively and quantitatively nested approach. Qualitative interviews on the social perception of SRI will help resolving societal losses imbued in the novelty of the phenomenon and aligning incoherent viewpoints on SRI.

Additional quantitative experiments may validate the proposed socio-psychological SRI framework to distinguish moderator variables of investors' willingness to trade off financial profits for social gratifications.

The current trends demand for the future study of SRI. In the light of the 2008/09 World Financial Recession, SRI appears as an idea whose time has come. Ever since its existence, SRI has been perpetuated by social and environmental deficiencies. The current stakeholders demand for transparent and accountable financial market transactions coupled with legislative reforms will prospectively galvanize SRI. As a crises-robust market option, SRI appears as a window of opportunity to help re-establish trust in financial market systems. Future studies must capture these predicted trends with attention to socio-economic success factors of financial social responsibility and stakeholder-specific SRI nuances. Additional investigations of the perception of SRI in the aftermath of the crisis could determine in what way the financial crisis has changed the financial community's view of market responsibility. Paying attention to the 2008/09 World Financial Recession, stakeholder interviews may also attribute the potential of SRI to re-establishing trust in financial markets and the optimum interplay of deregulated market systems and governmental control in providing financial social responsibility frameworks. Research-based transparency campaigns must promote SRI as a stable market option during times of crisis throughout the financial community and thereby raise the stakeholders' confidence in financial social responsibility. All these endeavors are aimed at fostering financial social responsibility as a future guarantor of economic stability and sustainable social progress throughout the world.

REFERENCES

Cuesta de la, G. M. & Martinez, V. C. (2004). Fostering corporate social responsibility through public initiative: From the EU to the Spanish case. *Journal of Business Ethics*, *55*, 275–293. doi:10.100710551-004-0994-y

Cuesta de la, G. M. & Valor, C. (2007). Fostering corporate social responsibility through public initiative: From the EU to the Spanish case. *Journal of Business Ethics*, *55*(3), 275–293.

Duncombe, W. (2008). *Program evaluation. Course Reader, Spring 2008, Maxwell School of Citizenship and Public Affairs*. Syracuse University.

Conclusion

This book explored corporate and financial social responsibility. The theoretical part discussed the human constituents of responsibility and the international emergence of CSR with special attention to multi-stakeholder partnerships. The rise of SRI in the international arena in the wake of stakeholder activism and intrinsic socio-psychological motives was outlined. Empirically expert interviews with public servants about CSR revealed opportunities of flexible corporate social service provision but also shed light on deficiencies of the authenticity of corporate social conduct. The potentials and downfalls of international PPPs were analyzed in the case of the currently launched UN multi-stakeholder network GAID. The meta-analysis of political divestiture from South Africa studies attributed methodological deficiencies to event study designs. Expert interviews about SRI featured the innovative potential but also revealed a lack of information about SRI and doubts as for efficiency considerations and fiduciary predicaments. Recommendations target at ingraining social responsibility in economic systems by global governance, multi-stakeholder management and governmental assistance of the implementation and administration of corporate and financial social responsibility. Transparency and accountability are key for monitoring corporate and financial social responsibility. As for the ongoing adaptation and adoption of CSR and SRI, the monograph investigated a current topic of concern. Future research on responsibility in the light of globalization and human boundedness will spearhead socio-economic responsibility models. In the wake of the 2008 financial crisis, research must attribute the newly defined role of social responsibility in the interplay of public and private sectors.

This book targeted at exploring innovative opportunities and revealing current challenges of corporate and financial social responsibility.

The theoretical part shed light on human foundations of responsibility. CSR was portrayed as a global governance and conflict resolution means. The international emergence of multi-stakeholder partnerships was discussed in the case of a currently set-up PPP network. The UNGC was introduced as an international social responsibility best practice guideline.

Financial social responsibility was attributed in the case of SRI. The emergence of SRI strategies was traced back to a combination of historical incidents, stakeholder pressure and legislative compulsion. Intercultural comparisons of North American and European policy frameworks led to conclusions about international differences in financial social investments. The analysis of the role of the UN in promoting SRI offered insights on the global governance of financial social responsibility. Political divestiture was outlined as an innovative stakeholder activism in financial markets. A framework of socio-psychological financial social responsibility motives complementing profit maximization investment models was proposed.

Empirically the book addressed up-to-date corporate and financial social responsibility conduct.

Expert interviews with public servants about CSR revealed the common body of knowledge and current trends but also opportunities and risks of public sector social welfare contributions. Public servants are critical about corporate social conduct. While CSR was honored to provide societal value and access to flexible resources, corporate social conduct is also associated with stakeholder management. As for recommendations, CSR must be fostered by global governance, governmental assistance and corporate social engagement. Transparency will allow accountability control.

The potentials and deficiencies of international PPPs were analyzed in the case of the currently launched UN multi-stakeholder network GAID. Since the inception GAID had leveraged its position as a UN-related organization that ingrains ICT for development in global governance and provided ICT for development best practices standards. During the start-up phase, some partners have successfully contributed to the network; others have experienced problems in connecting with GAID due to goal ambiguity and communication barriers. Transparent business planning fostered by stakeholder network management and ICT innovations will further advance the impact of GAID.

The meta-analysis of political divestiture from South Africa studies found event study designs methodologically challenged by uncontrollable lurking variables and sample selection deficiencies. While no stringent pattern of stakeholder activism, political divestiture and corporate values was determined, the evaluation identified areas for further research. Future studies must test the generalizability of the current findings on South African divestiture. The research on political divestiture must be extended to capture the long-term, socio-economic impact of divestiture.

Expert interviews on SRI outlined recent financial social responsibility advancements but also shed light on current deficiencies. Financial experts and practitioners are ambiguous about SRI – they are optimistic about the profitability and long-term perspectives of the innovative idea, but the lack of information about financial social responsibility raises doubts about the efficiency of SRI. Fiduciary predicaments and a loss of degrees of freedom of choice are mentioned downsides. SRI appears as a niche market solution for intrinsically responsible investors. Information campaigns and a higher degree of accountability on crises-robust SRI products in the aftermath of financial downturns but also SRI product innovations will leverage financial social responsibility into a mainstream financial investment means. Recommendations to ingrain social responsibility in economic systems concern public, private and civil actors. International governance and multi-stakeholder management are prerequisites for the adoption of social responsibility market economies. Governmental assistance is essential in the implementation and administration of corporate and financial social responsibility. Transparency and accountability are key for monitoring corporate and financial social market behavior.

As for the ongoing adaptation and adoption of CSR and SRI, the monograph investigated a current topic of concern for global governance, corporate management and financial investment. Future research on responsibility in the light of globalization and human boundedness will spearhead socio-economic responsibility models and lead to feasible changes in the market responsibility domain. In the aftermath of the 2008/09 World Financial Recession, research must attribute the newly defined role of social responsibility in the interplay of public and private sector social contributions. In the newly-restructured attempt to create a world of free men and economic markets that function based on the mutual responsibility of disciplined market actors, we must use our past experience to equip us for our future challenges. This piece hopefully contributes to a future rise of social responsibility in our currently globalizing, economically transforming and environmentally fragile world we simply must feel responsible about.

About the Author

Julia Margarete Puaschunder studied Philosophy/Psychology (MPhil, University of Vienna, 2003, highest entry exam), Business (MBA, Vienna University of Economics and Business, 2007), Public Administration (MPA, Maxwell School, 2008, full tuition waiver Fulbright Scholar with placements in Washington D.C. and New York City), Social and Economic Sciences (Doctor, Vienna University of Economics and Business, 2006, merit-based *ad personam* position, Dean's list), Natural Sciences (Doctor, University of Vienna, 2010, summa cum laude), Law, Economics and Sciences (pending).

Trained as a behavioral economist with Doctorates in Social and Economic Sciences as well as Natural Sciences and Masters in Business, Public Administration and Philosophy/Psychology, she has over 15 years of experience in applied social sciences empirical research in the international arena. Julia M. Puaschunder has launched and administered research projects in Australia, Austria, Canada, China, Germany, Indonesia, Switzerland, and the United States. She conducted interdisciplinary science and governance projects as well as held or holds advisory, board member, evaluator, committee, contributor, observer, referee and representative privileges for the Academic Council on the United Nations System, Academy of Behavioral Finance and Economics, Alpbach Laxenburg Group, Austrian Academy of Sciences, Austrian Chamber of Commerce New York, Austrian Economic Association, Austrian Federal Ministry of Science and Research, Austrian Federal Ministry of Science, Research and Economy, Austrian General Consulate New York, Austrian Office of Science and Technology Washington D.C., Austrian Scientists in North America Association, Austrian Society for New Institutional Economics, Cambridge Scholars Publishing, Discovery Innovation Growth (DiG) Talent Development Network, EURO working group on Behavioural Operational Research, European Corporate Governance Institute, European Horizons Conference, European Journal of

Economics, Law and Politics, European Union Commission, Finance, Risk and Accounting Perspectives Conference at University of Cambridge, Fritz Thyssen Foundation, Fulbright Commission, Harvard Association for Law and Mind Sciences, Harvard Club of Austria, Harvard University Center for the Environment, Horizon 2020, Human Resources Management and Services, International Institute for Applied Systems Analysis, International Journal of Environmental Protection and Policy, International Journal of Sustainable Entrepreneurship and Corporate Social Responsibility, Janeway Center, Kollegium Kalksburg Altkalksburger Vereinigung, Netherlands Organisation for Scientific Research, Oikos International New York City Chapter, Oxford Academic Research Network, Research in Management and Learning Education Unconference, Research Association for Interdisciplinary Studies, Society for International Development Vienna Chapter, Society of Authors, The Max Kade Foundation New York, The Neue Galerie New York, Tishman Environment and Design Center, U.S. Department of Education, Vienna Foundation, Vienna International Conference on Mathematical Modelling, Viennese Opera Ball New York International Business Committee and Virtus Corporate Governance Experts Global Repository. In 2011, she served as a participant in a U.S. White House conference call on environmental justice.

Before starting a Prize Fellowship in the Inter-University Consortium of New York working for the New School (Deans Office, Department of Economics, Department of Politics, Economics of Climate Change Project, Eugene Lang College, Parsons School of Design, School of Public Engagement and the Schwartz Center for Economic Policy Analysis) as well as Columbia University (Department of Economics, Graduate School of Arts and Sciences) and Princeton University, Julia M. Puaschunder held positions at the University of Vienna and the Vienna University of Economics and Business. For several years she was an Associate of the *Harvard University* Faculty of Arts and Sciences and serves as Contributor to the Harvard Law School and Mind Sciences Initiative Situationist. At the Harvard University Center for the Environment, she conducted research on intergenerational equity in cooperation with Harvard Business School and Harvard Kennedy School.

Apart from academic appointments in Austria, Julia was a scholar at The Australian National University, Columbia University in the City of New York, George Washington University, Harvard University, Haskayne School of Business, Ludwig-Maximilians-University of Munich, Princeton University, and The Open Society Institute & Soros Foundation New York.

Throughout her academic career, Julia was invited to present her research at Harvard University, Princeton University, Columbia University, Georgetown University, Brown University, Oxford University and Cambridge University as well as The Academic Council on the United Nations System. She published with Harvard University, Columbia University, Cambridge University and Oxford University outlets among other distinct journals and international publishing houses (e.g., Edward Elgar, Emerald, Palgrave Macmillan, Routledge, Springer International & Nature, Taylor & Francis, Vernon, Wiley). In 2018, she was invited to give a Keynote Speech at Wagner College in Staten Island, New York.

Julia organized conferences and public speakers from the Harvard Business School and Princeton University in North America and Europe. Since 2015 Julia Puaschunder supports the Economics of Climate Change Project Speaker Series hosted at The Schwartz Center for Economic Policy Analysis of The New School for Social Research in New York City. Julia helped initiate the 2017 Unconference at The New School New York in cooperation with the New School for Public Engagement and served on the Scientific Committee of the 2017 Finance, Risk and Accounting Perspectives Conference as well as the Social and Sustainable Finance and Impact Investing Conference 2017 at University of Cambridge. Julia served as a scientific board member of the 2018 Vienna International Conference on Mathematical Modelling at the Technical University Vienna and served as Proceedings Editor of the Research Association for Interdisciplinary Studies (RAIS) 2018 conference at the Erdman Center for Princeton University. Julia is scheduled to be Chairman Chief at the Research Association for Interdisciplinary Studies at the Erdman Center for Princeton University as well as a conference board member of the 2019 Annual Conference of the Academy of Behavioral Finance and Economics. Julia is included in the '2018 Marquis Who's Who in America and in the World' among the top 3% professionals around the globe. She was awarded the 2018 Albert Nelson Marquis Lifetime Achievement Award.

After having captured social responsibility in corporate and financial markets in Europe and North America with attention to Financial Social Responsibility and Socially Responsible Investment; Julia Puaschunder pursued the idea of Eternal Equity—responding to Western world intergenerational equity constraints in the domains of environmental sustainability, overindebtedness and demographic aging with focus on law and mind sciences. Currently, Julia dedicates interest to Humanness, Automated Control and Artificial Intelligence Ethics in the digital age.

Index

M

N

P

R

S

T

U

V

www.ingramcontent.com/pod-product-compliance
Lightning Source LLC
LaVergne TN
LVHW081333300926
849161LV00008B/1960
9781522576198